硕士博士研究生英语考试系列丛书

中国科学院博士研究生入学考试英语考试大纲及真题精解（2005—2017年）

主　编　于　华
主　审　高　原
编　者　（按姓氏笔画排列）
　　　　于　华　李利军　杨　莉
　　　　洪　雷　胡江波　钱玉彬
　　　　彭　宇

北京理工大学出版社
BEIJING INSTITUTE OF TECHNOLOGY PRESS

版权专有　侵权必究

图书在版编目（CIP）数据

中国科学院博士研究生入学考试英语考试大纲及真题精解．2005—2017年／于华主编．—北京：北京理工大学出版社，2018.1
　ISBN 978-7-5682-5236-2

　Ⅰ.①中…　Ⅱ.①于…　Ⅲ.①英语-博士生入学考试-自学参考资料　Ⅳ.①H31

中国版本图书馆CIP数据核字（2018）第010886号

出版发行 /	北京理工大学出版社有限责任公司
社　　址 /	北京市海淀区中关村南大街5号
邮　　编 /	100081
电　　话 /	（010）68914775（总编室）
	（010）82562903（教材售后服务热线）
	（010）68948351（其他图书服务热线）
网　　址 /	http://www.bitpress.com.cn
经　　销 /	全国各地新华书店
印　　刷 /	三河市华骏印务包装有限公司
开　　本 /	787毫米×1092毫米　1/16
印　　张 /	20.25
字　　数 /	471千字
版　　次 /	2018年1月第1版　2018年1月第1次印刷
定　　价 /	46.00元

责任编辑／梁铜华
文案编辑／梁铜华
责任校对／周瑞红
责任印制／王美丽

图书出现印装质量问题，请拨打售后服务热线，本社负责调换

前　　言

英语水平是衡量报考博士研究生的考生是否具备攻读博士学位的实力的一个重要尺度。为确保考生具有一定的英语能力，入学后能顺利攻读博士学位，中国科学院从1984年起对博士入学的英语考试实行统一命题和统一阅卷。中国科学院博士研究生招生入学考试英语考试实行春、秋季制，分别定在每年的3月和10月举行。2002—2013年，每年春秋两季博士入学英语考试的命题和阅卷工作全部由中国科学院大学外语系承担。从2014年起，中国科学院将一年两次的博士入学考试调整为一年一次，主要为春季招生，博士入学英语考试的命题仍旧由中国科学院大学外语系承担。

本书从2005年出版以来，逐年修订，以补充并增加新的博士入学英语考试真题及精解。该书的出版一直受到报考中国科学院研究生的考生热烈欢迎。随着入选真题套数的逐年增多，书的体积和重量已相当可观。为了便于考生携带，同时也为了突出近年真题的重要性，我们决定给书籍"瘦身"，即书的正文部分以2010年以后的博士入学英语考试真题及精解为主，而2005—2009年的真题及答案将以光盘的形式随书发售。

本书在策划上，除2005年9月考试大纲中的一套样题之外，共收录了22套真题，其中2005年10月—2009年10月的十套真题及答案以光盘形式出版并随书发售，2010年3月—2017年3月的十二套真题配有参考答案及试题精解。本书的试题精解部分由于华主编，策划、组织并审阅本书的编写工作。参加精解编写的老师有：钱玉彬（词汇）、洪雷（完形填空）、彭宇（阅读理解A）、于华（词汇、阅读理解A、阅读理解B）、杨莉（英译汉）、胡江波（写作）、李利军（写作）等多位教师。

本书是应广大考生的实际需求进行的一次尝试。由于教学任务繁重，时间仓促，疏漏不妥之处难免，敬请同行专家和读者不吝指正。

编　者
2017年11月

目 录

第一部分　中国科学院研究生院博士研究生入学考试英语考试大纲及样题　……………（1）
　　中国科学院研究生院博士研究生入学考试英语考试大纲　………………………………（3）
　　中国科学院博士研究生入学考试英语试卷（样题）　……………………………………（5）
　　中国科学院博士研究生入学考试英语试卷（样题）参考答案　…………………………（21）

第二部分　中国科学院博士研究生入学考试英语考试试题及参考答案
　　　　　　（2005—2009 年）　……………………………………………………………（23）

第三部分　中国科学院博士研究生入学考试英语考试试题及精解
　　　　　　（2010—2017 年）　……………………………………………………………（25）
　　中国科学院博士研究生入学考试英语试题（2010 年 3 月）　…………………………（27）
　　2010 年 3 月试题精解　……………………………………………………………………（41）
　　中国科学院博士研究生入学考试英语试题（2010 年 10 月）　…………………………（50）
　　2010 年 10 月试题精解　……………………………………………………………………（65）
　　中国科学院博士研究生入学考试英语试题（2011 年 3 月）　…………………………（74）
　　2011 年 3 月试题精解　……………………………………………………………………（88）
　　中国科学院博士研究生入学考试英语试题（2011 年 10 月）　…………………………（96）
　　2011 年 10 月试题精解　…………………………………………………………………（112）
　　中国科学院博士研究生入学考试英语试题（2012 年 3 月）　…………………………（122）
　　2012 年 3 月试题精解　……………………………………………………………………（137）
　　中国科学院大学博士研究生入学考试英语试题（2012 年 10 月）　……………………（146）
　　2012 年 10 月试题精解　…………………………………………………………………（161）
　　中国科学院大学博士研究生入学考试英语试题（2013 年 3 月）　……………………（170）
　　2013 年 3 月试题精解　……………………………………………………………………（185）
　　中国科学院大学博士研究生入学考试英语试题（2013 年 10 月）　……………………（194）
　　2013 年 10 月试题精解　…………………………………………………………………（209）
　　中国科学院大学博士研究生入学考试英语试题（2014 年 3 月）　……………………（219）
　　2014 年 3 月试题精解　……………………………………………………………………（234）
　　中国科学院大学博士研究生入学考试英语试题（2015 年 3 月）　……………………（244）
　　2015 年 3 月试题精解　……………………………………………………………………（259）
　　中国科学院大学博士研究生入学考试英语试题（2016 年 3 月）　……………………（268）
　　2016 年 3 月试题精解　……………………………………………………………………（284）
　　中国科学院大学博士研究生入学考试英语试题（2017 年 3 月）　……………………（294）
　　2017 年 3 月试题精解　……………………………………………………………………（309）

第一部分

中国科学院研究生院博士研究生入学考试英语考试大纲及样题

中国科学院研究生院
博士研究生入学考试
英语考试大纲

本大纲是在2002年10月起试行的原《中国科学院研究生院博士研究生入学考试英语考试大纲》的基础上修订的,自2005年10月起在中国科学院研究生院范围内试行。

考试对象

报考中国科学院所属各院、所、园、中心、站、台相关专业拟攻读博士学位的考生。

考试目的

检验考生是否具有进入攻读博士学位阶段的英语水平和能力。

考试类型、考试内容及考试结构

本考试共有5个部分:词汇(占10%)、完形填空(占15%)、阅读理解(占40%)、英译汉(占15%),写作(占20%)。试卷分为:试卷一(PAPER ONE)客观试题,包括前3个部分,共75题,顺序排号;试卷二(PAPER TWO)主观试题,包括英译汉和写作两个部分。

一、词汇

主要测试考生是否具备一定的词汇量和根据上下文对词和词组意义判断的能力。词和词组的测试范围基本以本考试大纲词汇表为参照依据。

共20题。每题为一个留有空白的英文句子。要求考生从所给的4个选项中选出可用在句中的最恰当词或词组。

二、完形填空

主要测试考生在语篇层次上的理解能力以及对词汇表达方式和结构掌握的程度。考生应具有借助于词汇、句法及上下文线索对语言进行综合分析和应用的能力。要求考生就所给篇章中15处空白所需的词或短语分别从4个选项中选出最佳答案。

三、阅读理解

本部分共分两节。要求考生能:

(1)掌握中心思想、主要内容和具体细节。

(2)进行相关的判断和推理。

（3）准确把握某些词和词组在上下文中的特定含义。

（4）领会作者的观点和意图，判断作者的态度。

A 节：主要测试考生在规定时间内通过阅读获取相关信息的能力。考生须完成 1 800～2 000 词的阅读量并就题目从 4 个选项中选出最佳答案。

B 节：主要测试考生对诸如连贯性和一致性等语段特征的理解。考生须完成 700～900 词的阅读量（2 篇短文），并根据每篇文章（约 400 词）的内容，从文后所提供的 6 段文字中选择能分别放进文章中 5 个空白处的 5 段。

四、英译汉

要求考生将一篇近 400 词的英语短文中有下划线的 5 个句子翻译成汉语。主要测试考生是否能从语篇的角度正确理解英语原句的意思，并能用准确、达意的汉语书面表达出来。

五、写作

要求考生按照命题、所给提纲或背景图、表写出一篇不少于 200 词的短文。目的是测试考生用英语表达思想或传递信息的能力及对英文写作基础知识的实际运用能力。

考试时间及计分

考试时间总计为 180 分钟，其中试卷一为 110 分钟，试卷二为 70 分钟。卷面总分 100 分。详见下表。

试卷一：

题号	名称	题量/道	分值/%	时间/min
Ⅰ	词汇	20	10	15
Ⅱ	完形填空	15	15	15
Ⅲ-A	阅读理解（A）	30	30	60
Ⅲ-B	阅读理解（B）	10	10	20
小计	—	75	65	110

试卷二：

题号	名称	题量/道	分值/%	时间/min
Ⅳ	英译汉——语篇中句子	5	15	30
Ⅴ	写作	1	20	40
小计	—	6	35	70

中国科学院
博士研究生入学考试
英语试卷

(样题)

考生须知：

一、本试卷由试卷一（PAPER ONE）和试卷二（PAPER TWO）两部分组成。试卷一为客观题，答卷使用标准化机读答题纸；试卷二为主观题，答卷使用非机读答题纸。

二、请考生一律用HB或2B铅笔填涂标准化机读答题纸，画线不得过细或过短。修改时请用橡皮擦拭干净。若因填涂不符合要求而导致计算机无法识别，责任由考生自负。请保持机读答题纸清洁、无折皱。答题纸切忌折叠。

三、全部考试时间总计180分钟，满分为100分。时间及分值分布如下：

试卷一：

	Ⅰ 词汇	15分钟	10分
	Ⅱ 完形填空	15分钟	15分
	Ⅲ 阅读理解	80分钟	40分
	小计	110分钟	65分

试卷二：

	Ⅳ 英译汉	30分钟	15分
	Ⅴ 写作	40分钟	20分
	小计	70分钟	35分

SAMPLE TEST
THE CHINESE ACADEMY OF SCIENCES ENGLISH ENTRANCE EXAMINATION FOR DOCTORAL CANDIDATES

PAPER ONE

PART I VOCABULARY (15 minutes, 10 points, 0.5 point each)

Directions: *Choose the word or expression below each sentence that best completes the statement, and mark the corresponding letter of your choice with a single bar across the square brackets on your Machine-scoring Answer Sheet.*

1. Ten years ago, a house with a decent bathroom was a _____ symbol among university professors.
   A. post   B. status   C. position   D. place
2. It would be far better if collectors could be persuaded to spend their time and money in support of _____ archaeological research.
   A. legible   B. legitimate   C. legislative   D. illicit
3. We seek a society that has at its _____ a respect for the dignity and worth of the individual.
   A. end   B. hand   C. core   D. best
4. A variety of problems have greatly _____ the country's normal educational development.
   A. impeded   B. imparted   C. implored   D. implemented
5. A good education is an asset you can _____ for the rest of your life.
   A. spell out   B. call upon   C. fall over   D. resort to
6. Oil can change a society more _____ than anyone could ever have imagined.
   A. grossly   B. severely   C. rapidly   D. drastically
7. Beneath its myriad rules, the fundamental purpose of _____ is to make the world a more pleasant place to live in, and you a more pleasant person to live with.
   A. elitism   B. eloquence   C. eminence   D. etiquette
8. The New Testament was not only written in Greek language, but ideas derived from Greek philosophy were _____ in many parts of it.
   A. altered   B. criticized   C. incorporated   D. translated

9. Nobody will ever know the agony I go _____ waiting for him to come home.
   A. over   B. with   C. down   D. through
10. While a country's economy is becoming the most promising in the world, its people should be more _____ about their quality of life.
    A. discriminating   B. distributing   C. disagreeing   D. disclosing
11. Cheated by two boys whom he had trust on, Joseph promised to _____ them.
    A. find fault with   B. make the most of
    C. look down upon   D. get even with
12. The Minister's _____ answer let to an outcry from the Opposition.
    A. impressive   B. evasive   C. intensive   D. exhaustive
13. In proportion as the _____ between classes within the nation disappears the hostility of one nation to another will come to an end.
    A. intolerance   B. pessimism   C. injustice   D. antagonism
14. Everyone does their own thing, to the point where a fifth-grade teacher can't _____ on a fourth-grade teacher having taught certain things.
    A. count   B. insist   C. fall   D. dwell
15. When the fire broke out in the building, the people lost their _____ and ran into the elevator.
    A. hearts   B. tempers   C. heads   D. senses
16. Consumers deprived of the information and advice they needed were quite simply _____ every cheat in the marketplace.
    A. at the mercy of   B. in lieu of   C. by courtesy of   D. for the price of
17. In fact the purchasing power of a single person's pension in Hong Kong was only 70 per cent of the value of the _____ Singapore pension.
    A. equivalent   B. similar   C. consistent   D. identical
18. He became aware that he had lost his audience since he had not been able to talk _____.
    A. honestly   B. graciously   C. coherently   D. flexibly
19. The novel, which is a work of art, exists not by its _____ life, but by its immeasurable difference from life.
    A. significance in   B. imagination at
    C. resemblance to   D. predominance over
20. She was artful and could always _____ her parents in the end.
    A. shout down   B. get round   C. comply with   D. pass over

PART II CLOZE TEST (15 minutes, 15 points)

Directions: *For each blank in the following passage, choose the best answer from the four choices given below. Mark the corresponding letter of your choice with a single bar across the square brackets on your Machine-scoring Answer Sheet.*

We are entering a period in which rapid population growth, the presence of deadly weapons, and dwindling resources will bring international tensions to dangerous levels for an extended period. Indeed, __21__ seems no reason for these levels of danger to subside unless population equilibrium is __22__ and some rough measure of fairness reached in the distribution of wealth among nations. __23__ of adequate magnitude imply a willingness to redistribute income internationally on a more generous __24__ than the advanced nations have evidenced within their own domains. The required increases in __25__ in the backward regions would necessitate gigantic applications of energy merely to extract the __26__ resources.

It is uncertain whether the requisite energy-producing technology exists, and more serious, __27__ that its application would bring us to the threshold of an irreversible change in climate __28__ a consequence of the enormous addition of manmade heat to the atmosphere. It is this __29__ problem that poses the most demanding and difficult of the challenges. The existing __30__ of industrial growth, with no allowance for increased industrialization to repair global poverty, hold __31__ the risk of entering the danger zone of climatic change in as __32__ as three or four generations. If the trajectory is in fact pursued, industrial growth will __33__ have to come to an immediate halt, for another generation or two along that __34__ would literally consume human, perhaps all life. The terrifying outcome can be postponed only to the extent that the wastage of heat can be reduced, __35__ that technologies that do not add to the atmospheric heat burden — for example, the use of solar energy — can be utilized. (1996)

21. A. one   B. it   C. this   D. there
22. A. achieved   B. succeeded   C. produced   D. executed
23. A. Transfers   B. Transactions C. Transports   D. Transcripts
24. A. extent   B. scale   C. measure   D. range
25. A. outgrowth   B. outcrop   C. output   D. outcome
26. A. needed   B. needy   C. needless   D. needing
27. A. possible   B. possibly   C. probable   D. probably
28. A. in   B. with   C. as   D. to
29. A. least   B. late   C. latest   D. last
30. A. race   B. pace   C. face   D. lace
31. A. on   B. up   C. down   D. out
32. A. less   B. fewer   C. many   D. little
33. A. rather   B. hardly   C. then   D. yet
34. A. line   B. move   C. drive   D. track
35. A. if   B. or   C. while   D. as

PART III READING COMPREHENSION

Section A (60 minutes, 30 points)

Directions: *Below each of the following passages you will find some questions or incomplete statements. Each question or statement is followed by four choices marked A, B, C, and D. Read each passage carefully, and then select the choice that best answers the question or completes the statement. Mark the letter of your choice with a single bar across the square brackets on your Machine-scoring Answer Sheet.*

Passage One

The writing of a historical synthesis involves integrating the materials available to the historian into a comprehensible whole. The problem in writing a historical synthesis is how to find a pattern in, or impose a pattern upon, the detailed information that has already been used to explain the causes for a historical event.

A synthesis seeks common elements in which to interpret the contingent parts of a historical event. The initial step, therefore, in writing a historical synthesis, is to put the event to be synthesized in a proper historical perspective, so that the common elements or strands making up the event can be determined. This can be accomplished by analyzing the historical event as part of a general trend or continuum in history. The common elements that are familiar to the event will become the ideological framework in which the historian seeks to synthesize. This is not to say that any factor will not have a greater relative value in the historian's handling of the interrelated when viewed in a broad historical perspective.

The historian, in synthesizing, must determine the extent to which the existing hypotheses have similar trends. A general trend line, once established, will enable these similar trends to be correlated and paralleled within the conceptual framework of a common base. A synthesis further seeks to determine, from existing hypotheses, why an outcome took the direction it did; thus, it necessitates reconstructing the spirit of the times in order to assimilate the political, social, psychological, etc., factors within a common base.

As such, the synthesis becomes the logical construct in interpreting the common ground between an original explanation of an outcome (thesis) and the reinterpretation of the outcome along different lines (antithesis). Therefore, the synthesis necessitates the integration of the materials available into a comprehensible whole which will in turn provide a new historical perspective for the event being synthesized.

36. The author would mostly be concerned with _____.
    A. finding the most important cause for a particular historical event
    B. determining when hypotheses need to be reinterpreted

C. imposing a pattern upon varying interpretations for the causes of a particular historical event
D. attributing many conditions that together lead to a particular historical event or to single motive

37. The most important preliminary step in writing a historical synthesis would be _____.
    A. to accumulate sufficient reference material to explain an event
    B. analyzing the historical event to determine if a "single theme theory" apples to the event
    C. determining the common strands that make up a historical event
    D. interpreting historical factors to determine if one factor will have relatively greater value

38. The best definition for the term "historical synthesis" would be _____.
    A. combining elements of different material into a unified whole
    B. a tentative theory set forth as an explanation for an event
    C. the direct opposite of the original interpretation of an event
    D. interpreting historical material to prove that history repeats itself

39. A historian seeks to reconstruct the "spirit" of a time period because _____.
    A. the events in history are more important than the people who make history
    B. existing hypotheses are adequate in explaining historical events
    C. this is the best method to determine the single most important cause for a particular action
    D. varying factors can be assimilated within a common base

40. Which of the following statements would the author consider false?
    A. One factor in a historical synthesis will not have a greater value than other factors.
    B. It is possible to analyze common unifying points in hypotheses.
    C. Historical events should be studied as part of a continuum in history.
    D. A synthesis seeks to determine why an outcome took the direction it did.

Passage Two

When you call the police, the police dispatcher has to locate the car nearest you that is free to respond. This means the dispatcher has to keep track of the status and location of every police car — not an easy task for a large department.

Another problem, which arises when cars are assigned to regular patrols, is that the patrols may be too regular. If criminals find out that police cars will pass a particular location at regular intervals, they simply plan their crimes for times when no patrol is expected. Therefore, patrol cars should pass by any particular location at random times; the fact that a car just passed should be no guarantee that another one is not just around the corner. Yet simply ordering the officers to patrol at random would lead to chaos.

A computer dispatching system can solve both these problems. The computer has no trouble keeping track of the status and location of each car. With this information, it can determine instantly which car should respond to an incoming call. And with the aid of a pseudorandom number generator, the computer can assign routine patrols so that criminals can't predict just when a police car will pass through a particular area.

(Before computers, police sometimes used roulette wheels and similar devices to make random assignments.)

Computers also can relieve police officers from constantly having to report their status. The police car would contain a special automatic radio transmitter and receiver. The officer would set a dial on this unit indicating the current status of the car — patrolling, directing traffic, chasing a speeder, answering a call, out to lunch, and so on. When necessary, the computer at headquarters could poll the car for its status. The voice radio channels would not be clogged with cars constantly reporting what they were doing. A computer in the car automatically could determine the location of the car, perhaps using the LORAN method. The location of the car also would be sent automatically to the headquarters computer.

41. The best title for this passage should be _____.
    A. Computers and Crimes
    B. Patrol Car Dispatching
    C. The Powerful Computers
    D. The Police with Modern Equipment

42. A police dispatcher is NOT supposed to _____.
    A. locate every patrol car
    B. guarantee cars on regular patrols
    C. keep in touch with each police car
    D. find out which car should respond to the incoming call

43. If the patrols are too regular, _____.
    A. the dispatchers will be bored with it
    B. the officers may become careless
    C. the criminals may take advantage of it
    D. the streets will be in a state of chaos

44. The computer dispatching system is particularly good at _____.
    A. assigning cars to regular patrols
    B. responding to the incoming calls
    C. ordering officers to report their location
    D. making routine patrols unpredictable

45. According to the account in the last paragraph, how can a patrol car be located without computers?
    A. Police officers report their status constantly.
    B. The headquarters poll the car for its status.
    C. A radio transmitter and receiver is installed in a car.
    D. A dial in the car indicates its current status.

Passage Three

A child who has once been pleased with a tale likes, as a rule, to have it retold in identically the same words, but this should not lead parents to treat printed fairy stories as sacred texts. It is always much better to tell a story than read it out of a book, and, if a parent can produce what, in the actual circumstances of the time and the individual child, is an improvement on the printed text, so much the better.

A charge made against fairy tales is that they harm the child by frightening him or arousing his sadistic impulse. To prove the latter, one would have to show in a controlled experiment that children who have read fairy stories were more often guilty of cruelty than those who had not. Aggressive, destructive, sadistic impulses every child has and, on the whole, their symbolic verbal discharge seem to be rather a safety valve than an incitement to overt action. As to fears, there are, I think, well-authenticated cases of children being dangerously terrified by some fairy story. Often, however, this arises from the child having heard the story once. Familiarity with the story by repetition turns the pain of fear into the pleasure of a fear faced and mastered.

There are also people who object to fairy stories on the grounds that they are not objectively true, that giants, witches, two-headed dragons, magic carpets, etc., do not exist; and that, instead of indulging his fantasies in fairy tales, the child should be taught how to adapt to reality by studying history and mechanics. I find such people, I must confess, so unsympathetic and peculiar that I do not know how to argue with them. If their case were sound, the world should be full of madmen attempting to fly from New York to Philadelphia on a broomstick or covering a telephone with kisses in the belief that it was their enchanted girl-friend.

No fairy story ever claimed to be a description of the external world and no sane child has ever believed that it was.

46. According to the author, the best way to retell a story to a child is to _____.
    A. tell it in a creative way
    B. take from it what the child likes
    C. add to it whatever at hand
    D. read it out of the story book

47. In the second paragraph, which statement best expresses the author's attitude towards fairy stories?
    A. He sees in them the worst of human nature.
    B. He dislikes everything about them.
    C. He regards them as more of a benefit than harms.
    D. He is expectant of the experimental results.

48. According to the author, fairy stories are most likely to _____.
    A. make children aggressive the whole life
    B. incite destructiveness in children

C. function as a safety valve for children

D. add children's enjoyment of cruelty to others

49. If the child has heard some horror story for more than once, according to the author, he would probably be _____.

A. scared to death

B. taking it and even enjoying it

C. suffering more the pain of fear

D. dangerously terrified

50. The author's mention of broomsticks and telephones is meant to emphasize that _____.

A. old fairy stories keep updating themselves to cater for modern needs

B. fairy stories have claimed many lives of victims

C. fairy stories have thrown our world into chaos

D. fairy stories are after all fairy stories

Passage Four

There has been a lot of hand-wringing over the death of Elizabeth Steinberg. Without blaming anyone in particular, neighbors, friends, social workers, the police and newspaper editors have struggled to define the community's responsibility to Elizabeth and to other battered children. As the collective soul-searching continues, there is a pervading sense that the system failed her.

The fact is, in New York State the system couldn't have saved her. It is almost impossible to protect a child from violent parents, especially if they are white, middle-class, well-educated and represented by counsel.

Why does the state permit violence against children? There are a number of reasons. First, parental privilege is a rationalization. In the past, the law was giving its approval to the biblical injunction against **sparing the rod**.

Second, while everyone agrees that the state must act to remove children from their homes when there is danger of serious physical or emotional harm, many child advocates believe that state intervention in the absence of serious injury is more harmful than helpful.

Third, courts and legislatures tread carefully when their actions intrude or threaten to intrude on a relationship protected by the Constitution. In 1923, the Supreme Court recognized the "liberty of parent and guardian to direct the upbringing and education of children under their control." More recently, in 1977, it upheld the teacher's privilege to use corporal punishment against schoolchildren. Read together, these decisions give the constitutional imprimatur to parental use of physical force.

Under the best conditions, small children depend utterly on their parents for survival. Under the worst, their dependency dooms them. While it is questionable whether anyone or anything could have saved Elizabeth Steinberg, it is plain that the law provided no protection.

To the contrary, by justifying the use of physical force against children as an acceptable method of education and control, the law lent a measure of plausibility and legitimacy to her parents' conduct.

More than 80 years ago, in the teeth of parental resistance and Supreme Court doctrine, the New York State Legislature acted to eliminate child labor law. Now, the state must act to eliminate child abuse by banning corporal punishment. To break the cycle of violence, nothing less will answer. If there is a lesson to be drawn from the death of Elizabeth Steinberg, it is this: spare the rod and spare the child.

51. The New York State law seems to provide least protection of a child from violent parents of _____.
    A. a family on welfare
    B. a poor uneducated family
    C. an educated black family
    D. a middle-class white family

52. "Sparing the rod" (in boldface) means _____.
    A. spoiling children
    B. punishing children
    C. not caring about children
    D. not beating children

53. Corporal punishment against schoolchildren is _____.
    A. taken as illegal in the New York State
    B. considered being in the teacher's province
    C. officially approved by law
    D. disapproved by school teachers

54. From the article we can infer that Elizabeth Steinberg is probably the victim of _____.
    A. teachers' corporal punishment
    B. misjudgment of the court
    C. parents' ill-treatment
    D. street violence

55. The writer of this article thinks that banning corporal punishment will in the long run _____.
    A. prevent violence of adults
    B. save more children
    C. protect children from ill-treatment
    D. better the system

Passage Five

With its common interest in lawbreaking but its immense range of subject-matter and widely-varying methods of treatment, the crime novel could make a legitimate claim to be regarded as a separate branch of literature, or, at least, as a distinct, even though a slightly disreputable, offshoot of the traditional novel.

The detective story is probably the most respectable (at any rate in the narrow sense of the word) of the crime species. Its creation is often the relaxation of university scholars, literary economists, scientists or even poets. Disastrous deaths may occur more frequently and mysteriously than might be expected in polite society, but the world in which they happen, the village, seaside resort, college or studio, is familiar to us, if not from our own experience, at least in the newspaper or the lives of friends. The characters, though normally realized superficially, are as recognizably human and consistent as our less intimate acquaintances. A story set in a more remote African jungle or Australian bush, ancient China or gas-lit London, appeals to our interest in geography or history, and most detective story writers are conscientious in providing a reasonably true background. The elaborate, carefully-assembled plot, despised by the modern intellectual critics and creators of "significant" novels, has found refuge in the murder mystery, with its sprinkling of clues, its spicing with apparent impossibilities, all with appropriate solutions and explanations at the end. With the guilt of escapism from real life nagging gently, we secretly take delight in the unmasking of evil by a vaguely super-human detective, who sees through and dispels the cloud of suspicion which has hovered so unjustly over the innocent.

Though its villain also receives his rightful deserts, the thriller presents a less comfortable and credible world. The sequence of fist fights, revolver duels, car crashes and escapes from gas-filled cellars exhausts the reader far more than the hero, who, suffering from at least two broken ribs, one black eye, uncountable bruises and a hangover, can still chase and overpower an armed villain with the physique of a wrestler, He moves dangerously through a world of ruthless gangs, brutality, a vicious lust for power and money and, in contrast to the detective tale, with a near-omniscient arch-criminal whose defeat seems almost accidental. Perhaps we miss in the thriller the security of being safely led by our imperturbable investigator past a score of red herrings and blind avenues to a final gathering of suspects when an unchallengeable elucidation of all that has bewildered us is given and justice and goodness prevail. All that we vainly hope for from life is granted vicariously.

56. The crime novel is regarded by the author as _____.

   A. a not respectable form of the traditional novel
   B. not a true novel at all
   C. related in some ways to the historical novel
   D. a distinct branch of the traditional novel

57. The creation of detective stories has its origin in _____.

   A. seeking rest from work or worries
   B. solving mysterious deaths in this society
   C. restoring expectations in polite society
   D. preventing crimes

58. The characters of the detective stories are, generally speaking, _____.

   A. more profound than those of the traditional novels
   B. as real as life itself

C. not like human beings at all

D. not very profound but not unlikely

59. The setting of the detective stories is sometimes in a more remote place because _____.

    A. it is more real

    B. our friends are familiar with it

    C. it pleases the readers in a way

    D. it needs the readers' support

60. The writer of this passage thinks _____.

    A. what people hope for from life can finally be granted if they have confidence

    B. people like to feel that justice and goodness will always triumph

    C. they know in the real world good does not prevail over evil

    D. their hopes in life can only be fulfilled through fiction reading

Passage Six

Whenever we are involved in a creative type of activity that is self-rewarding, a feeling overcomes us — a feeling that we can call "flow." When we are flowing we lose all sense of time and awareness of what is happening around us; instead, we feel that everything is going just right.

A rock dancer describes his feeling of flow like this: "If I have enough space, I feel I can radiate an energy into the atmosphere. I can dance for walls, I dance for floors. I become one with the atmosphere." "You are in an ecstatic state to such a point that you don't exist," says a composer, describing how he feels when he "flows." Players of any sport throughout the world are familiar with the feeling of flow; they enjoy their activity very much, even though they can expect little extrinsic reward. The same holds true for surgeons, cave explorers, and mountain climbers.

Flow provides a sort of physical sensation along with an altered state of being. One man put it this way: "Your body feels good and awake all over. Your energy is flowing." People who flow feel part of this energy; that is, they are so involved in what they are doing that they do not think of themselves as being separated from their activity. They are flowing along with their enjoyment. Moreover, they concentrate intensely on their activity. They do not try to concentrate harder, however; the concentration comes automatically. A chess player compares this concentration to breathing. As they concentrate, these people feel **immersed** in the action, lost in the action. Their sense of time is altered and they skip meals and sleep without noticing their loss. Sizes and spaces also seem altered: successful baseball players see and hit the ball so much better because it seems larger to them. They can even distinguish the seams on a ball approaching them at 165 kilometers per hour.

It seems then that flow is a "floating action" in which the individual is aware of his actions but not aware of his awareness. A good reader is so absorbed in his book that he knows he is turning the pages to go on reading, but he does not notice he is turning these pages. The moment people think about it, flow is destroyed, so they never ask themselves questions such as "Am I doing well?" or "Did everyone see my jump?"

Finally, to flow successfully depends a great deal on the activity itself; not too difficult to produce anxiety, not too easy to bring about boredom; challenging, interesting, fun. Some good examples of flow activities are games and sports, reading, learning, working on what you enjoy, and even day-dreaming.

61. What is the main purpose of the article?
    A. To illustrate the feeling of "flow."
    B. To analyze the causes of a special feeling.
    C. To define the new psychological term "flow."
    D. To lead people to acquire the feeling of "flow."
62. In this article, "flow" refers to a feeling which probably results from _____.
    A. awareness   B. ecstasy
    C. unconsciousness   D. self-rewarding
63. The word "immersed" (in boldface) is closest in meaning to _____.
    A. occupied   B. engrossed
    C. soaked   D. committed
64. What does one usually act while "flowing" in reading?
    A. Thinks what he is doing.
    B. Wonders how fast he can read.
    C. Turns the pages.
    D. Minds the page number.
65. The activity which can successfully bring about "flow" is most probably _____.
    A. gripping   B. difficult   C. boring   D. easy

Section B (20 minutes, 10 points)

Directions: *In each of the following passages, five sentences have been removed from the original text. They are listed from A to F and put below the passage. Choose the most suitable sentence from the list to fill in each of the blanks (numbered 66 to 75). For each passage, there is one sentence that does not fit in any of the blanks. Mark your answers on your Machine-scoring Answer Sheet.*

Passage One

A history of long and effortless success can be a dreadful handicap, but, if properly handled, it may become a driving force. When the United States entered just such a glowing period after the end of the Second World War, it had a market eight times larger than any competitor, giving its industries unparalleled economies of scale. ___66___ America and Americans were prosperous beyond the dreams of the Europeans and Asians whose economies the war had destroyed.

It was inevitable that this primacy should have narrowed as other countries grew richer. Just as inevitably, the retreat from predominance proved painful. By the mid-1980s Americans had found themselves at a loss over their fading industrial competitiveness. __67__ By 1987 there was only one American television maker left, Zenith. (Now there is none: Zenith was bought by South Korea's LG Electronics in July.) Foreign-made cars and textiles were sweeping into the domestic market. America's machine tool industry was on the ropes. __68__

All of this caused a crisis of confidence. Americans stopped taking prosperity for granted. They began to believe that their way of doing business was failing, and that their incomes would therefore shortly begin to fall as well. __69__ Their sometimes-sensational findings were filled with warnings about the growing competition from overseas.

__70__ In 1995 the United States can look back on five years of solid growth while Japan has been struggling. Few Americans attribute this solely to such obvious causes as a devalued dollar or the turning of the business cycle. Self-doubt has yielded to blind pride. "American industry has changed its structure, has gone on a diet, has learnt to be more quick-witted," according to Richard Cavanagh, executive dean of Harvard's Kennedy School of Government. "It makes me proud to be an American just to see how our businesses are improving their productivity," says Stephen Moore of the Cato Institute, a think-tank in Washington, DC. And William Sahlman of the Harvard Business School believes that people will look back on this period as "a golden age of business management in the United States."

A. For a while it looked as though the making of semiconductors, which America had invested and which sat at the heart of the new computer age, was going to be the next casualty.
B. Its scientists were the world's best, its workers the most skilled.
C. How things have changed!
D. The mid-1980s brought one inquiry after another into the causes of America's industrial decline.
E. Some huge American industries, such as consumer electronics, had shrunk or vanished in the face of foreign competition.
F. Some of the nation's largest businesses shrink in size when they appear on the government's database of federal contractors.

Passage Two

If sustainable competitive advantage depends on work force skills, American firms have a problem. __71__ Skill acquisition is considered an individual responsibility. Labor is simply another factor of production to be hired — rented at the lowest possible cost — much as one buys raw materials or equipment.

The lack of importance attached to human resource management can be seen in the corporate hierarchy. In an American firm the chief financial officer is almost always second in command. __72__ The executive who holds it is never consulted on major strategic decisions and has no chance to move up to Chief Executive Officer (CEO). By way of contrast, in Japan the head of human resource management is central — usually the second most important executive, after the CEO, in the firm's hierarchy.

While American firms often talk about the vast amounts spent on training their work forces, in fact they invest less in the skills of their employees than do either Japanese or German firms. __73__ And the limited investments that are made in training workers are also much more narrowly focused on the specific skills necessary to do the next job rather than on the basic background skills that make it possible to absorb new technologies.

As a result, problems emerge when new breakthrough technologies arrive. __74__ More time is required before equipment is up and running at capacity, and the need for extensive retraining generates costs and creates bottlenecks that limit the speed with which new equipment can be employed. __75__ And in the end the skills of the population affect the wages of the top half. If the bottom half can't effectively staff the processes that have to be operated, the management and professional jobs that go with these processes will disappear.

A. If American workers for example, take much longer to learn how to operate new flexible manufacturing stations than workers in Germany (as they do), the effective cost of those stations is lower in Germany than it is in the United Stated.
B. The head of human resource management is one of the most important executives in the firm.
C. The money they do invest is also more highly concentrated on professional and managerial employees.
D. Human resource management is not traditionally seen as central to the competitive survival of the firm in the United States.
E. The post of head of human resource management is usually a specialized job, off at the edge of the corporate hierarchy.
F. The result is a slower pace of technological change.

PAPER TWO

PART IV　TRANSLATION(30 minutes, 15 points)

Directions: *Read the following text carefully and then translate the underlined segments into Chinese. Write your pieces of Chinese version in the proper space on your Answer Sheet II.*

There is no greater power in the world today than that wielded by the manipulators of public opinion in America. (1) No king or pope of old, no conquering general or high priest ever disposed of a power even remotely approaching that of the few dozen men who control America's mass news and entertainment media.

(2) Their power is not distant and impersonal; it reaches into every home in America, and it works its will during nearly every waking hour. It is the power which shapes and molds the mind of

virtually every citizen, young or old, rich or poor, simple or sophisticated.

The mass media form for us our image of the world and then tell us what to think about that image. (3) Essentially everything we know — or think we know — about events outside our own neighborhood or circle of acquaintances comes to us via our daily newspaper, our weekly news magazine, our radio, or our television.

It is not just the heavy-handed suppression of certain news stories from our newspapers or the blatant propagandizing of history-distorting TV "docudramas" which characterizes the opinion-manipulating techniques of the media masters. They exercise both subtlety and thoroughness in their management of both the news and the entertainment which they present to us.

For example, the way in which the news is covered: (4) which items are emphasized and which are played down, the reporter's choice of words, tone of voice, and facial expressions; the wording of headlines; the choice of illustrations — all of these things subliminally(潜意识地) and yet profoundly affect the way in which we interpret what we see or hear.

On top of this, of course, the columnists and editors remove any remaining doubt from our minds as to just what we are to think about it all. (5) Employing carefully developed psychological techniques, they guide our thought and opinion so that we can be in tune with the "in" crowd, the "beautiful people," the "smart money." They let us know exactly what our attitudes should be toward various types of people and behavior by placing those people or that behavior in the context of a TV drama or situation comedy and having the other TV characters react to them in the politically correct way.

PART V WRITING (40 minutes, 20 points)

Directions: *Write an essay of no less than 200 words on the topic given below. Use the proper space on your Answer Sheet II.*

> Anything that is overdone may bring unwanted results. Addiction to the Internet is of no exception. Discuss the harmful effects on a person's life when he/she is indulged in the Internet.

中国科学院博士研究生入学考试英语试卷

(样题)

参考答案

PART I VOCABULARY

1. B   2. B   3. C   4. A   5. B   6. D   7. D   8. C
9. D   10. A   11. D   12. B   13. D   14. A   15. C   16. A
17. A   18. C   19. C   20. B

PART II CLOZE TEST

21. D   22. A   23. A   24. B   25. D   26. A   27. B   28. C
29. D   30. B   31. D   32. C   33. C   34. A   35. B

PART III READING COMPREHENSION

Section A

36. C   37. C   38. B   39. D   40. A   41. B   42. B   43. C
44. D   45. A   46. A   47. C   48. C   49. B   50. D   51. D
52. D   53. B   54. C   55. A   56. D   57. A   58. D   59. C
60. B   61. A   62. D   63. B   64. C   65. A

Section B

66. B   67. E   68. A   69. D   70. C   71. D   72. E   73. C
74. A   75. F

PART IV TRANSLATION

Suggested Chinese version for the 5 English Segments：

（1）过去的国王、教皇、征战他国的大将军或者基督教会的长老所行使的权力远远无法与当今那几十个控制着美国大众新闻、娱乐媒体的人手中的权力相比拟。

（2）他们的权力之手伸得很近,伸及每一个人,伸及美国的每一个家庭。人们除了睡眠之外,几乎无时无刻不在受着这个权力意志的影响。

（3）从根本上说,我们所了解的(或者说我们认为我们所了解的)一切有关我们居住地或者熟人圈之外发生的事件的信息,都是通过我们的新闻日报、周刊、广播或者电视而获得的。

（4）哪些是重点强调的、哪些是刻意低调报道的；报道者所用的词汇、语调；他(她)的面部表情；标题的用语、图片的选择；所有这一切,都不知不觉地但却根深蒂固地影响着我们对所见所闻的理解和解释。

（5）他们精心地运用现代心理技术引导我们的思想和看法,使我们与他们所宣扬的一些观点,如"时尚大众""美丽的人""聪明财富",相一致。

第二部分

中国科学院博士研究生入学考试英语考试试题及参考答案（2005—2009年）

（详情在本书所附的光盘里）

第三部分

中国科学院博士研究生入学考试英语考试试题及精解（2010—2017年）

中国科学院
博士研究生入学考试
英语试题

（2010年3月）

考生须知：
一、本试卷由试卷一（PAPER ONE）和试卷二（PAPER TWO）两部分组成。试卷一为客观题，答卷使用标准化机读答题纸；试卷二为主观题，答卷使用非机读答题纸。
二、请考生一律用HB或2B铅笔填涂标准化机读答题纸，画线不得过细或过短。修改时请用橡皮擦拭干净。若因填涂不符合要求而导致计算机无法识别，责任由考生自负。请保持机读答题纸清洁、无折皱。答题纸切忌折叠。
三、全部考试时间总计180分钟，满分为100分。时间及分值分布如下：

试卷一：

	Ⅰ 词汇	15 分钟	10 分
	Ⅱ 完形填空	15 分钟	15 分
	Ⅲ 阅读理解	80 分钟	40 分
	小计	110 分钟	65 分

试卷二：

	Ⅳ 英译汉	30 分钟	15 分
	Ⅴ 写作	40 分钟	20 分
	小计	70 分钟	35 分

GRADUATE UNIVERSITY, CHINESE ACADEMY OF SCIENCES ENGLISH ENTRANCE EXAMINATION FOR DOCTORAL CANDIDATES

March 2010

PAPER ONE

PART I VOCABULARY (15 minutes, 10 points, 0.5 point each)

Directions: *Choose the word or expression below each sentence that best completes the statement, and mark the corresponding letter of your choice with a single bar across the square bracket on your Machine-scoring Answer Sheet.*

1. Because of _____ reviews, the producer announced that the play will close with tonight's performance.
   A. adjacent   B. adequate   C. adhesive   D. adverse
2. Please don't interrupt me. If you have something to say, _____ your comment until I have finished speaking.
   A. withdraw   B. wither   C. withhold   D. withstand
3. The organ transplant community has _____ humans and monkeys for ethical reasons.
   A. knocked out   B. bailed out   C. pointed out   D. ruled out
4. Did the entertainer prepare his jokes before the program, or _____ them as he went along?
   A. envisage   B. visualize   C. improvise   D. mediate
5. This _____ is a national prize and is awarded for the best score by a player under 16 years of age.
   A. trophy   B. treat   C. trifle   D. tribute
6. Editors do think explicitly about timing and they are not motivated merely to be the first to print an exciting news story: they keep stories until the time is _____.
   A. prompt   B. ripe   C. enough   D. punctual
7. His short _____ in the living room had been long enough to keep him awake now.
   A. dove   B. dose   C. dole   D. doze

8. Suddenly one of the leaves begins to fly in a strong wind; the leaf is really no leaf at all — it's an insect _____ as a leaf.
   A. masked   B. disguised   C. repressed   D. assumed
9. Some children have amazed the world since their birth with their incredible intellect and abilities which can at times _____ even the brightest of adults.
   A. outdo   B. overtake   C. contend   D. enhance
10. When buying food, consumers are usually in a hurry, so they don't often _____ descriptions for motivating them to make a choice.
    A. cover up   B. get in   C. go after   D. linger over
11. Millions of people died in the 14th century as the result of a (an) _____ known as the Black Death.
    A. epidemic   B. antibiotics   C. pharmacy   D. contamination
12. While this arrangement was a major improvement over its _____, it still had drawbacks.
    A. premium   B. prevalence   C. premise   D. predecessor
13. The prime minister's proposal for new taxes created such a(n) _____ that his government fell.
    A. sensation   B. upheaval   C. withdrawal   D. outbreak
14. _____ sleep is crucial to the health of adults, new research suggests that lack of sleep may affect teens' health, too.
    A. Just as   B. As long as   C. Despite that   D. No matter how
15. He plans to _____ on hand surgery until September in hopes of winning his first gold medal in the Beijing Olympics.
    A. hold forth   B. hold out   C. hold off   D. hold down
16. To _____ American dollars into foreign currency, multiply the amount by the rate of exchange.
    A. compute   B. convey   C. convict   D. convert
17. The step was announced by the secretary of state in person and given maximum _____.
    A. publication   B. publicity   C. propaganda   D. promotion
18. It is only with further evolution and refinement that health plan report cards can _____ their potential and become a distinctive and useful tool.
    A. shed light on B. put up with   C. look forward to   D. live up to
19. In my twenties, I was _____ to anxiety and depression, which I experienced as a depletion of my self-esteem.
    A. inclined   B. accountable   C. prone   D. poised
20. Teachers complain that children _____ these tests without being able to write a decent essay, solve a multi-step math problem or construct a framework.
    A. look through   B. carry through   C. sail through   D. put through

PART II CLOZE TEST (15 minutes, 15 points)

Directions: *For each blank in the following passage, choose the best answer from the four choices given below. Mark the corresponding letter of your choice with a single bar across the square bracket on your Machine-scoring Answer Sheet.*

Time for another global-competitiveness alert. In the Third International Mathematics and Science Study — which last year tested a half-million students in 41 countries — American eighth graders __21__ below the world average in math. And that's not even __22__ part. Consider this as you try to __23__ which countries will dominate the technology markets of the 21st century: the top 10 percent of America's math students scored about the same as the average kid in the global __24__, Singapore.

It isn't exactly a news flash these days __25__ Americans score behind the curve on international tests. But educators say this study is __26__ because it monitored variables both inside and outside the classroom. Laziness — the factor often __27__ for Americans' poor performance — is not the culprit here. American students __28__ spend more time in class than pupils in Japan and Germany. __29__, they get more homework and watch the same amount of TV. The problem, educators say, is not the kids but a curriculum that is too __30__. The study found that lessons for U.S. eighth graders contained topics mastered by seventh graders in other countries.

Teachers actually agree that Americans need to __31__ their kids to more sophisticated math earlier. Unfortunately, experts say, the teachers don't recognize that __32__ these concepts are taught is as important as the concepts themselves. Most educators rely __33__ on textbooks and rote learning(死记硬背). While many textbooks cover __34__ ideas, most do so superficially, __35__ students with the techniques but not the mastery of the broader principles.

21. A. recorded   B. gained   C. climbed   D. scored
22. A. the least   B. the worst   C. the less   D. the worse
23. A. figure out   B. carry out   C. count up   D. show up
24. A. village   B. leader   C. friend   D. country
25. A. what   B. where   C. when   D. which
26. A. important   B. ineffective   C. comparable   D. delightful
27. A. ignored   B. blamed   C. exaggerated   D. viewed
28. A. vastly   B. accurately   C. actually   D. merely
29. A. To begin with B. As is known   C. Not only that   D. Even so
30. A. easy   B. small   C. short   D. poor
31. A. relate   B. expose   C. lead   D. instruct
32. A. where   B. why   C. how   D. whether
33. A. hardly   B. intentionally   C. consequently   D. exclusively

34. A. advanced   B. colorful   C. controversial   D. ambitious
35. A. carrying   B. leaving   C. expecting   D. shaping

PART III   READING COMPREHENSION

Section A (60 minutes, 30 points)

Directions: *Below each of the following passages you will find some questions or incomplete statements. Each question or statement is followed by four choices marked A, B, C, and D. Read each passage carefully, and then select the choice that best answers the question or completes the statement. Mark the letter of your choice with a single bar across the square bracket on your Machine-scoring Answer Sheet.*

Passage One

Most people lie in everyday conversation when they are trying to appear likable and competent, according to a study conducted by University of Massachusetts psychologist Robert S. Feldman. The study found that lies told by men and women differ in content, though not in quantity.

Feldman said the results showed that men do not lie more than women or vice versa, but that men and women lie in different ways. "Women were more likely to lie to make the person they were talking to feel good, while men lied most often to make themselves look better," Feldman said.

A group of 121 pairs of undergraduate UMass students were recruited to participate in the study. They were told that the purpose of the study was to examine how people interact when they meet someone new. Participants were told they would have a 10-minute conversation with another person. Some participants were told to try to make themselves appear likable. Others were told to appear competent. A third control group was not directed to present themselves in any particular way.

Participants were unaware that the session was being videotaped through a hidden camera. At the end of the session, participants were told they had been videotaped and consent was obtained to use the video-recordings for research.

The students were then asked to watch the video of themselves and identify any inaccuracies in what they had said during the conversation. They were encouraged to identify all lies, no matter how big or small.

Feldman said the students who participated in the study were surprised at their own results. "When they were watching themselves on videotape, people found themselves lying much more than they thought they had," Feldman said.

The lies the students told varied considerably, according to Feldman. Some were relatively minor, such as agreeing with the person with whom they were speaking that they liked someone when they really did not. Others were more extreme, such as falsely claiming to be the star of a rock band.

"It's so easy to lie," Feldman said. "We teach our children that honesty is the best policy, but we also tell them it's polite to pretend they like a birthday gift they've been given. Kids get a very mixed message regarding the practical aspects of lying, and it has an impact on how they behave as adults."

36. According to Feldman's study, men and women tell lies which differ in _____.
   A. the purpose to achieve   B. the amount of time taken
   C. the place of their occurrence   D. the people they're meant for
37. Paragraph 2 implies that _____.
   A. women wish to be unrestrained   B. women wish to be charming
   C. men wish to be impressive   D. men wish to be perceptive
38. Before the study of the interactions, two groups of participants were told _____.
   A. what they should discuss   B. whom they should talk to
   C. how they should behave   D. how fast they should speak
39. From the participants' response to the videotape, it can be said that they could hardly _____.
   A. believe they had told lies   B. tell where they had lied
   C. agree to make the tape public   D. tolerate their having been videotaped
40. Which word best describes the way the participants told lies, as observed by Feldman during the study?
   A. Hesitant.   B. Natural.   C. Embarrassed.   D. Hasty.
41. Feldman felt that the ideas told to the children about lie-telling were very _____.
   A. insincere   B. groundless   C. irresponsible   D. confusing

Passage Two

Modern Japan, despite its ready adoption of Western manners, is in things theatrical still faithful to the ancient feudal day. It is true that within the last few years, the old school drama has to some extent lost ground, and quite recently performances of Shakespeare's "Othello" and "Hamlet," and Daudet's "Sappho" have been received with favor by Tokyo audiences.

The explanation of this curious survival of the old form of play, at a time when all Japan is eagerly imitating the foreigner, is undoubtedly to be found in the peculiar customs of the country. The progressive Japanese finds it easier to change his mode of dress than to reform habits bred in the bone. The old plays, lasting, as they formerly did, from early morning until nearly midnight, just suited the Japanese play-goer, who, when he does go to the theatre, makes an all-day affair of it. Indeed, theatre-going in Japan is a very serious matter, and not to be entered upon lightly or without due preparation. Recently Sada Yoko and Oto Kawakami, who learned a good deal in their foreign travels, introduced the comparatively short evening performance of three or four hours, an innovation which was at once welcomed by the better class of people. But the new arrangement found little favor with the general public, and particular indignation was aroused in the bosom of the Japanese Matinee

Girl who loves to sit in the theatre as long as possible and weep over the play. For, to the young gentlewoman, the theatre is essentially the place for weeping. Japanese girls are extremely sentimental, and a play without tear-provoking situations would not appeal to them in the least.

The Japanese women are passionately devoted to the drama. It is usual for a party to book a box through a tea house connected with the theatre and at the same time make arrangements for what refreshments they wish served. The Japanese maiden makes the most elaborate preparations days beforehand. To be at the theatre on time, playgoers must rise with the sun, and all their meals, including breakfast, are eaten in the tiny box in the playhouse. It is not an easy task to reach one's seats and once the family has settled down, nothing but a catastrophe would induce it to leave its box. The women chew candy and the men freely drink sake as the play goes on.

42. Paragraph 1 stresses the idea that the general public in Tokyo _____.
    A. favors Shakespeare's masterpieces   B. enjoys Japanese old school drama
    C. appreciates Western classic theatre   D. likes performances of foreign styles
43. The peculiar custom of Japan is _____.
    A. making progressive changes in life   B. enjoying dressing in the latest fashion
    C. spending all day watching a drama   D. wearing formal clothes at the theatre
44. The emphasized difference between the Japanese play form and the foreign one is in _____.
    A. the length   B. the costume   C. the acting   D. the innovation
45. The Japanese Matinee Girl would most likely favor a play that centers on _____.
    A. the childhood of a naughty boy   B. the honeymoon of a young couple
    C. the trial of a serial murderer   D. the misfortunes of a big family
46. As playgoers, compared with Japanese men, Japanese women seem to be all the more _____.
    A. lighthearted about going to the theatre   B. emotionally involved with the play
    C. fond of eating food as the play goes   D. experienced in booking a play ticket
47. While watching a drama in the theatre box, the family would most UNLIKELY _____.
    A. go out for a drink   B. go to the restroom
    C. chat about the actors   D. show their inner feelings

Passage Three

Ever since the 1750s, when the writer, satirist, statesman and inventor Benjamin Franklin put political cartooning on the map by publishing the first cartoon of the genre in America, artists have combined their talent, wit and political beliefs to create cartoons that enrage, enlighten or simply engage the viewer.

A picture may paint a thousand words, but a cartoon provokes, protests and entertains all at once. It is this that makes cartoonists so valuable and influential in times of crisis. Today, that crisis is climate change, and clever imagery can give new impetus to our struggle to combat global warming. The organizers of Earthworks 2008, a global cartoon competition, believe that art and humor are simple ways to get the environmental message across.

"We set up the competition to give cartoonists around the world a platform on which to express themselves," says John Renard, one of the Earthworks organizers. "We hoped the competition would stimulate cartoonists to use their pens and wit to help combat environmental devastation and give new impetus to our desperate fight to stop global warming," he says. "After all, humor is often a valuable key in the struggle to win hearts and minds."

But despite **the sharp wit** that pervades the cartoons, climate change is no laughing matter for their creators. The 50 or so countries from which the 600 competition entries were sent are all suffering the effects of global warming, some more dramatically than others. Two cartoons were sent from Burma, where in May this year a tropical storm tore through five regions along the western coast, killing at least 100,000 people, and leaving millions more without shelter, food, or clean water.

Although governments around the world are reluctant to suggest, officially, that the disaster in Burma is a direct result of global warming, there's little doubt that it will have added to the tropical storm's destructive power.

Studies published in the journals *Nature* and *Science* have demonstrated a link between rising sea temperatures and increased wind-speed of tropical storms and hurricanes, and even US-government-funded organizations such as the National Oceanic and Atmospheric Administration admit that a warming of the global climate will affect the severity of storms. "Experiencing first-hand the catastrophic effects of climate change allowed these artists to give their cartoons a special sharpness," says Renard. "And it brought home to us the burden of responsibility to do our utmost to prevent such devastation from becoming more common."

48. In America, it was Benjamin Franklin who _____.
    A. invented satirical cartoons   B. started cartooning on the map
    C. initiated publishing cartoons   D. originated political cartooning
49. According to the Earthworks 2008 organizers, the fight against global warming _____.
    A. should be known to cartoonists worldwide
    B. may be simply described by means of cartoons
    C. could add to a cartoonist's sense of humor
    D. may arouse interest in cartoon competition
50. Cartoons' worth in promoting environmental protection, as emphasized by John Renard, lies in their quality of being _____.
    A. picturesque   B. provocative   C. entertaining   D. laughable
51. According to the passage, "**the sharp wit**" (boldfaced in Paragraph 4) that fills the competition entries refers to the cartoonists' _____.
    A. amusing expression   B. cutting criticism
    C. political keenness   D. bitter grievance
52. What does the passage say about the Burma disaster?
    A. Many governments denied its relevance to global warming.

B. Two Burmese cartoonists portrayed its devastating damage.

C. It was a political hot potato for many government officials.

D. The Burmese government was to blame for failing to predict it.

53. With respect to global warming, the passage suggests that political leaders should _____.

A. get aware of how cartoonists feel about it

B. experience its disastrous effects first-hand

C. learn from science how and why it occurs

D. take their responsibilities in combating it

Passage Four

The "issues" reported were unthinkable. The physician who enrolled the most patients in the study, an Alabama weight-loss doctor, allegedly forged scores of signatures, enrolling "volunteers" every few minutes.

By the time of the FDA review, she was under criminal investigation. (She's now in federal prison.) Another key researcher had been put on probation by the California medical board for gross negligence. He was arrested shortly after the study ended, when police, called to his home on a domestic violence complaint, found him with a bag of cocaine and waving a loaded gun at imaginary people. The study was so riddled with fraud and error that FDA reviewers decided it was useless.

Yet Dr. Ross says he was told to reveal nothing about those problems to the advisory board, which recommended that the drug be approved. Later, he says, he was pressured to soften his report about Ketek's liver toxicity to gain approval of higher-ups.

Six million Americans have now used the drug, including hundreds of infants in a clinical trial designed to test Ketek's effectiveness against ear infections. "How does one justify balancing the risk of fatal liver failure against one day less of ear pain?" one FDA scientist, Rosemary Johann-Liang, protested — to no avail — in a memo to her superiors. Most ear infections clear up in a few days on their own, she says.

The agency says the controversy is overblown. "There was enough good, solid scientific data to make that decision," says FDA spokeswoman Julie Zawisza, pointing to what appeared to be a history of safe use of Ketek in other countries. Ketek has now been linked to 18 deaths and at least 134 cases of liver damage, according to an independent analysis using FDA data. The real toll, some researchers say, may be far greater.

Last October the FDA sent a warning letter to Sanofi-Aventis, Ketek's maker, accusing the company of knowingly presenting compromised data to the agency, a charge the company denies. "We were not aware of the fraud," says spokeswoman Melissa Feltmann. "It was not until the FDA's criminal investigators uncovered it that we became aware of it."

The question remains, What did the FDA and the drugmaker know about the fake safety data, and when?

Congressmen John Dingell and Bart Stupak, both Michigan Democrats, are investigating that mystery right now in Congressional hearings.

"Unfortunately," Stupak says, "the truth comes too late for some victims."

54. According to Paragraph 1, the Alabama physician was accused of _____.
   A. forcing people to join his study
   B. administering illegal drugs to patients
   C. exaggerating some drug's effects
   D. inventing evidence for her research

55. The key researcher had probably been put on probation by the California medical board because he had _____.
   A. failed to fulfill his supervising duties
   B. threatened to kill some of his neighbors
   C. hidden a bag of cocaine in his office
   D. abused his wife and children at home

56. It can be inferred that Ketek is a medicine which _____.
   A. helps lose weight
   B. helps improve memory
   C. treats ear problems
   D. treats liver problems

57. What does the passage say about Rosemary Johann-Liang's protest?
   A. It was lodged in vain.
   B. It worried her superiors.
   C. It was found groundless.
   D. It aroused public attention.

58. FDA suspected Sanofi-Aventis of _____.
   A. being unqualified to make drugs
   B. scheming to do the fraud
   C. letting the misconduct go
   D. being unaware of the crime

59. The author obviously believes that, in the incident, FDA failed to _____.
   A. compensate the victims
   B. take immediate actions
   C. control the whole situation
   D. stick to its moral principles

Passage Five

One of Dara Torres' trainers is walking all over me. Literally, I'm lying on my stomach as Steve Sierra concentrates his entire 160 lb. on my glutei and hamstrings. It hurts, but in a good way.

It's all part of the flexibility — and strength-building regimen that Torres, who is making history as the oldest swimmer to compete in the Olympics, credits with getting her 41-year-old body in good-enough shape to race athletes half her age. But resistance stretching, as it is called, is not just for the Olympians among us. Its focus on maximizing muscle flexibility has been useful for everyone from injured NBA players to children with cerebral palsy. The exercises may not look like much — they generally require no equipment other than a mat and maybe a towel and some straps — and they may not feel that strenuous, but you know the next day that you've had a workout.

Resistance stretching centers on flexing your muscles even as you stretch them; for example, instead of simply releasing a leg lift, resist the urge to let your quad muscles relax on the way down. Unlike holding a muscle in a passively stretched position, the resistance route actively lengthens muscles through constant movement.

"Resistance stretching goes deep into the joints and grabs more muscle fibers to increase strength and flexibility," says Tierney, Sierra's partner. "It takes twice as much force to stretch a muscle as it does to contract it." I'm not convinced yet, but after they guide me through a few exercises my muscles do start to feel more energized. I can see why Torres likes to be worked on half an hour before she swims.

Although Tierney and Sierra have certified 250 trainers through weekend workshops, you might be hard-pressed to find a class at your local gym. That may have something to do with the fact that stretching has always been deemed the most disposable part of any exercise regimen. "People usually only think about flexibility and stretching when they are older and getting stiff or when they are injured," says Tierney. "It's just not considered sexy." That could change. As doctors urge even us non-Olympians to remain physically active throughout our lives, maybe we'll start to pay more attention to stretching. After all, look what it does for Torres.

60. From the passage we know that Dara Torres is _____.
    A. a sports historian   B. a swimming coach
    C. an Olympic champion   D. a professional athlete
61. As the author suggests, resistance stretching is an exercise _____.
    A. requiring little equipment B. beneficial to all of us
    C. for the strong-willed   D. to test our endurance
62. During the resistance stretching, one needs to _____.
    A. naturally let a lifted leg down   B. lengthen his muscles constantly
    C. contract the muscles hard   D. hold out against stretching
63. The benefit one gets from resistance stretching, as stressed by the author, is _____.
    A. his mental refreshment   B. his flexed bone joints
    C. his better body shape   D. his energized muscle
64. According to the author, the possible reason for the unpopularity of resistance stretching today is that it is thought to be _____.
    A. too painful to endure   B. causing too much hurt
    C. a trivial part of exercise D. too natural a physical act
65. Unlike most other people, the author insists that stretching may make one _____.
    A. live longer   B. look attractive   C. physically active   D. rid of disease

Section B (20 minutes, 10 points)

Directions: *In each of the following passages, five sentences have been removed from the original text. They are listed from A to F and put below the passage. Choose the most suitable sentence from the list to fill in each of the blanks (numbered 66 to 75). For each passage, there is one sentence that does not fit in any of the blanks. Mark your answers on your Machine-scoring Answer Sheet.*

Passage One

Swine flu has infected more than a million Americans and is infecting thousands more every week even though the annual flu season is well over.

That total of those who have already been infected is "just a ballpark figure," said Dr. Anne Schuchat, director of respiratory diseases at the Centers for Disease Control and Prevention, adding, "We know we're not tracking every single one of them." Only a tiny fraction of those million cases have been tested. __66__

A survey in New York City showed that almost 7 percent of those called had had flu symptoms during just three weeks in May when the flu was spreading rapidly through schools. If that percentage of the city has had it, then there have been more than 500,000 cases in the city alone. __67__

The flu has now spread to many areas of the country, Dr. Schuchat noted, and the C. D. C. has heard of outbreaks in 34 summer camps in 16 states. About 3,000 Americans have been hospitalized, and their median age is quite young, just 19. Of those, 127 have died.

The median age for deaths is somewhat higher, at 37, but that number is pushed up because while only a few elderly people catch the new flu, about 2 percent of them die as a result.

__68__ Even those victims, she said, "tend to be relatively young, and I don't think that they were thinking of themselves as ready to die."

The new flu has now reached more than 100 countries, according to the World Health Organization. __69__ Australia, Chile and Argentina are seeing a fast spread of the virus, mostly among young people, while one of the usual seasonal flus, an H3N2, is also active.

Five American vaccine companies are working on a swine flu vaccine, Dr. Schuchat said. The C. D. C. has estimated that once the new vaccine is tested for both safety and effectiveness, no more than 60 million doses will be available by September. __70__

A. The world's eyes are on the Southern Hemisphere, which is at the beginning of its winter, when flu spreads more rapidly.
B. Swine flu doesn't often infect people, and the rare human cases that have occurred in the past have mainly affected people who had direct contact with pigs.
C. That means difficult decisions will have to be made about whom to give it to first.
D. Of those who die, Dr. Schuchat said, about three-quarters have some underlying condition like morbid obesity, pregnancy, asthma, diabetes or immune system problems.
E. The estimate is based on testing plus telephone surveys in New York City and several other locales where the new flu has hit hard.
F. However, most of them have been mild enough that doctors recommended nothing more than rest and fluids.

Passage Two

Cultural knowledge consists of the rules, categories, assumptions, definitions, and judgments that people use to classify and interpret the world around them. __71__ To the members of that society, these cultural rules don't seem arbitrary at all, but logical, normal, right, and proper.

__72__ Each cultural system is different in this respect, with a logic and a consistency of its own. People in any given culture derive a large part of their personality and sense of group identity from these patterns, which have developed over a long period of time.

And this cultural pattern is learned, not innate. At birth, we are not Mexican, or Egyptian, or Japanese. __73__ We develop a particular cultural style, an inability, in Georges Braque's phrase, to do otherwise.

The cultural style that we absorb is therefore a kind of framework within which we develop a highly personal style. Although we remain individuals, we operate within a context which also marks us as Japanese, Mexican, or Egyptian.

As Japanese, Mexicans, or Egyptians, culture equips us with not only a special way of looking at life and the world, but with a problem-solving mechanism for finding our way through that world. It does so by providing us with categories for organizing our perception, and with a set of values for arranging these categories into basic groups: good and bad, better and worse, true and false, ugly and beautiful, and so on. __74__

You can easily see how useful culture is. The patterns developed within a social group over generations of interaction enable its members to generate meaning and structure very quickly from the plethora of daily events and occurrences. __75__

A. We learn to become these things, to perceive, value, and behave in certain ways, and not in others.
B. The knowledge of culture is basically a pattern of values, beliefs and expectations which underlie and shape the behavior of groups and individuals.
C. Although these are essentially arbitrary, they are shared among people, and form the basis for their life together.
D. Culture helps us achieve a level of security and predictability, to create and maintain order in large segments of our lives, thus freeing us to be more creative in other areas.
E. A foreign culture is therefore very much like a secret code.
F. Through the lens of our culture, we selectively perceive; we organize what we select; and we make judgments about these things.

PAPER TWO

PART IV TRANSLATION (30 minutes, 15 points)

Directions: *Read the following text carefully and then translate the underlined segments into Chinese. Write your Chinese version in the proper space on your Answer Sheet.*

I. Translate the underlined parts into Chinese:

The Internet is good at shame. 1) There are countless Web sites where people can post nasty complaints about ex-lovers and rude customers or, worse, push fragile teens over the edge, as in the recent case of a Missouri girl driven to suicide by online bullying. Now a new site aimed at college students is raising questions about the legality of online rumor mills. 2) JuicyCampus.com is a rapidly growing gossip site that solicits content with the promise of anonymity. But what began as fun and games — and now has sub-companies on seven college campuses, including Duke University, where it began — has turned ugly and, in many cases, to be flatly smearing others. The posts have devolved from innocuous tales of secret crushes to racist tirades and lurid finger-pointing about drug use and sex, often with the alleged culprit identified by first and last name. In one post, a nameless Loyola Marymount University student asks why so many African-Americans and Latinos are enrolled at the school: "I thought the high tuition was supposed to keep the undesirables OUT?" 3) It's gotten to the point, says Dan Belzer, a Duke senior who has written about the site for his school's newspaper, where "anyone with a grudge can maliciously attack defenseless students."

4) And get away with it, too. JuicyCampus — whose Duke-graduate founder, Matt Ivestor, declined to comment for this story — isn't sponsored by the schools it covers, so administrators can't regulate it. Neither does the law. Such sites are protected by a federal law that immunizes Web hosts from liability for the musings of their users — as long as the hosts themselves don't modify content. (And firmly establishing the identity of an individual poster would be next to impossible.) The rationale is to protect big companies like AOL from the actions of each and every user. But as a consequence, it means victims of a damaged rep have little legal recourse. "Courts tend to have antiquated understandings of privacy," says Daniel Solove, an expert in cyberlaw and the author of "The Future of Reputation." "Until that changes, we're going to see this keep happening." 5) At present, there's only one sure way to rein in a site like JuicyCampus: persuade everyone to stop using it. But you don't need a college degree to figure out that won't happen.

PART V WRITING (40 minutes, 20 points)

Directions: *Write an essay of no less than 200 words on the topic given below. Use the proper space on your Answer Sheet II.*

TOPIC

People often come up with different decisions when facing the same situation. Why?

2010年3月试题精解

第一部分 词 汇

1. 答案：D
    本题考查形容词的含义。A 邻近的；B 足够的，适当的；C 黏着的，有黏性的；D 不利的，敌对的，相反的。句子的意思是：因为没有得到好评，制作人宣布今晚将是这部戏的最后一次演出。

2. 答案：C
    本题考查动词的含义。A 收回，撤军，提款；B 枯萎，干枯，凋谢；C 抑制，阻挡；D 抵挡，反抗，禁得起。句子的意思是：别打断我，你要有话说，请等我说完。

3. 答案：D
    本题考查动词词组的含义。A (拳击比赛中)击倒，使昏迷；B 帮助摆脱困境；C 指出；D 排除。句子的意思是：器官移植有关方面出于道德原因排除使用人和猴子的器官。

4. 答案：C
    本题考查动词的含义。A 想象，设想；B 想象，设想；C 即兴发挥；D 调停解决。句子的意思是：表演者是在演出之前提前准备好笑话还是他即兴发挥的？

5. 答案：A
    本题考查名词的含义。A 战利品，胜利纪念品，奖品；B 请客；C 小事儿，小玩意儿，小装饰品；D 贡品。句子的意思是：这个奖杯是全国大赛的奖品，奖给16岁以下最佳进球者。

6. 答案：B
    本题考查形容词的含义。A 敏捷的，及时的，迅速的；B (果实、时机)成熟的；C 足够的；D 按时的，准时的。句子的意思是：编辑的的确确考虑时机的把握，他们并非只满足于第一时间发布刺激的新闻，他们等到时机成熟的时候才会把新闻发出去。

7. 答案：D
    本题考查名词的含义。A 和平鸽；B 药物的剂量；C 赈济品，施舍物；D 瞌睡，小睡。句子的意思是：他在起居室里睡的那点工夫够撑他醒一阵子了。

8. 答案：B
    本题考查过去分词的含义。A 掩饰，遮蔽；B 把……假扮起来；C 抑制，压制，约束；D 以为，假定为，(想当然地)认为。句子的意思是：强风中突然飞落一片树叶，那片树叶根本不是什么树叶——而是昆虫装出来的。

9. 答案：A
    本题考查动词的含义。A 胜过，超越；B 追上，赶上，超过；C 全力对付，竞争，奋斗；D 提高，增加(价值、品质、吸引力等)。句子的意思是：有些孩子从一出生就凭着他们时常超越最聪明的成人的难以置信的智慧和天赋惊诧了世人。

10. 答案：D

本题考查动词词组的含义。A 掩盖；B 进入；C 追逐；D 磨蹭,拖延。句子的意思是:购买食品时,顾客通常都比较匆忙,因此不会在食品说明上磨蹭来做出购买的决定。

11. 答案: A

本题考查名词的含义。A 传染病,瘟疫；B 抗生素；C 药房；D 污染。句子的意思是:14 世纪几百万人死于名叫黑死病的瘟疫。

12. 答案: D

本题考查名词的含义。A 保险费；B 盛行,普遍,广泛；C 假设,房屋及其地基,经营场地；D 前任,(被取代的)原有事物。句子的意思是:尽管现在的安排比以前的有了很大进步,但还是有些问题。

13. 答案: B

本题考查名词的含义。A 轰动,激动；B 动乱,激变,剧变；C 取钱,撤军；D (疾病、战争的)爆发。句子的意思是:首相新税提案引起动乱直接导致政府垮台。

14. 答案: A

本题考查句子逻辑关系。A 正如；B 只要；C 尽管；D 不管怎样。句子的意思是:正如睡眠对于成人的健康至关重要一样,新研究显示缺乏睡眠也会影响青少年的身体健康。

15. 答案: C

本题考查动词词组的含义。A 给予,提供；B 坚持到底,守住,提出；C 推迟,抵挡,不使……接近；D 保有(工作等),抑制(热情等)。句子的意思是:他打算把手术推迟到九月,希望在北京奥运会取得他的第一枚金牌。

16. 答案: D

本题考查动词的含义。A 计算；B 传递；C 犯罪；D 兑换,皈依,转变。句子的意思是:把美元兑换成外币,用汇率乘以兑换钱数。

17. 答案: B

本题考查名词的含义。A 出版；B 公开,宣传,尽人皆知；C (政治)宣传,宣传活动；D 促销,晋升。句子的意思是:这一措施由国务卿本人亲自宣布并予以最大程度的宣传。

18. 答案: D

本题考查动词短语的含义。A 提供说明、信息；B 容忍；C 期待；D 实践,不辜负。句子的意思是:只有通过进一步发展和改善,医保卡才会发挥潜质成为与众不同的有用的手段。

19. 答案: C

本题考查形容词的含义。A 倾向于；B 对于……负责；C 有……倾向的,易于……的；D 泰然自若的。句子的意思是:我二十几岁时经常易于焦虑、意志消沉,是一种缺乏自信的表现。

20. 答案: C

本题考查动词短语的含义。A 看一遍；B 使渡过难关(或麻烦)等；C 顺利地通过；D 接通电话,做妥一件工作。句子的意思是:老师抱怨,现在的孩子通过考试,却不能写成一篇像样的文章,解不出多步骤数学题,也建立不起任何架构。

第二部分 完形填空

21. 答案: D

本题考查的是习惯用法搭配。在谈论考试得分时,使用的习惯用法是 score high/low/

average。本句的意思是：美国八年级的学生在数学上的得分低于全球平均得分。

22．答案：B

本题考查的是词义辨析。四个选项的意思分别为 A 最少的；B 最差的；C 更少的；D 更差的。本句的意思是：这甚至还不是最糟的。

23．答案：A

本题考查的是动词短语语义辨析。A 想出来，考虑；B 实施；C 数到；D 出现，现身。本句是讲：当人们在考虑哪些国家会主宰 21 世纪的技术市场时，别忘了以下这些事实。

24．答案：B

本题考查的是语义辨析。本句的意思是说：在数学上得分前 10% 的美国学生的成绩仅和新加坡学生的平均成绩持平，而新加坡在数学上处于全球领导地位。

25．答案：C

本题考查的是定语从句中关系副词的使用。本句的意思是：在当下，当美国学生在世界性考试中的成绩处于下游的情况下，这就不再是一条新闻了。当先行词是表示时间的名词时，关系副词为 when。

26．答案：A

本题考查的是对文章上下文的理解以及语义辨析。四个选项的意思为：A 重要；B 无效；C 可比较的；D 令人高兴的。本句的意思是：研究者认为该研究很重要，因为它考虑到了学校内外多种因素变量。

27．答案：B

本题考查的是语义辨析。四个选项的意思分别为：A 忽视；B 批评；C 夸大；D 看作。本句话的意思是：懒惰经常被看成是美国学生学业成绩表现不佳的因素。

28．答案：C

本题考查的是对副词词义的辨析和对上下文的理解。A 大量地；B 准确地；C 事实上；D 仅仅。本句的意思是：其实，美国学生在课堂上花费的时间并不比日本和德国的学生花得少。

29．答案：C

本题考查的是连接词的使用。A 开始；B 众所周知；C 不仅如此；D 即使如此。本句是说：和日本、德国的学生相比，美国学生不仅花更多的时间学习，他们看电视的时间也不多，并且还得做更多的作业。

30．答案：A

本题考查的是形容词的词义辨析。A 容易；B 小；C 短；D 差。本句是讲：教育者们认为，出现这些问题的原因不在学生身上，而在于课程设置过于简单。

31．答案：B

本题考查的是动词的词义辨析。A 相关；B 使……接触；C 带领；D 教导。本句的意思是说：教师认为，美国民众需要让他们的孩子更早地接触到更为复杂的数学问题。

32．答案：C

本题考查的是连接副词的使用。A 在哪里；B 为什么；C 怎么样；D 是否。本句想表达的是：美国的教师没有意识到，与在课堂上教授什么概念一样重要的一点就是如何教授这些概念。

33．答案：D

本题考查副词的词义辨析。A 几乎不;B 故意地;C 于是;D 除……以外地。这句话是说:美国的大部分教育工作者完全依赖于教材和死记硬背。

34. 答案:A

本题考查形容词的词义辨析。A 高级的,深层的;B 绚丽多彩的;C 备受争议的;D 野心勃勃的。本句是说:尽管很多课本包括高等深层的概念,但大部分都讲得浮皮潦草。

35. 答案:B

本句考查现在分词的语义辨析。A 带着;B 留下;C 期望;D 塑造。这里是说:那些不能深刻地解释高等概念的书,只能让学生掌握一些技能,而不能掌握宽泛的理论。

第三部分 阅读理解

第一节 阅读理解 A

第一篇:

36. 答案:A

本题是细节题,考查第一段的最后一句话(第二段是对这句话的进一步解释):男人和女人谎言的区别在于内容,而不是数量。

37. 答案:C

本题是推理题,考查对第二段中引语部分的理解:男人说谎大都是为了让他们听起来更棒。

38. 答案:C

本题是细节题,考查对第一段倒数第二、三句话的理解。

39. 答案:A

本题是细节题,这道题的信息在第六段的引语部分。

40. 答案:B

本题是推理题,考查第六段第二句话,即引语部分的理解。

41. 答案:D

本题是推理题,考查对最后一段的理解,可用排除法。

第二篇:

42. 答案:C

本题是细节题,考查对第一段最后一句话的理解。

43. 答案:C

本题是细节题,考查第二段对第一、二、三句话的理解。

44. 答案:A

本题是推理题,考查对第二段后半段的细节归纳,尤其是"comparatively short"这一短语可以是答题的关键。

45. 答案:D

本题是推理题,考查对第二段倒数第二和第三句话的理解。

46. 答案:B

本题是推理题,考查对第二段倒数第一、二句话的理解或最后一段第一句话的理解。

47. 答案:A

　　本题是细节题,考查最后一段最后两句话的意思。

第三篇:

48. 答案:D

　　本题是细节题,考查对第一段第一句话的理解。

49. 答案:B

　　本题是细节题,考查对第二段最后一句话的理解。

50. 答案:C

　　本题是细节题,考查对第三段最后一句话的理解。

51. 答案:A

　　本题是指代题,这里的"the sharp wit"一定是前文提到过的。在这里指的是John Renard的话中提到的漫画家的幽默。

52. 答案:A

　　本题是细节题,考点在第五段。

53. 答案:D

　　本题是推理题,考查最后一段引语部分的含义。

第四篇:

54. 答案:D

　　本题是细节题,考查对第一段中"forged scores"(作假的成绩或记录)的理解。

55. 答案:A

　　本题是细节题,考查对第二段第二句话中"gross negligence"的理解。

56. 答案:C

　　本题是推理题,考点在第四段的第一句话中"to test Ketek's effectiveness against ear infections"。

57. 答案:A

　　本题是细节题,考查对第四段的倒数第二句话中词组 to no avail 的理解。

58. 答案:C

　　本题是细节题,考查对第六段第一句话的理解。

59. 答案:B

　　本题是作者态度题,考查倒数第三段作者发出的疑问的含义。

第五篇:

60. 答案:D

　　本题为细节题,考查对第二段第一句话的理解。

61. 答案:A

　　本题是细节题,考点是第二段最后一句话中的"they generally require no equipment…"。

62. 答案:B

本题是细节题,考查对第三段第二句话的理解。

63. 答案:D

本题是细节题,考查对第三段倒数第二句话的理解:"...my muscles do start to feel more energized..."

64. 答案:C

本题是细节题,考查对第四段第二句话的理解。

65. 答案:C

本题是细节题,考点是最后一段最后一句话中的"to remain physically active..."。

第二节 阅读理解 B

第一篇:

66. 答案:E

本题的答题关键在于把握该段以及下一段的主要内容——猪流感的传染人数多,并以纽约市的发病情况为例。因此,选项 E 中的"in New York City"与下一段的段首是连贯的。

67. 答案:F

本题的重点是把握句子之间的转折关系,选项 F 中的"However"一词是答题的突破口。

68. 答案:D

本题的答题关键是把握文章的结构:第 4、5、6 三个段落都讲到了猪流感的危害性大,即造成的死亡人数较多。选项 D 中的"Of those who die"在内容上与之契合。

69. 答案:A

本题的突破口是选项 A 中的"Southern Hemisphere"与第 7 段中提到的"Australia, Chile, Argentina"等国名的特征一致。

70. 答案:C

本题的答题要点是了解空格的前一句提示到:到 9 月份只能提供 6 000 万剂量的疫苗,因此疫苗的分配自然成了问题,这正是选项 C 的内容。

第二篇:

71. 答案:C

本题的答题突破口是"arbitrary"一词。

72. 答案:B

本题的答题要点是选项 B 与第二段的主题大意吻合,选项 B 的句子恰好是第二段的起始句。

73. 答案:A

本题的突破口是人称代词的一致性。只有第三段和第四段中人称代词为"we"。

74. 答案:F

本题的答题要点是前一句中"these categories"与选项 F 中的"these things"指的是同一内容。

75. 答案:D

最后一段的大意是文化的作用,而选项 D 也正是讲到这一点。

第四部分 翻　译

1）译文：

　　如今,有无数这样的网站,人们可在上面用污言秽语向过去的情人或向曾对自己无礼过的顾客发泄不满;更有甚者,他们会把脆弱的少年推向极端。最近,密苏里州就发生了这样的事,一个女孩不堪来自网络上的对她的咒骂和凌辱被逼自杀。

　　解析：

　　这句话在结构上没有什么复杂之处,在翻译时重点要把握的是以下词汇和短语:nasty意为下流的,肮脏的;over the edge 意为疯狂,精神错乱。如果此处把 push sb. over the edge 翻译为"把某人推向边缘",其意思是不完整的,最好在掌握短语本意的基础上,根据上下文领会出"把某人推向崩溃或疯狂的边缘"等就更好了。

2）译文：

　　JuicyCampus.com 是个欢迎用户发表攻击他人言论而保证不透露用户姓名的网站,其发展势头正猛。该网站目前在 7 所大学设有分部,包括它所起家的 DUKE 大学。它起初是为娱乐和好玩而设,如今却成了满是污言秽语且在许多时候纯粹是诽谤他人的场所。

　　解析：

　　在翻译这两句话的时候,要特别注意理解第二句话中两个破折号的含义。两个破折号之间的内容都是对 JuicyCampus.com 发展现状的补充和强调。在分析句子的时候,请先识别主语部分 what began as fun and games 和谓语 has turned ugly...,然后再处理破折号之间的内容,会有效降低本句话理解和翻译上的难度。

3）译文：

　　DUKE 大学有一位名叫 DAN BELZER 的高年级生,曾在校刊上发表过关于该网站的文章,他就此现象评论说:"这个网站已经发展到了这一地步,谁都可以在上面恶意攻击那些无力保护自己的学生。"

　　解析：

　　在结构上,本句话和上一句有相似之处,主句和从句被插入语隔开,增加了理解上的难度,也令大家对含义本来就丰富的 point 一词更加摸不着头脑。所以请大家阅读这句话的时候,暂时把插入语搁一边,先理解主句和从句的含义,这样对 point 的理解也就有了方向性,point 后接 where 从句,说明 point 此处的含义应该是"程度;地步"等。

4）译文：

　　而且他们还能免受惩罚,因为,JuicyCampus.com 网站覆盖的学校并未给其资助,所以,学校当局无权对其规范管理。(该网站是 DUKE 大学一个名叫 MATT IVESTOR 的毕业生创建的,他拒绝对整件事发表评论。)

　　解析：

　　第一句话和上文紧密相关。所以这样的句子提醒大家翻译之前最好先把全文通读一遍,否则就不好理解 And get away with it, too。在结构上,这句话也用了两个破折号,含义和第二句相似,是对 JuicyCampus 的补充说明,因此有了第二句的分析经验,这句话就比较好处理了。而参考译文把这一部分内容用括号的形式来处理的方法,也请大家参考。

5) 译文：

如今，要想控制 JuicyCampus.com 这样的网站，只有一种办法，即：劝说大家都不要再使用这个网站。但没有受过高等教育的人也看得出来，这种事不可能发生。

解析：

you don't need a college degree to 是翻译这句话的关键，此处作者的语调是玩笑式的，你看出来了吗？

第五部分 写 作

题目解析：

这个题目是哲学思辨类的题目，要求考生探讨一个具有哲理的生活现象："面对同一处境，不同的人有不同的选择。"哲学思辨性质的题目不是社会现实类题目，比如住房问题，高考问题，人口控制问题，等等。由于题目本身是抽象的，因此在写作的时候，除了做抽象的逻辑推理以外，最好能结合具体的实例来分析和佐证，以便虚实相生，加强说服力。否则容易陷入纯理论探讨的枯燥境地。对于题目中的问题，自然可以从很多方面来讨论；但不管从哪些方面来谈，都应注意并学会抽取几个主要的原因（这是题目中要求的重点内容），来进行针对性的分析，只要言之有理，语言流畅，就是好文章。

范文：

When facing the same situation, different people have different decisions. That is quite natural because there are many factors that could influence our final decisions, such as our cognitive abilities, our interests and our individual needs. I will analyze these in details in the following paragraphs.

The first plain truth, I am presenting here, is that people's cognitive abilities vary from gender, age and education levels. With different background of cognitive approaches, people have different points of view when looking at the same situation, so they come up with their own conclusions, and make different decisions. Even the same person will look at the same situation differently as he or she is aging. For example, when we are young, we may think love is all that we need to take into consideration. We can sacrifice everything for love. But when we get more mature and older, we may realize that love is only an episode in one's life and there are more crucial things than love in this world, such as one's responsibility, one's career.

Furthermore, people's interests influence their own decisions. When choosing their majors, college students often have various choices as a result of their own interests. Some people are fascinated by liberal arts, so they choose to study languages or literature; other people are intoxicated in exploring the mysteries in this planet, so they choose to study geology; still others are interested in researching this physical world, so they study physics.

Last, also a very important reason is that, different personal needs will be taken into account in decision making. Take a recent phenomenon as an example. The housing price in Beijing is now quite high; under such circumstances, some people choose to buy a flat, while others decide to rent their houses. Those who buy houses under the high prices may be in need of a house, or they may believe that the housing prices will continue to rise in the foreseeable future, which will turn out as an investment. While those who rent may choose to work in Beijing only for a couple of years, or they may believe that the current housing price will drop down some day, so they are just renting and waiting for that day. People's needs are varied, and behind each decision is usually an individual need.

In a word, the world is complex. There are no similar minds among people, just as there are never two similar leaves. It's this kind of distinction that makes our world more interesting. (419 words)

中国科学院
博士研究生入学考试
英 语 试 题

(2010 年 10 月)

考生须知：

一、本试卷由试卷一（PAPER ONE）和试卷二（PAPER TWO）两部分组成。试卷一为客观题，答卷使用标准化机读答题纸；试卷二为主观题，答卷使用非机读答题纸。

二、请考生一律用 HB 或 2B 铅笔填涂标准化机读答题纸，画线不得过细或过短。修改时请用橡皮擦拭干净。若因填涂不符合要求而导致计算机无法识别，责任由考生自负。请保持机读答题纸清洁、无折皱。答题纸切忌折叠。

三、全部考试时间总计 180 分钟，满分为 100 分。时间及分值分布如下：

试卷一：

	Ⅰ 词汇	15 分钟	10 分
	Ⅱ 完形填空	15 分钟	15 分
	Ⅲ 阅读理解	80 分钟	40 分
	小计	110 分钟	65 分

试卷二：

	Ⅳ 英译汉	30 分钟	15 分
	Ⅴ 写作	40 分钟	20 分
	小计	70 分钟	35 分

GRADUATE UNIVERSITY, CHINESE ACADEMY OF SCIENCES ENGLISH ENTRANCE EXAMINATION FOR DOCTORAL CANDIDATES
October 2010

PAPER ONE

PART I VOCABULARY (15 minutes, 10 points, 0.5 point each)

Directions: *Choose the word or expression below each sentence that best completes the statement, and mark the corresponding letter of your choice with a single bar across the square bracket on your Machine-scoring Answer Sheet.*

1. The dancers for the ballet were selected for similarity of height and build so that they might present a (an) _____ appearance.
   A. ultimate   B. deceptive   C. homogeneous   D. unanimous
2. It happened in a flash, although _____ everything seemed to occur in slow motion, as though I were watching from another planet.
   A. in return   B. in practice   C. in reality   D. in retrospect
3. A couple were holding each other close to _____ the cold wind that had sprung up.
   A. ward off   B. shake off   C. turn off   D. take off
4. The realization of all the potential profits _____ depends on sufficient spending by employers, by the government or by those purchasing exports.
   A. intimately   B. universally   C. ultimately   D. instinctively
5. The Association of University Teachers claims that taxpayers' money, _____ for basic research, is being used to prop up industrial and other applied research projects.
   A. designed   B. engaged   C. oriented   D. intended
6. History will always _____ any intended route and take an unforeseen one instead.
   A. lead to   B. deviate from   C. pass through   D. result from
7. There was something feverish, even _____, in the manner in which shoppers crowded into shops in the last days before Christmas.

A. desperate   B. courageous   C. discriminating   D. courteous

8. He received the Royal Swedish Academy of Sciences' 1983 Crafoord Prize, established to honor fields not _____ for the Nobel Prize.

    A. advisable   B. noticeable   C. eligible   D. favorable

9. On that trip, the loneliness was a little harder to handle, so I brought along our puppy to keep me _____.

    A. company   B. partner   C. attendant   D. fellowship

10. The most _____ example of water pollution occurred in 1969, when the Cuyahoga River in Ohio caught fire and helped shock America into adopting the Clean Water Act.

    A. concrete   B. precise   C. positive   D. notorious

11. They seek to _____ the long-term goals for what music education ought to be in our society.

    A. set out   B. set in   C. set apart   D. set back

12. Researchers found that teens who slept less than 6.5 hours a night were 2.5 times more likely than those who slept longer to have _____ blood pressure.

    A. alternated   B. accelerated   C. elevated   D. startled

13. Ricardo has shown great _____ in his determination to understand the theory of relativity.

    A. adherence   B. persistence   C. intuition   D. fantasy

14. Hosting the 2008 Olympics provided China with an opportunity to _____ its unprecedented progress.

    A. demonstrate   B. deduce   C. distinguish   D. disperse

15. The lawyer _____ his ideas loudly and clearly in court, which surprised her a great deal.

    A. acclaimed   B. admonished   C. addressed   D. asserted

16. Monique is studying business administration because she wants to be a highly paid _____ in a large company.

    A. primitive   B. executive   C. conservative   D. representative

17. Competent students are those who can see the application of a theory or a concept to a specific _____ example.

    A. empirical   B. academic   C. instinctive   D. impulsive

18. After negotiation for some time, all the members of the association promised to _____ to the strict code of practice.

    A. ascribe   B. confirm   C. adhere   D. confide

19. So many people are _____ with Google, the largest search engine that provides the most responses to search queries.

    A. haunted   B. obsessed   C. indulged   D. addicted

20. John has received offer letters from three companies, but he wants to _____ his options open, as he hasn't decided what kind of job he wants to do.

    A. take   B. leave   C. let   D. make

PART II CLOZE TEST (15 minutes, 15 points)

Directions: *For each blank in the following passage, choose the best answer from the four choices given below. Mark the corresponding letter of your choice with a single bar across the square bracket on your Machine-scoring Answer Sheet.*

In a move to disseminate faculty research and scholarship more broadly, the Faculty of Arts and Sciences (FAS) voted Tuesday to give Harvard University a worldwide license to make each faculty member's scholarly articles available and to exercise the copyright in the articles, __21__ that the articles are not sold for a profit.

"The goal of university research is the creation, dissemination, and __22__ of knowledge. At Harvard, __23__ so much of our research is of global significance, we have an essential responsibility to __24__ the fruits of our scholarship as widely as possible," said Provost Steven E. Hyman. "Today's __25__ in FAS will promote free and open __26__ to significant, ongoing research."

Harvard will take advantage of the __27__ by hosting FAS faculty members' scholarly articles in an open-access repository, making them available worldwide for __28__. The faculty member will __29__ the copyright of the article, __30__ the University's license. The repository contents can be made widely available to the __31__ through search engines such as Google Scholar.

This access will benefit scholars at all research __32__, which have seen their ability to __33__ subscriptions to a full __34__ of scholarly journals seriously compromised over the past few years. Research centers in poorer countries have been especially __35__ by the access limitations caused by the high cost of many journals, Shieber pointed out.

21. A. except	B. so	C. provided	D. despite
22. A. preservation	B. fascination	C. contribution	D. suspension
23. A. why	B. where	C. though	D. while
24. A. transmit	B. accommodate	C. transfer	D. distribute
25. A. action	B. campaign	C. election	D. function
26. A. atmosphere	B. access	C. attitude	D. acknowledgement
27. A. goal	B. promotion	C. license	D. research
28. A. fun	B. long	C. free	D. good
29. A. retain	B. remain	C. refrain	D. restrain
30. A. opposed to	B. similar to	C. pertinent to	D. subject to
31. A. staff	B. public	C. medium	D. authority
32. A. structures	B. markets	C. institutions	D. fragments
33. A. maintain	B. extend	C. cancel	D. combine
34. A. domain	B. range	C. report	D. board

35. A. privileged   B. sanctioned   C. punished   D. harmed

PART III   READING COMPREHENSION

Section A (60 minutes, 30 points)

Directions: *Below each of the following passages you will find some questions or incomplete statements. Each question or statement is followed by four choices marked A, B, C, and D. Read each passage carefully, and then select the choice that best answers the question or completes the statement. Mark the letter of your choice with a single bar across the square bracket on your Machine-scoring Answer Sheet.*

Passage One

The idea of building "New Towns" to absorb growth is frequently considered a cure-all for urban problems. It is erroneously assumed that if new residents can be diverted from existing centers, the present urban situation at least will get no worse. It is further and equally erroneously assumed that since European New Towns have been financially and socially successful, we can expect the same sorts of results in the United States.

Present planning, thinking, and legislation will not produce the kind of New Towns that have been successful abroad. It will multiply suburbs or encourage developments in areas where land is cheap and construction profitable rather than where New Towns are genuinely needed.

Such ill-considered projects not only will fail to relieve pressures on existing cities but will, in fact, tend to weaken those cities further by drawing away high-income citizens and increasing the concentration of low-income groups that are unable to provide tax revenues. The remaining taxpayers, accordingly, will face increasing burdens, and industry and commerce will seek escape. Unfortunately, this mechanism is already at work in some metropolitan areas.

The promoters of New Towns so far in the United States have been developers, builders, and financial institutions. The main interest of these promoters is economic gain. Furthermore, federal regulations designed to promote the New Town idea do not consider social needs as the European New Town plans do. In fact, our regulations specify virtually all the ingredients of the typical suburban community, with a bit of political rhetoric thrown in.

A workable American New Town formula should be established as firmly here as the national formula was in Britain. All possible social and governmental innovations as well as financial factors should be thoroughly considered and accommodated in this policy. Its objectives should be clearly stated, and both incentives and penalties should be provided to ensure that the objectives are pursued. If such a policy is developed, then the New Town approach can play an important role in alleviating American's urban problems.

36. As revealed in Para 1, the author considers the American New Town approach _____.

A. atypical   B. irrelevant   C. impractical   D. unprecedented

37. According to the author, the present New Town plan will _____.
    A. fail to bring about the intended results
    B. produce genuinely needed New Towns
    C. bridge the gap between the poor and the rich
    D. help resolve the spreading urban problems

38. The author believes that the New Town projects will lead to _____.
    A. more brisk commercial activities in the cities
    B. more low-income people living in the suburbs
    C. higher incidence of tax avoidance by industries
    D. heavier tax burdens on the remaining citizens

39. In the author's opinion, the European New Town plans are superior to the America's in their concern for _____.
    A. the typical suburban community   B. the interests of the promoters
    C. the welfare of the general public   D. the government's political achievement

40. Which of the following accords with the New Town formula in Britain, according to the passage?
    A. The accommodation of all the requests of low-income groups.
    B. The consideration of all possible aspects of urban problems.
    C. The explanation of all regulations concerning New Towns.
    D. The clarification of all the innovations at the national level.

Passage Two

It is a treasure hunt with a difference: conducted not with metal detectors, but by negotiation. Italy is at last reaping the benefits of a two-year campaign to regain smuggled antiquities. Five American museums have been talked into returning works that they claim to have acquired in good faith. Almost 70 of the finest are now on display in Rome — and they have just been joined by the only known intact work by Euphronios, an Athenian vase-painter.

New ground is also being broken with the return of nine items from the private collection of a New York philanthropist, Shelby White. This is the first pact negotiated with an individual. Francesco Rutelli, the culture minister, met Ms. White twice in America before the deal was done. She has always maintained that she and her late husband had no idea that the pieces were suspect. A tenth item from their collection, also by Euphronios, is being sent back to Italy in 2010. Under Italian law, any classical artifacts found on Italian soil belong to the state, even if (like Euphronios's vases) they originated in Greece. A former head of the J. Paul Getty Museum in Los Angeles and an American art dealer have been on trial for almost three years in Rome, charged with trafficking in illegally excavated objects. Both deny wrongdoing. Their charge was followed by a deal that officials say is crucial for efforts to curb the traffic in smuggled antiquities. Switzerland has undertaken to require importers of classical artifacts to produce proofs of origin and of legal export.

The deals with the museums have all involved give-and-take. In exchange for works claimed by

Italy, the museums have been given others on long-term loan. "Italian lovers of art and archaeology will get back what has been stolen, while others abroad will profit from the exhibition of sometimes even more beautiful works," says Mr Rutelli.

The deal with the Getty museum was the hardest to do but also the most productive: 40 of the works on show in Rome come from there. But they do not include the "Getty bronze," which the Italians had hoped to retrieve. This third-century BC statue, attributed to Lysippus, Greek sculptor, was caught by Italian fishermen in 1964. The Getty insists that it was found in international waters. The Italians say it was still illegally exported.

41. Paragraph 1 mainly focuses on Italy's _____.
    A. success in getting back some lost art treasures from abroad
    B. talk with foreign museums for returning its art treasures
    C. effort to find out where its smuggled art treasures are
    D. exhibition of some of its world-famous art treasures
42. What can be learned about Euphronios?
    A. His works have been scattered all over Europe.
    B. Ten of his works have been returned to Italy.
    C. His works have not been well preserved.
    D. None of his works has ever been exhibited.
43. Ms. White insisted that she got the Italian items _____.
    A. for charitable purpose   B. from her late husband
    C. by making a good deal   D. in ignorance of their identity
44. The trial of the two Americans in Italy helped to push some countries to _____.
    A. be strict with importing classical artifacts
    B. be tough to classical artifact traffickers
    C. require legal proof of all imported goods
    D. stop importing art works of foreign origin
45. To reclaim its treasures from foreign museums, Italy has chosen to _____.
    A. pay them for the long-time maintenance
    B. let them display some of its other works
    C. lend them money to buy some other works
    D. help them find some precious works to display
46. What is true about "Getty bronze" according to the passage?
    A. It was taken away from Greece.   B. It was found by some Italian fishermen.
    C. It was illegally exported to the U.S.A. D. It was buried somewhere in Italy.
47. The best title for this passage might be _____.
    A. Antiquity Smugglers Sentenced   B. Cost Paid for Wrongdoings
    C. Art Treasures Coming Home   D. Cultural Rarities on Display

Passage Three

Greg Gadson, a lieutenant colonel in the Army's Warrior Transition Brigade, is a natural leader — the kind of guy you'd be looking for on the battlefield. He's also the kind of guy Mike Sullivan, a coach for the New York Giants, whose thought could make a difference to his losing football team. The two men had gone to the US Military Academy at West Point together but hadn't been in touch much afterward, until Sullivan walked into Gadson's hospital room at Walter Reed Army Medical Center, outside Washington, D. C., last June. Friends had told Sullivan that his former Army football teammate had suffered serious injuries in Iraq — resulting in both of Gadson's legs being amputated above the knee.

"This man had suffered so much," Sullivan recalls, "yet he was so happy to see me." The coach, who brought his old friend a signed Giants jersey with the number 98 on it, watched as Gadson interacted with the other patients and the doctors and nurses, encouraging them all. "To see the impact he had on these people — the look in his eyes and how they responded — was overwhelming and inspirational."

Sullivan couldn't help but be impressed by Gadson's enthusiasm and lack of self-pity. When the Giants were scheduled to play the Redskins in Washington three months later, Sullivan sent his friend tickets — along with a request: Would Gadson speak to the team before they took the field? Having lost the first two games of the season, the Giants had already given up 80 points and, worse, seemed to be playing with no heart. The coach felt that Gadson was the perfect person to tell the players something they needed to hear about commitment, about perseverance, about teamwork.

Teamwork was everything to Gadson. He had played football at Indian River High School in the Tidewater region of Virginia and gone on to become a starting linebacker — No. 98 for West Point from 1986 to 1988, despite his relatively slight build of 190 pounds on a 5-foot-11 frame. Following his graduation, Gadson, the son of a hospital pharmacist and a teacher, planned to serve his compulsory five years and get out. But after tours in the Balkans and Afghanistan, he found himself hooked. "Serving my country is important," he says, "but for me it's about being a soldier, being there for each other in the biggest sense of the word. I love being part of that team."

48. In Paragraph 1, the word "amputated" most probably means _____.
    A. strained   B. cut off   C. held up   D. swollen
49. Greg Gadson used to be Mike Sullivan's _____.
    A. schoolmate   B. football coach
    C. superior in the army   D. fellow worker
50. According to the passage, "98" was Gadson's number as a football player in _____.
    A. the Redskins   B. the Giants   C. West Point   D. high school
51. Sullivan asked Gadson to speak to his losing team because Gadson _____.
    A. was his intimate friend   B. once played in the team
    C. won an honor in the army   D. could help motivate the team

52. Having visited the Balkans and Afghanistan, Gadson _____.
    A. had a new goal in life   B. felt sad about fighting wars
    C. decided to pursue his studies   D. expressed deep regret for his choice
53. "I love being part of that team" in the last paragraph means Gadson would like to _____.
    A. coach in Sullivan's team   B. fight for West Point again
    C. contribute to his country   D. be a sportsman forever

Passage Four

One of the appealing features of game theory is the way it reflects so many aspects of real life. To win a game, or survive in the jungle, or succeed in business, you need to know how to play your cards. You have to know when to hold 'em and know when to fold 'em. And usually you have to think fast. Winners excel at making smart snap judgments. In the jungle, you don't have time to calculate, using game theory or otherwise, the relative merits of fighting or fleeing, hiding or seeking.

Animals know this. They constantly face many competing choices from a long list of possible behaviors, as neuroscientists Gregory Berns and Read Montague have observed. "Do I chase this new prey or do I continue nibbling on my last kill? Do I run from the possible predator that I see in the bushes or the one that I hear? Do I chase that potential mate or do I wait around for something better?"

Presumably, animals don't deliberate such decisions consciously, at least not for very long. And even if animals could think complexly and had time to do so, there's no obvious way for them to compare all their needs for food, safety, and sex. Yet somehow animal brains add up all the factors and compute a course of action that enhances the odds of survival. And humans differ little from other animals in that regard. Brains have evolved a way to compare and choose among behaviors, apparently using some "common currency" for valuing one choice over others. In other words, not only do people have money on the brain, they have the neural equivalent of money operating within the brain. Just as money replaced the barter system — providing a common currency for comparing various goods and services — nerve cell circuitry evolved to translate diverse behavioral choices into the common currency of brain chemistry.

When you think about it, it makes a lot of sense. But neuroscientists began to figure it all out only when they joined forces with economists inspired by game theory. Game theory, after all, was the key to quantifying the faint notion of economic utility.

54. People will likely succeed if they are good at _____.
    A. adopting new theories for their work   B. identifying the details of a situation
    C. making quick and wise decisions   D. handling interpersonal relationships
55. In the jungle, there is usually little time to _____.
    A. recognize where a threat has come from
    B. compare the benefits of different actions

C. weigh merits and demerits of game theory

D. escape attacks from powerful predators

56. According to the passage, in the jungle, animals may face the question of whether to _____.

   A. join others to flee for safety
   B. continue to stay where they are
   C. hunt for food outside the bushes
   D. abandon what they have caught

57. A similarity between humans and animals is that both can _____.

   A. seriously examine present perils
   B. carefully choose their life partners
   C. immediately decide how to survive
   D. consciously prepare for emergencies

58. The last paragraph suggests that game theory _____.

   A. is useful in clarifying economic utility
   B. was developed from human activities
   C. was initiated by some neuroscientists
   D. is hard for the public to understand

59. The primary purpose of the passage is to _____.

   A. justify the application of game theory
   B. illustrate the concept of game theory
   C. trace game theory back to its origin
   D. compare different views on game theory

Passage Five

In the massive Zambezi River system, fish are not only vital to the ecosystem, but also a staple in the diet of millions of people. Yet, little is known about the species, their movements and the stocks. In hopes of ensuring that these fish stocks will continue to be around for many years to come, the African Wildlife Foundation has embarked on extensive research and monitoring efforts in the Zambezi River, its tributaries and related reservoirs.

While tracking the fish of the Zambezi River system, AWF learned of a sport-fishing tournament taking place on the river. AWF decided to join the tournament. All the tournament catches were carefully monitored and recorded, providing invaluable data on the health and size of key trophy specimens.

For the first time in history, real data is now available on the effect of the human population on the Zambezi River network, on the use of incompatible fishing methods, incompatible land uses (like deforestation, which leads to erosion and massive deposits of silt in the river), and overfishing. All this research will help AWF and its partners to help guide fishery policy and legislation — and help local communities create fishing strategies that are not just profitable, but truly sustainable.

For many years, the fish of the Zambezi River network have been bountiful. In fact, the upper part of the river alone feeds 300,000 people. The sardine catch in Lake Kariba yields more than 30,000 tons of fish annually — amounting to more than $55 million a year.

To manage the region's fisheries effectively, to monitor water quality, and to keep track of fish yields and fishing activities, AWF created the Aquatic Resources Working Group (ARWG). Its first priority was to gain a greater understanding of the fish that swim in the Zambezi River system as well as a clearer picture of the river system itself.

Although data collection will continue, the ARWG has already collected a significant amount of data. Now underway are pilot business ventures with fisheries and the creation of a formal fishing association in which registered fishermen drawn from the local community in Mozambique will undergo training in business skills, best-practice fishing, energy-efficient fish processing and marketing. The future is looking bright for both the fish and the communities along the Zambezi River system.

60. AWF's research on the Zambezi River system aims to _____.
    A. promote sustainable fishing there
    B. enhance wildlife conservation there
    C. protect the endangered fish species there
    D. know the fishing population density there

61. AWF made good use of the sport-fishing tournament by _____.
    A. finding out some rare species of fish
    B. collecting data about local fishing
    C. encouraging profitable fishing methods
    D. enjoying the native fishing culture

62. The study of the tournament catches reveals that _____.
    A. the fishing communities have expanded rapidly
    B. the fishermen have been using sustainable fishing strategies
    C. there has been no legislation on fishing in the Zambezi River
    D. the Zambezi area has been inappropriately exploited

63. By mentioning the bountiful fish in the Zambezi River network, the author intends to say that this bountifulness _____.
    A. needs to be ensured to continue
    B. will keep on for many years
    C. has been unknown to scientists
    D. enables the locals to live a carefree life

64. Which of the following is the least relevant information for ARWG's research?
    A. The streams of the Zambezi River.
    B. The fish species in the Zambezi River.
    C. The ways of fishing in the Zambezi River.
    D. The fishing harvest celebrations along the Zambezi River.

65. Through the pilot business ventures, the fishermen will learn how to _____.
    A. use the Zambezi aquatic resources in a cost-effective way
    B. cooperate with other fishing communities in the region
    C. make the most profit from the local fishing business
    D. engage in fishery activities for lasting benefit

Section B (20 minutes, 10 points)

Directions: *In each of the following passages, five sentences have been removed from the original text. They are listed from A to F and put below the passage. Choose the most suitable sentence from the list to fill in each of the blanks (numbered 66 to 75). For each passage, there is one sentence that does not fit in any of the blanks. Mark your answers on your Machine-scoring Answer Sheet.*

Passage One

To avoid the various foolish opinions to which mankind is prone, no superhuman genius is required. A few simple rules will keep you, not from all error, but from silly error. __66__ Aristotle could have avoided the mistake of thinking that women have fewer teeth than men, by the simple device of asking Mrs. Aristotle to keep her mouth open while he counted. He did not do so because he thought he knew.

Many matters, however, are less easily brought to the test of experience. If, like most of mankind, you have passionate convictions on many such matters, there are ways in which you can make yourself aware of your own bias. __67__ If someone maintains that two and two are five, or that Iceland is on the equator, you feel pity rather than anger, unless you know so little of arithmetic or geography that his opinion shakes your own contrary conviction. The most savage controversies are those about matters as to which there is no good evidence either way. Persecution is used in theology, not in arithmetic, because in arithmetic there is knowledge, but in theology there is only opinion. __68__

A good way of ridding yourself of certain kinds of dogmatism is to become aware of opinions held in social circles different from your own. When I was young, I lived much outside my own country. I found this very profitable in diminishing the intensity of the shared prejudice. __69__ If the people and the newspaper seem mad, perverse, and wicked, remind yourself that you seem so to them.

For those who have enough psychological imagination, it is a good plan to imagine an argument with a person having a different bias. __70__ I have sometimes been led actually to change my mind as a result of this kind of imaginary dialogue, and, short of this, I have frequently found myself growing less dogmatic through realizing the possible reasonableness of a hypothetical opponent.

A. This has one advantage, and only one, as compared with actual conversation with opponents; this one advantage is that the method is not subject to the same limitations of time and space.
B. If you cannot travel, seek out people with whom you disagree, and read a newspaper belonging to a party that is not yours.
C. If an opinion contrary to your own makes you angry, that is a sign that you are subconsciously aware of having no good reason for thinking as you do.
D. In this opinion both parties may be right, but they cannot both be wrong.

E. If the matter is one that can be settled by observation, make the observation yourself.
F. So whenever you find yourself getting angry about a difference of opinion, be on your guard; you will probably find, on examination, that your belief is going beyond what the evidence warrants.

Passage Two

No single element has tantalized and tormented the human imagination more than the shimmering metal known by the chemical symbol Au. For thousands of years the desire to possess gold has driven people to extremes, fueling wars and conquests, girding empires and currencies, leveling mountains and forests. __71__ Yet its chief virtues — its unusual density and malleability along with its imperishable shine — have made it one of the world's most coveted commodities, a transcendent symbol of beauty, wealth, and immortality. From pharaohs (who insisted on being buried in what they called the "flesh of the gods") to the forty-niners (whose mad rush for the mother lode built the American West) to the financiers (who, following Sir Isaac Newton's advice, made it the bedrock of the global economy): __72__

Humankind's feverish attachment to gold shouldn't have survived the modern world. Few cultures still believe that gold can give eternal life, and every country in the world — the United States was last, in 1971 — has done away with the gold standard. __73__ The price of gold, which stood at $271 an ounce on September 10, 2001, hit $1,023 in March 2008, and it may surpass that threshold again. Aside from extravagance, gold is still continuing to play its role as a safe haven in perilous times. __74__ In 2007 demand outstripped mine production by 59 percent. "Gold has always had this kind of magic," says Peter L. Bernstein, author of The Power of Gold. "But it's never been clear if we have gold or gold has us."

While investors flock to new gold-backed funds, jewelry still accounts for two-thirds of the demand, generating a record $53.5 billion in worldwide sales in 2007. __75__ However, such concerns don't ruffle the biggest consumer nations, namely India, where a gold obsession is woven into the culture, and China, which leaped past the U.S. in 2007 to become the world's second largest buyer of gold jewelry.

A. But gold's luster(光泽) not only endures; fueled by global uncertainty, it grows stronger.
B. Gold is not vital to human existence; it has, in fact, relatively few practical uses.
C. In the U.S. an activist-driven "No Dirty Gold" campaign has persuaded many top jewelry retailers to stop selling gold from mines that cause severe social or environmental damage.
D. Nearly every society through the ages has invested gold with an almost mythological power.
E. For all of its allure, gold's human and environmental toll has never been so steep. Part of the challenge, as well as the fascination, is that there is so little of it.
F. Gold's recent surge, sparked in part by the terrorist attack on 9/11, has been amplified by the slide of the U.S. dollar and nervousness over a looming global recession.

PAPER TWO

PART IV TRANSLATION (30 minutes, 15 points)

Directions: *Read the following text carefully and then translate the underlined segments into Chinese. Write your Chinese version in the proper space on your Answer Sheet.*

The image many of us may have of a language teacher is someone drilling a classroom full of teenagers in the finer points of French or German grammar in a way not self-evidently relevant to the outside world.

But the past decade has seen big changes to the way language teaching is organised and delivered in English schools. 1) <u>The age range of pupils where language teaching is compulsory has shifted downwards.</u> Now, all children start learning a foreign language, albeit gradually, when they're just seven and continue until they're 14. Previously the compulsory age range was between 11 and 16.

2) <u>At the same time, the methods of language teaching have become much more targeted towards enabling young people to communicate in the spoken word rather than to get every single dot and comma correct in the written form.</u> And the range of languages taught in schools has expanded enormously. Spanish, French and German remain the most popular choices, but Italian, Russian, Mandarin, Urdu, Bengali and a host of others are also taught in an increasing number of classrooms. 3) <u>So, for the graduate or native speaker of almost any world language, a career as a school teacher is a realistic and attractive prospect.</u> And it's one being followed by large numbers every year. Last September, around 1,700 graduates started one-year Postgraduate Certificate in Education (PGCE) training courses to become foreign language teachers in secondary schools, each offering competence in at least two foreign languages, French and Spanish being the most common.

And there are now increasing numbers training to become primary teachers with a language specialism, a training route introduced three years ago. 4) <u>Here, trainees prepare to handle all subjects across the timetable, as well as to develop an additional expertise in introducing foreign language learning to pupils.</u> Around 3,000 students have embarked on this route so far, most of whom are now working in primary schools.

5) <u>The embedding of language teaching in primary schools — a process which is still far from complete — has also created more localized links between teachers across the primary-secondary divide, as primary schools make use of the greater expertise in nearby secondary staffrooms.</u>

This has, in turn, introduced enrichment and variety to many experienced secondary teachers. One such example is Greg Horton, an advanced skills language teacher at Wildern School, a co-educational comprehensive, in Hampshire, who now frequently visits local primary schools to support teachers in language lessons.

PART V WRITING (40 minutes, 20 points)

Directions: *Write an essay of no less than 200 words on the topic given below. Use the proper space on your Answer Sheet II.*

TOPIC

According to some statistics, by the end of 2009, the resident population (常住人口) in Beijing has reached 17 million, not to mention the large floating population and the number is becoming bigger. Do you think the population in Beijing should be controlled? Why or why not?

2010年10月试题精解

第一部分　词　　汇

1. 答案：C
   本题考查形容词的含义。A 最终的；B 骗人的；C 一样的；D（意见、投票）一致（通过的）。句子的意思是：通过身高和体型的相似挑选芭蕾舞演员，这样就可以展现整齐划一的外表。

2. 答案：D
   本题考查介词短语的含义。A 作为回报；B 实际操作中；C 事实上；D 回想起来。句子的意思是：事情当时发生得很快，不过现在回想起来一切好像都是慢动作发生似的，就好像我是在外星看似的。

3. 答案：A
   本题考查动词词组的含义。A 避免（邪恶、寒冷）；B 摆脱；C 关掉；D 脱掉，起飞。句子的意思是：一对情侣紧紧拥在一起来抵御忽起的寒风。

4. 答案：C
   本题考查副词的含义。A 亲密地；B 普遍地；C 最终；D 本能地。句子的意思是：全部利润的实现最终取决于企业、政府或进口商足够的消费。

5. 答案：D
   本题考查过去分词的含义。A 设计来……；B 致力于……；C 以……为目的；D 计划用来……。句子的意思是：大学教师协会指出，本来计划用于基础研究的纳税款项都被用来搞工业和其他应用研究。

6. 答案：B
   本题考查动词词组的含义。A 导致；B 偏离；C 通过；D 导致。句子的意思是：历史总会避开任何设计好的走向而选择一条出乎意料的途径。

7. 答案：A
   本题考查形容词的含义。A 极度渴望的；B 勇敢的；C 歧视的，有鉴别力的；D 彬彬有礼的。句子的意思是：圣诞前最后几天，买东西的人蜂拥而入大小商店，那架势近乎狂热甚至就像要拼命似的。

8. 答案：C
   本题考查形容词的含义。A 可取的，适当的，明智的；B 明显的；C 有资格的，合格的；D 优惠的，有利的。句子的意思是：他获得了瑞典皇家科学院1983年颁发的克拉夫奖，该奖是为奖励诺贝尔奖以外的领域而设立的。

9. 答案：A
   本题考查固定搭配。Keep one company "陪某人做伴"。句子的意思是：那次旅行，孤单有些难以驾驭，于是我就带着我们的小狗给我做伴。

10. 答案：D

本题考查形容词的含义。A 具体的；B 精确的；C 积极的,正极的；D 臭名昭著的。句子的意思是：最臭名昭著的水污染事件发生在 1969 年,当年俄亥俄州的凯霍加河上起火,震惊了整个美国,导致《水净化法》的出台。

11. 答案：A

本题考查动词词组的含义。A 动身,起程；制定；B (雨、雪)开始降落,(季节)到来；C 拨出(时间、金钱等)；D 使受挫折。句子的意思是：他们试图从在我们这个社会中音乐教育应有的地位这一角度出发制定一个长期目标。

12. 答案：C

本题考查过去分词的含义。A 轮流的；B 提速的；C 升高的；D 受惊的。句子的意思是：研究人员发现,与睡眠多于 6.5 小时的青少年相比,睡眠不足 6.5 小时的青少年有大于 250% 的可能性患有高血压。

13. 答案：B

本题考查名词的含义。A 固执,黏着；B 持之以恒；C 直觉；D 幻想。句子的意思是：理查德显示出执着的决心来理解相对论。

14. 答案：A

本题考查动词的含义。A 展示,显示；B 演绎；C 区别；D 驱散,传播。句子的意思是：申办 2008 年奥运会为中国提供了展示国家进步的机会。

15. 答案：D

本题考查动词的含义。A 表扬；B 训诫；C 发言,解决；D 陈述。句子的意思是：律师在法庭上大声清楚地阐述了自己的想法,这使她大吃一惊。

16. 答案：B

本题考查名词的含义。A 原始的；B 行政官,业务主管；C 保守；D 代表。句子的意思是：莫妮卡正在学习工商管理,因为她想成为一个大公司的高薪业务主管。

17. 答案：A

本题考查形容词的含义。A 经验的,实证的；B 学术的；C 本能的；D 易冲动的。句子的意思是：能力强的学生是那些能够看出如何应用一个理论或如何将一个概念联系到一个特定的实例中的学生。

18. 答案：C

本题考查动词的含义。A 把……归因于；B 确认；C 恪守；D 吐露,承认。句子的意思是：磋商一段时间后,所有协会成员都承诺严格恪守职业道德标准。

19. 答案：B

本题考查动词的含义。A 闹鬼的,被困扰的；B 入迷的,一门心思的；C 沉迷于；D 上瘾的。句子的意思是：那么多人都一门心思地使用谷歌——为搜索提供最多结果的最大的搜索引擎。

20. 答案：B

本题考查动词和形容词的搭配。只有 leave 跟 open 搭配成立。句子的意思是：约翰得到三个公司的录用,但他保留选择余地,因为他还没有想清楚从事什么样的工作。

第二部分 完形填空

21. 答案：C
本题考查主从句的逻辑关系。A 除了；B 于是；C 只要；D 不管,尽管。原文是说：FAS 投票通过了一条规定,只要文章不是为了金钱而出售,哈佛大学拥有将其教工的学术成果在全球范围内发布的自由,并且拥有这些文章的版权。

22. 答案：A
本题考查名词的词义辨析。A 保存；B 着迷；C 贡献；D 暂停。本句是说：大学研究的最终目的是为了创造、传播和保存知识。

23. 答案：B
本题考查关系副词的用法。A 因为；B 那里；C 尽管；D 在……同时。先行词是表示地点状语的名词,因此关系副词只能选 where。本句意思是：哈佛大学的很多研究都具有全球性的影响力。

24. 答案：D
本题考查动词的词义辨析。A 传输；B 向……提供；C 转换,调动；D 散布,分发。本题的答题关键在于了解 distribute 与上文中的 disseminate 和 dissemination 是同义词。这句的意思是：哈佛人有义务将这些具有世界影响力的研究成果向全世界传播。

25. 答案：A
本句考查名词的词义辨析和对上下文的语义理解。A 行为；B 运动；C 选举；D 功能。本句讲的是 FAS 当下所作决策的重要性。

26. 答案：B
本句考查名词的词义与搭配。A 气氛；B 享用权；C 态度；D 承认。本题的答题关键在于 access to 这一固定搭配。本句和上句谈论的是 FAS 现在所采取的政策可以促进人们自由和开放地享用哈佛当下正在进行的重要研究。

27. 答案：C
本句考查名词的词义辨析。A 目标；B 升迁；C 许可；D 研究。本题的答题关键是该句与第一段中的"to give Harvard University a worldwide license to"的呼应关系。本句的意思是：哈佛将会利用这次获得许可的机会,将研究者的学术论文放在一个开放库中,使每个人都可以免费获取。

28. 答案：C
本题考查形容词的词义辨析。A 有趣的；B 很长的；C 免费的；D 永久的。这一句讲的是每个人都可以免费享用哈佛研究者的学术论文。

29. 答案：A
本题考查动词的词义辨析。A 保留；B 保持不变；C 忍住,节制；D 再紧张,再尽力。本句的意思是：哈佛的研究者可以保留自己所著文章的版权。

30. 答案：D
本题考查形容词词组的词义辨析。A 与……相反；B 与……相似；C 有关系的；D 视……而定,由……决定的。本句和上句的意思是说：根据哈佛的许可,哈佛的研究者可以保留自己所著文章的版权。

31. 答案：B

　　本题考查名词的词义辨析。A 教职员工；B 公众；C 媒体；D 权威机构。这句的意思是说：公众可以通过搜索引擎来查阅文献库中的内容。

32. 答案：C

　　本题考查名词的词义辨析。A 结构；B 市场；C 机构；D 片段，碎片。这句是说：如果公众可以通过搜索引擎来查阅文献库中的内容，那么在各个研究机构的研究者都会从中受益。

33. 答案：A

　　本题考查动词的词义辨析。A 保持；B 扩大……的范围；C 取消；D 联合。这句是说：在过去几年，各个研究机构保持订阅科技期刊的能力大受损害。

34. 答案：B

　　本题考查名词词组。A 领域；B 范围；C 报告；D 委员会。本句说的是研究机构对各行各业相关期刊的订阅。短语 a full range of 的意思是"各方面的，全部的，一整套的"。

35. 答案：D

　　本题考查动词的词义辨析。A 有特权；B 批准；C 受惩罚；D 受伤害。这句是说：由于订阅期刊的花费太高，贫困地区的研究中心尤其受到资源有限的限制。

第三部分　阅读理解

第一节　阅读理解 A

第一篇：

36. 答案：C

　　本题是推理题，答题关键在于是否理解第一段中作者两次用到"erroneously"（错误地）的用意。

37. 答案：A

　　本题是细节题，考查对第二段第一句话的理解。

38. 答案：D

　　本题是细节题，考查对第三段第二句话"The remaining taxpayers, accordingly, will face increasing burdens,..."的理解。

39. 答案：C

　　本题是推理题，考查对第四段第三句话"...do not consider social needs as the European New Town plans do"的理解。

40. 答案：B

　　本题是细节题，考查对第五段第二句话"all possible social and governmental innovations as well as financial factors..."的理解。

第二篇：

41. 答案：A

　　本题是大意题，考查对第一段第二句话（该段的主题句）的理解。

42. 答案：C

　　本题是推理题，考查对第一段最后一句话中"the only known intact work"（现在所知唯一保存完好的作品)言外之意的理解。
43. 答案:D
    本题是细节题,考点是第二段第三句话中的"...had no idea that the pieces were suspect"。
44. 答案:A
    本题是推理题,考查第二段最后一句话中的"to require importers of classical artifacts to produce proofs of origin and of legal export"。
45. 答案:B
    本题是推理题,考查对第三段引语的理解。
46. 答案:B
    本题是细节选择题,考点在第四段的第二句话:"This third-century BC statue,..., was caught by Italian fishermen in 1964."
47. 答案:C
    本题是全文大意题,考查对全篇文章的理解和归纳。

第三篇:
48. 答案:B
    本题是词汇题,考查这个词汇在上下文中可推理出的意思,考点在第一段的最后一句话。
49. 答案:A
    本题是推理题,考查第一段第三句话中的"The two men have gone to the US Military Academy at West Point together..."。
50. 答案:C
    本题是细节题,考点在最后一段的第二句话"No. 98 for West Point from 1986—1988"中。
51. 答案:D
    本题是细节题,考查对第三段最后一句话的理解。
52. 答案:A
    本题是细节题,考查对最后一段最后两句话的理解。
53. 答案:C
    本题是推理题,考查对最后一段最后一句话中"Serving my country is important."的理解。

第四篇:
54. 答案:C
    本题是细节题,考查对第一段中"...you have to think fast"和"Winners excel at making smart snap judgments"的理解。
55. 答案:B
    本题是推理题,考查第一段最后一句话的言外之意。
56. 答案:D
    本题是推理题,考查对第二段引语部分的归纳和推理能力。
57. 答案:C
    本题是细节题,考查对第三段中第三句和第四句话的理解。

58. 答案:A

　　本题是推理题,考点在最后一段中最后一句话"Game theory, after all, was the key to quantifying the faint notion of economic utility"。

59. 答案:B

　　本题是主旨大意题,考查对文章主要内容的概括能力。

第五篇:

60. 答案:A

　　本题为细节题,考点在第一段第三句话中的"In hopes of ensuring that these fish stocks will continue to be around for many years to come..."。

61. 答案:B

　　本题是细节题,考查对第二段最后一句话的理解。

62. 答案:D

　　本题属推理题,考查对第三段第一句话中"...incompatible fishing methods, incompatible land uses, and over-fishing..."的理解。incompatible 在这里是"不协调的,不适宜的"意思。

63. 答案:A

　　本题是推理题,考点是第四段与前后段落之间在内容上的衔接。第三段的结尾处作者讲到"create fishing strategies...truly sustainable",第五段的开始作者又提到"To manage the region's fisheries effectively",因此可以推断出作者介绍该水域渔业资源丰富的用意。

64. 答案:D

　　本题是细节题,考查对第五段第二句话的理解。本题的答题关键是要留意题干中的"the least relevant information"。

65. 答案:D

　　本题是长句理解题,考查对第六段第二句话的理解。

第二节　阅读理解 B

第一篇:

66. 答案:E

　　本题的答题关键是从该段的其余内容(亚里士多德的例子)推断出主旨大意,即起始句。

67. 答案:C

　　本题考查了空格与下一个句子之间的语义衔接。"angry/anger"是答题的要点。

68. 答案:F

　　本题的答题关键是把握空格上文的内容,并学会总结归纳,选项 F 中的"so"一词是答题的关键。

69. 答案:B

　　本题的下句"the people and the newspaper"中定冠词的使用,提示了空格中的句子中必然提到"people"和"newspaper"。

70. 答案:A

　　本题的答题要点是,空格上句中的"to imagine an argument"和下句中的"imaginary

dialogue"与选项 A 中的"actual conversation"形成了对照。

第二篇:
71. 答案:B
    本题的答题关键是句子之间的转折关系,空格下句中的"Yet"是突破口。
72. 答案:D
    本题的答题要点是空格前的标点为冒号,这说明冒号前后的两句话是互为解释说明,或者后句总结归纳前句的内容。
73. 答案:A
    本题的答题关键有两点:一是选项 A 中的"But"一词,表示与前一句转折;二是选项 A 中的"grows stronger",后一句的具体数据是为了进一步的解释。
74. 答案:F
    本题的答题要点是把握该段的大意——黄金价格上涨及背后可能的原因。选项 F 恰好是解释了前文提到的数据背后的原因。
75. 答案:C
    本题的突破口是空格下文中提到的"such concerns"与选项 C 中的"No Dirty Gold campaign"在语义上是连贯的。

第四部分 翻 译

1)译文:
   将语言作为必修课的学生,其年龄段已经下调了。
   解析:
   在这句话中,大家要正确理解 where 的含义。where 的先行词是 age range,即年龄范围,所以关系副词 where 也做同解,而不是指某个地方。

2)译文:
   同时,所实施的语言教学,其目的更趋于使学生能用口语交流,而非在书写方面连每一个标点都不能错。
   解析:
   围绕着比较级 more...than...理解这句话就不会有偏差;另外,请注意使役动词 get 的用法,在这句话中,get 的宾语是 every single dot and comma,宾语补足语是 correct。

3)译文:
   所以,对于几乎世界上任何一种语言的毕业生或以其为母语的人来说,当一名语言教师是一个很实际、很有吸引力、很有前途的职业。每年都有大量的人从事这个职业。
   解析:
   这句话看似理解起来不难,但翻译时表述比较别扭。理解上的重点是找对 it 的先行词——a career。

4)译文:
   这里,受培训者除了要掌握引导学生学习外语的额外专业知识和技能,还需学习教授课程表上的所有课程。

解析:

理解这句话的时候,请分清主和次。as well as 并非连接并列关系,而是主次关系,主是 trainees prepare to... 这一句,次是 as well as to develop... 所以在译文中要能体现出这种主次关系来。

5) **译文:**

把语言教学融入小学教育虽然还需进一步完善,但小学教育通过利用附近中学的师资及其更专业的知识和经验,当地的中小学教师之间就建立了更多的联系。

解析:

理解这句话的重点是 localized links,意即本地联系,而 across the primary-secondary divide 本意为"打破小学和中学之间的分界线",as 应理解为"因为"。

第五部分 写 作

题目解析:

仔细分析题目中的一句话"Do you think the population in Beijing should be controlled?"可以发现一个困惑:众所周知,北京的人口已经在受到限制,一方面我们国家已经有相应的计划生育政策,北京也不例外;另一方面,北京一直严格控制着进京指标,通过户籍调控限制北京的常住人口。那题目中为什么还说要控制北京人口呢? 可见,除了限制常住人口以外,更有可能的是指是否要限制北京的流动人口。这样的分析可以帮助我们从一个更为具体的角度考虑问题,从而文章更有针对性,文章的思路也更明晰。

同样,我们也可以根据题目中的提示,人口有常住人口和流动人口之分,分别从这两个不同的角度来分析并解释是否要控制北京的人口。

题目中要求陈述并解释个人的观点,因此论述原因是文章的主要侧重点,而不是分析如何控制人口,或是仅限于描述北京市人口拥挤的现状。

范文:

For a person who lives in Beijing, such kind of scenes would be very familiar: The buses and subways are always crowded every day; countless traffic jams in the rush hour turn Beijing into a big parking lot. All this happens mainly because there are too many people in this metropolitan. Some people then propose that the population in Beijing should be controlled, especially the large floating population should be controlled. However, I don't agree with this opinion for the following reasons.

First and foremost, controlling the floating population in Beijing is a kind of discrimination. In the history, no matter in China or in Western countries, big cities have always welcomed the social elites. However, how the society treats its grass-roots reflects that society's level of democracy. Beijing is our country's capital city, and every citizen has the right to come here. Its superior political, cultural and economic status makes it become many young people's promised land. Furthermore, it's the immigrants' incessant pouring into this city that has brought various talents and labor force to Beijing, which substantially boosts the city's development and brings a new vigor to the city. If we forbad people coming into Beijing, the city would lose its momentum in the long run.

Besides, we need to ask ourselves a crucial question: Why are there so many people crowded in Beijing, but not in other Chinese cities? What has caused this phenomenon? The answer is obvious. There are too many advantages in various industries of our capital city. In Beijing, there are more job opportunities, superior education resources, and better medical services than in other Chinese cities. Therefore, the population problem in Beijing is actually caused by its over-concentrated resources advantages. If we just control Beijing's population while ignore this over-concentrated resources phenomenon in Beijing, we wouldn't possibly solve this problem thoroughly. On the other hand, if we distribute parts of the over-concentrated resources of Beijing to other cities, people will spread to other cities and the population in Beijing will stop expanding accordingly.

  Therefore, we can't force the floating population to leave Beijing or stay away from it. The best way to control its population's expansion is not by limiting the floating population, but by implementing a fairer policy to make other cities develop as well as Beijing. (383 words)

中国科学院
博士研究生入学考试
英 语 试 题

（2011 年 3 月）

考生须知：
一、本试卷由试卷一（PAPER ONE）和试卷二（PAPER TWO）两部分组成。试卷一为客观题，答卷使用标准化机读答题纸；试卷二为主观题，答卷使用非机读答题纸。
二、请考生一律用 HB 或 2B 铅笔填涂标准化机读答题纸，画线不得过细或过短。修改时请用橡皮擦拭干净。若因填涂不符合要求而导致计算机无法识别，责任由考生自负。请保持机读答题纸清洁、无折皱。答题纸切忌折叠。
三、全部考试时间总计 180 分钟，满分为 100 分。时间及分值分布如下：

试卷一：

Ⅰ 词汇	15 分钟	10 分	
Ⅱ 完形填空	15 分钟	15 分	
Ⅲ 阅读理解	80 分钟	40 分	
小计	110 分钟	65 分	

试卷二：

Ⅳ 英译汉	30 分钟	15 分	
Ⅴ 写作	40 分钟	20 分	
小计	70 分钟	35 分	

GRADUATE UNIVERSITY, CHINESE ACADEMY OF SCIENCES ENGLISH ENTRANCE EXAMINATION FOR DOCTORAL CANDIDATES

March 2011

PAPER ONE

PART I VOCABULARY (15 minutes, 10 points, 0.5 point each)

Directions: *Choose the word or expression below each sentence that best completes the statement, and mark the corresponding letter of your choice with a single bar across the square bracket on your Machine-scoring Answer Sheet.*

1. My father was a nuclear engineer, a very academically _____ man with multiple degrees from prestigious institutions.
   A. promoted   B. activated   C. oriented   D. functioned

2. Public _____ for the usually low-budget, high-quality films has enabled the independent film industry to grow and thrive.
   A. appreciation   B. recognition   C. gratitude   D. tolerance

3. Dirty Jobs on the Discovery Channel, an unlikely television program, has become a surprising success with a _____ fan base.
   A. contributed   B. devoted   C. revered   D. scared

4. Pop culture doesn't _____ to strict rules; it enjoys being jazzy, unpredictable, chaotic.
   A. adhere   B. lend   C. expose   D. commit

5. Intellectual property is a kind of _____ monopoly, which should be used properly or else would disrupt healthy competition order.
   A. legible   B. legendary   C. lenient   D. legitimate

6. I am thankful to the company for giving me such a chance, and I earnestly hope that I will _____ everyone's expectations.
   A. boil down to   B. look forward to   C. live up to   D. catch on to

7. The image of an unfortunate resident having to climb 20 flights of stairs because the lift is

_____ is now a common one.

A. out of the way   B. on order   C. out of order   D. in no way

8. My eyes had become _____ to the now semi-darkness, so I could pick out shapes about seventy-five yards away.

A. inclined   B. accustomed   C. vulnerable   D. sensitive

9. Despite what I'd been told about the local people's attitude to strangers, _____ did I encounter any rudeness.

A. at no time   B. in no time   C. at any time   D. at some time

10. In times of severe _____ companies are often forced to make massive job cuts in order to survive.

A. retreat   B. retrospect   C. reduction   D. recession

11. Sport was integral to the national and local press, TV and, to a diminishing _____, to radio.

A. extent   B. scope   C. scale   D. range

12. Unless your handwriting is _____, or the form specifically asks for typewriting, the form should be neatly handwritten.

A. illegitimate   B. illegal   C. illegible   D. illiterate

13. The profession fell into _____, with some physicists sticking to existing theories, while others came up with the big-bang theory.

A. harmony   B. turmoil   C. distortion   D. accord

14. With the purchasing power of many middle-class households _____ behind the cost of living, there was an urgent demand for credit.

A. leaving   B. levering   C. lacking   D. lagging

15. Frank stormed into the room and _____ the door, but it wasn't that easy to close the door on what Jack had said.

A. slashed   B. slammed   C. slipped   D. slapped

16. When I was having dinner with you and Edward at his apartment, I sensed a certain _____ between the two of you.

A. intimacy   B. proximity   C. discrepancy   D. diversity

17. I decided to _____ between Ralph and his brother, who were arguing endlessly.

A. interfere   B. intervene   C. interrupt   D. interact

18. "I mean Gildas and Ludens are both wise, reasonable and tactful; but naturally they're _____, they want to know what's happening, and make judgments on it all."

A. indifferent   B. innocent   C. inquisitive   D. instinctive

19. In Africa HIV and AIDS continue to _____ the population; nearly 60 percent of those infected are women.

A. alleviate   B. boost   C. capture   D. ravage

20. By the end of the Spring and Autumn Period slave society was _____ disintegration.

A. on the ground of   B. on the top of

C. in the light of   D. on the verge of

PART II CLOZE TEST (15 minutes, 15 points)

Directions: *For each blank in the following passage, choose the best answer from the four choices given below. Mark the corresponding letter of your choice with a single bar across the square bracket on your Machine-scoring Answer Sheet.*

Tomorrow Japan and South Korea will celebrate White Day, an annual event when men are expected to buy a gift for the adored women in their lives. It is a relatively new __21__ that was commercially created as payback for Valentine's Day. That's __22__ in both countries, 14 February is all about the man.

On Valentine's Day, women are expected to buy all the important male __23__ in their lives a token gift: not just their partners, __24__ their bosses or older relatives too.

This seems __25__ enough. Surely it's reasonable for men to be indulged on one day of the year, __26__ the number of times they're expected to produce bouquets of flowers and __27__ their woman with perfume or pearls.

But the idea of a woman __28__ a man didn't sit easily with people. In 1978, the National Confectionery Industry Association (糖果业协会) __29__ an idea to solve this problem. They started to market white chocolate that men could give to women on 14 March, as __30__ for the male-oriented Valentine's Day.

It started with a handful of sweet-makers' producing candy __31__ a simple gift idea. The day __32__ the public imagination, and is now a nationally __33__ date in the diary — and one where men are __34__ to whip out their credit cards. In fact, men are now expected to give gifts worth __35__ the value of those they received. What a complication: not only do men have to remember who bought them what, they have to estimate the value and multiply it by three.

21. A. copy   B. concept   C. choice   D. belief
22. A. because   B. as   C. so   D. why
23. A. clients   B. friends   C. figures   D. colleagues
24. A. but   B. and   C. instead of   D. rather than
25. A. odd   B. good   C. fair   D. rare
26. A. given   B. if   C. but   D. though
27. A. attract   B. frustrate   C. surprise   D. touch
28. A. supporting   B. spoiling   C. comforting   D. fooling
29. A. came up with B. come out of   C. came up to   D. came along with
30. A. companion   B. compromise   C. competence   D. compensation
31. A. via   B. as   C. with   D. for
32. A. captured   B. appealed   C. favored   D. held

33. A. documented   B. recognized   C. illustrated   D. scheduled
34. A. volunteered   B. embarrassed   C. sponsored   D. obliged
35. A. triple   B. double   C. fourfold   D. equal

PART III READING COMPREHENSION

Section A (60 minutes, 30 points)

Directions: *Below each of the following passages you will find some questions or incomplete statements. Each question or statement is followed by four choices marked A, B, C, and D. Read each passage carefully, and then select the choice that best answers the question or completes the statement. Mark the letter of your choice with a single bar across the square bracket on your Machine-scoring Answer Sheet.*

Passage One

At many colleges, smokers are being run not just out of school buildings but off the premises. On Nov. 19, the University of Kentucky, the tobacco state's flagship public institution, launched a campus wide ban on cigarettes and all other forms of tobacco on school grounds and parking areas. Pro-nicotine students staged a "smoke-out" to protest the new policy, which even rules out smoking inside cars if they're on school property.

Kentucky joins more than 365 U.S. colleges and universities that in recent years have instituted antismoking rules both indoors and out. In most places, the issue doesn't seem to be secondhand smoke. Rather, the rationale for going smoke-free in wide open spaces is a desire to model healthy behavior.

Purdue University, which has 30-ft. buffer zones, recently considered adopting a campuswide ban but tempered its proposal after receiving campus input. Smoking will now be restricted to limited outdoor areas.

One big problem with a total ban is enforcing it. Take the University of Iowa. In July 2008, the school went smoke-free in accordance with the Iowa Smokefree Air Act, violations of which can result in a $50 fine. But so far, the university has ticketed only about 25 offenders. "Our campus is about 1,800 acres, so to think that we could keep track of who is smoking on campus at any given time isn't really feasible," says Joni Troester, director of the university's campus wellness program. Instead, the school helps those trying to kick the habit by offering smoking-cessation programs and providing reimbursement for nicotine patches, gum and prescription medications like Zyban.

The University of Michigan will probably take a similar approach when its ban takes effect in July 2011. "We don't have a desire to give tickets or levy punishments," says Robert Winfield, the school's chief health officer. "We want to encourage people to stop smoking, set a good example for students and make this a healthier community."

Naturally, there has been pushback from students. "Where do we draw the line between a culture of health and individual choice?" asks Jonathan Slemrod, a University of Michigan senior and president of the school's College Libertarians. "If they truly want a culture of health, I expect them to go through all our cafeterias and get rid of all our Taco Bells, all our pizza places." Students might want to enjoy those Burrito Supremes while they can. In today's health-obsessed culture, those may be next.

36. We can infer that the "newness" of the antismoking policy at the University of Kentucky lies in _____.
   A. its extended scope of no-smoking places
   B. its prohibition of cigarette sales on campus
   C. its penalty for bringing tobacco to school
   D. its ban on smoke when people are driving

37. By setting the antismoking rules the University of Kentucky mainly aims for _____.
   A. protecting students against passive smoking
   B. modeling itself on many other universities
   C. promoting the students' health awareness
   D. punishing those who dare smoke on campus

38. One of the problems enforcing the ban on smoking at the University of Iowa is _____.
   A. limiting the smoke-free areas   B. tracing smokers on campus
   C. forcing smokers to give up smoking   D. providing alternative ways for smokers

39. The word "levy" (in Paragraph 5) most probably means _____.
   A. impose   B. avoid   C. deserve   D. receive

40. According to Jonathan Slemrod, Taco Bell is _____.
   A. a tobacco shop   B. a school cafeteria
   C. an organic food store   D. an unhealthy food chain

41. The author's tone in the essay is _____.
   A. radical   B. optimistic   C. objective   D. critical

Passage Two

The familiar sounds of an early English summer are with us once again. Millions of children sit down to SATs, GCSEs, AS-levels, A-levels and a host of lesser exams, and the argument over educational standards starts. Depending on whom you listen to, we should either be letting up on over-examined pupils by abolishing SATs, and even GCSEs, or else making exams far more rigorous.

The chorus will reach a peak when GCSE and A-level results are published in August. If pass rates rise again, commentators will say that standards are falling because exams are getting easier. If pass rates drop, they will say that standards are falling because children are getting lower marks. Parents like myself try to ignore this and base our judgments on what our children are learning. But it's not easy given how much education has changed since we were at school.

Some trends are encouraging — education has been made more relevant and enthuses many children that it would have previously bored. My sons' A-level French revision involved listening to radio debates on current affairs, whereas mine involved rereading Molière. And among their peers, a far greater proportion stayed in education for longer.

On the other hand, some aspects of schooling today are incomprehensible to my generation, such as gaps in general knowledge and the hand-holding that goes with ensuring that students leave with good grades. Even when we parents resist the temptation to help with GCSE or A-level coursework, a teacher with the child's interests at heart may send a draft piece of work back several times with pointers to how it can be improved before the examiners see it.

The debate about standards persists because there is no single objective answer to the question: "Are standards better or worse than they were a generation ago?" Each side points to indicators that favor them, in the knowledge that there is no authoritative definition, let alone a measure that has been consistently applied over the decades. But the annual soul-searching over exams is about more than student assessment. It reveals a national insecurity about whether our education system is teaching the right things. It is also fed by an anxiety about whether, in a country with a history of upholding standards by ensuring that plenty of students fail, we can attain the more modern objective of ensuring that every child leaves school with something to show for it.

42. It can be concluded from Paragraph 1 that _____.
    A. SATs is one of the most rigorous exams mentioned
    B. it has been debated if children should be given exams
    C. few parents approve of the exam systems in England
    D. each year children have to face up to some new exams
43. Parents try to judge the educational standards by _____.
    A. whether their children have passed the exams
    B. what knowledge their children have acquired
    C. what educators say about curriculum planning
    D. whether their children's school scores are stable
44. To the author, the rereading of Molière was _____.
    A. dreary   B. routine   C. outmoded   D. arduous
45. To the author's generation, it is beyond understanding today why _____.
    A. teachers lay great stress on helping students obtain good grades
    B. teachers show much concern for students' future
    C. parents help little with their children's coursework
    D. parents focus on their children's general knowledge
46. According to the passage, with respect to educational standards in Britain, _____.
    A. no authorities have ever made a comment
    B. no one has ever tried to give them a definition
    C. no effective ways have been taken to apply them

D. no consistent yardstick has ever been used

47. In the author's opinion, the school education in Britain has been _____.

A. inflexible   B. irresponsible   C. unsuccessful   D. unforgivable

Passage Three

Suzan Fellman had a hard time with Laura Bush's redo of the famed guest quarters named for President Lincoln: "Looking at it, I thought I was in a Radisson lobby somewhere in the Midwest long ago. I could not imagine spending a night in that space."

Done up with Victorian furnishings, the Lincoln Bedroom is one of the residence's least-changed spaces, said Betty Monkman, formerly chief curator of the White House for nearly 40 years. "It's a quasi-museum room," she said, "with a lot of objects, such as the bed, that have symbolic importance."

The elaborately carved bed bought for Lincoln is the centerpiece of the room.

According to historian William Seale, the president was furious that his wife, Mary, spent so much money redecorating the White House during a time of war. He never slept in the bed, and the ornate piece eventually was moved to a spare room.

Los Angeles designer Fellman saw parallels, calling the Obama era a period of "pulling back on extravagance." It is a good time, she said, to revisit pieces in storage, to rearrange old furniture in a new fashion, and use paint and fabrics to bring life and fun into a room without spending a fortune.

In this re-imagining of the Lincoln Bedroom, Fellman would retain the legendary bed but paint the ceiling a sky blue and use a Cecil Beaton rose-print fabric for curtains. "Lincoln loved roses," Fellman said, "and this beige and ivory version keeps it from being too bold, modern or feminine." At a time when Americana is expected to stage a strong revival, Fellman said traditional styles such as Colonial and Federal can co-exist with European antiques if they are balanced in scale.

Mindful of the recession, the designer advocated selecting furniture with longevity in mind. "If you are going to spend money, buy quality things that you never want to get rid of," she said. "A couple of really good things can make all the difference in a room." Her splurges would include a camel-hair sofa, which Fellman said was long-lasting and timeless. As a Pop Art-influenced statement about thrift, a custom rug woven with a 6-foot-diameter medallion replicates the penny's image of Lincoln in subtle shades of ivory and copper.

In bad times as in good, spare rooms don't have to be grand to be effective, Fellman said. "A guest room should feel inviting and intimate," she said. "It has to exude serenity."

48. To Suzan Fellman, Laura Bush's redecoration of the Lincoln Bedroom could hardly be _____.

A. evaluated   B. imagined   C. understood   D. praised

49. The Lincoln Bedroom in White House is a place for _____.

A. the president to have a rest   B. visitors to stay overnight

C. storing Victorian furnishings   D. exhibiting classic objects

50. According to Fellman, the Obama era is similar to the Lincoln era in _____.
    A. decorating houses   B. respecting the past
    C. protecting the classic   D. encouraging thrift

51. The way Fellman would rearrange the Lincoln Bedroom includes _____.
    A. putting some roses on the table   B. omitting some European antiques
    C. adding to it some Federal styles   D. giving it the look of a strong America

52. In choosing the new furniture for the room, Fellman would give top priority to _____.
    A. its durability   B. its simplicity   C. its price   D. its color

53. Fellman would avoid making the Lincoln Bedroom look _____.
    A. tranquil   B. luxurious   C. hospitable   D. fascinating

Passage Four

Laurance Rockefeller, the middle brother of the five prominent and benevolent grandsons of John D. Rockefeller, who concentrated his own particular generosity on conservation, recreation, ecological concerns and medical research, particularly the treatment of cancer, died of pulmonary fibrosis at his home in Manhattan.

His career began on Wall Street almost 70 years ago, where he became a pioneer of modern venture capitalism, compounding his inherited wealth many times over. In the decades since he first took his seat on the New York Stock Exchange, he often used his native instinct for identifying the next big thing, not content simply to make more money but to make the money produce something of lasting value.

Less sociable than his older brother Nelson, who was a four-term governor of New York and the country's vice president under Gerald R. Ford, Laurance Spelman Rockefeller was also more reserved and private than his flamboyant younger brother Winthrop who was the governor of Arkansas. A philosophy major at Princeton he had long wrestled with the question of how he might most efficiently and satisfyingly use the great wealth to which he was born and which he later kept compounding as a successful pioneer of modern venture capitalism.

Using significant amounts of his money as well as his connections and prestige and negotiating skills he was instrumental in establishing and enlarging National Parks in Wyoming, California, the Virgin Islands, Vermont, Maine and Hawaii. As an active member of the Palisade Interstate Parkway Commission, he helped create a chain of parks that blocked the advance of sprawl, thus maintaining the majestic view that he first saw as a child looking out from Kykuit, the Rockefeller country home in Pocantico.

His commitment to wilderness, recreation and environmental conservation had many roots. Since childhood he liked to ride horses through unspoiled terrain. He was a passionate photographer in search of new landscapes. Even before Laurance reached adulthood the Rockefellers had included parks among their many philanthropic projects.

Laurance was born on May 26, 1910. As Laurance matured he came to more closely resemble his grandfather than did any other family member, having the same pursed and seemingly serious expression that John D. Rockefeller often showed in photographs. According to family accounts he was also the one who most closely revealed his grandfather's ability for profitable deals.

54. Paragraph 1 suggests that Laurance Rockefeller was a man who is _____.
    A. full of social responsibility   B. famous but short-lived
    C. successful in many fields   D. zealous in social activities
55. We can learn that, in making investments, Laurance Rockefeller was very _____.
    A. cold-hearted   B. close-fisted   C. far-sighted   D. half-witted
56. Compared with his two brothers, Laurance _____.
    A. often relied on himself   B. rarely appeared in public
    C. rarely voiced his opinions   D. often worried about his wealth
57. The word "instrumental" (boldfaced in Para 4) in this context can be replaced by "_____."
    A. generous   B. strategic   C. resolute   D. important
58. Laurance's childhood experience led him later to make significant contributions to _____.
    A. the building of national parks   B. the enlargement of urban areas
    C. the perfection of his hometown   D. the popularization of horse riding
59. According to the passage, Laurance resembled his grandfather in having _____.
    A. a contribution to public good   B. a talent of making money
    C. a passion for wilderness   D. a bias against political affairs

Passage Five

The first three days of July 1863 saw the bloodiest hours of the Civil War, in a battle that spilled across the fields and hills surrounding Gettysburg, Pa. The fighting climaxed in the bright, hot afternoon of the third day, when more than 11,000 Confederate soldiers mounted a disastrous assault on the heart of the Union line. That assault marked the farthest the South would penetrate into Union territory. In a much larger sense, it marked the turning point of the war.

No surprise, then, that the Battle of Gettysburg would become the subject of songs, poems, funeral monuments and, ultimately, some of the biggest paintings ever displayed on this continent. Paul Philippoteaux, famed for his massive 360-degree cyclorama paintings, painted four versions of the battle in the 1880s. Cycloramas were hugely popular in the United States in the last decades of the 19th century, before movies displaced them in the public's affection. Conceived on a mammoth scale, a cyclorama painting was longer than a football field and almost 50 feet tall. Little thought was given to preserving these enormous works of art. They were commercial ventures, and when they stopped earning they were tossed. Most were ultimately lost — victims of water damage or fire. One of Philippoteaux's Gettysburg renderings was cut up and hung in panels in a Newark, N. J., department store before finding its way back to Gettysburg, where it has been displayed off and on since 1913. Along the way, the painting lost most of its sky and a few feet off the bottom. Sections were cut and moved to patch holes in other sections. And some of the restorative efforts proved almost as crippling to the original as outright neglect. Since 2003, a team of conservators has labored in a $12 million effort to restore Philippoteaux's masterwork. They have cleaned it front and back, patched it, added canvas for a new sky and returned the painting to its original shape — a key part of a cyclorama's optical illusion was its hyperbolic shape: it bellies out at its central point, thrusting the image toward the viewer.

When restoration is completed later this year, the painting will be the centerpiece of the new Gettysburg battlefield visitors' center, which opens to the public on April 14. Much work remains to be done. But even partially restored, the painting seethes with life — and death.

60. With respect to the Battle of Gettysburg, Paragraph 1 mainly emphasizes _____.
    A. the reason for its occurrence   B. the significance of the battle
    C. the place where it broke out   D. the bloodiness of the battle
61. To the author, that Gettysburg Battle got reflected in many art works is _____.
    A. reasonable   B. meaningful   C. necessary   D. impressive
62. We can infer that cyclorama paintings _____.
    A. has regained their popularity since 1913
    B. were mostly destroyed by the Civil War
    C. more often than not lost than gained money
    D. had been popular before movies came in
63. Work done to restore the Philippoteaux's painting already began _____.
    A. before 1900   B. after 1913   C. in 2003   D. at its birth
64. According to the author, some previous efforts to restore the Philippoteaux's painting turned out to be _____.
    A. time consuming B. fruitless   C. destructive   D. a waste of money
65. What is true of the present state of the Philippoteaux's Gettysburg rendering?
    A. It is illusory in depiction.   B. It is a perfect restoration.
    C. It is a modified version.   D. It is incredibly lifelike.

Section B (20 minutes, 10 points)

Directions: *In each of the following passages, five sentences have been removed from the original text. They are listed from A to F and put below the passage. Choose the most suitable sentence from the list to fill in each of the blanks (numbered 66 to 75). For each passage, there is one sentence that does not fit in any of the blanks. Mark your answers on your Machine-scoring Answer Sheet.*

Passage One

Advertising is paid, nonpersonal communication that is designed to communicate in a creative manner, through the use of mass or information-directed media, the nature of products, services, and ideas. It is a form of persuasive communication that offers information about products, ideas, and services that serves the objectives determined by the advertiser. __66__ Thus, the ultimate objective of advertising is to sell things persuasively and creatively. Advertising is used by commercial firms trying to sell products and services; by politicians and political interest groups to sell ideas or persuade voters; by not-for-profit organizations to raise funds, solicit volunteers, or influence the actions of viewers; and by governments seeking to encourage or discourage particular activities, such as wearing seatbelts, participating in the census, or ceasing to smoke. __67__

The visual and verbal commercial messages that are a part of advertising are intended to attract attention and produce some response by the viewer. Advertising is pervasive and virtually impossible to escape. Newspapers and magazines often have more advertisements than copy; radio and television provide entertainment but are also laden with advertisements; advertisements pop up on Internet sites; and the mail brings a variety of advertisements. __68__ In shopping malls, there are prominent logos on designer clothes, moviegoers regularly view advertisements for local restaurants, hair salons, and so on, and live sporting and cultural events often include signage, logos, products, and related information about the event sponsors. __69__

Although the primary objective of advertising is to persuade, it may achieve this objective in many different ways. An important function of advertising is the identification function, that is, to identify a product and differentiate it from others; this creates an awareness of the product and provides a basis for consumers to choose the advertised product over other products. __70__ The third function of advertising is to induce consumers to try new products and to suggest reuse of the product as well as new uses; this is the persuasion function.

A. Another function of advertising is to communicate information about the product, its attributes, and its location of sale; this is the information function.
B. The forms that advertising takes and the media in which advertisements appear are as varied as the advertisers themselves and the messages that they wish to deliver.
C. An especially important issue in the creation of advertising is related to understanding how much information consumers want about a given product.
D. Advertising may influence consumers in many different ways, but the primary goal of advertising is to increase the probability that consumers exposed to an advertisement will behave or believe as the advertiser wishes.
E. Advertising also exists on billboards along the freeway, in subway and train stations, on benches at bus stops, and on the frames around car license plates.
F. The pervasiveness of advertising and its creative elements are designed to cause viewers to take note.

Passage Two

Few numbers tell a happier story than those that measure life expectancy. An American born in 1900 could expect to live 47 years. Thanks to colossal improvements in sanitation and medicine, that figure is now 75 for men and 80 for women. __71__

So it is both alarming and surprising when life expectancy falls, even for a small part of the population. Yet that is what some researchers at Harvard have found. They looked at death rates by county, having corrected for migration and merged sparsely populated ones so that America's 3,141 counties became 2,068 "county units."

__72__ But between 1983 and 1999, it fell significantly (by about a year) for women in 180 county units, and stagnated in another 783. Men fared less poorly: their life expectancy fell significantly in only 11 county units, and stagnated in another 48.

Put differently, life expectancy appears to have either stagnated or fallen slightly for some 4% of American men and 19% of women. The main culprits are diseases linked to smoking or obesity, such as lung cancer and diabetes. __73__

Majid Ezzati, one of the study's authors, says it is too soon to say. An optimist would point out that women took up smoking later than men. It was not until after the Second World War that they started puffing at anything like the male rate. The increase of poor women now dying of lung cancer may be a hangover from the end of the taboo on female smoking. __74__

A pessimist would reply that the other big killer, obesity, keeps spreading, especially among the poor. "We've been saying for ages that it must have peaked, but it keeps going up," says Dr Ezzati. Two decades ago, no state had an obesity rate above 15%. Now, 22 have passed the 25% mark. __75__ Neither is getting any smaller.

A. For most Americans, life expectancy continues merrily to rise.

B. And the poorest Americans have gained the most: blacks, for example, live more than twice as long now as they did a century ago.

C. Even though smoking takes an average of 14.5 years off women's lives, almost one in five American women age 18 and older smokes.

D. The counties where life expectancy has fallen are nearly all in the South or Appalachia, where huge deep-fried portions are the norm and waistlines are among America's widest.

E. But both sexes have quit in large numbers since the 1970s, so the death toll may fall in the future.

F. The crucial question is whether this represents a pause or the start of a trend.

PAPER TWO

PART IV TRANSLATION (30 minutes, 15 points)

Directions: *Read the following text carefully and then translate the underlined segments into Chinese. Write your Chinese version in the proper space on your Answer Sheet.*

Steve Jobs is an entrepreneur. And that is how history will long remember him. Not primarily as a fiduciary or an institution builder or an administrator, but rather as an individual who relentlessly pursued new opportunities. (1) From the first Apple computers to the breakthrough innovations of the past eight years, he has chased new possibilities without being discouraged by whatever obstacle he encountered. Over and over again he has turned his eye and his energy — and at times, it has seemed, his entire being — to what might be gained by creating a new offering or taking an unorthodox strategic path.

(2) That puts him in the company of great entrepreneurs of the past two centuries, each of whom — and especially Steve Jobs has been defined by the intense drive, tireless curiosity, and keen commercial imagination. That has allowed them to see products and industries and possibilities that might be. (3) Each of these individuals has also been extremely hardworking, demanding of themselves and others. All have been compelled more by the significance of their own vision than by their doubts.

(4) Jobs came of age in a moment of far-reaching economic, social, and technological change that we now call the Information Revolution. He has had a sense — analytic and intuitive — that in a time of great transformation, a lot is up for grabs. Imbued with a perception of his own importance on a stage where everything from telephony to music distribution to consumers' relationships with technology is being disrupted, Jobs felt there was simply no time to lose.

(5) This understanding has fueled the rapid-fire pace of his actions and his obsession with "What's next?" in products, which may have also fed his often harsh, dictatorial, and somehow still-inspiring management style.

PART V　WRITING (40 minutes, 20 points)

Directions: *Write an essay of no less than 200 words on the topic given below. Use the proper space on your Answer Sheet Ⅱ.*

TOPIC

"To get success, you need friends; to get huge success, you need enemies." Do you agree with this saying or not? Why or why not?

2011年3月试题精解

第一部分 词 汇

1. 答案：C
   本题考查过去分词的含义。A 晋升的,促销的；B 激活的；C 以……为导向的；D 有……功能的,运行的。句子的意思是：我父亲是位核工程工程师,一心扑在学术上,获得了多个名校的多个学位。

2. 答案：A
   本题考查名词的含义。A 欣赏,感激；B 识别,承认；C 感激,感谢；D 容忍。句子的意思是：公众对于低成本、高质量电影的欣赏促进了独立电影事业的繁荣发展。

3. 答案：B
   本题考查形容词组的含义。A 贡献的,造成的；B 忠实的,投入的；C 崇敬的,尊重的；D 害怕的。句子的意思是：《探索频道》播放的《干尽苦差事》,本不被看好,却取得了惊人的成功,拥有了一群忠实的观众。

4. 答案：A
   本题考查动词的含义和动词与介词的搭配。A 遵循,坚持；B 借出；C 暴露,置身于；D 做（坏事、傻事）,致力于。句子的意思是：大众文化不遵循教条,很花哨、经常出人预料甚至混乱无序。

5. 答案：D
   本题考查形容词的含义。A 字迹可辨的,可以认出的；B 传说中的；C 仁慈的,开恩的；D 合法的,正当的。句子的意思是：知识产权是种正当的垄断行为,应该恰当地使用,否则就会扰乱健康的竞争秩序。

6. 答案：C
   本题考查动词词组。A 归结为；B 期待；C 达到（期望值）,不辜负（期望）；D 跟上。句子的意思是：感谢公司给我这么一个机会,我真诚地希望达到大家的期望值。

7. 答案：C
   本题考查介词短语。A 使不妨碍；B 订购；C 出故障；D 绝对不。句子的意思是：因为电梯出了故障居民要爬20层楼的现象现在已经很普遍了。

8. 答案：B
   本题考查形容词的含义。A 倾向于；B 习惯；C 脆弱；D 敏感。句子的意思是：我的眼睛已经适应了这种半黑暗,可以辨别75码以内的东西。

9. 答案：A
   本题考查介词词组。A 从来,在任何时候都不；B 立即,马上；C 随时；D 有时,有朝一日。句子的意思是：尽管听到了很多当地人对待生人的态度如何如何,我从来都没有碰到不礼貌的待遇。

10. 答案:D

本题考查名词的含义。A 撤退;B 回想;C 减少,降低;D 衰退。句子的意思是:经济极度不景气的时候,公司经常不得不大批裁员来生存。

11. 答案:A

本题考查副词词组的含义。只有"A 在一定程度上"可以构成搭配。句子的意思是:体育是全国性和地方性的报纸、电视以及一定程度上广播中的必不可少的一部分。

12. 答案:C

本题考查形容词的含义。A 私生的,非法的;B 非法的;C 难以辨认的;D 文盲、不识字的。句子的意思是:除非你的字迹难以辨认,或者表格特别要求打印,否则表格应该工整填写。

13. 答案:B

本题考查名词的含义。A 和谐;B 动乱,混乱;C 扭曲,歪曲;D 和谐,一致。句子的意思是:这个行业乱了:有些物理学家坚持现有的理论,另外一些搞出了个大爆炸理论。

14. 答案:D

本题考查动词与介词(behind)的搭配。A 留下;B 杠杆;C 缺乏;D 落后。句子的意思是:许多中产阶级家庭购买力落后于生活成本,信贷要求变得迫切。

15. 答案:B

本题考查动词的含义。A 严厉斥责,乱砍;B 猛摔;C 溜走,滑倒;D 抽嘴巴。句子的意思是:弗兰克冲进屋子,摔上门,但想封住杰克的嘴不太容易。

16. 答案:A

本题考查名词的含义。A 亲昵行为;B 接近,临近;C 异议,差异;D 多样性。句子的意思是:我们在爱德华家一起吃饭的时候,我能察觉到你们俩挺亲密的。

17. 答案:B

本题考查动词的含义。A 干涉;B 干涉,介入;C 打断;D 互动。句子的意思是:拉尔夫和他兄弟吵得没完没了,我决定介入来劝阻他们。

18. 答案:C

本题考查形容词的含义。A 冷漠的;B 无辜的;C 好奇的;D 本能的。句子的意思是:我的意思是说基尔达斯和卢登思都很睿智、老练、通情达理;但自然地他们也很好奇,什么都想知道,还要指手画脚。

19. 答案:D

本题考查动词的含义。A 减轻;B 促进;C 抓住;D 摧残,践踏。句子的意思是:在非洲艾滋病病毒和艾滋病继续践踏着那里的居民,近 60% 的感染者是女性。

20. 答案:D

本题考查介词短语的含义。A 以……为理由;B 在……之上;C 鉴于;D 将近,即将。句子的意思是:春秋末期奴隶社会将近解体。

第二部分 完形填空

21. 答案:B

本题考查名词词义辨析。A 复制品;B 概念;C 选择;D 信念。原文是说:白色情人节是一个新概念,它是人们出于商业目的制造的一个节日,用于补偿女人在情人节的付出。

22. 答案：A

本题考查副词的词义辨析和上下文语义理解。从语义上讲，这里需要一个表示原因的副词，来表示为什么会有这么一个节日。故可以淘汰 C 和 D。A 和 B 选项的意思都是"因为"，但 because 的语气比 as 强，并且 because 表示直接原因，一般放在主句之后，也可独立存在。通常用于回答 why 的提问。

23. 答案：C

本题考查名词的语义辨析。A 顾客；B 朋友；C 人物；D 同事。这句的意思是说，在情人节那一天，女性要为她生活中的每一个重要男性购买一个象征性礼物。

24. 答案：A

本题考查连接词的用法。A. but，"not just…but…"是"not only…, but also…"的一个变体形式，表示，"不仅……而且……"；B. and，是表示并列的连接词；C. instead of，强调的是代替，表示"不是……而是……"；D. rather than 是一个并列连词，它表示"是……而不是……"。根据句意，"这些男性不仅只限于她们的配偶，还包括她们的老板或者其他年长的亲戚，"只有 A 选项符合。

25. 答案：C

本题考查形容词的词义辨析。A 怪异；B 好的；C 公平的；D 少见。本句的意思是说，给生活中的男性一年买一次纪念性的礼物看似很公平。

26. 答案：A

本题考查介词的词义辨析。A 考虑到；B 如果；C 但是；D 尽管。本句的意思是：考虑到男人一年当中的其他时间要给女人送花等因素，女人偶尔纵容一下男人也看似合理。

27. 答案：C

本题考查动词的词义辨析。A 吸引；B 使……沮丧；C 使……惊喜；D 触动。本句是说：男性要用香水或者珍珠等礼物使女人感到惊喜。

28. 答案：B

本题考查动名词的词义辨析和用法区分。A 支持；B 宠爱；C 安慰；D 愚弄。这句的意思是：女人去娇惯宠爱男人的这种想法让人感觉很不自在。

29. 答案：A

本题考查动词词组的语义辨析。A 想出；B 从……出来；C 拜访；D 与……一起来。这句的意思是：在 1978 年，全国糖果业协会想出了一个好办法来解决这个问题。

30. 答案：D

本题考查名词的词义辨析。A 陪伴；B 妥协；C 能力；D 补偿，赔偿，指对他人的损失给予价值相当的货币，或其他等价物，以使受损一方当事人回复其原有状况。本句的意思是：他们向男性推销白色巧克力，让他们在 3 月 14 日的时候送白色巧克力给女性，从而补偿女性在情人节那天的付出。

31. 答案：B

本题考查介词的词义辨析。A 通过；B 作为 C 与……一起；D 为了。这句是说：在开始时，男性在白色情人节送给女性一些白色的巧克力作为节日礼物。

32. 答案：A

本题考查动词的词义辨析。A 吸引；B 使……开心；C 偏爱；D 保持；本句意思是说，这个节日很快就捕获了公众的心。

33. 答案：B

　　本题考查过去分词转换形容词的词义辨析。A 记录的；B 认可的；C 阐明的；D 安排的。本句意思是：现在白色情人节已经是全国上下普遍认可的一个节日。

34. 答案：D

　　本题考查动词的词义辨析。A 自愿；B 尴尬；C 赞助；D 被迫，不得不。这句是说：白色情人节已经成为一个男人不得不去刷卡消费的日子。

35. 答案：A

　　本题考查形容词的词义辨析以及对下文内容的把握。A 三倍的；B 两倍的；C 四倍的；D 相同的。这句是说：男性送给女性的礼物价值是他们情人节所收到礼物价值的三倍。

第三部分　阅读理解

第一节　阅读理解 A

第一篇：

36. 答案：A

　　本题是细节题，考查对第一段最后一句话的理解。

37. 答案：C

　　本题是推理题，考查对第二段大意的归纳总结，并且提干中的"mainly"是答题的关键。

38. 答案：B

　　本题是细节题，考查对第四段中直接引语部分的理解。

39. 答案：A

　　本题是词汇题，这道题的关键是运用语法与搭配的知识，猜测出"levy"在短语"to give tickets or levy punishments"中的意思。

40. 答案：D

　　本题是推理题，文中讲到"get rid of all our Taco Bells"，可见 Taco Bells 与吸烟一样，都是不健康的。

41. 答案：C

　　本题是文体题，本文属于客观性的新闻报道。

第二篇：

42. 答案：A

　　本题是判断对错题，考查对第一段的理解。

43. 答案：B

　　本题是细节题，考查对第二段倒数第二句的理解。

44. 答案：A

　　本题是细节题，考查第三段的第一句与下文的联系。

45. 答案：A

　　本题是细节题，考点是第四段的第一句。

46. 答案：D

本题是细节题,考点是第五段第一句。
47. 答案:C
    本题是细节题,考查对最后一段倒数第二句中"a national insecurity"的理解。

第三篇:
48. 答案:D
    本题是推理题,需看完第一段才能做出正确的推测,尤其要了解"to have a hard time with"这一短语的含义。
49. 答案:B
    本题是细节题,考点是第一段第一句话中的"guest quarters named for President Lincoln"。
50. 答案:D
    本题是细节题,考查对第五段第一句话的理解。
51. 答案:C
    本题是细节题,考查对第六段最后一句的理解。
52. 答案:A
    本题是细节题,考点是第七段第一句中的"longevity"。
53. 答案:B
    本题是推理题,考查对最后一段最后一句话的理解。

第四篇:
54. 答案:A
    本题是推理题,答案在第一段中提到的"his own particular generosity on…"。
55. 答案:C
    本题是细节题,考查对第二段最后一句的理解。
56. 答案:B
    本题是推理题,考点在第三段中的"less sociable"和"more reserved and private"等表述上。
57. 答案:D
    本题是词汇题,考查根据上下文猜测词汇的意思的能力。
58. 答案:A
    本题是推理题,考查对第五段段首和后面几句话之间的语义理解能力。
59. 答案:B
    本题是细节题,考点是最后一段的最后一句。

第五篇:
60. 答案:B
    本题为推理题,考查对第一段中"the bloodiest","the turning point of the war"的理解。
61. 答案:A
    本题是推理题,考点是第二段段首中提到的"No surprise"。
62. 答案:D

本题属细节题,考点是第二段第三句话"before the movie displaced them in the public's affection"。
63. 答案:B
本题是推理题,考查对第二段后半部分关于该画颠沛流离经历的理解。
64. 答案:C
本题是细节题,考点是第二段的倒数第三句。
65. 答案:D
本题是推理题,考点是最后一段的最后一句。

第二节 阅读理解 B

第一篇:

66. 答案:D
本题的答题关键是下一句中的关联词"Thus"。另外,下一句中的"the ultimate objective of advertising"在语义上与选项 D 中的"the primary goal of advertising"相呼应。
67. 答案:B
本题的前一句中介绍了各种不同性质的广告,继而接下来介绍的是广告的形式多样化。
68. 答案:E
本题的答题关键是把握原文中第三段的主旨大意——广告无孔不入。选项 E 中的"also"一词的作用不可忽视。
69. 答案:F
本题所在的位置是第三段的最后一句话,很有可能是对整段内容的归纳总结。选项 F 恰好符合这一要求。
70. 答案:A
本题的答题要点是了解最后一段主要介绍了广告的三个功能。表示序列关系的词,例如,an important function, another function, the third function 是本题的解题突破口。

第二篇:

71. 答案:B
本题的答题关键是读懂第一段——用数字和事实说明美国人的寿命已经大幅度延长了。
72. 答案:A
本题的答题要点是下一句的"But"一词,提示这两句话之间是转折关系。
73. 答案:F
本题的答题关键是把握第四段和第五段之间的关系。第五段的段首讲到"it is too soon to say so"呼应的是第四段最后一句话的内容。
74. 答案:E
本题的答题要点是了解第五段中主要介绍了乐观者的看法,他们认为随着戒烟人数的大幅度增加,美国人的寿命还将延长。
75. 答案:D
本题的下一句中提到"Neither",这个词提示了空格中必定谈及了两个方面的情况。

第四部分　翻　译

(1) 译文：

　　从第一台苹果牌计算机问世到过去八年间各项突破性创新，乔布斯不畏任何艰难，捕捉新的机遇。

　　解析：

　　对这句话中 he 的处理：翻译时可以译成"他"，或"乔布斯"。

(2) 译文：

　　这就使他得以跻身于过去两个世纪伟大创业者的行列，他们——尤其是斯蒂夫·乔布斯——个个都因充沛的精力、持久的好奇心和旺盛的商业想象力而著称。

　　解析：

　　puts him in the company of 是翻译这句话的难点。很多考生把它理解成了"使他进入了……公司"，其实为"与……在一起"，引申为"跻身于"。

(3) 译文：

　　这些人全都格外勤奋，对己对人一丝不苟。不断激励他们的是高瞻远瞩，而不是迟疑不决。

　　解析：

　　在这句话中有两个词要重点理解：demanding 和 vision。demanding 意为：苛求的，高要求的。vision 意为：洞察力，想象力。

(4) 译文：

　　乔布斯青年时代，恰逢经济、社会和技术都在发生深远的变化，即我们所谓的信息革命时代。他有一种分析与直觉方面的天分，懂得在大变革时期有无数的机会可抓。

　　解析：

　　up for grabs 是这句话的理解重点。如果不认识这个短语，也别轻易放弃，至少你认识 grab：抓住。所以围绕着"抓住"理解这个短语不会有什么偏差。根据常理，在一个变革的年代，一个具有远见卓识，又极具创造力的人能抓住什么？所以 a lot 当然意指"机会"。

(5) 译文：

　　这种悟性促使他急如星火地行动起来，一心想的是产品"今后会怎样？"，这也促成了他那种常常是严厉、霸道但至今仍能给人以启发的管理风格。

　　解析：

　　请重点理解 fueled 意为刺激某种行为；the rapid-fire pace 意为快得像火一样的步伐；obsession with 意为迷恋；fed 意为滋养。

第五部分　写　作

题目解析：

　　这个题目比较有挑战性，乍看之下，两个分句自相矛盾。但是，既然有这种说法，就有它存在的理由，我们首先要找到人们这么说的理由是什么。找到了之后，才能够决定自己的立场，是赞成还是反对，理由分别又是什么。

　　首先审题发现，题目本身分成两个部分，一是"To get success, you need friends"，一是"to get huge success, you need enemies"。看起来像是一句似非而是的隽语,即看似矛盾而实际却可能成立的说法。对于题目中这两部分,考生可以分别表明态度,只支持其中一句而反对另一句;也可以全部赞成或反对,只要自己的立论站得住脚。一般而言,人们对第一句话没有太多异议,而第二句话才是争论的焦点。因此,题目中隐藏的重点是第二句话。此时,考生要细加思考的是:人们为什么会有第二句话这种说法?他们的理由是什么?这种观点真的可以成立吗?在什么样的条件下可以成立?在他们的逻辑中,有没有漏洞?……这样一步步追问下去,文章脉络就自然清晰了。提起笔来,也自然胸有成竹。

范文:

  I agree that we need friends to get success, but I don't agree that we need enemies to get huge success. The reasons can be listed as follows. Friends have a positive influence on people's lives. It's friends who give us courage, love and support when we are at a low tide. By contrast, enemies only set barriers in our ways to success and make us suffer from painful losses. Imagine when you are in a cold weather, which one would you embrace, a fire or cold water?

  It's true that sometimes we are subdued by our enemies, while sometimes we are defeated by ourselves. We easily become so proud and arrogant after we have achieved a little success that we can't accept others' unflattering advice; pride and prejudices have blinded our eyes with ease. At this time, the threat from an enemy may possibly keep us awake from the laziness and self-indulgence accompanied success, and work harder to achieve the next success. In this sense, an enemy can be said to contribute to our success a little bit.

  But can an enemy bring us huge success? Certainly not. A nation, as well as a person, gets huge success only from their hard work, ingenious minds and sometimes the help of chances. Enemies are always enemies. They may stimulate you to work hard, but it's unwise to expect an enemy to give you a hand when hardship arrives. During the difficult times, it's your friends who stand behind you and make strenuous attempts to help you. Success is hard to win, and huge success is even harder to secure. We can safely say that huge success can only come with your continuous efforts and generous help from your friends, family and associates; it will never be handed to you from an enemy, unless he or she purposely employs this as a strategy to confuse you. Besides, if you are strong enough in character, enemies can evoke your anger to fight against them hardly. But if your mind is not so strongly constituted, powerful enemies will destroy you effortlessly and utterly, leaving you little chance to bob up like a cork again. The contest between you and your enemies is often ruthless. Imagine you are in a battlefield now, do you believe that your enemies would make you win the battle? Definitely not. In this sense, enemies bring us not huge success, but desperation and destruction.

  So we can change the above mentioned words into this: "to get success, you need friends; to get huge success, you need more friends and few enemies." (421 words)

中国科学院
博士研究生入学考试
英语试题

(2011 年 10 月)

考生须知:

一、本试卷由试卷一（PAPER ONE）和试卷二（PAPER TWO）两部分组成。试卷一为客观题，答卷使用标准化机读答题纸；试卷二为主观题，答卷使用非机读答题纸。

二、请考生一律用 HB 或 2B 铅笔填涂标准化机读答题纸，画线不得过细或过短。修改时请用橡皮擦拭干净。若因填涂不符合要求而导致计算机无法识别，责任由考生自负。请保持机读答题纸清洁、无折皱。答题纸切忌折叠。

三、全部考试时间总计 180 分钟，满分为 100 分。时间及分值分布如下：

试卷一：

Ⅰ 词汇	15 分钟	10 分
Ⅱ 完形填空	15 分钟	15 分
Ⅲ 阅读理解	80 分钟	40 分
小计	110 分钟	65 分

试卷二：

Ⅳ 英译汉	30 分钟	15 分
Ⅴ 写作	40 分钟	20 分
小计	70 分钟	35 分

GRADUATE UNIVERSITY, CHINESE ACADEMY OF SCIENCES ENGLISH ENTRANCE EXAMINATION FOR DOCTORAL CANDIDATES

October 2011

PAPER ONE

PART I VOCABULARY (15 minutes, 10 points, 0.5 point each)

Directions: *Choose the word or expression below each sentence that best completes the statement, and mark the corresponding letter of your choice with a single bar across the square brackets on your Machine-scoring Answer Sheet.*

1. In swimming it is necessary to _____ the movement of the arms and legs.
   A. coordinate   B. harmonize   C. collaborate   D. mediate
2. Beijing's private cars will be banned from the roads _____ for one day a week during a six-month trial period.
   A. incidentally   B. occasionally   C. randomly   D. alternately
3. Joe puts too much _____ on pills from the drugstore and does not listen to his doctor.
   A. appliance   B. defiance   C. reliance   D. compliance
4. Among 169 cases, the smokers _____ 85.79%, and the ratio between males and females is 3.7 to 1.
   A. answer for   B. account for   C. take up   D. sum up
5. _____ inflation, driven by rising food and oil costs, is striking hardest at the world's very poor, who are forced to spend 60 to 80 percent of their income on food.
   A. Surging   B. Sprouting   C. Spilling   D. Spinning
6. Because the workers were new and inexperienced, the manager had to watch them and _____ their work closely.
   A. attend   B. demand   C. analyze   D. supervise
7. The department store guards were nearly _____ by the crowds of shoppers waiting for the sale to begin.

A. overflowed   B. overthrown   C. overturned   D. overwhelmed

8. All bad things are interconnected, and any one of them is _____ to be the cause of any other.
   A. subject   B. inferior   C. liable   D. vulnerable

9. Teachers have the authority to discipline pupils _____ their position as a teacher.
   A. by way of   B. by virtue of   C. in light of   D. in spite of

10. You can then eliminate all _____ the genuinely suitable applicants without having to interview an enormous number of people in person.
    A. of   B. that   C. for   D. but

11. Debt and the destruction of war have brought major economic setbacks, _____ damage to social services and human suffering.
    A. apart from   B. as good as   C. except for   D. rather than

12. On the whole it's a good book; and it would be unwise to _____ those small defects.
    A. dwell on   B. identify with   C. persist in   D. hack into

13. The main objective reason is that some developed countries _____ from the basic principle of anti-dumping and take the Anti-dumping Law as a tool for trade protection.
    A. derive   B. deviate   C. refrain   D. exempt

14. While big corporations _____ global business news, small companies are charging into overseas markets at a faster pace.
    A. overtake   B. occupy   C. dominate   D. reflect

15. He used to _____ his parents to help with the expenses.
    A. count on   B. take in   C. look into   D. get over

16. I was embarrassed when the _____ test paper my teacher spoke about turned out to be mine. I had forgotten to put my name on it.
    A. marked   B. branded   C. anonymous   D. fictitious

17. We _____ our voice depending on the circumstances, particularly in relationship to background noise.
    A. improve   B. modulate   C. rectify   D. temper

18. I'm far from certain that this group is going to be able to _____ what is necessary to gain complete control.
    A. carry out   B. tear down   C. break out   D. close down

19. I was lucky because I had turned my back on _____, pursuing instead common-sense reality.
    A. illustration   B. illusion   C. imagination   D. imitation

20. Excessive _____ in sweets and canned drinks and the lack of availability of fresh fruit and vegetables in the house can teach poor eating patterns.
    A. aspiration   B. intolerance   C. exposure   D. indulgence

PART II CLOZE TEST (15 minutes, 15 points)

Directions: *For each blank in the following passage, choose the best answer from the four choices given below. Mark the corresponding letter of your choice with a single bar across the square brackets on your Machine-scoring Answer Sheet.*

Adolescents are taking longer to become fully productive members of society, Reed Larson, professor of human development, University of Illinois, Champaign, told the World Future Society, Bethesda, Md. "What we expect of young people is __21__," he argued. They must go to school for 12 years or longer without any __22__ that their education will mean career success or relevance when they become adults. __23__, they do so without financial rewards, accept an identity __24__ by society, and delay starting a family, all of __25__ keeps adolescents in a kind of indeterminate state for years.

Larson says that "There should be way stations along the climb __26__ adulthood that allow young people to rest, gather themselves, and consider __27__." The success of government, business, and private life in the next 50 years __28__ it.

Education, literacy, and versatile interpersonal skills __29__ the list of necessary preparations for adulthood. Young people negotiating the complex worlds of home, work, and school __30__ use these skills in order to do so __31__ and competently. "The adolescent who is able to __32__ in only one world is increasingly __33__ for adult life," he warns.

As the time spent on the road to adulthood increases, so __34__ the danger that more youths will fall by the wayside. New and increased opportunities and initiatives will keep more youngsters focused, __35__ a smarter, more-versatile generation able to cope with the emerging global, high-tech world.

21. A. aggressive   B. original   C. rigid   D. extraordinary
22. A. qualification   B. guarantee   C. probability   D. recognition
23. A. However   B. Subsequently   C. Furthermore   D. Therefore
24. A. denied   B. defined   C. questioned   D. neglected
25. A. these   B. that   C. what   D. which
26. A. into   B. to   C. on   D. for
27. A. temptations   B. occasions   C. alternatives   D. inclinations
28. A. depends on   B. results in   C. longs for   D. copes with
29. A. top   B. cover   C. hold   D. rate
30. A. could   B. must   C. ought   D. shall
31. A. temporarily   B. smoothly   C. instantly   D. periodically
32. A. operate   B. engage   C. tackle   D. function
33. A. ill-prepared   B. ill-mannered   C. ill-informed   D. ill-advised

34. A. did B. does C. is D. was
35. A. created B. create C. creating D. to create

PART III READING COMPREHENSION

Section A (60 minutes, 30 points)

Directions: *Below each of the following passages you will find some questions or incomplete statements. Each question or statement is followed by four choices marked A, B, C, and D. Read each passage carefully, and then select the choice that best answers the question or completes the statement. Mark the letter of your choice with a single bar across the square brackets on your Machine-scoring Answer Sheet.*

Passage One

Everyone has been trying to understand Michael Jackson's death this summer. While medics are still picking at his slender corpse, cultural authorities argue like vultures over his reputation. Should he be remembered as a great singer, a man possibly sexually attracted to children, an emblematic black artist who tried to bleach his face white, the Fred Astaire (a major founder of stage dance) of the 1980s, the first to master the MTV pop video, or a troubled victim of a domineering father? His difficult journey from unhappy childhood, to weird quasi-adulthood has been told and re-told frequently and annoyingly across the world.

Yet Jackson's current crisis is an extreme version of a process that will happen to us all. For, as Jean-Paul Sartre (French existentialist philosopher) put it, at death we become prey to the "Other"— our identity dissipating into the sum total of what is thought about us. While we are alive, Sartre explained, we can resist this pressure: we can defy the opinions that other people try to project onto us. We can't erase our pasts, but we can always overturn future expectations. It's a struggle Sartre saw as central to our existence as moral beings: we must do more than act out the roles others have scripted for us.

This is the existential condition of humanity — we are the artists of our own lives, although with the anguish that comes from being condemned to be free. Given the weight of expectations heaped on his shoulders, it's something Michael Jackson felt more crushingly than most: a burden reflected in his lifelong modifications of his own appearance. The human body, Ludwig Wittgenstein (an Austrian-British philosopher) once declared, is the best picture we have of the human soul. And Jackson's body in his last days legibly expressed something very revealing.

Death, of course, takes everything away. The back catalogue of Jackson's songs is now the complete catalogue. Yet, according to Sartre, death is not the final chord of a melody that suddenly resolves and makes sense of what went before. Instead, it merely begins an endless new argument over meanings from which the core — the real person — is perpetually absent. Michael Jackson is no longer with us. Instead, "Michael Jackson" is becoming the sum of what others hope to make of him.

36. Paragraph 1 mainly tells that people have been trying to _____.
    A. define Jackson as a person
    B. speculate on Jackson's death
    C. stain Jackson's reputation
    D. question Jackson as a celebrity

37. According to Sartre, everybody at his death will surely _____.
    A. draw attention far and wide
    B. suffer immense defamation
    C. be the center of people's talk
    D. be put under others' judgment

38. Sartre held that, as a moral being, one should NOT _____.
    A. do simply as others expect
    B. conceal one's shameful past
    C. always defy others' opinions
    D. retreat from various pressures

39. As claimed by Wittgenstein, Jackson's dead body revealed that he _____.
    A. had worked too hard in pleasing his fans
    B. had fallen victim to public opinion
    C. had been an extremely sentimental guy
    D. had experienced both joys and sorrows

40. In the last paragraph, the "back catalogue" refers to Jackson's _____.
    A. albums released at his death
    B. MTV videos of his dancing
    C. music he had recorded before
    D. songs sung in his childhood

41. It can be concluded that today what we hear about Michael Jackson may NOT be _____.
    A. invented stories
    B. variable stories
    C. biased stories
    D. factual stories

Passage Two

Most graduate programs in American universities produce a product for which there is no market (candidates for teaching positions that do not exist) and develop skills for which there is diminishing demand (research in subfields within subfields and publications in journals read by no one other than a few like-minded colleagues), all at a rapidly rising cost.

Widespread hiring freezes and layoffs have brought these problems into sharp relief now. But our graduate system has been in crisis for decades, and the seeds of this crisis go as far back as the formation of modern universities. Kant, in his 1798 work "The Conflict of the Faculties," wrote that universities should "handle the entire content of learning by mass production, so to speak, by a division of labor, so that for every branch of the sciences there would be a public teacher or professor appointed as its trustee."

Unfortunately this mass-production university model has led to separation where there ought to be collaboration and to ever-increasing specialization. In my own department, for example, we have 10 faculty members, working in eight subfields, with little overlap. And as departments fragment, research and publication become more and more about **less and less**.

The emphasis on narrow scholarship also encourages an educational system that has become a process of cloning. Faculty members cultivate those students whose futures they envision as identical to their own pasts, even though their tenures will stand in the way of these students having futures as full professors.

The dirty secret of higher education is that without underpaid graduate students to help in laboratories and with teaching, universities couldn't conduct research or even instruct their growing undergraduate populations. That's one of the main reasons we still encourage people to enroll in doctoral programs. It is simply cheaper to provide graduate students with modest stipends and teaching assistants with as little as $5,000 a course — with no benefits — than it is to hire full-time professors.

The other obstacle to change is that colleges and universities are self-regulating or, in academic terms, governed by peer review. While trustees and administrations theoretically have some oversight responsibility, in practice, departments operate independently. To complicate matters further, once a faculty member has been granted tenure, he is functionally autonomous. Many academics who cry out for the regulation of financial markets vehemently oppose it in their own departments.

42. According to Paragraph 1, it seems to be NOT worthwhile to attend an American graduate program at a high cost if one wants to _____.
   A. pursue a teaching career   B. do business in the future
   C. become a prolific writer   D. engage in administrative work

43. Kant is quoted because _____.
   A. he pointed out why crises would arise in modern universities
   B. he proposed some idea of what a modern university should do
   C. he used to help relieve the problems universities had suffered
   D. he found how to cope with conflicts among the faculties

44. The boldfaced phrase "less and less" (in Paragraph 3) refers to _____.
   A. diminishing governmental support   B. publications in decreasing number
   C. theories with growing intelligibility   D. increasingly specialized knowledge

45. According to the author, in today's educational system, it's difficult to _____.
   A. attend courses of one's own choice
   B. get a scholarship in a desired specialty
   C. produce students with new horizons
   D. ask teachers to stay long in their jobs

46. Enrollments in doctoral programs are promoted by universities mainly because they need _____.
   A. the cheap labor of the students   B. to show high academic standard
   C. to attract enough full-time professors D. the talented hands to help with research

47. The author thinks it's bad for faculty members to be _____.
   A. free from the supervision of the trustees
   B. involved in any profit-making activities

C. subject to peer view on all academic matters
D. restricted to the work in their own departments

Passage Three

Next week, the European Parliament will debate stringent regulation of a number of effective pesticides. If this regulation is passed, the consequences will be devastating.

In the 1960s, widespread use of the potent and safe insecticide DDT led to eradication of many insect-borne diseases in Europe and North America. But based on no scientific evidence of human health effects, the U.S. Environmental Protection Agency banned DDT, and its European counterparts followed suit. Subsequently, more than 1 million people died each year from malaria — but not in America or Europe. Rather, most of the victims were children and women in Africa and Asia.

Today, even while acknowledging that indoor spraying of small amounts of DDT would help prevent many deaths and millions of illnesses, nongovernmental organizations continue — with great success — to pressure African governments not to allow its use. In order to stave off such pressure, African public health officials cave, and their children die needlessly. Yet, rather than learning the tragic lesson of the DDT ban, the European Union wants to extend this unscientific ban to other effective insecticides, including pyrethroids and organophosphates — further undercutting anti-malarial efforts.

The currently debated regulation would engender a paradigm shift in the regulation of chemicals, from a risk-based approach — based on real world exposures from agricultural applications — to a hazard-based standard, derived from laboratory tests and having little or no basis in reality as far as human health is concerned. Of course, this is fine with anti-chemical zealots. Their concern is bringing down chemical companies in the name of "the environment" — tough luck if African children have to be sacrificed to their agenda, as was the case with DDT (which is still banned in the EU and not under consideration in the current debate).

Most poignantly, the fight against malaria and other insect-borne tropical diseases would take another hit, with resulting illness, disability and death disproportionally affecting children under five and pregnant women.

And what, after all, is the "danger" of these chemicals being debated? In fact, there is no evidence to support the contention that insecticides pose a health threat to humans. Even DDT, one of the most studied chemicals of all time, has been conclusively shown to be safe for humans at all conceivable levels of exposure sufficient to control malaria and save millions of lives.

48. When the U.S. Environmental Protection Agency banned DDT in the 1960s, in Europe _____.
    A. the governments questioned the ban's effects
    B. the environmental authorities also banned it
    C. researchers paid more attention to the chemical

D. the general public showed support for the ban

49. Some nongovernmental organizations believe that DDT _____.
    A. is somewhat good for illness prevention
    B. threatens the health of African children.
    C. will regain popularity in Europe
    D. can soon become a political issue

50. According to the author, the "hazard-based standard" _____.
    A. can cause an increase in research expenses
    B. may lead to some environmental damage
    C. will be applied widely by researchers
    D. must be avoided in regulating chemicals

51. The author believes that the real intent of those supporting the regulation is to _____.
    A. help cure insect-born tropical diseases
    B. promote environmental protection
    C. stop the chemical companies' business
    D. protect African children against insects

52. After the debate, the European Parliament will _____.
    A. consider DDT's positive uses
    B. continue to keep DDT illegal
    C. remove some restrictions on DDT use
    D. study DDT's impact on human health

53. According to the author, the fight against malaria would _____.
    A. suffer another severe setback
    B. achieve another great success
    C. bring another round of problems
    D. produce another threat to people's health

Passage Four

In the post Cold War world few articles have influenced how Western policymakers view the world more than Samuel Huntington's 1993 article, "The Clash of Civilizations." Suggesting that the world was returning to a civilization dominated world where future conflicts would originate from clashes between 'civilizations,' the theory has been broadly criticized for oversimplification, ignoring local conflicts and for incorrectly predicting what has happened in the decade since its publication. The claim made by many that September the 11th has vindicated Huntington is simply not supported by the evidence.

Huntington's thesis outlines a future where the "great divisions among humankind and the dominating source of conflict will be cultural." He divides the world's cultures into seven current civilizations, Western, Latin American, Confucian, Japanese, Islamic, Hindu and Slavic-Orthodox. In addition he judged Africa only as a possible civilization depending on how far one viewed the development of an African consciousness had developed. These civilizations seem to be defined primarily by religion with a number of ad hoc exceptions.

Huntington predicts conflicts occurring between states from different civilizations for control of international institutions and for economic and military power. He views this mix of conflicts as normal by asserting that nation-states are a new phenomenon in a world dominated for most of its history by conflicts between civilizations. This is a dubious statement as the inter-civilizational conflict driven mainly by geo-political factors rather than cultural differences is an equally if not more persuasive way to view much of history.

The theory at least differentiates between non-Western civilizations rather than grouping them together. He also explains how the West presents pro-Western policies as positive for the entire world and that the very idea of a universal culture is a Western idea. However, his escape from a Eurocentric bias is only temporary. He completely fails to account for local cultures even though one can argue they collectively comprise a separate civilization. The article also predicts future conflicts will be started by non-Western civilizations reacting to Western power and values ignoring the equally plausible situation where Western states use their military superiority to maintain their superior positions. The policy prescriptions he suggests to counter this perceived threat equate to increasing the power of the West to forestall any loss of the West's pre-eminence. Thus he suggests the Latin American and Orthodox-Slavic civilizations be drawn further into the Western orbit and the maintenance of Western military superiority.

54. As stated in the passage, Huntington's article _____.
    A. advocated the interdependence of different cultures
    B. proposed a return of the world to its former state
    C. depicted the world in the post Cold War period
    D. stressed cultural aspects of international conflicts

55. According to the claim mentioned, an occurrence like "9 · 11" was what Huntington had _____.
    A. described   B. forecasted   C. criticized   D. ignored

56. Huntington's seven current civilizations excluded Africa because he deemed it as failing to _____.
    A. meet the criteria for being a civilization
    B. possess a uniform culture as its own
    C. reach a high level of development
    D. develop a mature cultural awareness

57. Huntington clearly held that _____.
    A. the world should be viewed without a Eurocentric bias
    B. the West seeks to promote a common culture
    C. policymakers should take local conflicts seriously
    D. non-Western cultures should quickly react to the West

58. Huntington proposed some measures to be taken against a perceived threat to _____.
   A. Latin-American countries   B. non-Western civilizations
   C. the West's pre-eminence   D. the Orthodox-Slavic world
59. According to the author, Huntington's theory is quite _____.
   A. provocative   B. ambiguous   C. questionable   D. high-sounding

Passage Five

The multibillion-dollar international pharmaceutical industry has been accused of manipulating the results of drug trials for financial gain and withholding information that could expose patients to possible harm.

The stranglehold the industry has on research is causing increasing alarm in medical circles as evidence emerges of biased results, under-reporting and selective publication driven by a market worth more than 10 billion pounds in Britain alone.

The industry has sponsored the trials of new drugs which have held out great promise for patients with cancer, heart disease, mental health problems and other illnesses.

But the tests on the same drugs in independent trials paid for by non-profit organizations — governments, medical institutions or charities — have yielded very different results.

The drugs for abnormal heart rhythm introduced in the late 1970s were killing more Americans every year by 1990 than the Vietnam War.

Yet early evidence suggesting the drugs were lethal, which might have saved thousands of lives, went unpublished.

Expensive cancer drugs introduced in the past 10 years and claiming to offer major benefits have increasingly been questioned.

Evidence published in the Journal of the American Medical Association showed that 38 per cent of independent studies of the drugs reached unfavorable conclusions about them, compared with 5 per cent of the studies paid for by the pharmaceutical industry.

In the latest case, the researchers commissioned by the National Institute for Clinical Excellence to develop guidelines for the prescribing of anti-depressant drugs to children say they were refused access to the unpublished trials of the drugs held by the pharmaceutical companies.

Published evidence suggested that the anti-depressant drugs were safe and effective for children.

But when they obtained the unpublished evidence by contacting individual researchers who had worked on the trials and other sources, a different picture emerged — one of an increase in suicidal thoughts and attempted suicide. Only one of the drugs, Prozac, emerged as safe.

Anti-depressant drugs, though not recommended for children, were widely prescribed in Britain until last year, when the Medicines and Healthcare Products Regulatory Agency issued a warning to doctors, prohibiting their use.

This followed the safety concerns raised by campaigners and taken up in two BBC TV Panorama broadcasts which brought the biggest response in the program's history.

Writing in the Lancet medical magazine, the researchers say: "On the basis of published evidence alone, we could have considered at least tentatively recommending use of these drugs for children and young people with depression."

60. The international pharmaceutical industry has been criticized for _____.
    A. controlling the drug market for its own profit
    B. overlooking its yield of destructive medicine
    C. neglecting research on the ill-effects of drugs
    D. covering up the adverse results of drug trials

61. The phrase "independent trials" (in Paragraph 4) in this context means "conducting the trials without _____."
    A. any financial involvement   B. any governmental funds
    C. the public's awareness   D. the authority's guidance

62. What was true about the drugs for abnormal heart rhythm?
    A. They killed lots of American soldiers in the Vietnam War.
    B. They were known to be harmful at the early stage of its use.
    C. They were illegally used due to their unpublished results.
    D. They claimed to save thousands of lives but did it in vain.

63. According to the passage, the unfavorable conclusions about drugs were kept a secret from _____.
    A. the general public   B. the drug companies
    C. the researchers   D. the authorities

64. The information unpublished about the anti-depressant drugs showed that _____.
    A. all but one drug were hazardous   B. only a few were good to children
    C. many of them could curb suicide   D. different drugs had varied results

65. It can be inferred that, 2 years ago, to the doctors prescribing anti-depressant drugs, the published evidence about the drugs would seem to be very _____.
    A. destructive   B. misleading   C. instructive   D. encouraging

Section B (20 minutes, 10 points)

Directions: *In each of the following passages, five sentences have been removed from the original text. They are listed from A to F and put below the passage. Choose the most suitable sentence from the list to fill in each of the blanks (numbered 66 to 75). For each passage, there is one sentence that does not fit in any of the blanks. Mark your answers on your Machine-scoring Answer Sheet.*

Passage One

Historically, the spread, prevalence, and very existence of contagious disease have wholly depended on the growth and concentration of human populations. ___66___ And though the last century has witnessed substantial worldwide success in combating many past scourges — such as polio and smallpox — infectious diseases still claim more lives than any other group of diseases. The prevailing demographic trends continue to create a crowded human "medium" that both invites and is vulnerable to infection.

The share of humanity living in cities with more than 1 million people has surged from less than 5 percent in 1900 to nearly 40 percent today, creating the ideal setting for the resurgence of old infectious diseases as well as the development of new ones. ___67___

Overcrowding — the increased proximity of susceptible individuals — is a principal risk factor for the incidence and spread of all major infectious diseases, including tuberculosis, dengue fever, malaria, and acute respiratory illnesses, which are unable to spread and survive in low population densities. ___68___

Aside from sheer growth and increasing density, the urbanization under way in developing nations is often accompanied by deteriorating health indicators and increased exposure to disease risk factors.

Access to clean water, good hygiene, and adequate housing are sorely lacking in developing nations. As a result, waterborne infections such as cholera and other diarrheal diseases account for 90 percent of all infectious diseases in developing countries — and 40 percent of all deaths in some nations. ___69___

In both industrial and developing nations, the incidences of a wide range of infectious diseases, including tuberculosis, diarrheal diseases, and HIV/AIDS, are considerably higher in urban slums — where poverty and compromised health define the way of life — than in the rest of the city. ___70___

A. Key disease carriers, such as insects and rats, thrive in crowded urban settings, further facilitating spread.
B. The unprecedented population densities in fourteenth-century Europe, for example, led to the plague outbreak that claimed the lives of one fourth of the population.
C. Although these infections are easily preventable if adequate water and sanitation are available, the vast majority of the world's population are lifelong victims.
D. While new global markets have created unprecedented economic opportunities and growth, the health risks of our increasingly interconnected and fast-paced world continue to grow.
E. Pathogens can more readily establish in large populations, since all infectious diseases require a critical number of vulnerable individuals in order to take root and spread.
F. These areas can serve as a perpetual reservoir of disease or disease vectors, placing other parts of the city at risk of an outbreak and allowing the disease to continue evolving, often into a deadlier strain.

Passage Two

When an eight-lane steel-truss-arch bridge across the Mississippi River in Minneapolis collapsed during the evening rush hour on August 1st 2007, 13 people were killed and 145 were injured. There had been no warning. The bridge was 40 years old but had a life expectancy of 50 years. The central span suddenly gave way after the gusset plates that connected the steel beams buckled and fractured, dropping the bridge into the river.

__71__ The St. Anthony Falls bridge, which opened on September 18th, 2008 and replaces the collapsed structure, should do just that. It has an embedded early-warning system made of hundreds of sensors. They include wire and fibre-optic strain and displacement gauges, accelerometers, potentiometers and corrosion sensors that have been built into the span to monitor it for structural weaknesses, such as corroded concrete and overly strained joints.

__72__ Another example is the six-lane Charilaos Trikoupis bridge in Greece, which spans the Gulf of Corinth, linking the town of Rio on the Peloponnese peninsula to Antirrio on the mainland. This 3km-long bridge, which was opened in 2004, has roughly 300 sensors that alert its operators if an earthquake or high winds warrant it being shut to traffic, as well as monitoring its overall health. These sensors have already detected some abnormal vibrations in the cables holding the bridge. __73__

The next generation of sensors to monitor bridge health will be even more sophisticated. For one thing, they will be wireless, which will make installing them a lot cheaper. __74__

Dr Lynch is the chief researcher on a project intended to help design the next generation of monitoring systems for bridges. He and his colleagues are also looking at how to make a cement-based sensing skin that can detect excessive strain in bridges. Individual sensors, says Dr Lynch, are not ideal because the initial cracks in a bridge may not occur at the point the sensor is placed.

__75__ He is also exploring a paint-like substance made of carbon nanotubes that can be painted onto bridges to detect corrosion and cracks. Since carbon nanotubes conduct electricity, sending a current through the paint would help engineers to detect structural weakness through changes in the paint's electrical properties.

A. The new Minneapolis bridge joins a handful of "smart" bridges that have built-in sensors to monitor their health.
B. The kilometers of wire needed to connect sensors to central computers can add significantly to the system's cost, according to Jerome Lynch of the University of Michigan, Ann Arbor.
C. By 2025 all bridges in America will have been equipped with this advanced technology.
D. A continuous skin would solve this problem.
E. In the wake of the catastrophe, there were calls to harness technology to avoid similar mishaps.
F. Engineers then installed additional weights as dampeners.

PAPER TWO

PART IV TRANSLATION (30 minutes, 15 points)

Directions: *Read the following text carefully and then translate the underlined segments into Chinese. Write your Chinese version in the proper space on your Answer Sheet.*

To most of us, nuclear is an all-or-nothing word. Nuclear war is unthinkable. Nuclear weapons must never be used. Nuclear power plants must be perfectly safe. (1) <u>Nuclear meltdown is the end of the world, and "Going nuclear" means you've hit the fatal button, and there's no turning back.</u>

The crisis in Japan is teaching us that this isn't true. Nuclear safety, like nuclear doom, is never certain. Too many things can go wrong. And then, just when catastrophe seems inevitable, things can go right. (2) <u>Our challenge in managing the current crisis, and in preparing for the next one, is to broaden our options.</u> We can't anticipate or prevent every scenario. But we can give ourselves a fighting chance.

(3) <u>Two days ago, I spoke highly of the reactor containment at the Fukushima Daiichi (福岛) power plant for surviving the earthquake and tsunami that knocked out their primary and backup cooling system.</u> "Everything that could go wrong did," I wrote. Hours later, and explosion damaged one of the containers. Now officials say a second container may have ruptured. Take that as a corollary to Murphy's Law. (4) <u>Anyone who says "Everything that could go wrong did" is overlooking something else that could go wrong.</u>

No one could have predicted every misfortune that hit this plant. (5) <u>First a quake bigger than any quake in Japan's history took out the power grid. Then a tsunami arrived with unprecedented speed and took out the backup diesel generators.</u> An explosion at one reactor knocked out four of five pumps at another. A valve malfunction blocked water from being pumped into one of the reactors. Gauges failed. Instrument panels failed. A fire erupted in a spent-fuel storage pool in a reactor that had been offline for months.

We don't know how this story will turn out. And that's the point. Failure is an option. So is success.

PART V WRITING (40 minutes, 20 points)

Directions: *Write an essay of no less than 200 words on the topic given below. Use the proper space on your Answer Sheet II.*

TOPIC

If your child were bullied (受欺负), what would you say to him or her? Tell why you would say so.

2011年10月试题精解

第一部分 词 汇

1. 答案:A
    本题考查动词的含义。A 协调,调节;B 使和谐;C 合作;D 调停,调解。句子的意思是:游泳时手臂与腿部动作要协调。
2. 答案:D
    本题考查副词的含义。A 附带地,顺便提及地;B 有时候,偶尔;C 随机地,任意地;D 交替地,轮流地。句子的意思是:北京的私家车将每周轮流一次禁止上路,试行6个月。
3. 答案:C
    本题考查名词的含义。A 用具,器具;B 挑战,挑衅,蔑视;C 依赖;D 遵从,依从。句子的意思是:乔过于依赖药店里的药,不听医生的话。
4. 答案:B
    本题考查动词词组的含义。A 负有责任;B (在数量、比例方面)占,提出理由,做出解释;C 开始从事,占去;D 总结,概括。句子的意思是:在169个案例中,烟民占85.79%,其中男女比例为3.7:1。
5. 答案:A
    本题考查现在分词的含义。A 急剧上升的,汹涌;B 发芽;C 溢出;D 旋转。句子的意思是:受食品价格和油价上升驱动的通胀不断飙升,对世界上最贫穷人口打击最大,他们被迫将其60%~80%的收入花在食物上。
6. 答案:D
    本题考查动词的含义。A 参加,照顾,看管;B 要求,强令,需求;C 分析;D 监督,管理,指导。句子的意思是:由于工人是新手没有经验,经理不得不仔细察看指导其工作。
7. 答案:D
    本题考查过去分词的含义。A 淹没的,泛滥的;B 被推翻的,被打倒的;C 被推翻的,颠倒的;D 使不安的,使不知所措的。句子的意思是:商场的保安被等待大减价开始的购物人群弄得几乎不知所措。
8. 答案:C
    本题考查形容词的含义。A 易遭受……的,受……影响的;B 次的,差的;C 有……倾向的,倾向于……,易于……的;D 脆弱的,易受攻击的。句子的意思是:所有糟糕的事情都是互相联系的,其中一个可能是另一个的原因。
9. 答案:B
    本题考查介词词组的含义。A 经由,通过……的方法;B 借助,由于;C 鉴于,基于……的考虑;D 尽管。句子的意思是:教师由于其教师地位有权严格要求学生。
10. 答案:D

本题考查固定搭配 all but 的含义。A 表示所属关系;B 那;C 对于,由于;D 除了,除……之外。句子的意思是:然后你不必面试大量的人就能够剔除真正合适的申请人以外的人。

11. 答案:A

本题考查介词词组的含义。A 除……外;B 和……几乎一样;C 除了……;D 而不……。句子的意思是:除了破坏社会服务并给人类带来痛苦以外,债务和战争破坏还使经济严重受挫。

12. 答案:A

本题考查动词词组的含义。A 详述;B 把……看成和……一样;C 坚持不懈;D 作为黑客进入。句子的意思是:总的来说它是本好书,再细说那些小的瑕疵就不明智了。

13. 答案:B

本题考查动词的含义。A 得到,源于,从……提取;B 偏离;C 克制;D 豁免,免除。句子的意思是:主要的客观原因是一些发达国家偏离反倾销的基本原则,把反倾销法当作贸易保护的工具。

14. 答案:C

本题考查动词的含义。A 赶上,追上,超车;B 占领;C 统治,控制,支配;D 反射,考虑。句子的意思是:在大公司世界商业新闻中占主导地位的同时小公司以更快的速度冲入海外市场。

15. 答案:A

本题考查动词词组的含义。A 依靠,指望;B 吸收,理解,欺骗;C 向……里面看,调查,窥视;D 克服。句子的意思是:过去他的开支都靠父母帮助。

16. 答案:C

本题考查形容词的含义。A 有标记的;B 标明……与众不同的;C 匿名的;D 虚构的,假的,非真实的。句子的意思是:结果老师所说的没写名字的试卷就是我的,我很不好意思,忘了写上名字。

17. 答案:B

本题考查动词的含义。A 改进,提高,好转;B 调节;C 改正,校正;D 调和,使缓和。句子的意思是:我们根据环境,尤其是根据与背景噪声的关系,来调节我们的声音。

18. 答案:A

本题考查动词短语的含义。A 进行,完成;B 拆除;C 爆发;D 关闭,倒闭。句子的意思是:我不能确定该集团会不会有能力采取必要的行动以获得完全控制权。

19. 答案:B

本题考查名词的含义。A 证明,例证;B 幻想;C 想象,想象力;D 模仿。句子的意思是:很幸运我放弃了幻想而去追求现实。

20. 答案:D

本题考查名词的含义。A 强烈的愿望,志向;B 不容忍,偏执,心胸狭隘;C 暴露,揭露;D 沉溺,沉迷,放纵。句子的意思是:过分爱吃糖果和灌装饮料、家里没有水果和蔬菜会培养糟糕的饮食方式。

第二部分　完形填空

本文主要讲的是为什么当下的年轻人需要更长的时间来成长为对社会有用的人以及整

社会应该怎样来帮助这些年轻人更为成功地完成这个过渡。

21. 答案：D

本题考查形容词的词义辨析以及对下文的理解。本句的意思是，"我们这个社会对年轻人有着非同寻常的高期望"。随后两句则较详细地介绍了社会对年轻人究竟有着什么样的期望。本句主语是"what we expect of young people"，是指社会对年轻人的期望。空格处需要的是一个做表语的形容词。4个选项均可做表语，但A选项用来描述人，而不是物；B选项"原创性的"和C选项"严格的，僵化的"虽然既可以用来修饰人，也可以修饰物，但都不符合句意。

22. 答案：B

本题考查名词的词义辨析。A 资历；B 保证；C 可能性；D 认可。从本句开始，作者介绍社会对年轻人的高期望：年轻人必须在学校待上12年或者更长时间，但这么长时间的教育也无法保证年轻人进入社会后迎接他们的是事业的成功或学有所用。

23. 答案：C

本题考查连接词的使用，本句与前句都是用来说明现代社会对年轻人的高期望。两句之间是并列和递进关系。因此选择C"还有"。

24. 答案：B

本题考查动词的词义辨析以及对句意的理解。四个选项的意思为：A 否认；B 定义；C 质疑；D 忽略。本句是讲年轻人在成长过程中所要经历的困难，其中包括没有经济回报、接受社会对他们身份的认定（即社会对他们的看法）以及推迟结婚生子。

25. 答案：D

本题考查定语从句及从句中关系代词的使用。该句的谓语动词为第三人称单数 keeps，故可以排除 A；本句是一个非限制性定语从句，故可以排除掉 B 选项；而 C 选项 what 则不能用在定语从句中。

26. 答案：B

本题考查介词的用法。本句的意思是，Larson 认为，在长大成人的这个过程中，应该有让青年人喘息的机会。climb to 意思是"向上爬"。

27. 答案：C

本题考查名词的词义。本句的意思是，"在中间站，年轻人可以休息，可以振作精神，还可以考虑成长道路上的其他可能性"，强调中间站在年轻人成长道路上的几个积极作用。四个选项的意思分别为：A 诱惑；B 场合；C 其他可能性；D 倾向性。

28. 答案：A

本题考查动词词组的语义辨析。四个选项的意思分别为：A 依赖于；B 导致；C 渴望；D 应对。本句的意思是，在接下来的50年中，政府、商业和个体生活的成功都依赖于此。即依赖于是否在年轻人成长过程中，给他们提供喘息的机会。

29. 答案：A

本题考查动词的词义辨析。本句的意思是，"受过良好教育、有文化、具有良好的人际技能占据了成为社会有用人才所需具备品质的前三位"。在本句中，top 用作动词，表示"为……之首；居……之冠"。

30. 答案：B

本题考查情态动词的使用。本句的意思是，"年轻人必须使用这些技能"，说明作者对这些技能的重视。作者认为,年轻人一定得使用这些技能。

31. 答案:B

   本题考查前后语义连贯。本句的意思,"为了能够顺利且成功地协调家庭、工作以及学校三个世界的关系,年轻人必须使用这些技能"。本题需要的是一个和 competently 并列的词或同义词,表示"成功地,胜任地"。四个选项的意思为:A 暂时地;B 顺利地;C 马上地;D 阶段性地。

32. 答案:D

   本题考查对文章上下文语义的理解。本句的意思是,"只能在家庭、工作及学校三个世界中的一个表现良好的年轻人越来越难以准备充分地成长为社会有用人才"。

33. 答案:A

   本题考查形容词的词义辨析。四个选项的意思是,A 准备不足的;B 态度恶劣的;C 消息不灵通的;D 不明智的。

34. 答案:B

   本题考查倒装句。这句的意思是,"年轻人成长为社会有用人才的时间拉长了,同样,更多年轻人中途放弃、误入歧途的风险也增大了"。前半句中的谓语用的是 increases 的现在时,那么后半句倒装句也用现在时,并用"does"替代动词 increases。

35. 答案:C

   本题考查分词短语的语法知识。现在分词 creating 的逻辑主语是句子的主语,并且两者是主动关系。本句大意是,更多更新的机会和倡议将使更多的年轻人专心致志、努力成长为对社会有用的人,从而造就能应对全球化高科技世界的更聪明、更多才多艺的一代人。

第三部分 阅读理解

第一小节 阅读理解 A

第一篇:

36. 答案:A

   本题是段落大意题,考查第一段中的问句:迈克尔·杰克逊到底是一个怎样的人?

37. 答案:D

   本题是细节题,考查对第二段第二句的理解:"as Jean-Paul Sartre put it, at death we become prey to the 'Other' — our identity dissipating into the sum total of what is thought about us." 意思是:正如萨特所说,人一去世,就会成为"另外一个个体"的猎物,即我们本体的猎物。

38. 答案:A

   本题是细节题,考查对第二段最后一句话的理解:人存在的核心是作为有精神、有道德的生物而存在的:我们必须超越别人对于我们的期待而存在。

39. 答案:B

   本题是推理题,这道题的关键是理解第三段的最后一句话 "And Jackson's body in his last days legibly expressed something very revealing" 的意思,即去世前的迈克尔·杰克逊身上明显地流露出了一些令人关注的情况。

40. 答案:C

   本题是词汇题,back 表示"以前的",也可用作副词,例如"back in 1980"。

41. 答案:D

本题是推理题,考查最后一段的最后一句话"'Michael Jackson'is becoming the sum of what others hope to make of him"的意思,即迈克尔·杰克逊正在成为我们每个人心里希望的那个迈克尔·杰克逊的总和。

第二篇:

42. 答案:A

本题是细节题,考查第一段中括号里的内容:candidates for teaching positions that do not exist。

43. 答案:B

本题是推理题,考查第二段第二句与第三句间的关系:第二句讲到"这一问题的祸根可追溯到现代大学的形成",紧接着第三句引用康德的文章。

44. 答案:D

本题是推理题,考查第三段的第一句中的"ever-increasing specialization"与下文的联系。

45. 答案:C

本题是推理题,考点是第四段中的"a process of cloning"和"those students whose futures they envision as identical to their own pasts",言下之意,老师是完全按照当年他们自己求学时的情况来培养学生的,这种教育是简单的"克隆"。

46. 答案:A

本题是细节题,考点是第五段的最后一句:It is cheaper to provide graduate students and teaching assistants than it is to hire full-time professors.

47. 答案:A

本题是推理题,考查对最后一段第二句中的"in practice, departments operate independently"的理解。

第三篇:

48. 答案:B

本题是推理题,考点在第二段第二句的后半部分:the U. S. Environmental Protection Agency banned DDT, and its European counterparts followed suit. 这里的European counterparts指的是与美国环保机构相对应的欧洲环境保护部门。

49. 答案:A

本题是细节题,考点是第三段第一句话中的从句部分:even while acknowledging that indoor spraying of small amounts of DDT would help prevent many deaths and millions of illnesses。

50. 答案:D

本题是推理题,考查第四段第一句话:The regulation would engender a paradigm shift in the regulation of chemicals, from a risk-based approach to a hazard-based standard。而这种危险分析方法只是基于实验室测试,没有基于现实中对人类健康影响的考虑。

51. 答案:C

本题是细节题,考查对第四段第三句中核心动词的理解:Their concern is bringing down

chemical companies。to bring down 是"使……倒下,击败"的意思。
52. 答案:B

本题是细节题,考点是第四段最后一句中括号的内容:which is still banned in the EU and not under consideration in the current debate。
53. 答案:A

本题是推理题,考查对第五段"the fight against malaria and other insect-borne tropical diseases would take another hit"的理解。短语"to take a hit"是"遭受重创"的意思。

第四篇:
54. 答案:D

本题是推理题,答案在第一段第二句:"where future conflicts would originate from clashes between 'civilizations'"。未来的冲突可能源于不同"文明"之间的碰撞。
55. 答案:B

本题是词汇题,考查第一段最后一句中"vindicate"(维护,证明……正确)的词义。
56. 答案:D

本题是推理题,考点在第二段第三句:"as a possible civilization depending on how far one viewed the development of an African consciousness had developed"。
57. 答案:B

本题是判断题,考点在第四段第二句的后半部分:"the very idea of a universal culture is a Western idea"。
58. 答案:C

本题是推理题,考查第四段第五句和第六句的内容。
59. 答案:C

本题是观点态度题,从文章第一段中的 ignoring 和 incorrectly predicting,以及第三段中的 a dubious statement 等用词中可以把握作者的观点和立场。

第五篇:
60. 答案:D

本题为推理题,考查对第一段话中后半部分"of manipulating the results of drug trials for financial gain and withholding information that could expose patients to possible harm"的理解。
61. 答案:A

本题是词汇题,考点是第四段中提到的"non-profit organizations",意为"非营利组织"。
62. 答案:B

本题属细节题,考点是第五段中的 every year 和第六段中的 early evidence。
63. 答案:C

本题是推理题,考查第九段中提到的"researchers say they were refused access to unpublished trials"。
64. 答案:A

本题是细节题,考点是第十一段最后一句:Only one of the drugs, Prozac, emerged as safe.

65. 答案:D

本题是推理题,考点是最后一段中的引语部分:at least tentatively recommending use of these drugs。

第二小节　阅读理解 B

第一篇：

66. 答案:B

本题的答题关键在于把握该段开始部分的结构:第一句为起始句,下面展开解释说明。并且我们可以看出第三句是举例解释第一句话,由此可判断第二句应该也是解释说明第一句的。选项 B 中的"in fourteenth-century Europe"与第三句中的"the last century"分别从两个历史时期举例解释段首。

67. 答案:E

本题的突破口是人口的数量,全文只有在本段中提到了具体的人口数量,与选项 E 中的"a critical number of vulnerable individuals"在内容上一脉相承。

68. 答案:A

本题的答题关键是把握本段的要点:城市人口密度大成为传染病流行的重要原因。因此段首的"overcrowding"和选项 A 中的"crowded"为本段的关键词。

69. 答案:C

本题的突破口是选项 C 中的"water and sanitation"与本段第一句中提到的"clean water, good hygiene"一致。

70. 答案:F

本题的答题要点首先要了解本段主要讲到城市贫民窟的情况。选项 F 中"These areas"与"other parts of the city"分别指的就是前文所说的贫民窟和城市的其他区域。

第二篇：

71. 答案:E

本题的答题关键是看懂第一段与第二段的内容。第一段讲旧桥的坍塌,第二段讲新桥的开通,以及新桥怎样才能避免发生同样的事故。

72. 答案:A

本题的答题要点是把握第三段的要点:希腊的一座桥梁也采用了相似的避险设计。选项 A 中的"a handful of 'smart' bridges"与下句中的"Another example"相呼应。

73. 答案:F

本题的关键是理解前一句的句意:这些感应器早已经探测到了一些支撑该桥的线缆中存在异常的震动。由此,发现问题之后就是对问题的解决。另外,选项 F 中的过去式应该引起同学们的注意。

74. 答案:B

本题的答题要点是下一段中直接讲到 Dr. Lynch 的工作,作为正式文体,没有对其进行必要的介绍,例如工作单位等信息是缺失的,这些细节的缺失让读者心存疑虑这位博士是不是桥梁建设或设计方面的专家,为什么要介绍他的工作。而选项 B 恰好填补了在这方面信息的缺失。

75. 答案:D

本题的前一句讲到单独的感应器的缺陷,那如何解决这一问题呢。这就是下文中讲到的解决方案。选项 D 中的 to solve this problem 是本题的突破口。

第四部分　翻　译

(1) **参考译文**:

　　核反应堆核心熔毁的灾难就是世界末日。"发展核"就意味着你按下了致命的按钮,没有回头路了。

　　解析:

　　该句理解上的重点和难点是"Going nuclear",这个短语的意思是"走核武器道路""拥有核武器"。

(2) **参考译文**:

　　在处理眼下的危机以及为下一次危机做好准备的过程中,我们面临的挑战是要增加我们的选择。

　　解析:

　　该句在翻译时容易引起歧义的地方是对"preparing for the next one"的处理,准确的理解应该是"为了应对第二次危机的到来"。

(3) **参考译文**:

　　两天前,我曾对福岛第一核电站的反应堆防泄漏控制装置加以赞扬,因为它经受住了将其主冷却系统和备用冷却系统都摧毁的地震和海啸。

　　解析:

　　该句理解上的重点有两个:"spoke highly of"和"survive"。"spoke highly of"意为"赞扬";"survive"此处为及物动词,意为"幸免于……"。

(4) **参考译文**:

　　谁要是说"所有可能出问题的地方都出问题了",那他就是忽视了其他可能出问题的地方。

　　解析:

　　该句难点有三处:一是主语部分中的替代句型,did 替代的是 go wrong 这一短语,引语部分的意思是"任何可能出错的地方一定会出错";二是 anyone 做主语,翻译时可以将英语中从句句式转换为汉语中的分句句式;三是主语部分的语法结构相对复杂。

(5) **参考译文**:

　　先是日本历史上空前的大地震摧毁了高压电力网。然后一场海啸以前所未有的速度袭来,摧毁了备用的柴油发电机。

　　解析:

　　该句的难点集中体现在专业学术词汇比较集中,例如:quake, the power grid, tsunami, backup, diesel generators 等。建议结合上下文,一目了然的语境有利于词义的确定。

第五部分 写 作

题目解析：

要写好此作文，考生有两部分内容要兼顾：第一，你将对孩子说什么，如何教育孩子？第二，解释你为什么要这样教育孩子。实际上第二部分内容更重要，需要花费更多的笔墨。因为此题考查的重点是阐释你在这件事上所具有的价值观以及教育理念。理性地看待孩子受欺负这个问题，教育孩子来应对成长过程中可能会遇到的人际关系危机，学习正确处理同伴之间的矛盾和纷争，这些都是孩子成长过程中不可缺少的一环，同时也是这篇作文内容充实、论述有理的重要基石。无论作者如何阐释，关键是要言之成理，使人信服，语言表达通顺流畅。

范文：

As Franklin Roosevelt once claimed, "We cannot always build the future for our youth, but we can build our youth for the future." Education for next generations is always man's major concern. Education covers many aspects, even including the way how a person gets along with others.

Suppose I had a little daughter, Yaoyao, and she was bullied by her classmate in her elementary school, I would first investigate the situation to find out who was right and who was wrong. If it was not her fault at all, I would speak to her like this: "Don't be frightened, Yaoyao. It's not right for your classmate to treat you like this, and we will find ways to deal with this sort of things." And then, I would suggest that she report this to her school, get support from her teacher, and ask that student to apologize to her.

Why would I say so? If a child were bullied, parents would tend to feel as if they themselves were hurt as well and easily became over emotional. Nevertheless, maintaining a reasonable and impartial attitude is extremely crucial at this moment, for parents' attitude also teaches children indirectly how they should behave in the future. Teaching takes place everywhere, whether in the family or in the school. Parents, as well as children's private teachers in building their characters, need to bear in mind that children learn to get along with others in their everyday contact. Undoubtedly, sometimes a child may suffer from being bullied by their schoolmates, and more often than not, that a schoolmate even isn't certain enough about his or her improper behavior, because most children are still in the process of learning the rules and disciplines of human society. So in the beginning, parents should teach their children what is right and what is wrong.

Furthermore, bullying is a detrimental way of behavior. If you bullied someone, you treated them in a very unpleasant way by using your strength or power to hurt or frighten them. So we should teach children how to assert their rights when being bullied. Injustice exists at the school as well as in a society. Therefore, learning how to fight against unfairness is also an essential part of the lesson for children. Parents should teach children not to lose their courage before the Might and fight against injustice in a reasonable way.

Besides, parents also need to protect children's self-esteem and let them know that being bullied is not a shameful thing. In history, many celebrities were also bullied when they were young, but they have instead achieved their self-fulfillments and became powerful later. A case in point is the story of the Ugly Duckling. It was also ridiculed and bullied by its peers in its childhood, but later it became a gorgeously beautiful swan.

In conclusion, when a child is bullied, parents should maintain a serene and impartial attitude, and guide the child in learning how to get along with others, how to fight against injustice, and how to build their self-esteem. (506 words)

中国科学院
博士研究生入学考试
英语试题

(2012 年 3 月)

考生须知:

一、本试卷由试卷一(PAPER ONE)和试卷二(PAPER TWO)两部分组成。试卷一为客观题,答卷使用标准化机读答题纸;试卷二为主观题,答卷使用非机读答题纸。

二、请考生一律用 HB 或 2B 铅笔填涂标准化机读答题纸,画线不得过细或过短。修改时请用橡皮擦拭干净。若因填涂不符合要求而导致计算机无法识别,责任由考生自负。请保持机读答题纸清洁、无折皱。答题纸切忌折叠。

三、全部考试时间总计 180 分钟,满分为 100 分。时间及分值分布如下:

试卷一:

Ⅰ 词汇	15 分钟	10 分
Ⅱ 完形填空	15 分钟	15 分
Ⅲ 阅读理解	80 分钟	40 分
小计	110 分钟	65 分

试卷二:

Ⅳ 英译汉	30 分钟	15 分
Ⅴ 写作	40 分钟	20 分
小计	70 分钟	35 分

GRADUATE UNIVERSITY, CHINESE ACADEMY OF SCIENCES ENGLISH ENTRANCE EXAMINATION FOR PH. D PROGRAMME
March 2012

PAPER ONE

PART I VOCABULARY (15 minutes, 10 points, 0.5 point each)

Directions: *Choose the word or expression below each sentence that best completes the statement, and mark the corresponding letter of your choice with a single bar across the square brackets on your Machine-scoring Answer Sheet.*

1. I had to _____ my desire to laugh while being scolded by my supervisor.
   A. repress B. depress C. compress D. distress
2. All living languages _____, and English seems to change more readily than some others.
   A. evoke B. evacuate C. evolve D. evade
3. He has always been a source of inspiration to me and I hope that he will take it as a _____ when I say that.
   A. compassion B. compliment C. complication D. supplement
4. The current financial crisis _____ a holistic, global approach to deal with all issues.
   A. cries out for B. gets hold of C. boils down to D. goes in for
5. If you see that the street is wet in the morning, you would _____ that it must have rained during the night.
   A. reduce B. seduce C. deduce D. induce
6. Even if she is responsible for the mistake, she is not likely to _____ it.
   A. own up to B. live up to C. hold on to D. get down to
7. The burst of growth and prosperity in America after 1945 had social consequences that were _____ anywhere in the world.
   A. unprecedented B. unidentified C. unaccountable D. unremarkable
8. Building the Bird's Nest calls for giant curving beams which crisscross in an _____ pattern of

woven steel.

   A. intuitive B. intensive C. intrinsic D. intricate

9. San Francisco was _____ by a terrible earthquake and fire in 1906.

   A. deprived B. detained C. devastated D. deported

10. Compared with his _____, Putin adopted a more active, flexible and pragmatic foreign policy.

    A. ancestor B. predecessor C. forerunner D. pioneer

11. We are a peaceful community but we cannot _____ and allow the people responsible to destroy the fabric of our society.

    A. start up B. start off C. stand by D. stick out

12. Language may be _____ of as a process which arises from social interaction.

    A. comprised B. conceived C. disposed D. deprived

13. Older, less dogmatic theories better explained how the problems in the financial _____ dragged down the rest of the economy.

    A. charter B. session C. chapel D. sector

14. These results should not be taken at face _____ — careful analysis is required to assess their full implications.

    A. revenue B. expense C. price D. value

15. Researchers are looking for new ways to _____ the problem.

    A. abridge B. approach C. condense D. dispose

16. Many writing experts think that intonation is used to _____ our feelings and attitudes; the same sentence can be said in different ways.

    A. convey B. convict C. conform D. conduct

17. Medical students learn to distinguish "acute," which means something of recent onset, from "chronic," which means a condition that will probably continue for a _____ period of time.

    A. gloomy B. temporary C. tough D. substantial

18. By analyzing the modern expansion of Western culture, this article concludes that it is of practical significance to _____ the dominant position of Chinese national culture.

    A. recall B. retort C. restore D. retard

19. There are few, if any, countries in the world in which sports _____ national life to the degree that they do in the US.

    A. permeate B. overwhelm C. submerge D. immerse

20. His violent behavior sometimes is _____ his personality of shyness and self-consciousness.

    A. on condition of B. in line with C. at odds with D. in disguise of

PART II CLOZE TEST (15 minutes, 15 points)

Directions: *For each blank in the following passage, choose the best answer from the four choices given below. Mark the corresponding letter of your choice with a single bar across the*

square brackets on your Machine-scoring Answer Sheet.

There have been five extinction waves in the planet's history — including the Permian extinction 250 million years ago, __21__ an estimated 70% of all land animals and 96% of all marine creatures vanished. The sample polling of animal populations so far suggests that we may have entered __22__ will be the planet's sixth great extinction wave.

Forests razed can grow back, polluted air and water can be cleaned — but __23__ is forever. And we're not talking about losing just a few species. In fact, conservationists quietly __24__ that we've entered an age of triage (治疗类选法), when we might have to decide which species can truly be __25__. The worst-case scenarios of habitat __26__ and climate change — and that's the pathway we seem to be __27__ — show the planet losing hundreds of thousands to millions of species, __28__ of which we haven't even discovered yet.

So __29__ you care about tigers and elephants, rhinos and orangutans, then you should be scared. But __30__ shouldn't leave us paralyzed. In hot spots like Madagascar and Brazil, conservationists are working with locals on the ground, __31__ that the protection of endangered species is tied to the welfare of the people who live closest to them. A strategy known as avoided deforestation goes __32__, encouraging environmental protection __33__ putting a price on the carbon locked in rain forests and allowing countries to trade credits in an international market, __34__ that the carbon stays in the forest and is not cut or burned. It's __35__ that any of this will stop the sixth extinction wave, let alone preserve the biodiversity we still enjoy, but we have no choice but to try.

21. A. when   B. because   C. there   D. so
22. A. that   B. what   C. when   D. which
23. A. earth   B. population   C. evolution   D. extinction
24. A. commit   B. acknowledge   C. rebuke   D. deny
25. A. sampled   B. surveyed   C. saved   D. tested
26. A. loss   B. shift   C. formation   D. exclusion
27. A. above   B. on   C. over   D. off
28. A. none   B. any   C. many   D. all
29. A. that   B. since   C. if   D. while
30. A. fear   B. rumors   C. species   D. climate
31. A. ensure   B. ensuring   C. ensured   D. having ensured
32. A. tougher   B. worse   C. further   D. closer
33. A. about   B. in   C. for   D. by
34. A. considering   B. indicating   C. supposed   D. provided
35. A. uncertain   B. unaware   C. unpleasant   D. unsuitable

PART III READING COMPREHENSION

Section A (60 minutes, 30 points)
Directions: *Below each of the following passages you will find some questions or incomplete statements. Each question or statement is followed by four choices marked A, B, C, and D. Read each passage carefully, and then select the choice that best answers the question or completes the statement. Mark the letter of your choice with a single bar across the square brackets on your Machine-scoring Answer Sheet.*

Passage One

Like so many things of value, truth is not always easy to come by. What we regard as true shapes our beliefs, attitudes, and actions. Yet we can believe things that have no basis in fact. People are capable of embracing horrific precepts that seem incredible in retrospect. In Nazi Germany, Adolf Hitler had millions of followers who accepted his delusions about racial superiority. As Voltaire put it long before Hitler's time, "Those who can make you believe absurdities can make you commit atrocities."

We are surrounded by illusions, some created deliberately. They may be subtle or may affect us profoundly. Some illusions, such as films and novels, we seek out and appreciate. Others can make us miserable and even kill us. We need to know if particular foods that taste perfectly fine can hurt us in the short term (as with Salmonella contamination) or in the long term (cholesterol), whether a prevalent virus is so dangerous that we should avoid public places, and what problems a political candidate may cause or resolve if elected. Gaining insights about the truth often is a challenge, and misconceptions can be difficult to recognize.

We often believe stories because they are the ones available. Most people would identify Thomas Edison as the inventor of the incandescent light bulb. Although Edison perfected a commercially successful design, he was preceded in the experimentation by British inventors Frederick de Moleyns and Joseph Swan, and by American J. W Starr.

The biggest enemies of truth are: people whose job is to sell us incomplete versions of the available facts, our willingness to believe what we want and the simple absence of accurate information. Companies advertising products on television do not describe the advantages of their competitors' products any more than a man asking a woman to marry him encourages her to date other men before making up her mind. It is a social reality that people encourage one another to make important decisions with limited facts.

Technology has simplified and complicated the fact-gathering process. The Internet allows us to check facts more easily, but it also **disburses** misinformation. Similarly, a belief that videos and photos necessarily represent reality ignores how easily they can be digitally altered. Unquestioning reliance on such forms of media makes us more susceptible to manipulators: those who want to deceive can dazzle us with a modem version of smoke and mirrors.

36. According to Voltaire, _____.
    A. Hitler was obsessed with violence   B. irrational ideas may be spread widely
    C. irrational ideas may lead to violence D. Hitler was misled by racism
37. Paragraph 2 shows that _____.
    A. truth is hard to get due to misconceptions
    B. public health deserves much attention
    C. political elections have profound impact
    D. illusions are helpful in gaining new insights
38. By mentioning Thomas Edison, the author seems to emphasize that _____.
    A. business successes may cover the truth
    B. commercial activities may involve cooperation
    C. irrational ideas may influence technological progress
    D. misconceptions may be due to lack of information
39. Advertising and making a marriage proposal are similar in that both _____.
    A. encourage fair competition   B. give partial information
    C. attack their enemies   D. take advantage of people's hesitation
40. The boldfaced word "disburses" in Paragraph 5 probably means "_____."
    A. spreads   B. disturbs   C. falsifies   D. corrects
41. The drawback brought by technology is that it makes people prone to _____.
    A. be addicted   B. be taken in   C. show off   D. decide hastily

Passage Two

All art booms are different. The previous one ended in 1989, when Japanese buyers withdrew from the Impressionist market. Interest rates rose in the slump that followed; there were plenty of sellers but no buyers. Today the reverse is true. Buyers are looking to diversify into alternative assets. The only problem is the sellers. There is plenty of money about, but little to buy.

It should follow, then, that buyers will snap up anything. But that is not quite the case, as the Old Master sales at Christie's in London on December 8th showed only too well. In the recent sales the best pieces sold brilliantly, and the rest hardly at all. The best included a rare Raphael drawing, and an elegant self-portrait by Sir Anthony van Dyck. Many of the leading dealers were present, including Philip Mould, known as the BBC's "art detective;" Alfred Bader, a rich American art-market broker; and the heirs to two important art-dealing businesses, William Noortman and Simon Green.

Van Dyck's oval shaped self portrait, painted in 1640, the year before he died, had been in the same family for almost 300 years. Mr. Mould joined forces with Mr. Bader to try and win the painting. Young Mr. Noortman, the underbidder who was trying to buy the picture for stock, did not stand a chance. The winning bid was £7.4m, nearly three times van Dyck's previous auction record.

The last lot in Christie's sale was a black chalk drawing, less than a foot square, by Raphael, an early 16th-century Italian master. It is the study of a head for one of the Greek muses. Its beauty, rarity and the sense that the study may well have been used by the artist himself when working on a larger painting drew collectors from far and wide.

Christie's had estimated the study would fetch £ 12m-16m. Bidding opened at £ 8.5m, with three buyers on the telephone. Jennifer Wright, Christie's New York-based drawings specialist, made a final bid for the Raphael of £ 26m — a world record for a work on paper.

After the sale, Christie's international co-head, Richard Knight, was quick to point out that, at £ 68.4m, theirs had been the biggest Old Master sale ever. "This result shows what a very solid market this is," he said. But that took no account of the failures, which were considerable. Fifteen of the 43 lots in Christie's auction failed to sell at all.

42. Unlike 1989, today, the art market is characterized by an increase of _____.
    A. sales   B. prices   C. buyers   D. supplies
43. Christie's sale showed that _____.
    A. many of the paintings were left on the shelf
    B. portraits were in greater demand than others
    C. buyers all found their favorite pieces
    D. sellers worried little about selling their lots
44. The self-portrait of Sir Anthony van Dyck was _____.
    A. kept in one home for three centuries   B. once sold for about 2.5 million pounds
    C. put up for auction for the first time   D. won by two American art dealers
45. Raphael's drawing at the sale was undoubtedly _____.
    A. the portrait of the artist himself   B. the part of a larger painting
    C. the copy of a Greek sculpture   D. the only one in the world
46. According to the passage, the £ 26m for the Raphael was most probably unexpected by _____.
    A. Alfred Bader   B. Jennifer Wright   C. Richard Knight   D. Simon Green
47. It can safely be concluded that the Old Master sale mentioned _____.
    A. reflected a very solid market   B. had both wins and losses
    C. turned out to be a total failure   D. sold more works than any other auctions

Passage Three

On the outside, Betsy Lueth's school looks like any other in this arty neighborhood of Minneapolis: a sprawling, boxy red brick building with plain steel doors. Yet inside, the blond, friendly Minnesotan presides over an institution unique in the heartland: Yinghua Academy, a charter public school where elementary students of every ethnicity study subjects ranging from math to American history in Mandarin.

The idea behind Yinghua, as with many immersion programs, is to introduce kids to the language and culture as early as possible — ideally, before age 12, while they're still absorbing information like sponges. Kindergartners and first-graders are taught exclusively in Mandarin, and a single period of English is introduced in the second grade. By the sixth grade, kids are learning half in English and half in Mandarin, with the expectation of proficiency in both.

The challenges at Yinghua are numerous. Most teachers come from Taiwan or mainland of China, and cultural misunderstandings prevail. Lueth's instructors are learning to be tolerant of local norms like nontraditional families and boys who cry — as well as a lot more parental input than they're used to. "In China, teachers are revered. They are not questioned," says Luyi Lien, Yinghua's Taiwan-born academic director. "In America, parents are more... expressive of their opinions."

Yinghua's student body, once 70% Asian, is now 50% white, black or Hispanic. The school has more than tripled its enrollment, to 300 kids, many of whom commute an hour each day. Research has shown that in the long run, immersion programs can provide cognitive benefits, including more flexible, creative thinking. Though students from the programs lag for a few years in English, by the fifth grade they perform as well as or better than their monolingual peers on standardized reading and math tests. For multicultural families, the psychological boost can also be important. Lueth's adopted daughter, Lucy, used to squirm when cousins asked why her skin color was different from theirs; Now, Lucy proudly answers them, "Yeah, I was born in China."

Lueth recently won an $800,000 grant from the Department of Education to develop a teaching model for immersion middle schools, and she advises educators around the country who are starting their own programs. If Yinghua can make Mandarin a success in Minnesota, so can they. "This is a glorious culture — and an increasingly important language — that we are meaningfully teaching to our children. And we're in the middle of nowhere."

48. According to the passage, Yinghua Academy is _____.
    A. an English language school for immigrants
    B. a high rise sticking out in the neighborhood
    C. a grade school with students of different races
    D. a unique institution with an Asian owner

49. In comparison with their counterparts in other schools around, Yinghua's twelve-year-old Asian children would most probably be _____.
    A. better at Western culture   B. more proficient in English
    C. better at acquiring knowledge   D. more bilingually competent

50. Most instructors at Yinghua are trying to adapt themselves to the local parents who are _____.
    A. soft with their children   B. unafraid to be critical
    C. as stubborn as a mule   D. respectful of nobody

51. According to the research, students from Yinghua will be more creative in thinking because _____.

A. they are taught there not only in English
B. they are not only learning languages there
C. they were not only born to White parents
D. they were raised not only nearby the school

52. Which word can best describe Lucy?
    A. Self-conscious. B. Self-assertive. C. Self-confident. D. Self-important.
53. In regard to the teaching of Mandarin, Lueth believes that Yinghua _____.
    A. has still a long way to go   B. deserves financial rewards
    C. plays a leading role in the US   D. shows what can be done anywhere

Passage Four

Fifty is the gateway to the most liberating passage in a woman's life. Children are making test flights out of the nest. Parents are expected to be roaming in their recreational vehicles or sending postcards of themselves riding camels. Free at last! Women can graduate from the precarious balancing act between parenting and pursuit of a career. That has been the message of my books since I wrote *New Passages* 15 years ago. What I didn't see coming was the **boomerang**.

With parents living routinely into their 90s, a second round of caregiving has become a predictable crisis for women in midlife. Nearly 50 million Americans are taking care of an adult who used to be independent. Yes, men represent about one third of family caregivers, but their participation is often at a distance and administrative. Women do most of the hands-on care.

It starts with the call. It's a call about a fall. Your mom has had a stroke. Or it's a call about your dad — he's run a red light and hit someone, again, but how are you ever going to persuade him to stop driving? Or your husband's doctor calls with news that your partner is reluctant to tell you: it's cancer.

When that call came to me, I froze. The shock plunges you into a whirlpool of fear, denial, and feverish action. You search out doctors. They don't agree on the diagnosis. You scavenge the Internet. The side effects make you worry. You call your brother or sister, hoping for help. Old rivalries flare up.

We'd like to think that siblings would be natural allies when parents falter. But the facts are quite different. Brothers bury their heads in the sand. The farther away a sister lives, the more certain she will call the primary caregiver and tell her she doesn't know what she's doing. A 1996 study by Cornell and Louisiana State universities concluded that siblings are not just inherent rivals, but the greatest source of stress between human beings.

There are many rewards in giving back to a loved one. And the short-term stress of mobilizing against the initial crisis jump-starts the body's positive responses. But this role is not a short race. It usually turns into a marathon, averaging almost five years. But most solitary caregivers will wait until the third or fourth year before sending out the desperate cry, "I can't do this anymore!"

54. As a writer, the author has for years focused on women's liberation from _____.

A. looking after their children B. taking care of their parents
C. earning a living for their families D. doing housework all day long

55. The word "boomerang" (boldfaced in Paragraph 1) refers to _____.
    A. husbands and wives giving different care to their weak parents
    B. women in their fifties taking all responsibilities for their families
    C. the elderly becoming dependent on their middle-aged children
    D. family caregiving having been shifted onto women's shoulders

56. To many women, the calls as described would most likely be very _____.
    A. invigorating   B. distressing   C. refreshing   D. confusing

57. Your brother or sister would be angry with your request for helping to _____.
    A. stop the quarrel between your parents
    B. find your husband a better doctor
    C. deal with your family problems
    D. take care of your Mom or Dad

58. According to the author, siblings tend to _____.
    A. live in different places after they form their own families
    B. stand on the same side when arguing with their parents
    C. compete with each other for being the primary caregiver
    D. shift onto each other the responsibilities for their parents

59. The author stresses that the process of giving back to a loved one is very _____.
    A. hopeless   B. rewarding   C. demanding   D. fruitless

Passage Five

Madonna seems like a person used to getting her own way. So the pop star must have been dismayed when a court in Malawi refused her request to adopt a three-year-old girl, Mercy James. The reason was that Madonna had not fulfilled residency requirements. The last time Madonna tried to adopt a Malawian child she met with more success and a heap of criticism.

By plucking David Banda from grinding poverty in Malawi in 2006 she provoked mixed reactions. Some praised the singer for offering a child an escape from a life of misery. Others suggested that the pop queen might have used her wealth and stardom to jump the queue. Detractors also suggested that it was wrong to take David away from his country of birth. The criticism grew louder when it emerged that David was not, in fact, an orphan.

That circumstance is not particularly uncommon. Children given up for adoption often do have a surviving parent but one who cannot provide adequate care. David's father was still alive but gave him up to an orphanage where he hoped his offspring would have a better life.

The number of families from rich countries wanting to adopt children from poor countries has grown substantially in the past 30 years. And there is little shortage of children who need additional help. In 2005, it was estimated that there were 132 million children who had lost at least one parent in sub-Saharan Africa, Asia, Latin America and the Caribbean. Around 13 million of these had lost both parents, although most of them lived with extended family.

But difficulties abound. Would-be parents typically want to adopt a healthy and young orphan, usually a small baby. Older children, or those who suffer chronic illnesses, are not in demand.

Governments are understandably uneasy about outsiders removing their citizens. And as the demand for children to adopt has grown, so have examples of abuse, including cases of children who have been kidnapped or parents who have been coerced or bribed. The absence of effective international regulation also allows middlemen to profit from the demand for children to adopt.

The Hague Convention on Inter-country Adoptions is intended to regulate international adoptions. It states that these can only go ahead if the parents' consent has been obtained without any kind of payment or compensation. Costs and expenses can be paid, and a reasonable fee may go to the adoption agency involved, but nothing more.

60. Paragraph 1 tells that Madonna _____.
    A. adopted a Malawian girl named Mercy James
    B. rarely failed to get whatever she wanted
    C. had an illegal adoption of a Malawian child
    D. regretted residing in a wrong community

61. We can infer that an adoption is generally acceptable if _____.
    A. the adopted has no close kin   B. the adopted is a foreign child
    C. the adopter is wealthy enough   D. the adopter has won some fame

62. Children like David are put on the list for adoption mostly because _____.
    A. their families suffer from poverty   B. they have lost both of their parents
    C. their parents neglect their growth   D. they have escaped from their home

63. Which can be concluded about the stated situation of adoption?
    A. Most children put up for adoption have found adopters.
    B. Those to be adopted outnumber those wanting to adopt.
    C. People are anxious to adopt healthy infants.
    D. The adopted rarely remain in their home country.

64. Paragraph 6 focuses on the corrupt practices concerning _____.
    A. choosing alien adoptees   B. caretaking of the adopted
    C. the search of suitable adopters   D. the growing demand for adoption

65. The adoption regulations in the Hague Convention will ban _____.
    A. charging the parents for giving up children
    B. adopting children for profit
    C. adopting 2 children in one family
    D. forcing one to accept any adoptee

Section B (20 minutes, 10 points)

Directions: *In each of the following passages, five sentences have been removed from the original text.*

They are listed from A to F and put below the passage. Choose the most suitable sentence from the list to fill in each of the blanks (numbered 66 to 75). For each passage, there is one sentence that does not fit in any of the blanks. Mark your answers on your Machine-scoring Answer Sheet.

Passage One

In June 2006, in Minato, Tokyo, a 16-year old high school student was killed by a Schindler elevator. He was backing out of it with his bicycle when the elevator suddenly rose with the doors still open, crushing his skull. Investigations began related to this fatality.

In the process of this investigation, the safety of elevators in Japan came under question. __66__ The Japan Elevator Association disclosed that 9,200 entrapments happened in Japan in 2004 in elevators of the big four Japanese elevator manufacturers (Mitsubishi Electric, Hitachi, Toshiba, and Fujitec).

Results from a recent investigation in Hiroshima showed that 34% of Schindler elevators in the city have had problems. __67__

As of June 14, 2006, the precise cause of the accident had still not been confirmed. __68__ The International Herald Tribune reported on June 14 that "Loose bolts and worn brake pads, evidence of poor maintenance, likely played a central role in the elevator accident."

__69__ The Asia Times Online reports that in response to a flood of inquiries from customers, the third-largest domestic elevator company, Toshiba Elevator and Building Systems Corp. is offering free inspections of their elevators, while Mitsubishi Electric Corp., the leading firm, and Hitachi Ltd, which is the second-largest, are responding to requests on a case-by-case basis.

In Hong Kong, many news agencies are finding similarities between the Minato case and the 2002 Fanling Hong Kong case. Thus, Hong Kong's Public Housing Authority has been questioned about the 33 public estates with Schindler elevators. __70__ In comparison, Hong Kong law requires a full annual examination every year, load testing every 5 years, and an inspection every month. Some buildings have inspections every 2 weeks.

A. There is a reported competition among elevator operators in Hong Kong, with some buildings opting to contract elevator maintenance to firms that offer low rates.
B. The Housing Authority has said that all of its elevators are maintained by the original manufacturer (in Hong Kong's case, by "Schindler Lifts Hong Kong Limited") and all elevators are inspected fully once every week.
C. It should be noted that elevator maintenance had been carried out by a Japanese maintenance company and not by Schindler since 2005.
D. That elevators are not infallible came as a surprise to many people, especially when it was discovered that of the 8,800 Schindler elevators installed in Japan, 85 have trapped people.
E. Japan has already ordered full inspections of the country's entire set of Schindler elevators, with

elevators of all manufacturers being inspected in government buildings.

F. Public concern over the Minato case has not been limited merely to Schindler elevators.

Passage Two

Like thousands of parents across Britain, I have been scanning the skies with some nervousness this week. My son and daughter are praying for the snow — and the school closures — to continue. And I'm praying for slush.

At a time when people are worried enough about keeping their jobs, the cost of school closure is immense. Parents unable to secure emergency childcare have no choice but to stay off work themselves. __71__ The Federation of Small Businesses reckons that by the end of the week our trembling economy will have suffered losses worth some £3.5bn.

__72__ Parenting websites abound with childhood memories of brave infants, battling their way to school in the Big Snow of the 1960s and 1970s and angry demands have been made for school staff to show courage and set an example. According to Margaret Morrissey of the Parents Outloud campaign group, "We are giving children the message that when things get difficult you should stay at home and have fun. __73__ "

I dare say I could have kept my pair indoors on Monday, reciting time tables instead of hurtling downhill on an offcut of laminate flooring, but it's not the effect on their characters I'm most concerned about. __74__ Back in the 1960s, local schools were largely staffed by local teachers. Today particularly in cities where property prices long ago outstripped the wages of public sector workers, teachers are frequently travelling vast distances to get to school.

If the transport system grinds to a halt, as it has across Britain this week, there's not a whole lot teachers, or dinner ladies, or cleaners, or any other workers on whom the smooth running of our schools depend, can do about it.

Put bluntly, it's not the teachers who were short of grit (勇气, 沙砾) this week, it was the roads. __75__ There are lessons that cannot be learned at school. Given the weather forecast, I call that fortunate.

A. Then, when they keep taking sick days from work when they grow up, we wonder why.
B. It's natural to look for the weak link in this chain of disaster and, not unusually, it's teachers who are being criticized.
C. This translates all too quickly into orders unfulfilled and contracts prejudiced.
D. Quite frankly, I don't blame thousands of teachers eagerly taking a couple of days off when faced in front by mob of badly behaved, obese and foul-mouthed children.
E. For the want of some sand for the roads, £3.5bn was lost.
F. And it seems unfair to impose our comfortable schoolroom nostalgia on a profession facing peculiar contemporary challenges.

PAPER TWO

PART IV   TRANSLATION (30 minutes, 15 points)

Directions: *Read the following text carefully and then translate the underlined segments into Chinese. Write your Chinese version in the proper space on your Answer Sheet.*

   In order to think about the possibility of a science of virtues, we must, of course, reflect on what we mean by virtue. In the simplest sense virtues are dispositions to act in certain morally good ways. 1) Thus, a courageous person is disposed to face danger without fleeing, and we would be hesitant to characterize as courageous someone who runs away from danger. Yet, strangely enough, a person characterized by courage might in some circumstances flee from danger without causing us to doubt that he possessed the virtue. And, on the other hand, a person who lacked the virtue of courage might on occasion face danger without fleeing. 2) Sometimes, therefore, we will discover no perfect fit between virtuous character and a disposition to act in specific ways.

   A little better characterization of virtues is to think of them as something like skills that we acquire through habituation. The pitcher (棒球投手) who throws a low strike over the outside corner of the plate may just be lucky. If, however, he can do it time after time — habitually — he has acquired a skill. Virtues are something like that, though also a bit different. 3) They are not simply skills that, like technical competence, enable us to carry out a particular task with proficiency; rather, they are skills that fit us for life generally. Acquiring virtues is more like learning to drive a car than it is like merely being able to parallel park. Driving requires a capacity to respond in fitting ways to countless circumstances that arise along the way, not just the ability to carry out a single maneuver.

   This account of virtues as something like skills more closely approximates a reasonable description of what we mean by virtue, but even habituation cannot be the complete story. It is hard for a pitcher to become skilled, because throwing that low, outside strike is inherently difficult, no matter how badly he wants to throw it. 4) In virtuous action, however, much of the difficulty may come precisely from what we want, from our own contrary inclinations. If I deliberately throw a pitch outside the strike zone, that does not mean I lack the capacity to throw a strike. But if I deliberately cheat the opposing team, I seem to lack a certain virtue. 5) Thus, virtues are not only habitual; they also engage the will in a way that skills do not.

PART V   WRITING (40 minutes, 20 points)

Directions: *Write an essay of no less than 200 words on the topic given below. Use the proper space on your Answer Sheet II.*

TOPIC

Do you agree that history repeats itself? Provide examples to support your viewpoints.

2012年3月试题精解

第一部分 词 汇

1. 答案：A

   本题考查动词的含义。A 抑制，镇压；B 压抑，使沮丧；C 压缩，浓缩；D 使苦恼，使痛苦。句子的意思是：主管训斥我的时候，我不得不忍住想笑的欲望。

2. 答案：C

   本题考查动词的含义。A 唤起，引起，博得；B 疏散，撤出；C 发展，进化；D 规避，逃避，躲避。句子的意思是：所有现存的语言都进化，英语似乎比一些语言更为易变。

3. 答案：B

   本题考查名词的含义。A 同情，怜悯；B 赞美(话)，恭维(话)；C 复杂，纠纷；D 补充。句子的意思是：他一直是我的灵感来源，我说这话时希望他当作是赞美之词。

4. 答案：A

   本题考查动词词组的含义。A 迫切需要；B 抓住，掌握；C 意味着，归结为；D 从事，致力于，追求。句子的意思是：现在的金融危机急需一个全球一体化的方法来解决所有问题。

5. 答案：C

   本题考查动词的含义。A 减少，降低；B 引诱，诱导；C 演绎，推断；D 归纳，引起，导致。句子的意思是：早晨的时候如果你看到街道是湿的，就会推断出前一天晚上肯定下了雨。

6. 答案：A

   本题考查动词词组的含义。A 坦白，爽快承认；B 真正做到，不辜负；C 紧紧抓住，坚持；D 开始认真对待(工作等)，开始认真注意(细节等)。句子的意思是：她即使真的犯了错误，也不可能承认。

7. 答案：A

   本题考查形容词的含义。A 无先例的，空前的；B 身份不明的，未辨别出的；C 无责任的，不负责任的，难以说明的，不能解释的；D 平凡的，不出色的，不引人注目的。句子的意思是：1945 年之后美国的快速发展与繁荣产生了世界上任何地方都未曾有过的社会影响。

8. 答案：D

   本题考查形容词的含义。A 直觉的；B 加强的，集中的，深入细致的；C (指价值、性质)固有的，内在的，本质的；D 错综复杂的，复杂精细的。句子的意思是：建筑鸟巢需要巨型马鞍形钢桁架复杂的编织式结构。

9. 答案：C

   本题考查动词的含义。A 夺去，使丧失；B 耽搁，扣留，扣押；C 使荒芜，毁坏；D 驱逐。句子的意思是：1906 年可怕的大地震和大火使旧金山市成了废墟。

10. 答案：B

    本题考查名词的含义。A 祖先；B 前任，前身，(被取代的)原有事物；C 先驱，预兆；D 先驱,创始人,开拓者。句子的意思是:与其前任相比,普京采取了更为积极、灵活和实用的外交政策。

11. 答案:C

　　本题考查动词词组的含义。A 开业;B 开始;C 袖手旁观;D 突出。句子的意思是:我们是和平社区但不能袖手旁观、坐视人们破坏社会秩序。

12. 答案:B

　　本题考查动词的含义。A 包含,包括,构成,组成;B 设想,构思,想象,认为;C 处理,处置,安排,布置;D 剥夺。句子的意思是:语言可以被视为一个起源于社交的过程。

13. 答案:D

　　本题考查名词的含义。A 宪章,共同纲领;B 时间段,会议;C 小教堂,祈祷室;D 部分,部门。句子的意思是:较为古老、不那么教条的理论更好地解释了金融方面的问题是如何拖垮整个经济的。

14. 答案:D

　　本题考查名词的含义。A 收入;B 花费,消费,消耗;C 价格,代价;D 价值。句子的意思是:这些结果不应该凭表面意义来判断,需要进行细致分析以评估其全部含义。

15. 答案:B

　　本题考查动词的含义。A 缩短,减少,限制;B 着手处理,靠近,接近;C 浓缩,压缩,精练;D 处理,处置,安排(一般的用法是 dispose of something,或 dispose someone)。句子的意思是:研究人员正在寻找新方法解决问题。

16. 答案:A

　　本题考查动词的含义。A 传达,传播;B 证明……有罪,宣判……有罪;C 遵守,依照,符合;D 管理,指挥,引导。句子的意思是:很多写作专家认为语调是用来传达情感和态度的;同一个句子可以用不同的语调说出来。

17. 答案:D

　　本题考查形容词的含义。A 阴沉的,阴暗的;B 暂时的,临时的;C 困难的,坚强的,牢固的;D 充足的,大量的,相当程度的。句子的意思是:医科学生懂得区别急性和慢性:急性即最近突发,慢性即很可能持续相当长时间的状况。

18. 答案:C

　　本题考查动词的含义。A 回忆,收回;B 反驳;C 恢复,修复;D 延迟。句子的意思是:通过分析西方文化在现代的发展,本文得出结论:重建中国文化的主导地位具有重大实际意义。

19. 答案:A

　　本题考查动词的含义。A 弥漫,遍布,渗入;B 制服,使不知所措;C 浸没;D 使浸没,使沉浸在……之中。句子的意思是:若有,也很少有国家像美国那样,其体育运动如此渗入国民生活。

20. 答案:C

　　本题考查介词短语的含义。A 在……条件下;B 符合,与……一致;C 与……不一致,与……不和;D 伪装。句子的意思是:他的暴力行为有时候与其腼腆和自觉的个性大相径庭。

第二部分　完形填空

本文主要阐述在面临历史上可能已出现的第六次物种灭绝时,人们的态度以及生态环境保护者所采取的种种举措。

21. 答案:A

本题考查定语从句以及定语从句中关系副词的使用。本句的意思是,"二叠纪物种灭绝事件发生在两亿多年前。那时,地球上70%的陆生动物和96%的海洋生物消失"。

22. 答案:B

本题考查宾语从句以及引导宾语从句的关系代词的使用。本句的意思是,"到目前为止,对动物的取样调查表明,我们可能已经进入了将成为地球上第六次物种灭绝的时期"。

23. 答案:D

本题考查对文章主题词的把握。本文的核心是物种的灭绝,本句的意思是,"森林砍伐后,可以再长回来;空气污染了,可以再净化回来;但物种灭绝后,就永远灭绝了,无法返回"。

24. 答案:B

本题考查对上下文句意的理解及动词语义辨析。本句用到了 in fact,表示一种转折,意思是,即使主张对物种进行保护的生态环境保护者也默默地承认了这样的现实,即我们现在已经进入到了一个治疗类选法阶段。

25. 答案:C

本题考查动词的词义辨析。本题主要是对前文提到的治疗类选法时代的一个解释,"在这样的阶段或时代,我们可能需要选择究竟哪些物种可以真正地被拯救"。四个选项的意思为:A 取样;B 调查;C 拯救;D 测试。

26. 答案:A

本题考查对上下文句意的理解。"生物栖息地的消失"和"环境的变化"是两个同义并列成分,对"最糟糕的情景"(the worst-case scenarios)进行修饰。

27. 答案:B

本题考查介词搭配用法。本句的意思是,我们似乎就在这样一条道路上。

28. 答案:C

本题考查代词的词义辨析和对上下文的理解。本句的意思是,有些物种我们人类还没有来得及发现。

29. 答案:C

本题考查条件从句的用法。本句的意思是,"如果你关心老虎、大象、犀牛和猩猩的生存,那么你一定会被吓到"。

30. 答案:A

本题考查上下文词义的呼应。上一句讲到如果人们关心这些物种,那么就会被现状所吓到。这一句表示即使被吓到了,也不要被吓得目瞪口呆,无所作为。两句之间是转折关系。

31. 答案:B

本题考查动词的分词用法。本句的意思是,"在马达加斯加和巴西这样的热带区域,生态环境保护者们正在和当地的居民一起工作,从而确保对濒危物种的保护,这与当地居民的福利紧密相关"。

32. 答案:C

本题考查对上下文语义的理解。四个选项都可以和 go 组成搭配,意思分别为:A 变强硬; B 变糟;C 更近一步;D 接近。但本句意思是,"避免毁林策略和前一句提到的其他环境保护方法相比,更进一步,更胜一筹"。

33. 答案:D

本题考查介词的用法辨析。这句是说,"避免毁林策略通过对热带雨林地区的碳资源进行标价来鼓励人们进行环境保护"。

34. 答案:D

本题考查句子的逻辑关系。前面的主句是说,"避免毁林策略鼓励人们保护环境,它所使用的方法是对雨林地区的碳资源进行标价"。后面的从句讲道,"对碳资源进行标价的前提是这些资源是存在的,没有被砍伐或烧毁"。两句之间是条件或假设关系。

35. 答案:A

本题考查形容词的词义辨析。前文提到的是人们为了保护物种所采取的种种措施。本句则是讲以上措施是否能否保存物种的多样性,阻止第六次物种灭绝的到来的可能性。"尽管人们也不确定这些措施是否有效,但除此之外,人类别无选择"。

第三部分 阅读理解
第一小节 阅读理解 A

第一篇:

36. 答案:C

本题是细节题,考查第一段最后一句:那些能让你相信谬论的人也能让你犯下暴行。

37. 答案:A

本题是段落主旨题,考查对第二段中心大意的掌握,在第二段最后一句:要深刻了解真理往往是个挑战,而且错误的观念也不易识别。

38. 答案:D

本题是例证题,考查对爱迪生的例子说明观点的理解,即第三段第一句。

39. 答案:B

本题是例证题,这道题的信息在第四段第二句,但二者的共同之处却是本段第一句,即本段的主题句。

40. 答案:A

本题是词汇题,考查第五段第二句的前半句和后半句的关系。

41. 答案:B

本题是细节题,考查对最后一段最后一句的理解。

第二篇:

42. 答案:C

本题是细节题,考查对第一段第三句和第四句的理解:there were plenty of sellers but no buyers. Today the reverse is true.

43. 答案:A

本题是细节题,考查对第二段第一句和第二句的理解:It should follow that buyers will snap up anything. But that is not quite the case.

44. 答案:A

本题是细节题,考查对第三段第一句的理解:Van Dyck's oval shaped self portrait,..., had been in the same family for almost 300 years.

45. 答案:D

本题是细节题,考查对第二段第四句的理解。本题答题可以用排除法,只有选项 D 最接近原文中所提到的 a rare Raphael drawing。

46. 答案:C

本题是推理题,考查对第五段第一句的理解:拍卖行对此画作的估价在 1 200 万～1 600 万英镑之间,最后几乎以 3 倍的价格成交,自然是 Christie 拍卖行始料不及的。

47. 答案:B

本题是细节题,考查最后一段最后两句的意思。

第三篇:

48. 答案:C

本题是细节题,考查对第一段最后一句的理解:a charter public school where elementary students of every ethnicity study subjects in Mandarin。

49. 答案:D

本题是推理题,考查对第二段最后一句的理解:with the expectation of proficiency in both. 这里的 both 指的是英语和汉语这两种语言。

50. 答案:B

本题是推理题,考查对第三段最后一句的理解:American parents are expressive of their opinions.

51. 答案:A

本题是细节题,考查对第四段第三句的理解:immersion programs can provide cognitive benefits, including more flexible, creative thinking.

52. 答案:C

本题是推理题,考查对第四段最后一句的理解,考点在 proudly 一词上。

53. 答案:D

本题是推理题,考查对最后一段第二句和第三句话的理解:If Yinghua can make Mandarin a success in Minnesota, so can they.

第四篇:

54. 答案:A

本题是指代题,考查对第一段第五句中"that"(妇女不用在追求事业和养育孩子之间权衡挣扎)的理解。

55. 答案:C

本题是词汇题,考查对第一段最后一句中"boomerang"(飞去来器)的比喻意义的理解。

56. 答案:B

　　本题是主旨大意题,考点为对第四段的大意理解。

57. 答案:D

　　本题是细节题,考查对第四段最后两句的理解:你给你的兄弟姐妹打电话,希望他们伸出援手。从前的对手(指兄弟姐妹)又开始剑拔弩张。

58. 答案:D

　　本题是推断题,考查对第五段第一句和第二句的理解。

59. 答案:C

　　本题是推断题,考查对最后一段第三句和第四句的理解。

第五篇:

60. 答案:B

　　本题为细节题,考查对第一段第一句的理解:a person used to getting her own way。

61. 答案:A

　　本题是推断题,考点是对第三段第二句的理解:offering a child an escape from a life of misery。

62. 答案:A

　　本题是细节题,考查对第三段第三句的理解:他的生父将他交给孤儿院抚养。

63. 答案:C

　　本题是推断题,考查第五段第二句的理解:to adopt a healthy and young orphan, usually a small boy。

64. 答案:D

　　本题是推理题,考查对第六段最后一句的理解。

65. 答案:B

　　本题是细节题,考点在最后一段的第二句和第三句。

第二小节　阅读理解 B

第一篇:

66. 答案:D

　　本题的答题关键是把握空格前一句中提到的"the safety of elevators in Japan came under question"(日本的电梯安全受到了质疑),与选项 D 中的"elevators are not infallible"相呼应。

67. 答案:E

　　本题的突破口是内容衔接。空格的前一句提到"problems",因此顺其自然,空格中应围绕问题是什么或如何解决问题。

68. 答案:C

　　本题的答题关键是把握空格上文的内容:2006 年 6 月 14 日的电梯事故原因至今不详。选项 C 中解释了这其中的部分隐情:从 2005 年起,电梯的维护不再是 Schindler 公司,而是一家日本的公司。

69. 答案:F

本题所在的第五段中讲到了其他一些电梯生产厂家的情况，与选项 F 是总分的逻辑关系。

70. 答案：B

本题所在的最后一段讲到了在香港发生的类似电梯事故。选项中只有 B 提到了香港。

第二篇：

71. 答案：C

本题的答题关键是理解选项 C 中 That 指代的是前一句中的内容：没有能力聘请临时保姆的父母别无选择，只能自己离职（以便照看放假在家的孩子）。

72. 答案：B

本题的答题要点是选项 B 中提到的"一般情况下，老师们往往受批评"，这一内容与下文中"angry demands made for school staff"呼应。

73. 答案：A

本题的答题关键是理解前一句中提到的、我们给孩子的教育理念：事情不顺利的时候，你应该在家里歇着。选项 B 中讲到的是这种教育的结果。

74. 答案：F

本题的答题要点是把握空格的下文：回顾了今昔教学环境的变化给老师们带来的不便。选项 F 中"nostalgia"一词是突破口。

75. 答案：E

本题的突破口是空格前一句中提到的"grit"，选项 E 中"some sand"与之呼应。

第四部分　翻　译

1) **参考译文：**

因此，一个勇敢的人会面对危险而不逃跑；而是否把一个逃避危险的人称为勇敢，我们会迟疑不决。

解析：

该句理解上的重点有二：一是"be disposed to"；二是"characterize someone as something"。它们的意思分别是"愿意做某事"和"把某人描述成……"。此外，还请注意原文中 characterize 的宾语 someone who runs away from danger 由于过长而后置倒装的现象。

2) **参考译文：**

所以，有时候我们会发现，在美德与具体的行为倾向之间并非存在完美的吻合。

解析：

理解该句的关键是"fit"，此处意为：If there is a fit between two things, they are similar to each other or are suitable for each other. 例如：We must be sure that there's a fit between the needs of the children and the education they receive. （我们必须要确保孩子的需要和他们所受的教育是相互吻合的。）所以原文中的"perfect fit"的意思为"完美的吻合"。

3) **参考译文：**

(说)美德是技能，并非简单地指像我们的业务能力一样使我们能熟练地完成某项任务,而是指那种让我们在生活中普遍受用的技能。

解析:
理解该句的重点是 not... rather...,意为"不是……而是……"。另外,第一个分句中的插入语(like technical competence)和修饰 skills 的定语从句也是造成阅读理解难度的因素。

4) **参考译文:**
在施行一种美德时,我们所遇到的大部分困难可能恰恰因为我们想要得到什么而起,因为我们自己有种种自相矛盾的意愿。

解析:
翻译该句时,请注意"precisely"一词的准确意思,此处不再是"精确的,准确的"的意思,而是 used to emphasize that a particular thing is completely true or correct,意为"恰恰,正好"。

5) **参考译文:**
因此,美德不仅是习惯,而且还涉及意志,这是技能所不能及的。

解析:
该句的理解重点是"engage"一词,此处的意思是"运用,利用"。

第五部分 写 作

题目解析:
这是一道哲学思辨题。由于需要进行一番抽象的思辨论证,考生的逻辑思维过程要清晰,分析要中肯。正如题目中所要求的,同时也需辅以具体的例证。事实上,写作这个题目本就离不开对具体例子的分析,因为这里讨论的是"历史",而历史总是由过去的一些具体事例所组成。历史是否总是在重复?观点可以见仁见智,关键是如何来证明观点。哲学思辨类题目,一般要求考生平时有较为广博的知识积累,否则会有"巧妇难为无米之炊"之感。在写作的结构方面,文章需要构思明晰,布局合理,论点明确,论述充分。在语言方面,注意句式变化、表达的多样化,尤其要求准确地运用逻辑关联词来连接段落和句子。

范文:

I agree that history repeats itself. Lots of examples in the history can justify this argument, among which I will only choose a few here.

The past is not just ancient incidents that sit quietly in a textbook. Our history is a living part of ourselves. Careful study of the past can help us understand that our present situations are similar to our past, for history is a continuous process. Although from a microscopic perspective, human society is so complicated that it seems impossible to repeat the past. It is undeniable that during different historical stages, people's conditions of material life, social mores, and customs, vary a lot. However, if we examine human history from a macroscopic perspective, we can find that human history tends to come in cycles, often problems and issues return that share striking similarities with events in the past. Indeed many of today's problems may have manifested themselves in some similar ways in the past. Take ancient Chinese history as an example. Every dynasty in the history has undergone a process of starting from birth, flourishing and then declining. Each old dynasty was then overthrown and replaced by a new one, which has been shown clearly in Tang, Song, Yuan, Ming and Qing Dynasties.

Why did this happen? In view of Marx's Historical Materialism, history is created by people, and the economical basis determines the superstructure of a society. If we analyze the economical basis of each dynasty, we will find the reasons behind these vicissitudes. Usually at the beginning of a new dynasty, the rulers would organize the country reasonably to make people relax from the past tumults, and the society gradually developed into a prosperous period. Then in this prosperous society, some people became much richer and they bought more lands to hire more people to work as farmers. As more landlords exploited the farmers' labor, the gap between the rich and the poor was widened and scaled to such a limit that the poor felt living was more miserable than death. Hence the uprising took place, making the current dynasty coming to an end. A new dynasty then appeared in the ruins of the old one, repeating the same process.

Therefore, history does repeat itself, although this repetition is not a simple one. Understanding the past is a crucial way to solve the problems of the present and the future. (398 words)

中国科学院大学
博士研究生入学考试
英语试题

(2012年10月)

考生须知：

一、本试卷由试卷一（PAPER ONE）和试卷二（PAPER TWO）两部分组成。试卷一为客观题，答卷使用标准化机读答题纸；试卷二为主观题，答卷使用非机读答题纸。

二、请考生一律用 HB 或 2B 铅笔填涂标准化机读答题纸，画线不得过细或过短。修改时请用橡皮擦拭干净。若因填涂不符合要求而导致计算机无法识别，责任由考生自负。请保持机读答题纸清洁、无折皱。答题纸切忌折叠。

三、全部考试时间总计 180 分钟，满分为 100 分。时间及分值分布如下：

试卷一：

Ⅰ 词汇	15 分钟	10 分
Ⅱ 完形填空	15 分钟	15 分
Ⅲ 阅读理解	80 分钟	40 分
小计	110 分钟	65 分

试卷二：

Ⅳ 英译汉	30 分钟	15 分
Ⅴ 写作	40 分钟	20 分
小计	70 分钟	35 分

UNIVERSITY OF CHINESE ACADEMY OF SCIENCES ENGLISH ENTRANCE EXAMINATION FOR PH. D PROGRAM

October 2012

PAPER ONE

PART I VOCABULARY (15 minutes, 10 points, 0.5 point each)

Directions: *Choose the word or expression below each sentence that best completes the statement, and mark the corresponding letter of your choice with a single bar across the square bracket on your Machine-scoring Answer Sheet.*

1. John made _____ keys for the house: one for his wife and one for himself.
   A. facilitated   B. sophisticated   C. duplicate   D. intricate
2. It's difficult to be great without being _____: a doctor should never belittle a patient's concerns, regardless of how trivial they may seem to the doctor.
   A. pathetic   B. compassionate   C. fussy   D. sentimental
3. Marriage is based upon the complete willingness of the two parties. Neither party shall use _____ and no third party is allowed to interfere.
   A. collision   B. compensation   C. compulsion   D. collaboration
4. They would be _____ buying a product if it had not been tested on animals.
   A. deterred from   B. derived from   C. dismissed from   D. deserted from
5. As long as students can form a sound personality and _____ future well-being, the university has served its purpose.
   A. persevere in   B. convert into   C. live through   D. strive for
6. This is a _____ misconception in many people's minds — that love like merchandise can be "stolen."
   A. populated   B. prevalent   C. plagued   D. pretentious
7. Language may be _____ of as a process which arises from social interaction.
   A. comprised   B. conceived   C. disposed   D. deprived
8. Some companies are making _____ efforts to increase the proportion of women at all levels of employment.

A. solitary   B. statistical   C. susceptible   D. strenuous

9. _____, Mr. Hall admits that he pushed too hard, and ultimately his efforts failed.
   A. In retrospect   B. In due course   C. In vain   D. In essence

10. The final _____ cry comes when he complains about her selling their story to a newspaper; she was endangering his future and freedom.
    A. patient   B. patriotic   C. pathetic   D. prominent

11. When a failing plant began to _____, she believed it was her good work that somehow brought about good results.
    A. perish   B. shoot   C. wither   D. thrive

12. As rumor is ungrounded, it can't spread _____; a person is speechless when justice is not on his side.
    A. by and large   B. far and wide
    C. back and forth   D. hot and cold

13. Japanese firms in the late 1980s used shady accounting practices to _____ financial problems.
    A. conclude   B. compromise   C. conceal   D. contaminate

14. Most earthquakes are in remote areas; but every now and then a quake may _____ volcanic eruptions or drown the coastlines with tsunamis, death-dealing tidal waves.
    A. yield   B. trigger   C. transmit   D. evolve

15. However, very interesting dynamics regarding the competition and market structure are _____.
    A. seeing the light   B. shedding light
    C. bringing to light   D. coming to light

16. The politicians also _____ a mixture of tactics in a campaign to defend the Prime Minister.
    A. employed   B. mobilized
    C. endeavored   D. experienced

17. Cancers are described as being more or less _____ in proportion to their more or less rapidly growing and being invasive.
    A. mischievous   B. miscellaneous   C. malicious   D. malignant

18. Some manufacturers have tried to partially _____ the pain to buyers through straightforward price increases.
    A. put out   B. hold up   C. pass on   D. hand over

19. The company has had a lot of problems in the past, but it has always managed to _____.
    A. turn over   B. hold up   C. set up   D. bounce back

20. Public interest in and support for film festivals have grown throughout the US, giving new filmmakers broad _____.
    A. exposure   B. horizon   C. reputation   D. revelation

PART II CLOZE TEST (15 minutes, 15 points)

Directions: *For each blank in the following passage, choose the best answer from the four choices given below. Mark the corresponding letter of your choice with a single bar across the square bracket on your Machine-scoring Answer Sheet.*

Kevin Davies sent a sample of his saliva to a genetic testing laboratory in Iceland to learn about his health risks. When he received his results, Mr. Davies learned that, __21__ his genetic makeup, he had an above-average risk of __22__ prostate cancer.

Out of __23__, he checked back three months later and found that the company, called deCODE, had changed its assessment: His risk was now __24__ average.

DeCODE had recalculated its algorithm, based on new data. Davies, who is himself a geneticist by training, wasn't too __25__ by this about-face: "The information that these companies can give you can change and evolve __26__ time," he says.

That isn't the only way today's genetic tests offer __27__ conclusions. According to a US government study, results often vary __28__ among genetic-testing companies, largely because __29__ has its own way of choosing and analyzing data.

When the project to __30__ human DNA was finally completed in 2003, many predicted a revolution. Drugs could be chosen to match individual patients with maximum therapeutic effect and minimum side effects, the __31__ of so-called personalized medicine.

__32__ a summer downpour of troubling stumbles for genetic-testing companies and programs shows just how long and twisting the road can be __33__ advances in basic scientific research and their application.

It also has __34__ the question of how medicine will be practiced in an era __35__ anyone can research ailments and treatments on the Internet, sometimes becoming more familiar with new therapies and tests than their physicians.

21. A. despite   B. based on   C. in line with   D. in contrast to
22. A. contracting   B. affecting   C. intervening   D. associating
23. A. excitement   B. pleasure   C. curiosity   D. irritation
24. A. above   B. below   C. on   D. off
25. A. satisfied   B. captivated   C. encouraged   D. surprised
26. A. on   B. in   C. over   D. by
27. A. slippery   B. positive   C. complicated   D. convincing
28. A. gradually   B. intensely   C. highly   D. widely
29. A. that   B. each   C. it   D. such
30. A. remove   B. transplant   C. calculate   D. map
31. A. advent   B. censorship   C. cultivation   D. methodology

32. A. But   B. For   C. Thus   D. Though
33. A. at   B. with   C. between   D. on
34. A. enlightened B. spotlighted C. provoked   D. modified
35. A. that   B. which   C. where   D. when

PART III READING COMPREHENSION

Section A (60 minutes, 30 points)

Directions: *Below each of the following passages you will find some questions or incomplete statements. Each question or statement is followed by four choices marked A, B, C, and D. Read each passage carefully, and then select the choice that best answers the question or completes the statement. Mark the letter of your choice with a single bar across the square bracket on your Machine-scoring Answer Sheet.*

Passage One

The Super Bowl and the Oscars are the moon and the sun of American communal rituals. Together, more Americans watch them than attend church or vote in presidential elections.

Like it or not, they are America's preeminent means of announcing itself to the world; we can share our ideals with hundreds of millions of our friends (and enemies) around the planet.

Of the two events, one emphasizes the spirit of collective effort, by gathering anonymous men in identical uniforms to sacrifice themselves for the shared ideals of the tribe. The other glorifies the exceptional individual, who is celebrated for the very beauty and talent that sets him or her apart from lesser members of the species. Virtually anywhere there is a television — in Afghanistan, in Uruguay — these grand pageants are watched.

The Super Bowl offers us a model of the kind of moral clarity that can be elusive on the playing fields of our lives. Its scores are settled on neutral territory, and its teams are governed by inflexible rules. There is little room for favoritism or sentimentality or emotional nuance. Football knows right from wrong. The Super Bowl shows us a world we all can agree on — one in which, far removed from the messiness of everyday life, strength and skill and practical intelligence prevail. Its champions earn their trip to Disneyland, because they prove themselves to be rulers of a magical kingdom.

The Oscars, on the other hand, restore us to the commotion of the social world. They allow charm, money, fame and influence to matter. Sex and youth count above all, which is why, to the Oscars' disgrace, women over 40 are rarely on display. Like Greek gods, the stars of the show are magnifications of the best and worst in all of us. No matter that they arrive bedecked with jewels or with a supermodel on their arm or with a complexion whose glow is suspiciously youthful, at the Oscars they are stripped to their most vulnerable selves, utterly at the mercy of the unpredictable. The Oscars give us unfiltered human spectacle, in which one is either called to the stage to meet with approval or forced to sit and contend with feelings of neglect and disappointment.

36. The author holds that the Super Bowl and the Oscars are _____ .
    A. two key events that draw most of the world's attention to America
    B. the moon and the sun to Americans as well as to the rest of the world
    C. the rituals that are much more important than presidential elections
    D. two important occasions for the realization of American dreams
37. The Super Bowl and the Oscars are similar in _____ .
    A. giving recognition of many personal sacrifices
    B. conferring an honor on certain achievements
    C. encouraging an endeavor for national glory
    D. placing a high priority on individual talent
38. The kind of moral clarity showed in the Super Bowl most probably refers to a sense of _____ .
    A. fair play   B. social responsibility
    C. self-discipline   D. collective identity
39. According to the author, what we all agree on about the world shown by the Super Bowl is _____ .
    A. the possibility that everyone can win   B. the types of award to the champions
    C. the ways of showing one's strength   D. the criteria for judging success
40. The author emphasizes that the stars at the Oscars are _____ .
    A. a symbol of human dignity   B. images of Greek gods
    C. a mirror of ourselves   D. ideals of social elite
41. According to the author, the Oscars offer us a human scene that shows a contrast between _____ .
    A. trust and suspicion   B. justice and injustice
    C. wealth and poverty   D. delight and dismay

Passage Two

More than 50 years ago, the psychologist Carl Rogers suggested that simply loving our children wasn't enough. We have to love them unconditionally — for who they are, not for what they do.

As a father, I know this is a tall order, but it becomes even more challenging now that so much of the advice we are given amounts to exactly the opposite. In effect, we're given tips in conditional parenting, which comes in two flavors: turn up the affection when they're good, withhold affection when they're not.

Conditional parenting isn't limited to old-school authoritarians. Some people who wouldn't dream of spanking choose instead to discipline their young children by forcibly isolating them, a tactic we call "time out." Conversely, "positive reinforcement" teaches children that they are loved only when they do whatever we decide is a "good job." The primary message of all types of conditional parenting is that children must earn a parent's love.

The child psychologist Bruno Bettelheim, who readily acknowledged that the version of negative conditional parenting known as time-out can cause "deep feelings of anxiety," nevertheless endorsed it for that very reason. "When our words are not enough," he said, "the threat of the withdrawal of our love and affection is the only sound method to impress on him that he had better conform to our request."

But research suggests that love withdrawal isn't particularly effective at getting compliance, much less at promoting moral development. Even if we did succeed in making children obey us, is obedience worth the possible long-term psychological harm? Should parental love be used as a tool for controlling children?

Albert Bandura, the father of the branch of psychology known as social learning theory, declared that unconditional love "would make children directionless and quite unlovable" — an assertion entirely unsupported by empirical studies. The idea that children accepted for who they are would lack direction or appeal is most informative for what it tells us about the dark view of human nature held by those who issue such warnings.

In practice, unconditional acceptance should be accompanied by actively imagining how things look from the child's point of view. Most of us would protest that of course we love our children without any strings attached. But what counts is how things look from the perspective of the children — whether they feel just as loved when they mess up or fall short.

42. The author thinks what Carl Rogers suggested is _____.
    A. hard to practice today
    B. unlikely to work
    C. harmful to children
    D. unpopular among parents
43. In conditional parenting, when children don't behave themselves, parents will _____.
    A. warn them of the consequences
    B. give them a physical punishment
    C. hold back their love of them
    D. stress their good behavior
44. Bettelheim believes that time-out _____.
    A. is a useful means in some cases
    B. causes psychological disorder
    C. is an unconditional parenting style
    D. causes children's disobedience
45. According to research, love withdrawal would _____.
    A. help children build a sense of independence
    B. improve a long-term parent-child relation
    C. do little for fostering children's ethical values
    D. cause children to develop an aggressive tendency
46. In Albert Bandura's opinion, children accepted for who they are would _____.
    A. disrespect their parents
    B. lack a sense of responsibility
    C. be inconsiderate of others
    D. be disliked by others
47. According to the passage, in practicing unconditional acceptance it is essential for parents to _____.
    A. show respect for children's ideas
    B. set a moral example for children
    C. consider environmental factors
    D. watch for children's frustrations

Passage Three

It's a Monday night at MIT, just a few weeks before final exams. Grad students Tegin Teich and Todd Schenk could be studying or relaxing. Instead, they're hustling through a maze of basement hallways in search of notorious energy hogs: vending machines. The average soda dispenser consumes 3,500 kilowatts a year — more than four times the juice for a home refrigerator. To conserve electricity, MIT's administrators have been installing devices called Vending Misers, which use motion detectors to turn off a machine's lights and cooling systems when people aren't nearby, cutting energy consumption by 50%. Trouble is, MIT isn't exactly sure where all its vending machines are located, or which ones already have the devices installed. So tonight it's enlisted the MIT Energy Club to help figure it out.

It's just one event on the club's very busy calendar. With 750 students, the four-year-old group is MIT's fastest-growing extracurricular organization. Many of its members aim to build careers in "green tech" fields, and club events offer a chance to network and learn about the challenges and opportunities in emerging energy fields. In recent weeks, members had lunch with the U.S. Energy Secretary and toured a nuclear reactor. Others discussed national biofuel policy as part of a biweekly discussion held over beer and pizza at a local pub. Club members say the group exposes them to people and ideas from other disciplines; as a result, M.B.A. types become better versed in the science of climate change, while science geeks get comfortable reading business plans and understanding concepts like return on investment. In contrast to left-leaning campus environmentalists of a decade ago, who might have joined Greenpeace after school, "most of our members really believe in the power of the tools of capitalism to solve the problem," says founder Dave Danielson, who earned a Ph.D. in material sciences last fall.

Down in the basement at MIT, Teich and Schenk have found a group of eight vending machines. Four of them are hooked up to Vending Misers, but only one is functioning. "This is like wiring a stereo," Schenk says, untangling wires to make the devices work. Teich climbs on top of a different machine to pick off layers of masking tape left over from a paint job that had rendered the gizmo's sensor inoperable. "We probably just saved MIT $100 in reduced electricity bills," Teich says. It won't save the planet — but every bit counts.

48. Tegin Teich and Todd Schenk are _____.
    A. fourth-year students at MIT
    B. members of the MIT Energy Club
    C. good at machine maintenance
    D. environmental engineering majors

49. What does the passage say about Vending Misers?
    A. They failed to function well as expected.
    B. They were designed by the MIT Energy Club.
    C. They can detect the presence of people.

D. They keep soda dispensers working consistently.

50. Many members join the club's events for _____.
   A. career preparations
   B. leisure enjoyments
   C. answering Greenpeace's call
   D. opposing nuclear energy

51. The club has enabled its members to _____.
   A. help the government with decision-making
   B. become brave enough to challenge the authorities
   C. decide to invest in biofuel in the future
   D. acquire much interdisciplinary knowledge

52. It is implied that Greenpeace _____.
   A. suffered some business losses
   B. prefers to recruit science students
   C. is suspicious of capitalism
   D. was founded by Dave Danielson

53. What does the last paragraph imply about "a paint job"?
   A. It caused a problem to the Vending Miser.
   B. It was needed for repairing the Vending Miser.
   C. It improved the Vending Miser's efficiency.
   D. It was part of what the Vending Miser did.

Passage Four

No doll outshines Barbie's celebrity. If all the Barbies and her family members — Skipper, Francie and the rest — sold since 1959 were placed head to toe, they would circle the Earth more than seven times. And sales boomed in 2009, when the fashion doll celebrated her 50th birthday on March 9th.

Barbie starred at an array of global events honouring her milestone, including a glamorous affair at New York's Fashion Week in February. On her birthday, Mattel, the company that makes her, launched a souvenir doll honouring the original Barbie in her black-and-white striped swimsuit and perfect ponytail. It was available for purchase only that one day. Another Golden Anniversary doll targets collectors. Barbie fans planned hundreds of events, including the National Barbie Doll Collectors Convention in Washington, D.C., which was sold out.

When Ruth Handler created Barbie in 1959, a post-war culture and economy thrived but girls still played with baby dolls. These toys limited the imagination; so Handler introduced Barbie the Teen-Age Fashion Model, named after her daughter, Barbara. Jackie Kennedy soon walked onto the world stage and Barbie already had a wardrobe fit for a first lady. Barbie bestowed on girls the opportunity to dream beyond suburbia, even if Ken (Barbie's fictional boyfriend) at times tagged along.

Barbie entranced Europe in 1961 and now sells in 150 countries. Every second three Barbies are sold around the world. Her careers are myriad — model, astronaut, Olympic swimmer, palaeontologist and rock star, along with 100 others, including president. Like any political candidate, controversy hit Barbie in 1992 when Teen Talk Barbie said "Math class is tough" and girls' education became a national issue. She has been banned (in Saudi Arabia), tortured (by pre-teen girls, according to researchers at the University of Bath's School of Management) and fattened (in 1997).

Feminists continue to batter Barbie, claiming that her beauty and curves treat women as objects. But others see her as a pioneer trendsetter, crashing the glass ceiling long before Hillary Clinton cracked it.

High-tech entertainment now attracts girls and Barbie also faces fierce competition from various copycats including the more fashionable, but less charming, Bratz dolls. The Bratz suffered a setback in 2008. Mattel sued MGA Entertainment, Bratz's producer, for copyright infringement. A judge awarded Mattel $100m in damages.

54. According to Paragraph One, Barbie _____.
   A. was born earlier than the dolls of any other brands
   B. has long been number one in the world of dolls
   C. has beaten other dolls in sales 7 times since 1959
   D. was once taken aboard a spaceship circling the earth

55. To celebrate Barbie's 50th birthday, _____.
   A. a Barbie fan club was set up in Washington, D. C.
   B. the original Barbie was displayed in New York
   C. fashion shows were held worldwide on March 9th
   D. Barbies based on its original design appeared on the market

56. Ruth Handler created Barbie in the hope that it would _____.
   A. dress as attractively as Jackie Kennedy did
   B. encourage girls to become fashion models
   C. help girls generate new ideas and wishes
   D. become her daughter's constant companion

57. We can infer from Paragraph 4 that Barbie used to _____.
   A. cause a debate in the U. S. about girls learning math
   B. act as a role model in more than 100 occupations
   C. face denial by the parents of many pre-teen girls
   D. become fatter to cater to the overweight girls

58. Feminists hate Barbie mostly because it symbolizes women's _____.
   A. material comforts   B. sexual attraction
   C. political power   D. multiple talents

59. According to the passage, MGA Entertainment _____.
   A. lost a fortune by losing a lawsuit
   B. sold a toy cat to compete with Barbie
   C. beat traditional Barbie with hi-tech
   D. filed a lawsuit against Mattel

Passage Five

As he has done frequently over the last 18 months, Andy Roost drove his blue diesel Peugeot 205 onto a farm, where signs pointed one way for "eggs" and another for "oil."

He unscrewed the gas cap and chatted casually as Colin Friedlos, the proprietor, poured three large jugs of used cooking oil — tinted green to indicate environmental benefit — into the Peugeot's gas tank.

Mr. Friedlos operates one of hundreds of small plants in Britain that are processing, and often selling to private motorists, used cooking oil, which can be poured directly into unmodified diesel cars, from Fords to Mercedes.

The global recession and the steep drop in oil prices have now killed many of those large refining ventures. But smaller, simpler ones like Mr. Friedlos's are moving in to fill the void with their direct-to-tank product, with a flood of offers of free oil from restaurants.

Used cooking oil has attracted growing attention in recent years as a cleaner, less expensive alternative to fossil fuels for vehicles. In many countries, including the United States, the oil is collected by companies and refined into a form of diesel. Some cities use it in specially modified municipal buses or vans. And the occasional environmentalist has experimented with individually filtering the oil and using it as fuel.

Peder Jensen, a transport specialist at the European Environment Agency, said that cooking oil fuel was "feasible" for diesel engines — Rudolf Diesel predicted that his engine, patented in the 1890s, would run on it — and that it was, "from an environmental point of view, a good idea, taking this waste and making it useful."

Others disagree. Stuart Johnson, manager of engineering and environment at Volkswagen of America, called putting raw vegetable oil in cars "a bad idea" and said, "We don't recommend it." The inconsistent quality of cooking oil fuel, he said, means that "it may contain impurities and it may be too viscous," especially for newer, more complex diesel engines with injection systems.

"None of that seems to stir concern in Mr. Nicholson, the Welsh entrepreneur." He said. "There is a lot of resistance," he said, "to putting something into your precious car that you brewed in the kitchen sink."

60. What is true about Andy Roost with respect to using cooking oil fuel for his diesel Peugeot?
   A. He's been relying on it.   B. He's just started to try it.
   C. He's keen on its green color.   D. He's curious about its effect.

61. Unlike those large refining ventures, Mr. Friedlos's plant _____.
   A. has been enjoying an economic revival   B. operates for protecting the environment
   C. produces its product at a very low cost   D. has switched to serve private motorists

62. As to the advantage of used cooking oil over fossil fuels, the former is _____.
   A. based on greater sources of raw material   B. more easily processed into a form of fuel
   C. purer so that it is better for diesel engines   D. used more widely in the world as car fuel

63. According to the passage, Rudolf Diesel was _____.
   A. an environmentalist   B. a car owner
   C. an engine designer   D. a car producer
64. Some people oppose the use of cooking oil fuel because it may _____.
   A. give little help to environmental protection
   B. pose a threat to some fossil fuel businesses
   C. do damage to some kinds of diesel engines
   D. contain things harmful to the user's health
65. Mr. Nicholson thinks that the negative opinions about the use of used cooking oil are _____.
   A. understandable   B. unimaginable   C. unreasonable   D. unacceptable

Section B (20 minutes, 10 points)

Directions: *In each of the following passages, five sentences have been removed from the original text. They are listed from A to F and put below the passage. Choose the most suitable sentence from the list to fill in each of the blanks (numbered 66 to 75). For each passage, there is one sentence that does not fit in any of the blanks. Mark your answers on your Machine-scoring Answer Sheet.*

Passage One

In a survey last year the bosses of small businesses overwhelmingly came out in favour of hard work and a strong character over formal qualifications. Two thirds rated character and attitude as very important, whereas only 3 per cent considered university degrees to be a real asset. __66__

Historically, it can be summarised like this: on the one hand the self-educated leaders of small businesses have viewed graduates as time-wasting and costly upstarts, while graduates have sneered at the provincial mindset and paltry pay of the non-corporate office.

But according to David Bishop, of the Federation of Small Businesses, it has got more to do with practical issues. "Because of their size, small businesses look for generalists with broader responsibilities rather than specialists," he says. "They are not like a major employer with hundreds of employees each assigned a specific role."

Take IT, for example. __67__

Certainly, there is resistance within the SME (small and medium-sized enterprises) community to employing graduates. The most frequently cited reasons reported by owner managers are: perceived high costs, worries about recruitment, retention and the graduate's commitment, and concern about the high risk of recruiting graduates who are seen as inexperienced and often too academic.

__68__ "Recruitment is a challenge in terms of competition and costs when you can't offer the package of an international bank, but graduates are valuable because they are on top of innovative research and development."

___69___ Afzal Akram, chairman of Business Link for London, says that small businesses are beginning to realise the potential employee resources found in universities.

"In today's business environment, people are the real differentiator, so getting the best is crucial. Tapping the graduate recruitment market allows small businesses to access candidates with excellent skills, training and education, who are hungry and motivated."

___70___ They undertake projects that benefit the host business, ranging from website design, marketing and accounting system implementation to product development.

A. It is difficult for small manufacturers to find a graduate who can deal with all the equipment across the business, but it is easy to find one with in-depth knowledge.
B. There is also a lack of awareness of what universities and graduates have to offer.
C. This data seemed to confirm a longstanding mistrust between small businesses and graduates.
D. Small businesses know that graduates offer them a great opportunity and want to see more graduates going into small firms in intern positions.
E. Nonetheless, Bishop says that more and more graduates are finding employment in small businesses.
F. They can bring fresh ideas and skills to a business, boosting performance and profitability.

Passage Two

Women could increase their retirement benefits by 30 per cent if they work as many years as men, expert says.

Latin American and Caribbean women could probably get a 30% higher payout if their retirement age were changed to equal men's retirement age, noted specialist Truman Packard of the World Bank during a recent presentation at IDB headquarters. His new analysis sheds a bit more light on the differences between men's and women's participation in Latin American pension systems.

Is leveling the retirement age for working men and women an equitable and efficient solution for society? ___71___

Traditionally, women have retired earlier than men, but they tend to live longer than their male counterparts. Thus, most women are in need of a pension guarantee. But few actually have one.

___72___ While most men are covered by self-financed or independent pensions, over half of women are covered only through survivor's benefits, due to the contribution of their husbands.

The results from Argentina tell the story of the two informal sectors of society that are outside of the social security system: one chooses not to contribute and is largely made up of men who were either self-employed, independent or employers; and the other is composed mostly of women who were employees of small firms and/or employed without a contract and benefits. ___73___

Additionally, more women than men fail to work the minimum number of years required to be eligible for the pension guarantee. ___74___

Throughout Latin America and the Caribbean there are significant behavioral differences between men and women in regard to contribution levels. ___75___

A. Many of these women would have liked to contribute to pension plans, but could not because their employment circumstances excluded them from participating, noted Packard.
B. Packard conducted a survey in 2000 in Santiago, Chile, showing that while some 30 percent of men who participate in the social security system never become eligible to receive the minimum government pension guarantee, as many as 50 percent of participating women do not.
C. Packard said his findings indicate that equalizing retirement ages for both genders is not only a worldwide trend, but a logical option.
D. Data from a 2003 survey of older adults (average age 60) in Argentina showed a striking difference in pension coverage between men and women.
E. Packard also suggested moving from the old pay-as-you-go public systems to multi-pillar model private systems based on contribution density.
F. Packard's study shows that contribution density — the ratio of contributing months to total months worked in the labor force — is lower for women than for men.

PAPER TWO

PART IV TRANSLATION (30 minutes, 15 points)

Directions: *Read the following text carefully and then translate the underlined segments into Chinese. Write your Chinese version in the proper space on your Answer Sheet.*

For a certain breed of consumers, the arrival of Apple's new generation iPad is an occasion of monomaniacal focus and intense anticipation. Visions of how the shiny new gadget will revolutionize their lives fill their heads. (1) They're willing to sacrifice hours waiting in line and hard-earned cash that they can hardly afford to spare, all to get their hands on Apple's hot new toy. Why is it that some consumers are constantly driven to possess the newest and hottest gadget?

The lure of the new applies to consumers with a particular personality style. Psychology researchers have shown that each of us has our own level of craving for new things. They call this "novelty-seeking," or the sexier alternative, "neophilia." (2) The curiosity motive, long known to cause both humans and non-humans to seek mental stimulation, exists to different degrees in all of us.

People with high degrees of novelty-seeking are drawn to new situations, experiences, and, of course, possessions. (3) They tend to make impulsive decisions, be disorganized, and are highly oriented toward seeking and getting rewards. Research also shows that novelty-seeking is associated to addictive disorders, including substance abuse.

(4) Generally speaking, people high in neophilia, are among those compelled to be on the lookout for the newest, highest-profile technological advances. They are first in line when the newest gadget shows up in stores. The "high" they experience while cradling their latest gadget is similar to

the rush of pleasure that occurs in the reward centers of the brain when any type of addiction is satisfied. (5) Techno-gadgets are particularly appealing because they themselves have addictive qualities. Unfortunately, the "high" will fade quickly as the brain adapts and seeks the next rewarding novelty.

PART V   WRITING (40 minutes, 20 points)

Directions: *Write an essay of no less than 200 words on the topic given below. Use the proper space on your Answer Sheet II.*

TOPIC

What is the true spirit of the Olympic Games? Please use examples to illustrate your points.

2012年10月试题精解

第一部分 词 汇

1. 答案:C
   本题考查形容词的语义,同时也是一道语境题。A 便利的;B 老于世故的,复杂的、精密的;C 复制的,完全一样的;D 错综复杂的。该句的大意为:约翰配了两把完全一样的家里钥匙:一把给他太太;另一把他自己留着。

2. 答案:B
   本题考查形容词的语义。A 引起怜悯的,可怜的;B 有同情心的;C 易激怒的,爱挑剔的;D 感情用事的。该句的大意为:伟大的人都具有同情心;医生绝不应该轻视病人所担心的事,不管他们担心的事儿在医生看来有多么的不重要。

3. 答案:C
   本题考查题干中两句话的逻辑关系和名词语义,是一道语境题。A 碰撞、互撞,冲突、抵触;B 补偿物,补偿金;C 强制,强制力;D 合作,协作。原文的大意为:婚姻建立在双方完全自愿的基础之上。任何一方都不应强迫对方,任何第三方也不得干涉。

4. 答案:A
   本题考查动词短语的语义和句子的逻辑关系。A 威慑住……不……,阻止……不……;B 从……中提取,从……中得到;C(从头脑中)去除,不再考虑;D 擅离(职守),开小差。该句的大意为:他们不会购买未进行动物实验的产品。

5. 答案:D
   本题考查动词短语的语义。A 坚持;B 转变,使皈依,兑换;C 经历过……,经受住……;D 为……而奋斗;争取;谋求。该句的大意为:只要学生们能够形成良好的性格,并能够为未来的美好生活而努力奋斗,那么他们的大学就起到了作用。

6. 答案:B
   本题考查句子的逻辑关系和形容词语义辨析,是一道语境题。A 人口密集的;B 流行的,盛行的,普遍的;C 令人痛苦的,令人烦恼的;D 矫饰的,做作的。该句的大意为:许多人都持有一种普遍的错误观点,认为爱情和商品一样会被"偷走"。

7. 答案:B
   本题考查动词的语义。A 由……构成,由……组成;B 认为;C 处理、处置,安排;D 夺去,剥夺。该句的大意为:语言可以被视为在社会交往中出现的一种过程。

8. 答案:D
   本题考查形容词与名词的搭配。A 单独的,独自的;B 统计的,统计学的;C 易受感动的,易受影响的;D 劲头十足的;紧张的,艰苦的;费劲的,费力的。该句的大意为:一些公司正在竭尽全力地提高女性在各个岗位上的受聘比例。

9. 答案:A

本题考查介词与名词构成的固定短语。A 回想起来,回顾往事;B 到时候,在今后适当的时候;C 徒然,白费力;D 本质上,实质上,基本上。该句的大意为:回想起来,霍尔先生承认他当时推得过猛,最终他的努力失败了。

10. 答案:C

本题考查形容词的形近词词义辨析。A 有耐心的,忍耐的,容忍的;B 爱国的;C 引起怜悯的,可怜的;D 突起的;突出的,杰出的。该句的大意为:当他抱怨她把他们俩的事情卖给了一家报纸,使得他的未来和自由陷入了困境时,听者发出了怜悯的一声长叹。

11. 答案:D

本题考查动词的语义,也是一道语境题。A 丧生,凋谢;B 射中;C 凋谢,枯萎;D 茁壮成长,茂盛生长。该句的大意为:濒临枯萎的植物重新茂盛生长时,她相信这是自己的努力得到了回报。

12. 答案:B

本题考查固定短语。A 大体上,总的说来,一般地说;B 到处,各处,广泛地;C 来回地,反复地;D(旅馆等的)冷热水;忽冷忽热。该句的大意为:无凭无据的谣言传不远,无情无义的人们难自圆。

13. 答案:C

本题考查动词的形近词辨析。A 推断出,推论出;B 通过互让解决(争执、分歧等),妥协;C 隐藏,掩盖,隐瞒;D 弄脏,污染。该句的大意为:20世纪80年代末期的一些日本公司运用隐蔽的会计手段来掩盖他们的财务问题。

14. 答案:B

本题考查动词与名词的搭配。A 出产,产生;B 扣扳机开(枪),触发;C 传送,输送,传递;D 使逐步形成,进化。该句的大意为:大多数地震都发生在偏僻的地区;但是时不时地,地震可能会激发火山爆发或以极其危险的海浪——海啸淹没海岸线。

15. 答案:D

本题考查与名词 light 有关的动词短语。A 明白过来,领悟,同意;B 使某事显得非常清楚,一般后接介词 on;C 揭露,暴露,揭示;D 显露,为大家所周知,出现。该句的大意为:但是,与竞争及市场结构相关的非常有趣的动态模型显现出来了。

16. 答案:A

本题考查动词与名词的搭配。A 雇用,利用、使用;B 动员,调动;C 努力,尽力尝试;D 经历,体验。该句的大意为:政客们同样调动了各种各样的策略来保护首相。

17. 答案:D

本题考查形容词的形近词辨析。A 恶作剧的,顽皮的;B 混杂的,各色各样混在一起的;C 恶意的,恶毒的;D 恶性的,致命的。该句的大意为:癌细胞生长的速度越快,侵略性越强,则癌细胞的致命性越大。

18. 答案:C

本题考查动词短语。A 伸出,拿出;B 举起,支撑;C 向前移动,把……传给另一个;D 交出,交付,让与。该句的大意为:一些生产商通过直接涨价的方式在一定程度上将痛苦传给了(或:转嫁给了)购买者。

19. 答案:D

本题考查动词短语和句子的转折关系,是一道语境题。A 移交,(使)翻转,仔细考虑;B 举起,支撑;C 建立、成立、创立,准备、安排;D 弹回,迅速恢复元气,(经济等的)复苏。该句的大意为:这个公司在过去确实有过许多问题,但是它早已试图东山再起。

20. 答案:A

本题考查动词的语义。A 暴露,公开露面;B 地平线;C 名气,名声;D 揭示,揭露,被揭示的真相。该句的大意为:在全美各地,公众涌现出对电影节的兴趣和支持,这给了新生的电影制片人很多崭露头角的机会。

第二部分 完形填空

本文主要阐述当前基因测试的不稳定性,以及基因测试研究所面临的种种困难。

21. 答案:B

本题考查介词/介词短语的语义辨析。A 尽管;B 在……基础上;C 与……一致,符合;D 相比之下。原文是说,凯文·戴维斯(Kevin Davies)将他的唾液样本送到冰岛一家基因检测实验室,以了解自己有无健康隐患。接到结果后戴维斯获悉,根据他的基因构成,他患前列腺癌的风险在平均水平之上。

22. 答案:A

本题考查动词的词义辨析。A 染上(恶习、疾病等);B (疾病)侵袭;C 介入,干预;D 使发生联系。本句是说,他患有(染上)前列腺癌这种疾病的风险高于平均水平。

23. 答案:C

本题考查名词的词义辨析。A 兴奋;B 享受;C 好奇;D 恼怒。本句意思是,出于好奇,他三个月后再次送检。

24. 答案:B

本题考查介词与名词的搭配以及上下文的理解。前文指出,第一次基因测试的分析报告显示,他得癌症的风险高于平均水平。三个月后,同一家实验室给出的分析报告和第一次不同。既然前次是高于风险,第二次与第一次不同,那么这次的结果应该是不高于平均水平,即 below average 或者 average。

25. 答案:D

本句考查过去分词转换来的形容词词义辨析和对上下文的语义理解。A 对……感到满意;B 被……吸引;C 被……鼓励;D 对……感到惊奇。本句讲的是 Kevin Davies 对于结果的大变脸并不感到太惊讶。

26. 答案:C

本句考查介词的用法。本句的意思是,这些基因公司所提供的测试结果会随着时间而发展和变化。over time 这个词组表示"随着时间的流逝",符合句意。

27. 答案:A

本句考查形容词的词义辨析和对文章上下文的理解。A 不可靠的;B 正面的;C 复杂的;D 令人信服的。由前文我们可以了解到,基因测试的结果会随着时间而发展变化,也就是不可靠。本句的大意是,当前基因测试的结果不可靠是比较常见的情况,并不仅仅体现在 Kevin Davies 的这两次基因测试报告的结果不同。

28. 答案:D

本题考查副词语义辨析以及对上下文的理解。A 慢慢地；B 强烈地；C 高度地；D 广泛地。这一句讲的是根据美国政府的一项研究报告,各个基因测试公司的测试结果往往迥然不同。

29. 答案：B

本题考查代词的指代。本句的意思是,各个基因测试公司的测试结果间存在广泛的差异主要是因为每一家公司都有自己选择数据和分析数据的方法。这里需要的代词表示"每一家公司",在这四个选项中,只有 B 选项符合句意。

30. 答案：D

本题考查动词与名词的搭配。A 脱掉；B 移植；C 计算；D 绘制。本句说的是对人类 DNA 的图谱绘制。

31. 答案：A

本题考查名词的词义辨析以及对上下文语义的理解。A 到来；B 审查制度；C 培植；D 方法。这句的意思是:可以根据病人的个体情况来选择用药,从而使治疗效果最大化而副作用最小化,这标志着所谓个性化医疗时代的来临。

32. 答案：A

本题考查连接词的使用及对上下文的理解。前文说,基因图谱的绘制使很多人以为个性化医疗时代即将来临。本句是对前一句的转折:但是基因检测公司和项目接二连三地碰到了让人头疼的失误。

33. 答案：C

本题考查介词的使用和对语篇上下文的理解。这句是说,由此看出,在基础科学研究与科研成果应用之间还有一条漫长而曲折的道路要走。本句考查重点 between... and...。

34. 答案：B

本题考查动词的词义辨析。A 启发；B 使突出醒目；C 激起,挑起；D 修饰,改变。本句说的是,在人人都能在互联网上研究小病和疗法,有时甚至比医生还要熟悉新疗法和新检测的时代,医生该如何行医这个问题已经成为公众注意的焦点。

35. 答案：D

本题是一道语法题,考查关系词的用法。A 和 B 是关系代词；C 和 D 是关系副词,分别表示地点和时间。该空白处需要的是一个时间关系副词。

第三部分 阅读理解
第一节 阅读理解 A

第一篇：

36. 答案：A

本题是细节事实题,考查对第一段最后一句话中"more Americans watch them"的理解。

37. 答案：B

本题是推理题,要求能够从第三段中归纳出超级杯和奥斯卡之间的相似之处——表彰体育或演艺方面的杰出成就。

38. 答案：A

本题是细节事实题,考查对第四段中第二句和第四句话的理解,关键点:...inflexible rules...,...knows right from wrong...。

39. 答案:D

本题是长句理解题,考点是第四段中的长句——第五句,关键点:...strength and skill and practical intelligence prevail...。"prevail"一词在这里是"获胜、占优势"的意思。

40. 答案:C

本题是推理题,考查对第五段第四句话的理解,关键点:...the stars of the show are magnifications of the best and worst in all of us...。

41. 答案:D

本题是长句理解题,考查对第五段最后一句话的理解,关键点:...either called to the stage to meet with approval or forced to sit and contend with feelings of neglect and disappointment...。

第二篇:

42. 答案:A

本题是推理题,从第二段的第一句话中我们得知这一要求现在变得更加具有挑战性(more challenging),由此可以推断出,其本身已经非常难以实现。另外,本题也考查了短语"a tall order"中"tall"的意思,意为"不可能的、过分的"。

43. 答案:C

本题是细节事实题,考查对第二段第二句话的理解,关键点在于理解冒号的作用。

44. 答案:A

本题是推理题,考查对第四段最后一句话的理解,关键点:...the only sound method...。

45. 答案:C

本题是长句理解题,考查对第五段第一句话的理解,关键点:...much less at promoting moral development...(更不用说在促进孩子的道德成长方面了)。

46. 答案:D

本题是长句理解题,考查对第六段第二句话的理解,关键点:...children accepted for who they are would lack direction or appeal...。

47. 答案:A

本题是推理题,考查对第七段第一句和第三句话的理解,关键点:...actively imagining how things look from the child's point of view...,...how things look from the perspective of the children...。

第三篇:

48. 答案:B

本题是推理题,第一段的最后一句话透露了这两位学生的身份:the MIT Energy Club。

49. 答案:C

本题是长句理解题,考查对第一段第五句话的理解,关键点是定语从句的理解。

50. 答案:A

本题是细节事实题,考查对第二段第三句话的理解,关键点:Many of its members aim to build careers in "green tech" fields...。

51. 答案:D

本题是长句理解题,考查对第二段第六句话的理解,关键点:...the group exposes them to people and ideas from other disciplines....。

52. 答案:C

本题是推理题,考查对第二段最后一句话的理解,原句大意为:和十几年前的左翼绿色和平组织的成员不同,麻省理工学院能源协会的成员们相信资本运作在解决环保问题方面可以发挥重要的作用。由此我们可以推断出,绿色和平组织的成员并不相信资本的力量。

53. 答案:A

本题是细节事实题,考查对第三段第四句话的理解,关键点:...a paint job that had rendered the gizmo's sensor inoperable。

第四篇:

54. 答案:B

本题是推理题,考查第一段第一句话的意思,这是一个双重否定句。同时,本题还考查了第一句话和第二句话之间的逻辑关系,第二句话中用所有芭比娃娃头脚相连的长度来强调第一句话中提到的"No doll outshines Barbie's celebrity",言下之意,芭比娃娃的销售量是其他玩家无法匹敌的。

55. 答案:D

本题是细节事实题,考查对第二段第二句话的理解,关键点:...honouring the original Barbie。

56. 答案:C

本题是推理题,考查对第三段第二句话的理解,关键点:These toys limited the imaginations...。

57. 答案:A

本题是推理题,考查对第四段第四句话的理解,关键点:...controversy hit Barbie when Teen Talk Barbie said "Math class is tough"...。

58. 答案:B

本题是细节事实题,考查对第五段第一句话的理解。

59. 答案:A

本题是推理题,考查对第六段第二句话、第三句话和第四句话的理解,从中可以推断出这场官司中谁赢谁输。

第五篇:

60. 答案:A

本题是推理题,考查对第一段第一句话的理解,关键点:...frequently over the last 18 months...。

61. 答案:C

本题是细节事实题,考查对第四段最后一句话的理解,关键点:...with a flood of offers of free oil from restaurants...。

62. 答案:B

本题是细节事实题,考查对第四段最后一句话的理解,关键点:...direct-to-tank product...。

63. 答案:C

本题是长句理解题,考查对第六段中连线号部分的理解,关键点:Rudolf Diesel predicted that his engine, patented in the 1890s...。

64. 答案:C

本题是细节事实题,考查对第七段最后一句话的理解。

65. 答案:A

本题是态度立场题,考查对第八段第一句话的理解,关键点:None of that seems to stir concern...。

第二节 阅读理解 B

第一篇:

66. 答案:C

本题的答题关键在于:选项 C 中的 this data 指代了空格的前一句提到的 2/3 和仅 3% 这两个数据。

67. 答案:A

本题的答题关键在于:理解第三段和第四段之间的逻辑关系,即第三段举例说明第四段中的观点。因此两段在内容上是一致的。

68. 答案:E

本题的上下文中都涉及了"recruit"一词,由此可见,本题中的内容应该与此紧密相关。

69. 答案:B

本题的答题关键是空格后一句中的"universities"一词。

70. 答案:F

本题的答题关键是把握最后一段的主要内容——高学历毕业生的优势。

第二篇:

71. 答案:C

本题的答题关键是了解空格的前一句是个问句,所以选项 C 中的 trend 对应了问句中的 solution。

72. 答案:D

本题的答题关键是理解空格的后一句的作用——具体地分析了男女在享受退休金的比例方面存在差距。

73. 答案:A

本题的答题关键在于了解选项 A 中"these women"的指代作用。

74. 答案:B

本题的答题关键在于把握空格的前一句中介绍的第六段的主要内容:更多的女性由于未能满足最低的工作年限而无法享受退休金的待遇,相比之下,男性的人数较少。

75. 答案:F

本题的答题关键是 contribution levels 和 contributing months。

第四部分 翻 译

(1) 译文：

他们愿意牺牲数小时排队，拿出他们辛苦赚来、花着心疼的钱，就为得到苹果公司的时髦新物件。

解析：

理解该句的关键在于找出 sacrifice 的两个宾语——hours and hard-earned cash；另一个难点是副词"all"，在文中相当于副词"completely"，意为"完全地，彻底地"。

(2) 译文：

我们早就知道，好奇动机使得人类和非人类寻求精神刺激，而这种动机不同程度地存在于我们所有人身上。

解析：

本句阅读的难点在于插入语切断了句子的主干和语流，分析该句的关键在于找出句子的谓语动词 exists；其次要知道 long known to cause both humans and non-humans to seek mental stimulation 是主语 The curiosity motive 的修饰语，而 to different degrees 和 in all of us 都是修饰 exists 的状语。

(3) 译文：

他们往往会做出冲动的决定、缺乏条理、高度渴望寻求和获得奖赏。

解析：

该句的理解重点是平行结构（A）make impulsive decisions，（B）be disorganized，（C）and are highly oriented toward seeking and getting rewards。而 A，B，C 这三点正是喜新癖者人群的特点。

(4) 译文：

通常来说，具有严重喜新癖的人（或称喜新癖者）不由自主地关注最新和最广受瞩目的技术进步，当最新的玩意出现在商店里，他们得首先拿到。

解析：

该句的难点是生词"neophilia"。在本文的第二段第三句话中可以找到该词的解释。建议考生在做英译汉时，先把原文通读一遍，学会利用上下文，从而能够充分而透彻地理解个别词句的含义。

(5) 译文：

科技玩意尤其具有吸引力，因为它们本身就具有让人上瘾的特质。可惜的是，随着大脑对其适应并寻找下一种令人满足的新东西，"快感"会迅速消退。

解析：

该句的理解重点是单词"high"。如果通读过全文，大概不会把它理解为高低的"高"，因为本段的第三句话对"high"做了解释，即"similar to the rush of pleasure"，意为"快感"。

第五部分　写　作

题目解析：

分析题目中的关键词 true spirit of the Olympic Games，发现 true spirit 应该比 spirit 有更深一层的含义。既然有"真正的"奥运精神，那么一般人通常误解的奥运精神是什么呢？不难想象，人们会注重比赛的胜负，但一味求胜并不是奥运会提倡的精神。首先，我们要对真正的奥运精神有所思考和认识。其次，对具体的奥运精神的表述，可能不止一种，在写作的时候要选择一种自己觉得最有说服力因而最能阐述清楚的。比如，奥运宪章里说的"相互了解、友谊、团结和公平竞争"的精神；或者奥林匹克原则里体现出来的参与精神："奥运会重在参与，而不是胜利，正如生活中最重要的不是取胜，而是奋斗本身。"选择好阐述的着眼点之后，再由所选的这一点引申开去，联系实际，以寻找这一精神在实际生活中的运用。另外，按题目要求，还要举例子来说明论点，注意例子的选取要具有说服力和代表性。

范文：

　　The true spirit of the Olympic Games, as far as I am concerned, is best expressed in the Olympic Creed: "The most important thing in the Olympic Games is not to win but to take part, just as the most important thing in life is not the triumph but the struggle. The essential thing is not to have conquered but to have fought well." This spirit has impelled athletes to constantly strive to become stronger. Moreover, the true spirit of the Olympic Games can inspire us to make never-ending efforts to improve ourselves in various competitions in our lives.

　　Thousands of athletes have participated in the Olympic Games, but obviously only a few can be winners. If our goal is only a medal, then we can get very little from the competition and are bound to miss the spirit of the Olympic Games. Olympic spirit is participation, while fame and fortune is less important. Take John Stephen Akhwari for example, who participated in marathon in the 1968 Mexico City Olympic Games. When he ran at 19 kilometers, he was unfortunately injured, but he finished the entire race with his strong will. Although he was the last one to complete the game, he became a real hero in the history of the Olympic Games.

　　For an athlete, to fight for a better record is their goal and profession. For us average people, to struggle for a better life is our destiny. We tend to think that triumph is our goal in life, but more often than not we have found that after one conquest there come more tasks and challenges. The endless challenges in life require perseverance and a spirit of Sisyphus. Every time after the rock falls back from the top of a mountain, we have to continue to roll it to the top again. Absurd as it seems, this is not a meaningless process, because we have grown mature and become wiser in this struggling process of life.

　　Remember, the most important thing in the Olympic Games is not to win but to take part, and the most important thing in life is not the triumph but the struggle. (360 words)

中国科学院大学
博士研究生入学考试
英语试题

(2013年3月)

考生须知：

一、本试卷由试卷一（PAPER ONE）和试卷二（PAPER TWO）两部分组成。试卷一为客观题，答卷使用标准化机读答题纸；试卷二为主观题，答卷使用非机读答题纸。

二、请考生一律用 HB 或 2B 铅笔填涂标准化机读答题纸，画线不得过细或过短。修改时请用橡皮擦拭干净。若因填涂不符合要求而导致计算机无法识别，责任由考生自负。请保持机读答题纸清洁、无折皱。答题纸切忌折叠。

三、全部考试时间总计180分钟，满分为100分。时间及分值分布如下：

试卷一：

	Ⅰ 词汇	15分钟	10分
	Ⅱ 完形填空	15分钟	15分
	Ⅲ 阅读理解	80分钟	40分
	小计	110分钟	65分

试卷二：

	Ⅳ 英译汉	30分钟	15分
	Ⅴ 写作	40分钟	20分
	小计	70分钟	35分

UNIVERSITY OF THE CHINESE ACADEMY OF SCIENCES ENGLISH ENTRANCE EXAMINATION FOR PH. D PROGRAM

March 2013

PAPER ONE

PART I VOCABULARY (15 minutes, 10 points, 0.5 point each)

Directions: *Choose the word or expression below each sentence that best completes the statement, and mark the corresponding letter of your choice with a single bar across the square bracket on your Machine-scoring Answer Sheet.*

1. Between 1981 and 1987, the number of permanent jobs had increased by only 1,000, although training has been substantially _____ by the corporation.
   A. boosted　　　B. curtailed　　　C. plunged　　　D. expended
2. It is a touching scene that every parent can immediately _____ because they have gone through the same ritual with their own children.
   A. come through　　　　　　B. identify with
   C. take up　　　　　　　　　D. refer to
3. In ancient mythology there were no impassable _____ separating the divine from the human beings.
   A. polarity　　　B. split　　　C. gulf　　　D. void
4. Guarantees and warranties tell buyers the repairs for which a manufacturer is _____ .
   A. qualified　　　B. agreeable　　　C. compatible　　　D. liable
5. The oil spill had a _____ effect on sea birds and other wildlife.
   A. reluctant　　　B. mischievous　　　C. devastating　　　D. malignant
6. A friend is, _____, a second self.
   A. as it is　　　B. as it were　　　C. as well as　　　D. as though
7. He leaned out of an upstairs window and felt a current of warm air _____ from the street.
   A. exalting　　　B. ascending　　　C. swaying　　　D. fluctuating
8. In a market economy, it is impractical to _____ big banks to reduce the qualification to provide financial support for small and medium-sized enterprises.

  A. take on   B. bear on   C. hold on   D. count on

9. The author _____ us as consistently fair and accurate about the issues.
  A. dismissed   B. agitated   C. struck   D. seized

10. The new system is similar to the old one _____ there is still a strong central government.
  A. now that   B. so that   C. in case that   D. in that

11. In the final analysis, it is our _____ of death which decides our answers to all the questions that life puts to us.
  A. conception   B. deception   C. reception   D. presentation

12. The great tragedy of life is not that men _____, but that they cease to love.
  A. terminate   B. expire   C. perish   D. wither

13. His doctor has told him he mustn't drink, but he still has the occasional brandy _____.
  A. on the spot   B. on the sly   C. in nature   D. in short

14. In some African countries, the cost of treating an AIDS patient may _____ his or her entire annual income.
  A. exploit   B. expel   C. expire   D. exceed

15. The current _____ with exam results is actually harming children's education.
  A. intervention   B. manipulation   C. obsession   D. domination

16. Sometimes certain families adhered _____ the same religious beliefs for several generations.
  A. to   B. for   C. after   D. with

17. He knew that the area's rich plant life had been severely _____ by the huge herds of cows grazing the land.
  A. depleted   B. decomposed   C. corrupted   D. corroded

18. The long wait for news of my exam results has already set my nerves _____.
  A. on fire   B. on edge   C. on earth   D. on impulse

19. A solution must be found that doesn't _____ too many people in this group, otherwise it cannot work.
  A. arouse   B. offend   C. spur   D. violate

20. The Federal Government _____ farmers by buying their surplus crops at prices above the market value.
  A. pirates   B. mediates   C. supplements   D. subsidizes

PART II   CLOZE TEST (15 minutes, 15 points)

Directions: *For each blank in the following passage, choose the best answer from the four choices given below. Mark the corresponding letter of your choice with a single bar across the square bracket on your Machine-scoring Answer Sheet.*

  Parents who believe that playing video games is less harmful to their kids' attention spans than watching TV may want to reconsider. Some researchers __21__ more than 1,300 children in different grades for a year. They asked both the kids and their parents to estimate how many hours per week the kids spent watching TV and playing video games, and they __22__ the children's attention spans by __23__ their schoolteachers. __24__ studies have examined the effect of TV or video games on attention problems, but not both. By looking at video-game use __25__ TV watching, these scientists were able to show for the first time that the two activities have a similar relationship __26__ attention problems.

Shawn Green, a psychologist at the University of Minnesota, points out that the study doesn't distinguish between the type of __27__ required to excel at a video game and that required to excel in school.

"A child who is capable of playing a video game for hours __28__ obviously does not have a __29__ problem with paying attention," says Green. "__30__ are they able to pay attention to a game but not in school? What expectancies have the games set up that aren't being delivered in a school __31__?" Modern TV shows are so exciting and fast paced that they make reading and schoolwork seem __32__ by comparison, and the same may be true __33__ video games, the study notes.

"We weren't able to break the games down by educational versus non-educational __34__ nonviolent versus violent," says Swing, __35__ that the impact that different types of games may have on attention is a ripe area for future research.

21.	A. followed	B. trained	C. questioned	D. challenged
22.	A. provoked	B. speculated	C. formulated	D. assessed
23.	A. surveying	B. considering	C. persuading	D. guiding
24.	A. Continued	B. Previous	C. Later	D. Ongoing
25.	A. far from	B. except for	C. as well as	D. instead of
26.	A. for	B. to	C. on	D. of
27.	A. competition	B. technique	C. attention	D. strategy
28.	A. on end	B. at length	C. now and then	D. in and out
29.	A. similar	B. relevant	C. serious	D. tricky
30.	A. What	B. Why	C. When	D. Where
31.	A. setting	B. scene	C. frame	D. platform
32.	A. industrious	B. limited	C. dull	D. funny
33.	A. on	B. at	C. in	D. for
34.	A. or	B. against	C. while	D. with
35.	A. adding	B. adds	C. added	D. having added

PART III   READING COMPREHENSION

Section A (60 minutes, 30 points)
Directions: *Below each of the following passages you will find some questions or incomplete statements. Each question or statement is followed by four choices marked A, B, C, and D. Read each passage carefully, and then select the choice that best answers the question or completes the statement. Mark the letter of your choice with a single bar across the square bracket on your Machine-scoring Answer Sheet.*

Passage One

Ever since the early days of modern computing in the 1940s, the biological metaphor has been irresistible. The first computers — room-size behemoths — were referred to as "giant brains" or "electronic brains," in headlines and everyday speech. As computers improved and became capable of some tasks familiar to humans, like playing chess, the term used was "artificial intelligence." DNA, it is said, is the original software.

For the most part, the biological metaphor has long been just that — a simplifying analogy rather than a blueprint for how to do computing. Engineering, not biology, guided the pursuit of artificial intelligence. As Frederick Jelinek, a pioneer in speech recognition, put it, "airplanes don't flap their wings."

Yet the principles of biology are gaining ground as a tool in computing. The shift in thinking results from advances in neuroscience and computer science, and from the push of necessity.

The physical limits of conventional computer designs are within sight — not today or tomorrow, but soon enough. Nanoscale circuits cannot shrink much further. Today's chips are power hogs, running hot, which curbs how much of a chip's circuitry can be used. These limits loom as demand is accelerating for computing capacity to make sense of a surge of new digital data from sensors, online commerce, social networks, video streams and corporate and government databases.

To meet the challenge, without gobbling the world's energy supply, a different approach will be needed. And biology, scientists say, promises to contribute more than metaphors. "Every time we look at this, biology provides a clue as to how we should pursue the **frontiers** of computing," said John E. Kelly, the director of research at I. B. M.

Dr. Kelly points to Watson, the question-answering computer that can play "Jeopardy!" and beat two human champions earlier this year. The I. B. M. 's clever machine consumes 85,000 watts of electricity, while the human brain runs on just 20 watts. "Evolution figured this out," Dr. Kelly said.

Several biologically inspired paths are being explored by computer scientists in universities and corporate laboratories worldwide. One project, a collaboration of computer scientists and neuroscientists begun three years ago, has been encouraging enough that in August it won a $21 million round of government financing. In recent months, the team has developed prototype "neurosynaptic" microprocessors, or chips that operate more like neurons and synapses than like conventional semiconductors.

36. Paragraph 1 mainly tells _____ .
    A. what the biological metaphor is
    B. how computers have improved
    C. when modern computing began
    D. why DNA is the original software
37. Frederick Jelinek's quotation implies that _____ .
    A. technology is created by humans rather than by God
    B. airplanes differ from birds when using their wings
    C. computers can hardly match human brains
    D. biology can barely serve to explain computing
38. To meet growing demands computers need to be _____ .
    A. more complex in circuitry
    B. smaller in chip size
    C. more energy efficient
    D. more heat-sensitive
39. The boldfaced word "frontiers" (in Para. 5) refers to _____ .
    A. computing problems
    B. networking regulations
    C. streaming restrictions
    D. online shopping benefits
40. The human brain is superior to Watson in _____ .
    A. question generation
    B. power consumption
    C. event organization
    D. speech recognition
41. In pushing the boundaries of computing, biology serves as a(n) _____ .
    A. initiator
    B. director
    C. accelerator
    D. contributor

Passage Two

South Korea's *hagwon* (private tutoring academies) crackdown is one part of a larger quest to tame the country's culture of educational masochism. At the national and local levels, politicians are changing school testing and university admissions policies to reduce student stress and reward softer qualities like creativity. "One-size-fits-all, government-led uniform curriculums and an education system that is locked only onto the college-entrance examination are not acceptable," President Lee Myung-bak vowed at his inauguration in 2008.

But cramming is deeply embedded in Asia, where top grades — and often nothing else — have long been prized as essential for professional success. Modern-day South Korea has taken this competition to new extremes. In 2010, 74% of all students engaged in some kind of private after-school instruction, sometimes called *shadow education*, at an average cost of $2,600 per student for the year. There are more private instructors in South Korea than there are schoolteachers, and the most popular of them make millions of dollars a year from online and in-person classes. When Singapore's Education Minister was asked last year about his nation's reliance on private tutoring, he found one reason for hope: "We're not as bad as the Koreans."

In Seoul, large numbers of students who fail to get into top universities spend the entire year after high school attending *hagwons* to improve their scores on university admissions exams. And they must compete even to do this. At the prestigious Daesung Institute, admission is based on students' test scores. Only 14% of applicants are accepted. After a year of 14-hour days, about 70% gain entry to one of the nation's top three universities.

From a distance, South Korea's results look enviable. Its students consistently outperform their counterparts in almost every country in reading and math. In the U. S., Barack Obama and his Education Secretary speak glowingly of the enthusiasm South Korean parents have for educating their children, and they lament how far the U. S. students are falling behind. Without its education obsession, South Korea could not have been transformed into the economic powerhouse that it is today. But the country's leaders worry that unless its rigid, hierarchical system starts to nurture more innovation, economic growth will stall — and fertility rates will continue to decline as families feel the pressure of paying for all that tutoring. "You Americans see a bright side of the Korean system," Education Minister Lee Ju-ho tells me, "but Koreans are not happy with it."

42. South Korea's educational system _____.
   A. gives much weight to exams   B. stresses students' creativity
   C. shames the country's culture   D. offers easy admissions

43. *Shadow education* _____.
   A. casts a shadow in students' minds
   B. makes the students' scores level
   C. stimulates competition among teachers
   D. takes the form of private tutoring

44. In Seoul, students who fail to get into top universities _____.
   A. can only go to private universities
   B. must spend one more year in high schools
   C. may choose any *hagwon* they like
   D. need to fight for good private tutoring

45. Parents in South Korea _____.
   A. usually supervise their children from a distance
   B. only focus on their kids' reading and math
   C. devote much of their energy to their kids' education
   D. lament the way the US parents educate their children

46. South Korea's education obsession _____.
   A. has failed to nurture any creative students
   B. has contributed to the country's economic growth
   C. has led to an increase in the nation's fertility rates
   D. has won world notoriety for South Korean parents

47. With respect to the future of the educational system, South Korean politicians _____.

A. are concerned about its rigidity
B. see it as a model for other cultures
C. wish to encourage the birth of more children
D. hope to expand the scope of private tutoring

Passage Three

A dispute that, according to Members of Parliament (MPs), threatens the very survival of London Metropolitan University (London Met), the capital's biggest higher education institution, is spilling over onto London's streets. Last week lorry drivers on Holloway Road in Islington watched as a group of students and staff marched in protest against a meeting of London Met's governors.

"Save our Staff" and "London Met on the Roper," a reference to the university's vice-chancellor, Professor Brian Roper, screamed the banners.

The university, which has 34,000 students, has long attracted controversy for the militancy of its staff and students, but the latest row is a more serious matter. This crisis is over an attempt by the Higher Education Funding Council (Hefc) to claw back more than £50m that London Met should not have received. It is believed that as many as 500 jobs could go as a result of the university having been overpaid for student dropouts since 2005, and the unions are furious, claiming at the same time that the university is being unfairly treated by Hefc but that neither the managers nor the governors have explored the alternatives to job cuts.

"The University and College Union (UCU) is very concerned that the Hefc regulations appear to discriminate against widening participation," said a UCU spokesperson. "But we also feel very strongly about the fact that the management are not consulting the unions as they are required to do in law and that they have not considered alternatives like a freeze on new appointments."

One of the issues in dispute is whether students who did not take their assessments at the end of the year but were intending to take them the following year should be classified as drop-outs. Hefc considers them to have dropped out and says that its funding definitions apply to all universities regardless; UCU believes they should not be classified in this way on the grounds that they need all the help they can get to complete the course.

The dispute has also hit the House of Commons. An early day motion signed by MPs says that the scale of the cuts — an 18m reduction in teaching budgets and 38m in claw-backs for previous years —"throws the future operability of the university into doubt at a time when education and training are vital to the capital's economic health."

48. The dispute mentioned is partly between _____.
    A. MPs and UCU
    B. MPs and the Hefc
    C. London Met's staff and its governors
    D. London Met's students and lorry drivers
49. "London Met on the Roper" implies that _____.

A. Brian Roper is in power
B. London Met is at risk
C. London Met is facing a brain drain
D. Brian Roper is losing credibility

50. Hefc is to take back over £50m from London Met, believing that, for years, the latter _____.
    A. has practiced low standards of teaching
    B. has overpaid its governors and staff
    C. has been unfair to some instructors
    D. has had lots of students quitting school

51. The unions are angry with the school management because the latter _____.
    A. has been indifferent to the possible job cuts
    B. has been negligent in approving appointments
    C. has unwisely widened the student enrollment
    D. has unreasonably forced its 500 staff to leave

52. According to UCU, Hefc should include in its funding system the students who choose to take their assessments _____.
    A. several times   B. outside school
    C. in later years   D. at a lower cost

53. It is likely that the House of Commons will _____.
    A. urge Hefc to be reconciled to London Met
    B. intervene concerning Hefc's decisions
    C. back up the governors of London Met
    D. question London Met's qualifications

Passage Four

After years of defensiveness, a siege mentality and the stonewalling of any criticism, a quiet revolution is under way in animal research.

What has triggered this change of heart? It's partly down to the economic climate plus fewer new medicines and the removal of much of the threat from animal rights extremism, in the UK at least.

Until recently the only criticism of animal research came from antivivisection groups who persistently complained about a lack of transparency. Now criticism is coming from researchers too, with the recognition that not all aspects of animal experimentation are as robust as they should be and that something needs to change.

That is why we have published new guidelines aimed at improving the quality of reporting on animal experiments in research papers. These have been met with support, notably from the major funding bodies and many international journals. This is indicative of the new climate in which we operate.

Five years ago the guidelines would have been met with scepticism and accusations of increased bureaucracy from some within the scientific community.

The difference is that these guidelines come in the wake of recent studies, which reveal serious shortcomings in animal research. One by my own organisation, the UK's NC3Rs, found that key information was missing from many of the 300 or so publications we analysed that described publicly funded experiments on rodents and monkeys in the UK and the US.

The new guidelines should ensure the science emerging from animal research is maximised and that every animal used counts. Better reporting will allow greater opportunity to evaluate which animal models are useful and which are not. One way of doing this is through the systematic reviews that are the gold standard in clinical studies but rarely undertaken for animal studies due to the lack of information published.

Animal research has been a thorn in the side of researchers for many years. We can't afford to get this wrong, scientifically, ethically or financially. Failings in reporting animal data properly can be perceived as an attempt to hide something, either about the quality or value of what is being done. When animal research is funded from the public purse a public mandate is essential. There is much scope for improvement. It is time for scientists — funders, researchers and editors — to use the new guidelines to put our house in order.

54. According to the passage, those who had long blamed animal research are _____.
    A. those ignorant of science
    B. government officials
    C. some of their colleagues
    D. antivivisection groups

55. The passage suggests that the change of heart among animal researchers refers to _____.
    A. their reconsideration of their research
    B. their resistance to their greater enemies
    C. their giving in to animal right groups
    D. their confession to their work failures

56. The new guidelines mostly stress that the report on animal research needs to be _____.
    A. directive
    B. comprehensive
    C. affirmative
    D. authoritative

57. The UK's NC3Rs research is mentioned to illustrate that animal research _____.
    A. needs government funding
    B. needs publishing guidelines
    C. involves some serious problems
    D. involves analyses and variations

58. For animal researchers, to put their work under systematic review would be something _____.
    A. new
    B. hard
    C. pleasant
    D. unthinkable

59. The best title for this passage is _____.
    A. Make the Most of Animal Experiments
    B. Improve the Quality of Animal Research
    C. Make Every Animal Experiment Count
    D. Give Public Support to Animal Research

Passage Five

Likenesses of Buddha are these days so commonplace — the casual adornment of fashionable spas, fusion restaurants and Parisian nightclubs — that it is strange to think that artists once hesitated, out of reverence, to portray the Buddha in corporeal form. In 2nd century India, judging by a 2nd century sandstone carving excavated from Mathura, it was sufficient to simply depict an empty throne — the implication that the Buddha was a spiritual king being very clearly understood by anyone who saw it.

But as the stunning new gallery of Buddhist sculpture at London's Victoria and Albert Museum makes plain, somewhere along the line the reticence (沉默) about rendering the Buddha's likeness gave way, and the world embarked on two millenniums of rich iconography and statuary. The gallery's 47 masterworks, chosen from the museum's renowned Asian collections, trace the Buddha's portrayal from the 2nd to the 19th centuries, in places as diverse as India, Java and Japan.

Inspiration came from unexpected sources. Some sculptors in Sri Lanka and China simply shaped the Buddha in their own likenesses. A 4th century stucco bust unearthed in Afghanistan features the full lips associated with Indian Gupta art, but also fulsome curls that reflect the Greco-Roman artists brought to the region by Alexander the Great.

Other enlightened souls are shown beside the Buddha. Among the gallery's most glorious artifacts are depictions of bodhisattvas — those who deliberately postpone their passage to nirvana (涅槃), Buddhists believe, in order to help others along the eightfold path. In the 14th century, metalworkers from Nepal's Kathmandu Valley crafted the Bodhisattva Avalokiteshvara, a manifestation of the Buddhist lord of compassion, in gilded copper and precious-stone inlay. An androgynous-looking deity with wide hips and sensuous form (in Chinese tradition, Avalokiteshvara or Guan Yin is female, in others male), Avalokiteshvara's serene face projects the harmony to which all Buddhists aspire.

John Clarke, the gallery's principal curator, says that Avalokiteshvara is sometimes depicted holding a blooming lotus — a symbol of spiritual purity. "It comes up from the mud, flowers, and remains untouched by the dirt that surrounded it," he says. You could say the same thing for the wonderful richness of Buddhist art.

60. Spas, restaurants and nightclubs are stated to show that _____.
    A. images of Buddha are often seen in those places
    B. those places are frequented by many Buddhist artists
    C. those places are filled with flavor of Buddhist culture
    D. Buddhist worshippers regularly go to those places

61. The 2nd century Indian case mentioned denotes that artists at that time considered it disrespectful to _____.
    A. depict the figure of Buddha   B. reflect things about Buddhism
    C. paint Buddha in a vague form   D. distort Buddhist spirituality

62. The new gallery at London's Victoria & Albert Museum indicates that _____.
    A. Buddha's portrayal came to a surge in the year of 2000
    B. some Buddha sculptures have a history of about 2,000 years
    C. the image of the Buddha has been distorted for 2,000 years
    D. the silence on portraying Buddha was broken in 2000
63. The gallery's sculptures of Buddha reflect _____.
    A. the sculptors' secular views about Buddhism
    B. the sculptors' imitation of an alien culture
    C. something about the sculptors' own cultures
    D. something associated with modern art
64. To Buddhists, Avalokiteshvara is a deity that can help one _____.
    A. against arrogance   B. control his temper
    C. out of greediness   D. out of sufferings
65. The last sentence of the passage implies that Buddhist art _____.
    A. emerges from other art forms but retains its own features
    B. needs to be further explored in its complex structures
    C. keeps its dominant position over any other form of art
    D. remains a symbol of spiritual purity in the world of artists

Section B (20 minutes, 10 points)

Directions: *In each of the following passages, five sentences have been removed from the original text. They are listed from A to F and put below the passage. Choose the most suitable sentence from the list to fill in each of the blanks (numbered 66 to 75). For each passage, there is one sentence that does not fit in any of the blanks. Mark your answers on your Machine-scoring Answer Sheet.*

Passage One

In August 1969 an unmarried pregnant woman living in Texas wanted to terminate her pregnancy by having an abortion. Her doctor refused this request because Texas law made it a crime to have an abortion unless the operation was necessary to save the mother's life. __66__ Throughout the legal proceedings, the woman was identified as Jane Roe to protect her anonymity. Roe's lawyers claimed that the Texas abortion laws violated her rights under the due process clause of the 14th Amendment, which prohibited states from depriving their citizens of life, liberty, or property without due process of law.

__67__ Justice Harry Blackmun recognized that a woman's right to an abortion could be limited by "a compelling state interest" to protect her health and life. Based on medical evidence, Justice Blackmun concluded that during the "second trimester" of a woman's pregnancy (months 4 to 6), the state might intervene to regulate abortion to protect the mother's well-being. And the state could regulate or prohibit abortion during the third trimester (months 7 to 9). __68__

The *Roe* decision has generated continuing controversy. __69__ Its critics can be roughly divided into two groups: those who oppose the decision because they believe abortion is murder and those who believe that the Court improperly substituted its policy preference for the will of the people as expressed through their elected representatives in state governments. __70__ And so it has been since 1973, when the *Roe* case was decided. Efforts to modify or overturn the *Roe* decision have continued. In *Webster v. Reproductive Health Services* (1989), for example, the Court upheld provisions of a Missouri law that restricted the right to an abortion, a retreat from the *Roe* decision that stopped short of overturning it.

A. However, during the first trimester (months 1 to 3) of a pregnancy, it seemed unlikely that there would be "a compelling state interest" to restrict abortion rights to protect the health and life of the mother.

B. Abortions performed in the first trimester (months 1 to 3) pose virtually no long-term risk of such problems as infertility, ectopic pregnancy, spontaneous abortion (miscarriage) or birth defect, and little or no risk of preterm or low-birth-weight deliveries.

C. So the woman sought legal help and filed suit against Henry Wade, district attorney for Dallas County, Texas.

D. The Supreme Court ruled that the Texas statutes on abortion were unconstitutional and that a woman did have the right to terminate her pregnancy.

E. Justice Byron White accurately remarked in his dissent that the right to an abortion is an issue about which "reasonable men may easily and heatedly differ."

F. Women's rights advocates have hailed *Roe* as a landmark victory.

Passage Two

In 1998, a Belgian student named Sacha Klein left Brussels and enrolled as a four-year student at a U.S. university, graduating with a computer-science degree, and landing a summer internship at Virginia-based consulting firm Booz Allen Hamilton, where management liked him enough to offer him a full-time position. Today, he designs information systems for Booz Allen, and studies toward a master's degree in business.

He is deaf.

__71__ In 1990, the Americans with Disabilities Act (ADA) opened the door for people like Klein to contribute to the U.S. economy in ways no one imagined before. The ADA requires businesses to make accommodations to allow a person with a disability to do a job for which he or she is qualified.

In addition, the ADA requires public facilities to remove architectural barriers that hinder people with disabilities from shopping, going to the theater, or using public toilets.

__72__ Katherine McCary, president of a business group that promotes hiring people with disabilities, said European managers tell her they want to hire people with disabilities, but that they can't get to work.

___73___ Had he stayed in Europe, he said, he would not have been able to become a white-collar professional, but would have been put on track for factory work.

___74___ A federal hotline offering advice on workplace accommodations went from handling 3,000 calls per year before the law to 40,000 calls per year in the mid-1990s.

The cost of accommodations turned out to be zero in half the cases and averaged about $500 in the other half, according to the Labor Department. ___75___

Compliance with the law is good for business: 87 percent of consumers prefer to patronize companies that hire people with disabilities, according to a January 2006 survey by the University of Massachusetts. In addition, workers with disabilities could help relieve a labor shortage.

A. Klein thinks attitudes matter, too.
B. Employers report that workers with disabilities are loyal and productive.
C. Klein said he has learned a lot at Booz Allen about teamwork and communication.
D. While one can paint a rosy picture of the U.S. companies embracing people with disabilities, in the early 1990s, the ADA was greeted with panic by the business community, which predicted enormous costs and out-of-control litigation.
E. Since the Rehabilitation Act of 1973, which obligated government agencies to hire people with disabilities, Congress has passed 11 major laws to improve access to education, transportation, technology, and housing.
F. Some experts believe such widespread architectural changes have put the United States ahead of the 44 other countries with disability-discrimination laws.

PAPER TWO

PART IV TRANSLATION (30 minutes, 15 points)

Directions: *Read the following text carefully and then translate the underlined segments into Chinese. Write your Chinese version in the proper space on your Answer Sheet.*

Mary Barra made history last year when she became the first woman to lead the development of new cars and trucks at General Motors, the world's largest automaker. In January, Virginia Rometty took over as CEO of IBM, the first woman to head the technology giant in its 101-year history. (1) These milestones in male-dominated industries are raising new questions about women's advancement in the workplace. Does the glass ceiling still exist, or is it an outdated metaphor that fails to acknowledge the progress women have made?

(2) Nearly three decades after the introduction of the glass ceiling metaphor, many women say the glass ceiling is very much intact, pointing to the data that show women last year held just 14 per

cent of all executive officer positions at Fortune 500 companies. But others disagree, citing advances made by women in recent years. And some contend that the glass ceiling should be replaced by a different metaphor. When asked if a glass ceiling still exists for women, Barra said, "I don't think so. I've never seen it or felt it in my career." She acknowledged the small percentage of women in top executive positions but said she expects the situation will improve, noting that "it's just a matter of time."

Linda Carli, a psychology professor at Wellesley College and an expert on gender discrimination, sees things differently. (3) She said women still face major workplace hurdles, but she wouldn't describe them as a glass ceiling. She thinks a labyrinth is a better metaphor. (4) "There are women getting to very high places, and yet the rest of us are still floundering," Carli said. (5) No matter where you stand on the issue of a glass ceiling, there's no denying that women are underrepresented in the top ranks of corporate America.

PART V WRITING (40 minutes, 20 points)

Directions: *Write an essay of no less than 200 words on the topic given below. Use the space provided on your Answer Sheet II.*

TOPIC

What is the one thing that you've learned from doing sports which applies to all aspects of your life? Please use examples to illustrate your points.

2013 年 3 月试题精解

第一部分 词 汇

1. 答案:A

    本题考查句子的让步逻辑关系和动词语义,是一道语境题。A 促进,提高;B 剪短,截短,减少;C 把……投入,使突然陷入;D 花费,消费。该句的大意为:在 1981—1987 年,尽管公司的培训项目得到了显著的促进和提高,固定工作的数量仅仅增加了 1 000 个。

2. 答案:B

    本题考查句子的因果逻辑关系和动词短语,是一道语境题。A 胜利,成功,安然度过;B 认识自我与他人的同一性;C 从事;D 指的是……。该句的大意为:每个父母都会立刻认同这感人的一幕,因为父母们都在自己孩子成长过程中经历过相同的仪式。

3. 答案:C

    本题考查名词的语义。A 极,(性质、特点等的)正好相反,截然对立;B 裂口,裂缝;C 海湾,不可逾越的鸿沟;D 空间;真空;空白。该句的大意为:在古代神话中,神与人之间有一道无法逾越的鸿沟。

4. 答案:D

    本题考查形容词的语义。A 合格的;B 令人愉快的,惬意的;C 合得来的,协调的;D 负有法律责任的。该句的大意为:担保书和使用保证书告诉购买者生产商有责任提供的维修服务。

5. 答案:C

    本题考查形容词与名词的搭配。A 不情愿的,勉强的;B 恶作剧的,顽皮的;C 破坏性极大的,毁灭性的;D 恶毒的,恶性的。该句的大意为:漏油事件给海鸟和其他野生动物造成了毁灭性的影响。

6. 答案:B

    本题考查固定短语。A 实际上;B 可以说,在某种程度上;C 和……一样(程度),除……之外(也),和;D 好像,仿佛。该句的大意为:在某种程度上,朋友就是另一个自己。

7. 答案:B

    本题是一道语境题,考查动词的及物性/不及物性用法。A 使升高,高举,为及物动词;B 上升,升高,为不及物动词;C 摇摆,摆动;D 波动,起伏。该句的大意为:他从楼上的一扇窗户探出身来,感觉到一股热气从街道中涌上来。

8. 答案:D

    本题考查动词短语。A 穿上;采用,采纳;B 压在……上,使难以承受负荷;C 抓牢,继续、坚持;D 依靠,指望。该句的大意为:在市场经济中,依赖大银行降低向中小企业提供金融支持的门槛,这是不切实际的。

9. 答案:C

    本题考查动词的语义。A 把……打发走,解散;B 使激动,使狂躁不安;C 打中、击中,给……印象、让……觉得……；D 抓住。该句的大意为：令我们印象深刻的是，该作者对于事件的描述一贯公正准确。

10. 答案：D

本题考查连接词的固定短语。A 既然，由于；B 所以，因此；C 假使，免得、以防、以防万一，该短语大多数情况下省略 that；D 因为。该句的大意为：新的体系与原有的相似，因为强大的中央政府依旧存在。

11. 答案：A

本题考查名词的形近词辨析。A 思想，观念，想法；B 欺骗；C 接待，迎接，欢迎；D 赠送，呈现。该句的大意为：在最后的分析中，正是我们关于死亡的观念决定了我们在生活中遇到的所有问题的答案。

12. 答案：C

本题考查动词的语义。A 停止，结束；B 满期，届期；C 丧生，凋谢；D 凋谢，枯萎。该句的大意为：生活中可怕的悲剧并不是人们的死亡，而是人们不再爱别人。

13. 答案：B

本题考查介词短语的语义。A 在场，立即、马上；B 诡秘地，偷偷地；C 实际上，无论如何、根本；D 简言之。该句的大意为：他的医生告诉他，他不得饮酒，但他仍然时不时偷偷地喝上几口白兰地。

14. 答案：D

本题考查动词的形近词辨析。A 开发、开采、开拓、利用；B 驱逐、赶；C 满期、届期；D 超过，胜过。该句的大意为：在一些非洲国家，治疗艾滋病的费用可能会超过患者全年的总收入。

15. 答案：C

本题考查名词的语义。A 插入、介入、干涉；B 操作、使用、操纵、控制；C 着迷，困扰；D 支配，统治。该句的大意为：目前人们对于考试结果过于看重，这实际上不利于孩子的教育。

16. 答案：A

本题考查介词与动词的搭配。该句的大意为：有时一些家庭的好几代人都信奉同一种宗教信仰。

17. 答案：A

本题考查动词与名词的搭配。A 耗尽……的资源，使枯竭；B 分解，使腐烂，使腐败；C 腐蚀，使堕落；D 腐蚀，侵蚀。该句的大意为：他了解到该地区大量放牧牛群，这严重耗尽了当地丰饶的植被。

18. 答案：B

本题考查介词短语。A 起火，着火；B 竖着、直立着，紧张不安、烦躁；C 世界上，人世间；D 一时冲动，一时心血来潮。该句的大意为：我一直在等待我的考试结果，这令我非常烦躁不安。

19. 答案：B

本题考查句子的逻辑关系和动词语义，是一道语境题。A 使奋发，引起、唤起、激起；B 冒犯，得罪，使生气；C 用踢马刺策（马）前进，促进、激励；D 违反、违背、违犯。该句的大意为：必须想出一种让这组人中的大多数不会反感的方法，否则就行不通。

20. 答案：D

本题考查动词的语义。A 以海盗方式劫掠，抢劫；B 调解，调停；C 增补，补充；D 给……

津贴(或补贴),补助,资助。该句的大意为:联邦政府通过以高于市场价的价格购买农民手中剩余的粮食来补贴他们。

第二部分 完形填空

本文主要阐述看电视和打电子游戏对儿童注意力的影响。

21. 答案:A

本题考查动词的词义。A 追踪;B 训练;C 质疑;D 挑战。原文是说研究者对1 300 名不同年级的儿童进行了长达一年的跟踪调查研究。

22. 答案:D

本题考查动词的词义。A 煽动;B 猜测;C 制定;D 评估,评定。本句是说,研究者们对儿童的注意力广度(或注意力持续的时间)进行了评估。

23. 答案:A

本题考查动词的词义。A 调查;B 考虑;C 劝说;D 引导。本句意思是,通过问卷调查学校老师来评估儿童的注意力广度(或注意力持续的时间)。

24. 答案:B

本题考查形容词的词义辨析和对上下文的理解。A 持续的;B 先前的;C 以后的;D 正在进行的。本句的意思是,先前的研究已经调查了电视或电子游戏对注意力问题的影响,但没有同时调查两者的共同影响。

25. 答案:C

本句考查介词短语的语义辨析。A 远离,一点也不;B 除……之外;C(除……之外)还;D 是……而不是……。本句讲的是,除了调查看电视对注意力广度的影响之外,研究者还调查了打电子游戏对它的影响。

26. 答案:B

本句考查介词与名词的搭配。本句的意思是,通过调查看电视与玩电子游戏对注意力广度的影响,研究者们首次发现这两种活动与儿童的注意力问题有相似的关系。have a relation to (with)表示有关系,其中,to 后面接事,with 后接人。

27. 答案:C

本句考查对文章上下文的理解和文章主题的把握。A 竞争;B 技术;C 注意力;D 策略。本句的意思是,Shawn Green 指出这个研究没有区分使儿童在电子游戏中胜出和在学业中胜出所需要的注意力有什么不同。本文主要介绍了看电视和打电子游戏对儿童注意力的影响,注意力的问题是调查研究的主要方面,也是这篇文章的关键词。

28. 答案:A

本题考查固定搭配的语义辨析。A 连续地;B 详尽地;C 不时地;D 进进出出地。这一句的意思是,一个能连续几个小时玩电子游戏的儿童显而易见不会有太严重的注意力问题。

29. 答案:C

本题考查形容词的词义辨析和对文章下文的理解。A 相似的;B 相关的;C 严重的;D 狡猾的。本句的意思是,一个能连续几个小时玩电子游戏的儿童显而易见不会有太严重的注意力问题。

30. 答案:B

本题考查疑问副词的用法,是一道语法题。本句意思是,为什么儿童能在玩电子游戏时专注,却不能专注于学业?

31. 答案:A

本题考查名词的近义词辨析。A 环境;B 场景,现场;C 框架;D 平台。这句的意思是,电子游戏引出了儿童们的哪些期望,而这样的期望在学校环境中却没有出现?

32. 答案:C

本题考查形容词的词义辨析和对文章上下文的理解。A 勤奋的;B 有限的;C 无趣的;D 有趣的。这句的意思是,现代快节奏的电视节目让人兴奋;相比之下,读书和学校作业显得枯燥无趣。

33. 答案:D

本题考查介词的使用和对文章上下文的理解。前文提到,快节奏的电视节目让人兴奋;相比之下,读书和学校作业显得枯燥无趣。本句呼应前句,意思是,电子游戏也有这些特点。

34. 答案:A

本题考查连接词的用法。这句的意思是,我们不能将电子游戏划分为教育与非教育类,也不能将之划分为暴力的和非暴力的。本句考查 not A or B 句型。

35. 答案:A

本题考查现在分词的用法,是一道语法题。在本句,adding 是现在分词状语,表示伴随。本句的意思是,Swing 还提到(或,补充道),不同类型电子游戏对儿童注意力的影响是今后研究的一个重要问题。

第三部分 阅读理解

第一节 阅读理解 A

第一篇:

36. 答案:A

本题是主旨大意题,考查了第一段的主要内容,关键点是把握第一段的结构:首句是起始句,接下来的几句话起到了展开论述起始句的作用。

37. 答案:D

本题是细节事实题,貌似考查第二段中引语部分的含义,实则考查第二句话的意思,因为引语部分的作用是为了进一步解释这一句。关键点:Engineering, not biology, guided the pursuit of artificial intelligence。

38. 答案:C

本题是推理题,考查对第五段第一句话的理解。关键点:... without gobbling the world's energy supply。

39. 答案:A

本题是词汇题,考查对第五段的理解,原文中 frontiers 一词与段首第一句话中 challenge 对应。

40. 答案:B

本题是细节事实题,考查对第六段第二句话的理解,关键点是要求学生在阅读过程中学会对比两个悬殊巨大的数字。

41. 答案:D

本题是主旨大意题,考查对全文主要内容的把握。关键点是要读懂第三段在文章中的作用。另外,从最后一段的第一句话中的"biologically inspired paths"也可以推断出本题的答案。

第二篇:

42. 答案:A

本题是推理题,考查对第一段第三句话的理解,关键点:...an education system that is locked only onto the college-entrance examination...。

43. 答案:D

本题是词汇题,考查第二段第三句话的语义,关键点是把握 private after-school instruction 与 shadow education 之间解释与被解释的关系。

44. 答案:D

本题是细节事实题,考查对第三段第二句话的理解,关键点:...they must compete even to do this...。

45. 答案:C

本题是细节事实题,考查对第四段第三句话的理解,关键点:...the enthusiasm South Korean parents have for educating their children...。

46. 答案:B

本题是长句理解题,考查第四段第四句话的意思,这是一个双重否定句。

47. 答案:A

本题是观点态度题,考查对第四段最后一句话的理解,关键点:...but Koreans are not happy with it...。

第三篇:

48. 答案:C

本题是细节事实题,考查对第一段最后一句话的理解,关键点:...a group of students and staff marched in protest against a meeting of London Met's governors...。

49. 答案:B

本题是推理题,考查第一段和第二段的内容,要求学生可以联系上下文,推断出游行人群所举标语的含义。

50. 答案:D

本题是长句理解题,考查对第三段第三句话的理解,关键点:...as a result of the university having been overpaid for student dropouts since 2005...。

51. 答案:A

本题是长句理解题,考查对第三段第三句话的理解,关键点:...but that neither the managers nor the governors have explored the alternatives to job cuts...。

52. 答案:C

本题是推理题,考查对第五段第二句话的理解,关键点:...they need all the help they can

get to complete the course....。

53. 答案:B

本题是推理题,考查对第六段第一句话的理解,关键点:...also hit the House of Commons。

第四篇:

54. 答案:D

本题是推理题,考查对第三段第一句话的理解,关键点在于副词"persistently"。

55. 答案:A

本题是长句理解题,考查对第三段第二句话的理解,关键点:...with the recognition that... and that...。

56. 答案:B

本题是推理题,考查第七段第一句话的意思,关键点是理解动词"maximised"(最大限度地利用)。

57. 答案:C

本题是推理题,考查第六段第二句话的意思,关键点:...found that key information was missing...。

58. 答案:A

本题是细节事实题,考查第七段第三句话的意思,关键点在于副词"rarely"。

59. 答案:C

本题是主旨大意题,要点是准确把握文章的关键词或主题词。

第五篇:

60. 答案:A

本题是细节事实题,考查第一段第一句话中连线号的作用,关键点:Likenesses of Buddha are these days so commonplace。

61. 答案:A

本题是推理题,考查对第一段的整体把握,关键点有两处:...once hesitated...to portray the Buddha in corporeal form;...sufficient to simply depict an empty throne....。

62. 答案:B

本题是细节事实题,考查时间信息,第二段最后一句中提到有些佛像为公元2世纪的作品。

63. 答案:C

本题是推理题,考查对第三段第二句话和第三句话的理解,关键点:...simply shaped the Buddha in their own likenesses;...reflect the Greco-Roman artists....。

64. 答案:D

本题是推理题,考查第四段第二句话的意思,关键点:...in order to help others along the eightfold path....。

65. 答案:A

本题是细节事实题,考查第五段第一句话的意思,关键点:...a symbol of spiritual

purity...。

第二节 阅读理解 B

第一篇：

66. 答案：C

本题的突破口在空格的后一句,关键点是短语"the legal proceedings",定冠词 the 的使用说明上文已经提到过法律诉讼程序。

67. 答案：D

本题的突破口是考查学生是否把握了第二段的叙事顺序,另一个突破口是空格后一句中提到的"a women's right to an abortion"。

68. 答案：A

本题的答题关键是理解第二段中作者讲到了女性怀孕的三个阶段,其中第二阶段和第三阶段在空格的上文已经提到。为什么最后谈到第一阶段呢? 因为孕期的第一阶段是可以实施人工流产的,相反,第二阶段和第三阶段出于对孕妇健康等的考虑,是不允许流产的。

69. 答案：F

本题的答题关键是空格前一句中讲到的"controversy"一词,自然而然,接下来的这一句中要谈到有人支持、有人反对的情况。

70. 答案：E

本题的难度较大,突破口在空格后一句中的"...so it has been since 1973",其中"so"一词是用替代的手段加强了两句之间的衔接。

第二篇：

71. 答案：E

本题的突破口是把握文章第三段的主要内容,该段介绍了前两段中提到的个案的新闻背景,按照时间顺序介绍了和保障残疾人权益有关的一些法案法令。时间节点是答题的关键。

72. 答案：F

本题的答题关键是第四段中提到的"architectural barriers",选项 F 中的"such widespread architectural changes"与之呼应。

73. 答案：A

本题的答题重点是要了解从第六段开始作者又回到了个案,结合个案深度分析现状。

74. 答案：D

本题的突破口是空格的后一句,要理解法律颁布之后,投诉电话的猛增这一情况。

75. 答案：B

本题的答题关键是把握第八段和第九段(即紧挨空格的前后位置),它们介绍了雇用残疾人对公司和社会来说益处多、好处多。

第四部分 翻 译

(1) 译文：

这些女性在男性主导的种种行业中所创下的里程碑,让人们对女性在职场晋升产生新疑问:玻璃天花板是否依然存在?或者它已经是个过时的说法,无法表现出女性职业生涯的发展?

解析:

这部分的翻译包括两个句子,前一个句子相对容易一些,后一句中理解的重点是"glass ceiling",直译为"玻璃天花板"即可领会其比喻义———一种无形的、看不见的、却难以突破的障碍。

(2) **译文:**

玻璃天花板这个比喻说法提出了已有大约三十年了,许多女性表示这个现象毫无改变,她们引用数据指出,去年所有《财富》杂志五百强公司首席执行官中只有14%是女性。

解析:

该句的特点是长,要学会把原文拆分成三个部分:第一部分介绍了玻璃天花板这个说法源于何时;第二部分是原句中主干部分;第三部分为现在分词短语,补充说明许多女性的观点。不拘泥于英语原句的句法结构,通顺流畅地表达出原文的意思是英译汉考查的重要方面。

(3) **译文:**

她表示,女性在职场上依然面对重大阻碍,但她不会用"玻璃天花板"一词来形容。

解析:

该句中的"hurdle"是理解和翻译的难点,意为"障碍"。可以结合上下文的逻辑关系得知,"hurdle"一词对应的信息为玻璃天花板的本意。

(4) **译文:**

她说,"有些女性晋升到非常高的职位,然而我们其他人都在挣扎中。"

解析:

该句中的生词"flounder"是可以根据句子本身提供的逻辑关系推测出词义的。上文大意是有些女性升了,而我们还在……。"..., yet... still..."这两个副词告诉读者这两者之间很可能存在截然相反的情况。通过这种对比的关系,可以大致推测出"而我们其他人仍在为升职而苦恼着"。

(5) **译文:**

不管你对玻璃天花板议题持何种立场,不可否认的是,女性在美国企业高级主管中比例偏低。

解析:

考生不要被该句中最长的单词"underrepresented"吓倒。这是个合成词,由 under 和 represented 两部分构成,顾名思义,其意为"未被充分代表的"或"代表名额不足的"。

第五部分 写 作

题目解析:

题目中,关键词 one thing 指的是我们从参加体育运动中所体会、领悟到的一个人生道理。另一短语 you've learned from doing sports,则指必须是你亲自经历过的一项体育运动,而不是指观察别人的体育锻炼。由于题目针对的是"你"个人的经历,因此,需要从自己的体育经历中找一个或几个例子来阐明"你"所感悟到的哲理或想法。事实上,体育运动益处很多,也能给我们带来很多有益的人生启示，比如，"坚持就是胜利"，"熟能生巧"，"过程胜过结果"，等等。选取其中的一个道理或启示进行阐述即可。范文中选取的是坚持对于成功的必要性。另外，这篇作文可以用举例法来具体阐明主旨观点，例如从自身体育运动的例子到生活中的例子，例子的选取恰好可以对应题目的要求。

范文：

  From my personal experience in doing sports, I have learned a lesson that perseverance is the key to success. This notion of life, as far as I observe, could be applied to almost all aspects of my life.

  I once had a very unforgettable experience in doing sports. When I was still a college student, I once took part in a running competition. In order to prepare for this race, I had practiced running for almost a month. At the day of the game, I did my utmost to run in order to win a prize for our class. At the end of the race, I was so exhausted and thirsty that I desperately wanted to give up, but my classmates in the playground all encouraged me to carry on. Finally I persevered and won a third prize. This experience has taught me that perseverance is the key to success. When the situation turns so difficult that we think we won't be able to succeed, perseverance will bring us hope and even a surprising reward.

  Success is not easy to come in everybody's life. Therefore the preparation for it is often a long process. Sometimes what helps people to succeed is not so much a person's intelligence as his or her spirit of perseverance. Later in my life, I have used this experience again to face another significant challenge. After working for several years, I decided to apply to a Ph. D. program. It was not easy for me to prepare for the entrance exam because I was still at work and had to squeeze time for it. There were so many subjects for me to review and I was almost on the verge of breakdown. Just a few days before the examination, high pressure made me so exhausted that I decided to quit. But then, a friend of mine encouraged me to carry on. So I persevered to the last minute and finally passed the entrance examination. Now I am a Ph. D. candidate in my ideal university.

  No doubt, it's difficult to persevere when the situation is really hard. But as a Chinese saying goes, "Do nothing by halves." Perseverance is the key to success. This is a valuable lesson that I have learned from doing sports. (377 words)

中国科学院大学
博士研究生入学考试
英语试题

(2013年10月)

考生须知：

一、本试卷由试卷一（PAPER ONE）和试卷二（PAPER TWO）两部分组成。试卷一为客观题，答卷使用标准化机读答题纸；试卷二为主观题，答卷使用非机读答题纸。

二、请考生一律用HB或2B铅笔填涂标准化机读答题纸，画线不得过细或过短。修改时请用橡皮擦拭干净。若因填涂不符合要求而导致计算机无法识别，责任由考生自负。请保持机读答题纸清洁、无折皱。答题纸切忌折叠。

三、全部考试时间总计180分钟，满分为100分。时间及分值分布如下：

试卷一：

Ⅰ 词汇	15 分钟	10 分
Ⅱ 完形填空	15 分钟	15 分
Ⅲ 阅读理解	80 分钟	40 分
小计	110 分钟	65 分

试卷二：

Ⅳ 英译汉	30 分钟	15 分
Ⅴ 写作	40 分钟	20 分
小计	70 分钟	35 分

UNIVERSITY OF CHINESE ACADEMY OF SCIENCES ENGLISH ENTRANCE EXAMINATION FOR PH. D PROGRAM

October 2013

PAPER ONE

PART I VOCABULARY (15 minutes, 10 points, 0.5 point each)

Directions: *Choose the word or expression below each sentence that best completes the statement, and mark the corresponding letter of your choice with a single bar across the square bracket on your Machine-scoring Answer Sheet.*

1. Abruptly the ground fell away from our feet, and an _____ void opened before us.
   A. anxious　　　B. audible　　　C. awesome　　　D. amiable
2. Autobiographical advertising can _____ consumers' past memories about the product or brand.
   A. exaggerate　　B. excavate　　　C. extract　　　D. evoke
3. Many animals are on the _____ of disappearing from the face of the earth and zoos can provide them with a safe place to live and breed.
   A. range　　　　B. verge　　　　C. part　　　　D. link
4. If costs continue to _____, the state will not be able to afford this scheme for long, and it will become unpopular.
   A. soar　　　　B. shoot　　　　C. swing　　　　D. settle
5. There's a _____ in the fact that although we're living longer than ever before, people are more obsessed with health issues than they ever were.
   A. paradox　　　B. dilemma　　　C. polarity　　　D. misconception
6. _____, Mr. Hall admits that he pushed too hard, and ultimately his efforts failed.
   A. In essence　　B. In due course　　C. On average　　D. In retrospect
7. A taxicab and a laundry truck missed each other by inches on Sixth Avenue, stopping in such a position that each _____ the other's progress.
   A. implored　　　B. implemented　　C. impeded　　　D. imparted
8. In her new novel, "Annabel," reviewed this week in the magazine, Kathleen Winter _____

the nature-nurture divide.

   A. outgrows   B. explores   C. perceives   D. contends

9. They drifted on the lake, fishing and catching shrimp to _____.

   A. get by   B. get over   C. get along   D. get across

10. In some California housing estates, a key alone is insufficient to get someone in the door; his or her voiceprint must also be _____.

    A. duplicated   B. perceived   C. acquired   D. verified

11. France will lower its tax rate on food and drinks at restaurants in hopes of _____ tourists and locals to struggling cafés, which means a saving of $7.05 on a $50 meal.

    A. ushering   B. initiating   C. luring   D. trapping

12. In a global economy that has produced more dramatic ups and downs than anyone thought possible, Asia may be _____ another disheartening plunge.

    A. taking in   B. heading for   C. longing for   D. spreading out

13. In the 1970s, he became a tireless promoter for the drug as a cure for depression — which he once suffered from — and other _____.

    A. ailments   B. therapies   C. tolls   D. addictions

14. Hearing the news, she could feel anger _____ inside her.

    A. stumbling   B. staggering   C. twisting   D. surging

15. Many advertisers remain _____ of the Internet and question how heavily to rely on it.

    A. inconsistent B. supportive   C. skeptical   D. prospective

16. If the expert advice is more positive, will the parents be able to _____ attitudes which have built up over decades in a few days?

    A. approve of   B. shrug off   C. show off   D. pick up

17. It will be very helpful if parents have seen the school environment and know what kind of tasks the school will _____ on the daily life of their child.

    A. compose   B. impose   C. dispose   D. expose

18. The author skillfully fuses these fragments into a _____ whole.

    A. congestive   B. corporate   C. collaborative D. cohesive

19. _____ his seeming rebellion against middle-class values, he remains essentially middle-class.

    A. Instead of   B. As for   C. For all   D. But for

20. It's very difficult to _____ the exact meaning of an idiom in a foreign language.

    A. exchange   B. transfer   C. convert   D. convey

PART II CLOZE TEST (15 minutes, 15 points)

Directions: *For each blank in the following passage, choose the best answer from the four choices given below. Mark the corresponding letter of your choice with a single bar across the*

square bracket on your Machine-scoring Answer Sheet.

"Pain," as Albert Schweitzer once said, "is a more terrible lord of mankind than even death itself." Prolonged pain destroys the quality of life. It can __21__ the will to live, at times __22__ people to suicide. The physical effects are equally __23__. Severe, persistent pain can spoil sleep and appetite, __24__ producing fatigue and reducing the availability of nutrients to organs. It may __25__ delay recovery from illness or injury and, in weakened or elderly patients, may make the difference between life and death.

__26__, there are some kinds of pain that existing treatments cannot ease. __27__ doctors can do little in these cases is terribly distressing for everyone involved but is certainly __28__. What seems less understandable is that many people suffer not because their discomfort is untreatable but because physicians are often reluctant to __29__ morphine. Morphine is the safest, most effective painkiller known for constant, severe pain, but it is also __30__ for some people. __31__, it is rarely prescribed.

Indeed, concern over addiction has __32__ many nations in Europe and elsewhere to ban __33__ any uses of morphine and related substances, including their medical applications. Even __34__ morphine is a legal medical therapy, as it is in Great Britain and the U.S., many doctors, afraid of turning patients into addicts, __35__ amounts that are too small to control pain.

21. A. boost   B. erode   C. wear   D. distract
22. A. driving   B. drive   C. drives   D. driven
23. A. compound   B. comprehensible C. exhaustive   D. profound
24. A. with   B. whereby   C. thereby   D. as
25. A. thus   B. though   C. along   D. instead
26. A. Fortunately   B. Sadly   C. Notably   D. Promptly
27. A. Though   B. Which   C. That   D. While
28. A. understandable B. shameful   C. worrying   D. puzzling
29. A. promote   B. produce   C. prescribe   D. present
30. A. strong   B. costly   C. ineffective   D. addictive
31. A. Consequently B. Conclusively   C. However   D. Meanwhile
32. A. urged   B. enhanced   C. led   D. stimulated
33. A. presently   B. virtually   C. decisively   D. promptly
34. A. when   B. though   C. which   D. where
35. A. administering B. administer   C. administered   D. to administer

PART III   READING COMPREHENSION

Section A (60 minutes, 30 points)

Directions: *Below each of the following passages you will find some questions or incomplete* statements. Each question or statement is followed by four choices marked A, B, C, and D. Read each passage carefully, and then select the choice that best answers the question or completes the statement. Mark the letter of your choice with a single bar across the square bracket on your Machine-scoring Answer Sheet.

Passage One

Germany, Europe's economic powerhouse, does not lack courage: it rebounded from two world wars, digested reunification and has now powered ahead of neighbors still reeling from the financial crisis. It overhauled a rigid labor market and raised the retirement age to 67 with little fuss. Most recently, it simply decided to abandon nuclear power.

With this boldness at the top comes obedience at the bottom — 82 million Germans will wait at a pedestrian red light, even with no car in sight.

But when it comes to empowering women, no Teutonic drive or respect seems to work — even under one of the world's most powerful women, Chancellor Angela Merkel.

Despite a batch of government measures and ever more passionate debate about gender roles, only about 14 percent of German mothers with one child resume full-time work, and only 6 percent of those with two. All 30 German stock index companies are run by men. Nationwide, a single woman presides on a supervisory board: Dr. Simone Bagel-Trah at Henkel.

Eighteen months after the *International Herald Tribune* launched a series on the state of women in the 21st century with a look at Germany, the country has emerged as a test case for the push-and-pull of economics and tradition.

For the developed world, Germany's situation suggests that puzzling out how to remove enduring barriers to women's further progress is one of the hardest questions to solve.

In all European countries, from the traditionally macho southern rim to more egalitarian Nordic nations, the availability and affordability of child care, intertwined with traditional ideas about gender roles, have proved key factors in determining gender equality. The nature of male networks is another telling factor.

Women remain a striking minority in top corporate circles, even in fiercely egalitarian countries like Sweden or the US where opportunities often go with one's abilities. Very few countries approach 20 percent female representation on corporate executive boards.

Yet if Swedish executive suites boast 17 percent women and the United States and Britain 14 percent, in Germany it is 2 percent — as in India, according to McKinsey's 2010 Women Matter report.

One of the countries in most need of female talent — the German birthrate is among the lowest in Europe and labor shortages in skilled technical professions are already 150,000 — Germany is a place where gender stereotypes remain engrained in the mind, and in key institutions across society.

36. The first two paragraphs describe _____.

A. practical German leadership in various fields

B. retired German workers' lives

C. a successful Germany since World War I

D. a German style of dealing with crises

37. According to the author, under the leadership of Chancellor Angela Merkel _____ .

A. females must have been allowed to take some full-time jobs

B. women might have been supported to become stronger

C. discussions should have been held about women's importance

D. women should have become more powerful than they are now

38. The author mentions Dr. Simone Bagel-Trah in order to show _____ .

A. the potential for females to become top executives

B. the scarcity of female CEOs in the country

C. the inferiority of female CEOs to male ones

D. the strength of a company led by a female

39. The phrase "the push-and-pull of economics and tradition" (in Paragraph 5) refers to the fact that _____ .

A. economic progress needs efforts by both genders

B. traditional gender roles remain in modern society

C. economic needs conflict with traditional mindsets

D. traditional gender bias makes an economy even worse

40. Which of the following situations forms a barrier to European women's progress?

A. A woman may feel very proud with all her colleagues being male.

B. A babysitter may find it very hard to make the hostess satisfied.

C. Men's friendship is thought to be much stronger than women's.

D. Women are deemed more capable than men only at home.

41. By writing this passage, the author aims to suggest that in Germany the improvement of women's social roles is _____ .

A. essential   B. debatable   C. hopeless   D. formidable

Passage Two

Lately I got a chance to read People magazine's most recent compilation of "The 50 Most Beautiful People in the World." It was fabulous. In addition to offering helpful grooming tips, the issue involves an attempt to answer one of the most difficult questions of our time: Which is ultimately more influential, nature or nurture?

Consider first the extreme nurturists, who abstain from the notion that anything is biologically fixed. There's John Watson, famous for the statement: "Give me a child and let me control the total environment in which he is raised, and I will turn him into whatever I wish."

A nurture viewpoint is also advanced by TV star Jenna Elfman, who attributes her beauty to drinking 100 ounces of water a day, and using a moisturizer that costs $1,000 a pound. However, even a beginner in the study of human developmental biology might easily note that no degree of expensive moisturizers would get, say, me on People's beauty list.

Naturally, similarly strong opinions come from the opposing, nature faction — the genetic determinists among the Most Beautiful. Perhaps the cockiest of this school is Josh Brolin, an actor whose statement could readily serve as a manifesto for those in his profession: "I was given my dad's good genes."

One searches the pages for a middle ground, for the interdisciplinary synthesizer who perceives the contributions of both nature and nurture. At last, we find Monica, a singer, who has an absolutely wondrous skill for applying makeup. This, at first, seems like just more nurture propaganda. But where does she get this cosmetic aptitude? Her mother supplies the answer: it's something that's inborn. One gasps at the insight: There is a genetic influence on how one interacts with the environment. Too bad a few more people can't think this way when figuring out what genes have to do with intelligence, substance abuse, or violence.

In matters of human beauty, hardwired preferences matter but can be overcome. Novelist George Eliot was strikingly homely, but her magnetic character inspired Henry James to write in a letter: "She is magnificently ugly — deliciously hideous. She has a dull grey eye, a vast pendulous nose, a huge mouth, and full of uneven teeth… Now in this vast ugliness resides a most powerful beauty which, in a very few minutes, steals forth and charms the mind, so that you end as I ended, in falling in love with her."

42. The article suggests that People magazine regularly _____.
    A. provides a list of the most beautiful people in the world
    B. gives advice about how to look like international beauties
    C. provides guidance on answering complex questions
    D. offers help in dealing with marriage or family problems
43. What John Watson said can best be interpreted as _____.
    A. parents' oversight guides a child's growth
    B. one's upbringing determines what they become
    C. a change of environment affects one's health
    D. child-raising is by no means easy
44. According to Paragraph 3, the author believes _____.
    A. one can get prettier if drinking enough water every day
    B. Jenna Elfman's experience is worth publicizing
    C. the secrets of beauty are found in human biology
    D. beauty must depend on more than one or two factors
45. According to the author, Josh Brolin's statement shows that the actor is _____.
    A. over-charming   B. over-assertive
    C. over-confident   D. over-sensitive
46. As an example in favor of both nature and nurture, the author feels that Monica's mother is

rather _____.

    A. insightful   B. absurd   C. justifiable   D. irrelevant

47. As he wrote, Henry James fell in love with George Eliot because of _____.

    A. her unique ugliness   B. her attractive character

    C. her masculine beauty   D. her skillful writing

Passage Three

All countries have obvious incentives to learn from past mistakes, but those that have successfully risen to the status of great powers may be less inclined to adapt quickly in the future. When it comes to learning the right lessons, paradoxically, nothing fails like prior success.

This wouldn't seem to make sense. After all, strong and wealthy states can afford to devote a lot of resources to analyzing important foreign-policy problems. But then again, when states are really powerful, the negative consequences of foolish behavior rarely prove fatal. Just as America's "Big Three" automakers were so large and dominant they could resist reform and innovation despite ample signs that foreign competition was rapidly overtaking them, strong and wealthy states can keep misguided policies in place and still manage to limp along for many years.

The history of the Soviet Union offers an apt example of this phenomenon. Soviet-style communism was woefully inefficient and brutally inhumane, and its Marxist-Leninist ideology both alarmed the capitalist world and created bitter splits within the international communist movement. Yet the Soviet Union survived for almost 70 years and was one of the world's two superpowers for more than four decades. The United States has also suffered serious self-inflicted wounds on the foreign-policy front in recent decades, but the consequences have not been so severe as to compel a broader reassessment of the ideas and strategies that have underpinned many of these mistakes.

The tendency to cling to questionable ideas or failed practices will be particularly strong when a set of policy initiatives is bound up in a great power's ruling ideology or political culture. Soviet leaders could never quite abandon the idea of world revolution, and defenders of British and French colonialism continued to see it as the "white man's burden." Today, U.S. leaders remain stubbornly committed to the goals of nation-building and democracy promotion despite their discouraging track record with these endeavors.

Yet because the universal ideals of liberty and democracy are core American principles, it is hard for U.S. leaders to acknowledge that other societies cannot be readily remade in America's image. Even when U.S. leaders recognize that they cannot create "some sort of Central Asian Valhalla," as Defense Secretary Robert Gates acknowledged in 2009, they continue to spend billions of dollars trying to build democracy in Afghanistan, a largely traditional society that has never had a strong central state, let alone a democratic one.

48. Concerning improvement based on past history, great powers often _____.

    A. fail to distinguish right from wrong

    B. understate all their wrongdoings

C. mention their prior success alone

D. ignore having made mistakes

49. America's "Big Three" automakers are used as an example to show that _____.

A. nations would need to adapt for their future

B. businesses would learn from failures

C. countries could survive their faults

D. enterprises could defeat their rivals

50. The passage suggests that the Soviet Union _____.

A. had long been in crisis before it fell

B. used to be number one in the world

C. lasted for a long time because of its brutality

D. caused separatism in western countries

51. The US sees the troubles with its foreign affairs as _____.

A. a vital blow to its world position

B. resulting from its ideological flaws

C. suffering temporary setbacks

D. a sign of deficiencies in its policies

52. Britain and France are mentioned as those who _____.

A. had their own forms of democracy

B. used to be enemies of the Soviet Union

C. were once superior to the US

D. wanted to be world leaders

53. The author most likely intends to give great powers _____.

A. advice B. support C. sympathy D. threats

Passage Four

Much of the debate about multiculturalism in the UK is crass, ignorant and misconceived. The new critics, from the left in particular, risk contributing to the very processes they decry, since they are so dismissive of the achievements that mark this country out from others, particularly in Europe. I can't think of any other EU state that has been more successful than the UK in managing cultural diversity.

In this country, we need more multiculturalism, not less. That is to say, we should concentrate upon developing further links between different ethnic and cultural communities, and upon dialogue even when on the surface it seems to create problems. Jack Straw's remarks about women who wear the veil have provoked huge controversy. But he was right to raise the issue, because he was emphasizing the importance of connection and communication. In a pluralistic society all groups should accept the need for interrogation from others — it is the condition of producing mutual respect, rather than undermining it. He was not suggesting any sort of coercion.

Pakistani groups in particular featured in the riots that happened in Oldham, Leeds and

Bradford in the 1990s and early 2000s. At that time as well, multiculturalism came in for a bashing: it was widely blamed in the press for creating segregation between Pakistani and local white communities. These claims were made, however, by writers with scant knowledge of the neighbourhoods in question.

A sociologist at the University of Leeds, Ludi Simpson, later studied the communities concerned in depth and — something often neglected — over time. He found that segregation was far lower than most outside commentators had suggested. Many Pakistani families originally living in the inner-city areas had in fact moved out across the years to middle-class neighbourhoods or rural areas. Contrary to the idea that the Asian (mostly Muslim) groups wanted to keep to themselves, the evidence showed a desire for more mixing, with most wanting independent lifestyles away from too much ethnic clustering.

For much of the 20th century the main perceived social problem was that of class conflict. Class differences continue to overlap with cultural and ethnic divisions. But for us today the perceived social problem is that of the management of diversity: delivering its benefits, which are many, while **containing** the conflicts and costs that it can incur. We shan't get anywhere in pursuing such goals if we abandon multiculturalism.

54. According to the author, the new critics are _____.
    A. reluctant to understand the differences between cultures
    B. getting into a position contrary to their own argument
    C. ignorant of the reasons why UK stands out in Europe
    D. going to the extreme left in criticizing multiculturalism
55. Jack Straw's remarks as mentioned probably convey the idea that _____.
    A. any kind of culture in the world deserves respect
    B. gender bias remains the obstacle to women's liberation
    C. women's veil wearing shows cultural backwardness
    D. social hierarchy remains a problem in Islamic countries
56. As suggested by the author, the Pakistani groups in the 1990s and early 2000s _____.
    A. suffered from wide blame in the media
    B. made strong criticism of multiculturalism
    C. had conflicts with the local white communities
    D. rose in rebellion against the government
57. The author suggests that the blame put on multiculturalism was due to the lack of _____.
    A. close investigation into the reasons for the racial segregation
    B. in-depth knowledge about the cultural groups involved
    C. an acute awareness of the feelings of the inner-city dwellers
    D. a full understanding of the gap between different social classes
58. Ludi Simpson's study showed that _____.
    A. the cluster of mixed ethnic groups likely gave rise to ethnic tension

B. the Pakistani groups tended to live peacefully much more than before
C. the Muslim community mostly kept separate from other communities
D. the wish to live exclusively with one's own ethnic groups was a myth

59. The boldfaced word "containing" in the last paragraph can best be replaced by the word "_____."

A. controlling   B. compromising   C. covering   D. considering

Passage Five

NASA's new Mars probe, a $2.5 billion, nuclear-powered rover the size of a small car, is at the Florida launch site being prepared for its nine-month journey to the red planet, with one key issue still unresolved — where to land.

The Mars Science Laboratory, nicknamed Curiosity, will delve deeper than any previous science mission to answer the age-old question about whether there is life beyond Earth. The goal of the project is to determine if the region where Curiosity lands has or ever had the right conditions to support microbial life.

Scientists spent years poring over pictures and analyzing chemical data collected by a fleet of robotic spacecraft circling Mars before narrowing down the options to four finalists: Eberswalde Crater, Mawrth Vallis, Holden Crater and Gale Crater.

"Each site has things that make it good and things that make it not quite so good," said planetary scientist Matt Golombek. "It's kind of hard to select because it boils down to which kind of science is important to you, and that's almost personal."

The rover will touch down within a 12.4-by-15.5 mile targeted area, a relatively small patch of real estate for interplanetary travel. Being able to make a precision touchdown hasn't made things easy for scientists tapped to choose Curiosity's landing spot. In the past, lots of scientifically interesting sites were eliminated because of concerns the spacecraft wouldn't be able to make a safe landing.

Eberswalde Crater stands out among the four contenders because of a single, stunning geologic feature — a delta, believed to be a buildup of sediment left by flowing water.

"If you want a site that probably has the highest chance of preserving organics and biosignatures that might have existed, this is the place," Golombek said. "It's just a spectacular example where water came and built up a sediment."

The attractive Eberswalde site, however, has a serious drawback as well. If its deposits turn out to be nothing more than clay-dusted rocks, the mission would be largely a **bust**.

The next candidate site, Mawrth Vallis, is an open book of **Martian history**, with exposed valley walls that date back about 3.7 billion years, nearly as old as the planet itself. Its clays, known as phyllosilicates, form in the presence of water, believed to be a necessary ingredient for life. Mawrth's short-coming is that scientists don't understand how it formed. Water that once flowed in the valley could have been far too acidic for life to flourish.

60. The primary purpose of the passage is to discuss _____ .
    A. the controversy over the mission carried out by Curiosity
    B. the age-old efforts to search for life beyond the earth
    C. the power of the nuclear-driven probe in collecting data
    D. the best place for the landing of a new Mars probe

61. According to the passage, the four options _____ .
    A. cater to a small group of scientists' tastes
    B. represent different disciplines of science
    C. have advantages as well as disadvantages
    D. differ from others in the goals that they serve

62. What is true about Eberswalde Crater?
    A. The delta shows that life might have existed there.
    B. Clay-dusted rocks characterize the deposits there.
    C. The sediment must have resulted from acidic water.
    D. Having water makes it the best choice for the mission.

63. The boldfaced word "bust" (in the next to the last paragraph) is closest in meaning to "_____ ."
    A. financial burden   B. daydream
    C. vain attempt   D. tough task

64. In the last paragraph, "Martian history" probably refers to the history of _____ .
    A. fiction-writing about space   B. Martian-led missions
    C. Martian geology   D. Mars exploration

65. The passage will probably continue with the description of _____ .
    A. other key ingredients for life besides water
    B. Holden Crater and Gale Crater respectively
    C. scientists' further analysis of Mawrth Vallis
    D. different difficulties in making the decision

Section B (20 minutes, 10 points)

Directions: *In each of the following passages, five sentences have been removed from the original text. They are listed from A to F and put below the passage. Choose the most suitable sentence from the list to fill in each of the blanks (numbered 66 to 75). For each passage, there is one sentence that does not fit in any of the blanks. Mark your answers on your Machine-scoring Answer Sheet.*

Passage One

There is an immense and justified pride in what our colleges have done. At the same time there is a growing uneasiness about their product. The young men and women who carry away our degrees are a very attractive lot — in looks, in bodily fitness, in kindliness, energy, courage, and buoyancy. 66 That too is in some ways admirable; for in spite of President Lowell's remark that the university should be a repository of great learning, since the freshmen always bring a stock with them and the seniors take little away, the fact is that our graduates have every chance to be well informed, and usually are so. 67 When it becomes articulate, it takes the form of wishes that these attractive young products of ours had more intellectual depth and force, more freedom from trouble and worry in dealing with the different ideas, more of the firm, clear, quiet thoughtfulness that is a very potent and needed guard against fraudulence and deception which exist around them and keep harassing them constantly. 68 Firstly, granting that our graduates know a good deal, their knowledge lies about in fragments and never gets welded together into the stuff of a tempered and mobile mind. Secondly, our university graduates have been so busy boring holes for themselves, acquiring special knowledge and skills, that in later life they have astonishingly little in common in the way of ideas, standards, or principles. Thirdly, it is alleged that the past two decades have revealed a singular want of clarity about the great ends of living, attachment to which gives significance and direction to a life. 69 My argument will be simple, perhaps too simple. What I shall contend is that there is a great deal of truth in each of them, and that the remedy for each is the same. 70

A. Yet the uneasiness persists.
B. It is larger infusion of the philosophic habit of mind.
C. But what of their intellectual equipment?
D. Our colleges have failed.
E. Here are three grave charges against American education, and I want to discuss them briefly.
F. The complaint commonly breaks itself up into a list of three particulars.

Passage Two

Woody Allen, in earlier, funnier days, told a joke about two women in a resort in the Catskills complaining about the cuisine: "The food at this place is really terrible," says one. "Yeah, and such small portions," replies her friend. 71 They are dangerous things, their production and transport often unpleasant, the less visible environmental consequences of their use worse still. And there is not enough of them. The current boom in "unconventional" gas seems likely to provide good news on both fronts.

 72 Oil is found in relatively few places, and its energy density, pumpability and ease of use in internal-combustion engines make it particularly well suited as a transportation fuel. Coal is found in many more places and it cannot be pumped around, but can be crushed and burned and so produces baseload power. Gas, typically found and exploited in the same sort of places as oil, is easily moved around through plumbing but is not, usually, seen as a transportation fuel.

 73 Other innovations, such as producing liquefied natural gas from offshore sources and shipping it to its destinations directly, and technologies that might allow exploitation of the natural

gas that is frozen into some permafrosts, further increase the scope for new production. __74__

   Coal, unlike oil, is hard to embargo: and an obvious consequence of the changes in gas production is that they make gas supply a less potent political tool. __75__ But countries can benefit from unconventional reserves without actually having any. More producers and a larger capacity to ship the fuel in its liquefied form will make gas a more fungible commodity. That continuing trend will mean that very few countries will ever be locked into a single source.

A. Now new drilling technologies pioneered in America are allowing gas to be extracted from more types of rock, and thus from much more widespread sources.
B. In Europe, where Russia has used supply cut-offs to put pressure on neighbouring Ukraine, discoveries of shale gas in eastern Europe could diversify supply in a useful way.
C. All told, this transition to more plentiful, diverse and widespread reserves in effect makes gas a bit more like coal, and a bit less like oil.
D. Gas that's now being unconventionally extracted isn't lying there underground in big natural pools near the earth's surface, and it's not easy to collect.
E. Thus the current thinking about fossil fuels.
F. The three conventional forms of fossil carbon — oil, coal and gas — differ both in the way the earth stores them and the way its people use them.

PAPER TWO

PART IV   TRANSLATION (30 minutes, 15 points)

Directions: *Read the following text carefully and then translate the underlined segments into Chinese. Write your Chinese version in the proper space on your Answer Sheet.*

   Do today's kids make terrible entry-level workers? (1) That's a question much on employers' minds as graduation season kicks off and young adults begin their first full-time jobs. We've all heard the stories: assistants who won't "assist," new workers who can't set an alarm, employees who can't grasp institutional hierarchies.
   Bosses who toiled in the pre-Self Esteem Era salt mines have little patience for these upstarts. (2) A popular advice columnist had some choice words last week for a young employee who dismissively waved her sandwich at a superior requesting back-up during a critical meeting. The young woman explained that she was on her lunch break. Moreover, she noted, being "errand girl" wasn't in her job description.
   It's easy to laugh off these anecdotes, but there are some complex reasons for the lack of familiarity with work norms. (3) For one thing, many twenty-something adults have never held a menial summer job, once considered training wheels for adult life in the American middle class. It

was once common to see teenagers mowing lawns, waiting tables, digging ditches, and bagging groceries for modest wages in the long summer months. (4) Summer employment was a social equalizer, allowing both rich and financially strapped teenagers to gain a foothold on adulthood, learning the virtues of hard work, respect and teamwork in a relatively low-stakes atmosphere. But youth employment has declined precipitously over the years and young people are losing a chance to develop these important life skills in the process. (5) Teenagers and twenty-somethings are the least skilled members of the work force, so it's not surprising that they would be edged out in a recession by more reliable full-time workers.

PART V WRITING (40 minutes, 20 points)

Directions: *Write an essay of no less than 200 words on the topic given below. Use the space provided on your Answer Sheet II.*

TOPIC

People who claim to have supernatural powers, like Wang Lin, Yan Xin and many others, have come and gone in the past few decades and have always had a large following. What conclusion may be drawn from this phenomenon?

2013年10月试题精解

第一部分　词　　汇

1. 答案:C

   本题考查形容词的语义。A 焦虑的,发愁的;B 听得见的;C 令人敬畏的,令人惊叹的;D 和蔼可亲的,令人愉悦的。该句的大意为:突然大地从我们脚下陷落下去,一块可怕的凹陷出现在我们面前。

2. 答案:D

   本题考查动词与名词的搭配。A 夸张,夸大;B 挖空,挖掘;C(费力地)取出;采掘,提炼;D 唤起,引起;使人想起。该句的大意为:自传性质的广告可以唤起消费者对于该产品或该品牌的回忆。

3. 答案:B

   本题考查介词与名词的搭配。A 山脉,排、行,走向;B 边,边沿,边缘;C 一部分,组成部分;D 连接,纽带。该句的大意为:许多动物濒临灭绝,动物园可以为它们提供一个安全的地方生存、繁衍。

4. 答案:A

   本题考查名词与动词的搭配。A 猛增,剧增;B 射中;C 摇摆,摆动;D 安顿,使安居,确立(制度等)。该句的大意为:如果费用继续猛增的话,国家将无法长期承担这一计划,该计划(最终)将无人问津。

5. 答案:A

   本题考查名词的语义和句子的逻辑关系,是一道语境题。A 似是而非的矛盾说法;B 进退两难的困境,窘境;C 极,(性质、特点等)正好相反,截然对立;D 误解,错误印象。该句的大意为:矛盾的是,尽管我们现在比任何时候都更长寿,但是人们也比任何时候都更困扰于健康问题。

6. 答案:D

   本题考查介词短语。A 本质上,大体上,其实;B 到时候,在今后适当的时候;C 平均起来;D 回想起来,回顾往事。该句的大意为:回想起来,霍尔先生承认当时推得过猛,最终他的努力失败了。

7. 答案:C

   本题考查动词的形近词辨析。A 恳求,乞求;B 使生效,履行,实施;C 妨碍,阻碍,阻止;D 给予、传授,告知、通知。该句的大意为:一辆出租车和一辆洗衣店的卡车在第六大道以毫厘之差几乎相撞,并且两辆车停的位置都阻碍了对方的通行。

8. 答案:B

   本题考查动词的语义。A 长大(或发展)得使……不再适用;B 探索,探究,调查研究;C 感知、感觉,认识到、意识到;D 搏斗,争斗。该句的大意为:在凯瑟琳·温德的新小说《安娜贝尔》一书中,作者探讨了先天与后天的区别。

9. 答案:A

  本题考查动词短语。A 通过,设法,继续存在;B 克服,使度过,走完;C 相处,进展,前进;D 横过(马路、河流等),使被理解,使被接受。该句的大意为:他们在湖上漂流着,依靠打鱼捕虾度日。

10. 答案:D

  本题考查动词的语义和句子的逻辑关系,是一道语境题。A 复制;B 感知,感受;C(尤指通过努力)取得,获得,学到;D 证明、证实,核实,查清。该句的大意为:在加州的一些住房里,单靠钥匙是开不了门的,还需验证房主的语音信息。

11. 答案:C

  本题考查动词与名词的搭配。A 引,领,招待;B 开始,创始;C 吸引、引诱,诱惑;D 设陷阱捕捉。该句的大意为:为了吸引游客和其他人,从而拯救艰难度日的餐馆,法国将降低餐饮业中食品和酒水的税率。这样一来,50 美元的一顿饭可以节省 7.05 美元。

12. 答案:B

  本题考查动词短语。A 吸引,领会,包括;B 朝……进发,奔,走向;C 渴望,羡慕,憧憬;D 伸展,延长,分散。该句的大意为:如今的全球经济已经产生了更多的任何人都无法想象的大起大落,而亚洲可能会面临一个更令人沮丧的经济猛跌。

13. 答案:A

  本题考查名词语义和句子中的并列关系,是一道语境题。A 疾病,病痛;B 疗法,治疗;C(事故等)伤亡人数;D 入迷,嗜好。该句的大意为:在 20 世纪 70 年代,他一直不知疲倦地宣传这种药物,认为它可以用来治疗抑郁症(他自己曾得过)和其他疾病。

14. 答案:D

  本题考查名词与动词的搭配。A 绊脚,绊倒,结结巴巴地说;B 摇晃,蹒跚;C 使转动,使盘绕,使扭转;D 起伏,汹涌、猛冲。该句的大意为:听到这个消息,她感觉到自己怒火中烧。

15. 答案:C

  本题考查形容词的语义。A 不一致的,不协调的;B 支持的,维持的;C 惯于怀疑的,表示怀疑的;D 预期的,未来的,即将发生的。该句的大意为:许多广告商依旧对互联网持怀疑态度,质疑人们对网络的依赖。

16. 答案:B

  本题考查动词短语。A 赞成,赞同;B 耸肩表示蔑视或表示对……不屑理睬,摆脱;C 炫耀,卖弄;D 捡起,(尤指偶然地、无意地、不费劲地)得到,学会。该句的大意为:如果专家的建议更积极,家长们会在短短几天内就能摆脱几十年形成的观点吗?

17. 答案:B

  本题考查动词与介词的搭配。A 组成、构成,作曲;B 征税,加(负担、惩罚等)于……、把……强加于;C 排列、布置,安排、处理;D 暴露,使遭受,使处于……作用(或影响)之下。该句的大意为:如果父母已经亲眼看到学校的环境,并且了解学校将给他们的孩子布置什么样的作业,这会非常有用。

18. 答案:D

  本题考查形容词的语义。A 充血的,引起拥堵的;B (结成)社团的,合伙的;C 合作的,协

作的,协力完成的;D 团结的,有聚合性的。该句的大意为:作者巧妙地将这些片段融合成一个连贯统一的整体。

19. 答案:C

本题考查连接词的用法。A(用……)代替……,(是……)而不是……;B 至于、关于,就……方面来说;C 尽管,虽然;D 要不是。该句的大意为:尽管他的价值观看上去和中产阶级的格格不入,本质上来讲他仍是中产阶级。

20. 答案:D

本题考查动词的近义词辨析。A 更换,交换;B 改变,转变;C 使转变、使转化,使改变信仰;D 传播,传递,表达,传达。该句的大意为:很难将外语中俗语的意思精准地传达出来。

第二部分 完形填空

本文主要阐述疼痛对人类生命质量的负面影响,以及医生为什么不给病人使用吗啡来止痛的原因。

21. 答案:B

本题考查动词的词义辨析及对语句的理解。A 促进(及物动词);B 削弱(及物动词);C 磨损(不及物动词);D 使……分散(及物动词)。原文是说长时间的疼痛能削弱人的求生意愿。

22. 答案:A

本题考查现在分词做状语的用法,是一道语法题。在这里,需要一个现在分词做主句的结果状语,表示长时间的疼痛能削弱人的求生意愿,有时甚至迫使人自杀。

23. 答案:D

本题考查形容词的词义辨析。A 复合的;B 可理解的;C 详尽的;D 深远的。本句的意思是,疼痛对身体的影响同样巨大。

24. 答案:C

本题考查连接词的词性和用法。A 介词,随着;B 关系副词,凭……,由此;C 表目的连词,借以、从而、由此;D 连接副词,当。本句的意思是,持续剧烈的疼痛会影响人们的睡眠和胃口,从而让人疲惫不堪并减少了身体各器官可吸收的营养物质。

25. 答案:A

本句考查连词的用法和上下文的逻辑关系。本句接着上句,意思是,由于以上情形的出现,于是疼痛拖延了病人从疾病和伤势中恢复健康的时间。

26. 答案:B

本句考查对上下文的理解。前句是说,疼痛对人体有很大的伤害,本句意思是,有很多种疼痛是现在的治疗技术无法缓解的,从前后的逻辑关系,可以看出,这是一种让人无能为力的、悲伤的现实。

27. 答案:C

本句考查对主语从句的掌握,是一道语法题。在句中,That doctors can do little in these cases 作主语,是主语从句。当主语从句放在主语位置时,that 不能省。另外,四个选项中,只有 C that 是引导主语从句的关联词。

28. 答案:A

本题考查对句意的理解。可以从该句中 but 一词表明的逻辑关系来理解。本句是说,医生对有些疼痛无能为力这个事实虽让人沮丧,但也能得到人们的理解。

29. 答案:C

本题考查动词的形近词辨析。A 促进;B 产生;C 开处方;D 呈现。本句的意思是,让人不太能理解的是,很多病人忍受疼痛的折磨不是因为他们的疼痛不可治疗,而是因为医生不愿意给他们开出吗啡这个处方。

30. 答案:D

本题考查形容词词义辨析及对文章上下文的理解。A 强烈的;B 昂贵的;C 无效的;D 成瘾的。本句意思是,对付长期性的剧烈疼痛,吗啡是最安全、最有效的止痛药,但对有些人而言,这种药又是上瘾的。另外,可以从接下来一段的第一句话来确定对本句的理解:对吗啡成瘾的关注导致欧洲和其他地方的很多国家禁止使用它。

31. 答案:A

本题考查上下文句子的逻辑关系和连接副词的使用。前文提到,对付长期性的剧烈疼痛,吗啡是最安全、最有效的止疼药,但对有些人而言,这种药又是上瘾的。由此可以得出一个合乎逻辑的结论,吗啡很少被医生用于处方。

32. 答案:C

本题考查动词的词义辨析。A 强烈要求;B 加强;C 引导,导致;D 促进。这句的意思是,对吗啡成瘾性的关注导致欧洲和其他地方的很多国家禁止使用它。

33. 答案:B

本题考查副词的语义。A 马上;B 实际上;C 决定性;D 及时。这句话是说,对吗啡成瘾性的关注导致欧洲和其他地方的很多国家禁止对吗啡及其相关物质的任何使用。

34. 答案:D

本题考查关系副词的使用,是一道语法题。在 where morphine is a legal medical therapy 中,where 是关系副词,引导一个状语从句修饰主句。这句的意思是,即使是在英国和美国这些将吗啡视为一种合法治疗手段的地方,很多医生还是担心把病人变成瘾君子,因此给病人开的吗啡量太小以至于根本无法控制疼痛。

35. 答案:B

本题考查动词不同时态和形态的用法,是一道语法题。在本句中,句子的主语是 many doctors,afraid of turning patient into addicts 是插入成分,amounts that are too small to control pain 是宾语,可见句子缺少一个谓语。

第三部分　阅读理解

第一节　阅读理解 A

第一篇:

36. 答案:A

本题是例证题,要求考生可以从第一段和第二段中提到的各个例子中总结出共同的相似点:即德国政府在各方面施政效率都很高。关键点:... with this boldness at the top....。

37. 答案:D

本题是细节事实题,考查对第三段的理解,关键点在 even 这个副词上,同时需要注意选项中虚拟语气的含义。

38. 答案:B

本题是细节事实题,考查对第四段最后一句话的理解,关键点:...a single women...。

39. 答案:C

本题是词汇题,考查该短语在第五段中的语义。短语本身并不费解,答题关键是将短语放在文章的上下文中理解。本题也可以利用排除法,看哪一个选项与文章的主题大意最接近。

40. 答案:D

本题是长句理解题,考查第七段第一句话的意思。关键点:...intertwined with traditional ideas about gender roles...。

41. 答案:A

本题是推理题,考查第十段第一句话的意思。关键点:...in most need of female talent...。

第二篇:

42. 答案:A

本题是细节事实题,考查第一段第一句话的意思,关键点:...most recent compilation of...。

43. 答案:B

本题是例证题,考查第二段的结构,看懂 John Watson 这个例子是为了说明极端后天论者的观点。关键点:... the extreme nurturists...。

44. 答案:D

本题是推理题,考查第三段最后一句话的意思,注意一般 however 后面的信息往往是作者重点论述的内容或观点。

45. 答案:C

本题是词汇题,考查第四段中 cockiest 一词的含义。我们可以利用构词法和联想法大致推出该词的意思。首先,-est 可能是形容词最高级的后缀;其次,我们可以联想到 cock 一词表示"公鸡",可比喻趾高气扬的人。

46. 答案:A

本题是细节事实题,考查第五段第五句和第六句的意思,关键点:...one grasps at the insight...。

47. 答案:B

本题是长句理解题,考查第六段第二句话的意思,关键点:...her magnetic character inspired Henry James...。

第三篇:

48. 答案:D

本题是推理题,考查第一段第二句话的意思,关键点:...nothing fails like prior success...。

49. 答案:C

本题既是例证题,又是长句理解题,考查第二段最后一句的意思以及与前一句的逻辑关系。该句的大意是:尽管种种迹象显示国外竞争对手正在快速地取代美国的三大汽车厂商,他们依然没有进行改革和创新;同样,强大而富裕的国家就算政策失误,依旧可以向前发展,只不过速度会减缓而已。

50. 答案：A

本题是主旨大意题，考查第三段的前半段的主要内容，关键点：...woefully inefficient and brutally inhumane...。

51. 答案：C

本题是长句理解题，考查第三段最后一句话的意思，关键点：...suffered serious self-inflicted wounds...，...but the consequences have not been so severe...。

52. 答案：D

本题是推理题，考查第四段第二句话的意思，关键点：...defenders of British and French colonialism continued to see it as the "white man's burden"...。

53. 答案：A

本题是写作目的题，考查对文章主要内容和写作意图的把握。

第四篇：

54. 答案：B

本题是长句理解题，考查第一段第二句话的意思，关键点：...contributing to the very processes they decry...。

55. 答案：A

本题是细节事实题，考查第二段倒数第二句话的意思，关键点：...it is the condition of producing mutual respect...。

56. 答案：C

本题是细节事实题，考查第三段第一句话的意思，关键点：...featured in the riots...。

57. 答案：B

本题是推理题，考查对第三段最后一句话的理解，关键点：...by writers with scant knowledge of the neighbourhoods in question...。

58. 答案：D

本题是细节事实题，考查第四段最后一句话的意思，关键点：Contrary to the idea...。

59. 答案：A

本题是词汇题，考查第五段第三句话中 delivering 与 containing 两个词之间的逻辑关系，关键是通过逻辑关系把握 containing 一词在这句话中的含义。

第五篇：

60. 答案：D

本题是推理题，考查第一段最后一行中"...with one key issue still unresolved"的意思。

61. 答案：C

本题是细节事实题，考查第四段第一句话的意思。

62. 答案：A

本题是正误判断题，考查第六段至第九段中提到的一些信息，可以用"找错、排除"的方法确定最佳选项。

63. 答案:C

本题是词汇题,考查第八段第二句话与第一句话之间的关系,第一句话中的"a serious drawback"是该段的核心词。

64. 答案:C

本题是词汇题,考查第九段第一句话的意思:选择这一环形山着陆的优势在于从这里可以看出火星地质变化发展的历史。

65. 答案:B

本题是文章结构题,考查整篇文章的行文脉络。另外,第三段最后一行中提到四个环形山,本文已经讨论了前两个,很可能接下来要提到后两个。

第二节　阅读理解 B

第一篇:

66. 答案:C

本题的答题关键是空格后一句中的"That"。另外,仔细阅读前一句,可以发现这里罗列了年轻人的各种优势,唯独没有提到空格后一句中重点讲到的"知识能力"这一方面,由此可见,这两句之间需要一个过渡和连接。

67. 答案:A

本题的突破口是把握这个语篇的结构。空格的上文主要讲的是年轻人的优势,而下文讲的是年轻人的抱怨和问题,这两者之间是强烈的对比。因此,空格处的句子应是该语篇的分水岭。

68. 答案:F

本题的答题关键是把握空格后的部分按照序列的方法讲的三个方面的问题。选项 E 和 F 中都提到了这三点,要求区分哪一个选项更适合统领下文,哪一个更适合总结归纳上文。

69. 答案:E

本题的答题关键是理解选项 E 既是总结归纳了上文,又引出下文——作者将要简要地提出解决方法。

70. 答案:B

本题的答题要点是前一句中提到的"the remedy for each is the same",选项 B 中的 it 呼应了"the remedy"一词。

第二篇:

71. 答案:E

本题的答题关键是了解第一段的结构。空格的上文从一个笑话幽默地引出文章真正的话题,笑话与话题之间的衔接需要一个过渡句。

72. 答案:F

本题的答题要点是把握一个自然段的起始句有可能统领下文。本题所在的第二段便是如此。

73. 答案:A

本题的突破口是下一句中的"other innovations",言下之意,空格中的句子一定谈到了某种技术或技术创新。

74. 答案：C

本题的突破口是选项 C 中的"this transition"呼应了空格前一句中提到的物质形态的转变。

75. 答案：B

本题的答题关键是把握空格所要填写的内容与上文之间的可能的关系，在这里，空格中的句子举例说明了前一句话的内容，两者之间是解释与被解释的关系。

第四部分 翻　译

(1) 译文：

随着毕业季节来临，年轻人开始从事他们第一份全职工作，这是许多雇主脑海里都有的一个问题。

解析：

该句中的动词词组"kick off"是理解的重点和难点。根据本句主语"graduation season"——"毕业季节，毕业季"这一敏感词汇，考生也应该能够顺理成章地猜测出"kick off"意为"到来，来临"；另外，根据 as 从句中的 and 一词连接的并列关系，也可以大致猜出"kick off"的语义。

(2) 译文：

上周，一名很受欢迎的忠告专栏作家针对一名年轻雇员的经历发表了一些精辟的见解，后者曾在一次至关重要的会议上向一名要求她帮忙的上司轻蔑地挥舞了手中的三明治。

解析：

该句的理解重点有二。一是能理解"choice words"，意为"一针见血的话，精辟的见解"。二是能看出"requesting back-up during a critical meeting"是名词"superior"的后置定语。

(3) 译文：

首先，许多20多岁的年轻人从来没有当过干粗活的暑期工，而暑期工曾经被美国中产阶级视为准备踏入成人生活的演练方式。

解析：

该句的理解重点同样有二。一是考生能根据"summer job"这个线索推测出"menial"意为"辛苦的，卑微的，不体面的"。二是能理解"training wheel"意为"用以训练的车轮"，而暑期工就像正式踏足职场前的训练一样，是中产阶级认为的步入成人生活的前奏。

(4) 译文：

暑期打工促进社会平等，使家境富足和经济窘困的青少年都能在一个相对低风险的环境中了解到努力工作、尊重和团队合作的价值。

解析：

理解该句的难点是"strapped"和"low-stakes"两处。根据前后文，考生应该能领会和富人相比较而言,普通青年时常面临的就是经济上的"困境"。而暑期工相比较正式的职场而言,其氛围还是相对轻松很多,"风险低"很多的。

(5) 译文:

二十几岁的年轻人是掌握技能最少的劳动力,因此在经济衰退时期他们便会被更加可靠的全职工作者所取代。

解析:

理解该句的重点是词组"edge out"。根据本句中因果关系,考生不难理解,在遭遇经济衰退的时候,职场上掌握技能最少的新手可以和熟练的全职工相抗衡吗?当然不行,新手是首当其冲被"排挤出去"的人。

第五部分 写 作

题目解析:

本题目试图探讨的是过去几十年里一些宣称具有特异功能的人士在社会上引起众人追随的现象。题目中的关键词,除了 supernatural powers 以外,还有题目中的 conclusion。写作文时一定要注意题目中的提问方式,此处问的是从此现象中可以得出什么"结论",而不是引起此现象的原因,因此,在写作的时候要针对结论来写。当然,在实际写作的时候,可以先扼要地分析原因,但落脚点和重点一定要放在结论上,也就是要点题。具体结论可以见仁见智,重要的是语言流畅,内容贴切,论述合乎逻辑,具有说服力。范文中的结论是特异功能并不存在,人们的盲从说明了科普知识的欠缺。

范文:

Wang Lin, a Qigong Master who claims to have supernatural power, has a large following in China nowadays. Many people, even some high officials or celebrities, come to visit Wang Lin. But he has finally been proved to be a cheat. One conclusion may be drawn from this phenomenon: people's scientific thinking still needs to be enhanced.

When some mysterious phenomena occur in society, ordinary people tend to believe it without critical thinking or scientific reasoning. Wang Lin, the so-called Qigong Master, was actually playing some tricks before the public. The supernatural power he claimed to possess was actually a hypnosis, which he had taken advantage of to control the audience's psychology. After a successful show, he claimed to possess a supernatural power which could help people to achieve success easily. This has greatly catered to people's unconscious desire to take a short cut to succeed, or get rich overnight. The promise of success brought them a very good feeling, hence caused them to turn a blind eye to the fact that Wang Lin's show of supernatural power was actually a magic show.

For decades, Chinese people have tended to believe in supernatural powers but not scientific knowledge. Qigong Masters like Yan Xin and Wang Lin have always had a large following. One reason why Qigong Masters always have a large following is that ordinary people have known very little scientific knowledge. This has led to the prevalence of pseudoscience in our society. If they had some scientific sense, these Masters of Qigong would not be able to cheat them so easily. We live in a physical world which is controlled by physical laws. Science has a very detailed explanation for most of the phenomena in this world. Supernatural power exists only in people's imagination, just as Wang Lin's case has shown.

From the above analysis, we may arrive at the conclusion that because of their psychological needs, people choose to believe in the existence of supernatural power. There is an urgent need to disseminate scientific ideas to the public. (340 words)

中国科学院大学
博士研究生入学考试
英语试题

（2014年3月）

考生须知：
一、本试卷由试卷一（PAPER ONE）和试卷二（PAPER TWO）两部分组成。试卷一为客观题，答卷使用标准化机读答题纸；试卷二为主观题，答卷使用非机读答题纸。
二、请考生一律用HB或2B铅笔填涂标准化机读答题纸，画线不得过细或过短。修改时请用橡皮擦拭干净。若因填涂不符合要求而导致计算机无法识别，责任由考生自负。请保持机读答题纸清洁、无折皱。答题纸切忌折叠。
三、全部考试时间总计180分钟，满分为100分。时间及分值分布如下：

试卷一：

Ⅰ 词汇	15 分钟	10 分
Ⅱ 完形填空	15 分钟	15 分
Ⅲ 阅读理解	80 分钟	40 分
小计	110 分钟	65 分

试卷二：

Ⅳ 英译汉	30 分钟	15 分
Ⅴ 写作	40 分钟	20 分
小计	70 分钟	35 分

UNIVERSITY OF CHINESE ACADEMY OF SCIENCES ENGLISH ENTRANCE EXAMINATION FOR PH. D PROGRAM
March 2014

PAPER ONE

PART I VOCABULARY (15 minutes, 10 points, 0.5 point each)

Directions: *Choose the word or expression below each sentence that best completes the statement, and mark the corresponding letter of your choice with a single bar across the square brackets on your Machine-scoring Answer Sheet.*

1. The old bridge is not strong enough to allow the _____ of heavy vehicles.
   A. passage   B. route   C. tunnel   D. pressure
2. The widowed old woman was so lonely that she would talk _____ to the strangers in the supermarkets about her pets.
   A. at best   B. at length   C. in bulk   D. in effect
3. Citizens of developed and developing nations alike face dangers from _____ medicines; they pose a terrible hazard to public health.
   A. distinctive   B. proliferating   C. fraudulent   D. ineffective
4. It must be much tougher than I realized, _____ on just 10,000 Yuan a year.
   A. getting by   B. getting away   C. getting around   D. getting along
5. When the relationship of parents and children is at this low _____, mutual love and respect need careful maintenance and rebuilding.
   A. rate   B. rank   C. scale   D. ebb
6. To have a knowledge-based economy and a scientifically _____ population, developing countries must invest in fundamental science and blue skies research.
   A. moderate   B. obsolete   C. literate   D. desperate
7. New Zealanders colloquially refer to themselves as "Kiwis," _____ the country's native bird.
   A. for   B. by   C. with   D. after

8. These are students who, at some stage of their undergraduate careers, leave class, either _____, or because they are asked to do so.
   A. voluntarily   B. selectively   C. compulsorily   D. necessarily

9. The sanctions are designed to force Libya to _____ the two Lockerbie suspects and to co-operate in the investigation in a similar case.
   A. hand in   B. hand out   C. hand down   D. hand over

10. I could then realize that he was a fever specialist of world _____.
    A. renown   B. domain   C. prominence   D. authority

11. The Labour defeat was a disaster, but it might be a blessing _____.
    A. at liberty   B. in disguise   C. at risk   D. in sequence

12. Science suggests that the greater part of an optimistic outlook can be _____ with the right instruction.
    A. acquired   B. imposed   C. traced   D. fabricated

13. True modesty does not _____ an ignorance of our merits, but in a due estimate of it.
    A. count in   B. fall in   C. consist in   D. rein in

14. Nearly 4 out of 5 workers at the company take unpaid _____ at least once a week.
    A. leave   B. shift   C. change   D. slot

15. She walked round to the _____ of the car and stood silently while he undid the boot and picked up her bag.
    A. ream   B. ranch   C. rear   D. realm

16. Good leadership requires you to surround yourself with people of _____ perspectives who can disagree with you without fear of revenge.
    A. cynical   B. diverse   C. dominant   D. indifferent

17. The small supplier firm will often be located near to the big firm, and will be expected to provide supplies _____.
    A. on duty   B. on demand   C. on purpose   D. on record

18. Operations which left patients _____ and in need of long periods of recovery time now leave them feeling relaxed and comfortable.
    A. ignored   B. exhausted   C. deserted   D. alienated

19. Disobedience will bring _____ on the nation: fatal disease, famine, wild beasts ravaging the land, and war leading to exile.
    A. calamity   B. provision   C. rivalry   D. revival

20. Obama reiterated his call today for Republicans and Democrats to _____ their differences in the face of the economic crisis.
    A. lean on   B. leak out   C. leave out   D. lay aside

PART II CLOZE TEST (15 minutes, 15 points)

Directions: *For each blank in the following passage, choose the best answer from the four choices* *given below. Mark the corresponding letter of your choice with a single bar across the square brackets on your Machine-scoring Answer Sheet.*

The relationship between husbands and wives is one of the strongest bonds in our society. It is deep, passionate, and often __21__. The exact amount of husband-wife violence is difficult to __22__, but it is one of the most common of all forms of violence. More calls to the police involve family disturbances __23__ all other forms of violent behavior __24__. In 1993, New York city police __25__ received 300,000 domestic violence calls. But researchers deemed that it was still an __26__. They estimate that it actually occurs in about one of __27__ two marriages.

In many societies, husbands have traditionally had the legal right to physically punish wives who refuse to accept male __28__. Although this practice is no longer __29__ in Western culture, it still occurs. __30__, many victims of spousal abuse find that the police are reluctant to be of much help. Battered women report that abusive husbands are merely given a lecture or spend the night in jail and are soon back to their __31__ ways. There appear to be two major reasons for this. First, most police officers are male, and they tend to hold a traditional view of gender roles. Even assaults that do serious physical harm to the __32__ are often seen as private matters that should be __33__ by the married partners, not the police. Second, __34__ other violent crimes, a significant percentage of the victims of spousal abuse drop the charges __35__ their attackers, some officers feel that even a vigorous enforcement effort is likely to produce few results.

21. A. fantastic   B. alien   C. violent   D. stressful
22. A. control   B. prove   C. suppose   D. determine
23. A. than   B. over   C. above   D. upon
24. A. documented   B. committed   C. classified   D. combined
25. A. alone   B. else   C. itself   D. only
26. A. understatement B. underestimate   C. underground   D. underproduction
27. A. those   B. both   C. all   D. every
28. A. prestige   B. authority   C. hierarchy   D. temperament
29. A. referred to   B. approved of   C. carried out   D. interfered with
30. A. Therefore   B. However   C. Moreover   D. Meanwhile
31. A. everlasting   B. continuing   C. threatening   D. misunderstanding
32. A. victim   B. children   C. society   D. police
33. A. disposed   B. resolved   C. promised   D. concerned
34. A. regarding   B. unlike   C. rather than   D. as to
35. A. against   B. to   C. for   D. about

PART III READING COMPREHENSION

Section A (60 minutes, 30 points)
Directions: *Below each of the following passages you will find some questions or incomplete statements. Each question or statement is followed by four choices marked A, B, C, and D. Read each passage carefully, and then select the choice that best answers the question or completes the statement. Mark the letter of your choice with a single bar across the square brackets on your Machine-scoring Answer Sheet.*

Passage One

Mark Kelly is originally from Lancashire in England. He has been living in Japan for six years and, at the weekend, he is a fake priest. "I was living in Sapporo, studying Japanese, and I needed the money. It's far better paid than teaching in a language school," he said. "Being a fake priest is big business in Japan—I've done a TV commercial for one company," he added. "In Sapporo, there are five agencies employing about 20 fake priests. In a city like Tokyo, there must be hundreds."

The fake Western priests are employed at Western-style weddings to give a performance and add to the atmosphere. These are not legal ceremonies—the couples also have to make a trip to the local registrar. "In the past almost all weddings in Japan were Shinto, but in the last few years Western-style weddings have appeared and become very popular," said one Japanese priest. "Most couples are trying to re-create a European wedding, so they overwhelmingly ask for a foreign priest instead of a Japanese one," he added.

The fake priests in Japan sometimes have to deal with difficult situations. Mr. Kelly has often presided over ceremonies where the bride is pregnant. "It is common. Once, the bride vomited on me and then fainted. It wasn't very romantic," he said. Another difficulty is meeting genuine Japanese priests. "We do occasionally bump into the real thing. They are very much against us, but there are not enough genuine Japanese priests to meet the demand," he said.

One Japanese Christian priest spoke out. "It is a real problem for us. They are not genuine and they give us a bad name," he said. "It is important for the bride and groom to have a proper wedding, and they are not getting it from these foreign priests. I have even heard of hotels using staff when they can't find anyone else."

But Mr. Kelly argues that the ceremony is not about religion, but about image. "I give a good performance. I use an Apache wedding prayer in my ceremony. It works very well, although I had to take out the part about the bear god in the sky," he said. "If people are crying by the end of the wedding, I think I have done a good job."

36. What do we know about Mark Kelly?

A. He's a professional priest. B. He's a language student.
C. He's working for a TV station. D. He's earning a living in Japan.

37. The fake Western priests are in great demand in Japan because of _____.
    A. the popularity of Western-style weddings
    B. the bad reputation of Japanese priests
    C. the decline of the traditional religion, Shinto
    D. the low prices at which they are hired

38. Using a foreign priest at a wedding in Japan is _____.
    A. forbidden according to criminal law
    B. meant for having a Western atmosphere
    C. aimed to save a trip to a registrar
    D. deemed necessary to add to the solemnity

39. According to the passage, Mr. Kelly considers his job rather _____.
    A. demanding   B. amusing   C. sacred   D. creative

40. Japanese priests are angry with those fake foreign priests because they are _____.
    A. bringing an end to the occupation   B. misleading the bride and groom
    C. damaging the image of the former   D. corrupting the morals of weddings

41. According to Mr. Kelly, what mostly interests a Japanese couple at the wedding is _____.
    A. how well the priest can perform his role
    B. what religious rituals are being followed
    C. whether other participants can be moved
    D. who can make them burst into tears

Passage Two

There are already drugs that brighten moods, like Prozac, and other antidepressants that control levels of a brain chemical called serotonin. While originally meant to treat depression, these drugs have been used for other psychological conditions like shyness and anxiety and even by otherwise healthy people to feel better about themselves.

But is putting people in a better mood really making them happy? People can also drown their sorrows in alcohol or get a **euphoric** feeling using narcotics, but few people who do so would be called truly happy.

The President's Council on Bioethics said in a recent report that while antidepressants might make some people happier, they can also substitute for what can truly bring happiness: a sense of satisfaction with one's identity, accomplishments and relationships.

"In the pursuit of happiness human beings have always worried about falling for the appearance of happiness and missing its reality," the council wrote. It added, "Yet a fraudulent happiness is just what the pharmacological management of our mental lives threatens to confer upon us."

Now the race is on to develop pills to make people smarter. These drugs aim at memory loss that occurs in people with Alzheimer's disease or a precursor called mild cognitive impairment.

But it is lost on no one that if a memory drug works and is safe, it may one day be used by healthy people to learn faster and remember longer.

Studies have already shown that animals can be made to do both when the activity of certain genes is increased or decreased. Dr. Tom Tully, a professor at Cold Spring Harbor Laboratory, created genetically engineered fruit flies that he said had "photographic memory." They could, in one session, learn something that took normal flies 10 sessions.

"It immediately convinced everyone that memory was going to be just another biological process," Dr. Tully said. "There's nothing special about it. That meant that it was going to be treatable and manipulable."

But experts say that improving memory will not necessarily make one smarter, in the sense of IQ, let alone in wisdom. "It would be a mistake to think that drugs that have an impact on memory necessarily will have an effect on intelligence," said Dr. Daniel L. Schachter, chairman of psychology at Harvard.

"Is it a good thing to remember everything?" Dr. Tully asked. Could a brain too crammed with information suffer some sort of overload?

42. Talking of antidepressants, the author expresses dissatisfaction with _____.
    A. their wide promotion   B. their original aim
    C. their extended use   D. their free prescription

43. The word "euphoric" (boldfaced in Paragraph 2) can be replaced by the word "_____."
    A. refreshed   B. deceptive   C. regenerative   D. delighted

44. According to the Council's report, for those who seek contentment with their lives, antidepressants can _____.
    A. cheat them   B. please them   C. facilitate them   D. scare them

45. The example of fruit flies is given to show that _____.
    A. medication for improving memory is safe
    B. animals can do something humans cannot
    C. drugs can help healthy people learn faster
    D. medical science can work some wonders

46. The author thinks that, to one, remembering everything could be _____.
    A. damaging   B. deluding   C. discouraging   D. dissatisfying

47. From the passage we can infer that medicines have little power in _____.
    A. bringing one mixed feelings   B. solving psychological problems
    C. making people remember better   D. manipulating brain disorders

Passage Three

The staff of Normandy Crossing Elementary School outside Houston eagerly awaited the results of state achievement tests this spring. For the principal and assistant principal, high scores could buoy their careers at a time when success is increasingly measured by such tests. For fifth-grade math and science teachers, the rewards were more tangible: a bonus of $2,850.

But when the results came back, some seemed too good to be true. Indeed, after an investigation by the Galena Park Independent School District, the principal and three teachers resigned May 24 in a scandal over test tampering.

The district said the educators had distributed a detailed study guide after stealing a look at the state science test by "tubing" it — squeezing a test booklet, without breaking its paper seal, to form an open tube so that questions inside could be seen and used in the guide. The district invalidated students' scores.

Of all the forms of academic cheating, none may be as startling as educators tampering with children's standardized tests. But investigations in many states this year have pointed to cheating by educators. Experts say the phenomenon is increasing as the **stakes** over standardized testing become higher — including, most recently, taking student progress on tests into consideration in teachers' performance reviews.

Many school districts already link teachers' bonuses to student improvement on state assessments. Houston decided this year to use the data to identify experienced teachers for dismissal, and New York City will use it to make tenure decisions on novice teachers.

The federal No Child Left Behind law is a further source of pressure. Like a high jump bar set intentionally low in the beginning, the law — which mandates that public schools bring all students up to grade level in reading and math by 2014 — was easy to satisfy early on. But the bar is notched higher annually, and the penalties for schools that fail to get over it also rise: teachers and administrators can lose jobs and see their school taken over.

No national data is collected on educator cheating. Experts who consult with school systems estimated that 1 percent to 3 percent of teachers — thousands annually — cross the line between accepted ways of boosting scores, like using old tests to prepare students, and actual cheating.

"Educators feel that their schools' reputation, their livelihoods, their psychic meaning in life are at stake," said Robert Schaeffer, public education director for Fair Test.

48. Paragraph 1 stresses the relationship between students' test results and _____.
    A. their teachers' interest
    B. their families' prestige
    C. their own future success
    D. their school's reputation
49. According to the passage, the cheating was that _____.
    A. the test supervisors provided hints during the test
    B. the test designers trained the testees before the test
    C. the students exchanged their notes during the test
    D. the students were given the answers before the test
50. It is commonly believed that _____.
    A. educators rarely get involved in academic cheating
    B. children's standardized tests have many drawbacks
    C. teachers play a key role in their students' cheating

D. school intervention helps reduce academic cheating

51. In Paragraph 4, the boldfaced word "stakes" refer to "_____."
    A. opportunities   B. responsibilities   C. benefits   D. achievements

52. In some places in the US, students' test assessments _____.
    A. indicate if the students have been effectively taught
    B. decide whether the teachers can remain in their jobs
    C. help identify who are fit to pursue a teaching career
    D. influence how to improve curriculums in the future

53. What kind of role does the author think the government plays as associated with educator cheating?
    A. They are adding to it.   B. They are lenient with it.
    C. They are overlooking it.   D. They are serious about it.

Passage Four

The debate as to whether the Internet or books are a boon to school education is conducted on the supposition that the medium is the message. But sometimes the medium is just the medium. What matters is the way people think about themselves while engaged in the two activities. A person who becomes a citizen of the literary world enters a hierarchical universe. There are classic works of literature at the top and beach reading at the bottom.

A person enters this world as a novice, and slowly studies the works of great writers and scholars. Readers immerse themselves in deep, alternative worlds and hope to gain some lasting wisdom. Respect is paid to the writers who transmit that wisdom.

A citizen of the Internet has a very different experience. The Internet smashes hierarchy and is not marked by respect. Maybe it would be different if it had been invented in Victorian England, but Internet culture is set in contemporary America. Internet culture is egalitarian. The young are more accomplished than the old. The new media is supposedly cleverer than the old media. The dominant activity is free-wheeling, disrespectful, antiauthority disputation.

These different cultures foster different types of learning. The great essayist Joseph Epstein once distinguished between being well informed, being hip and being cultivated. The Internet helps you become well informed — knowledgeable about current events, the latest controversies and important trends. The Internet also helps you become hip — to learn about what's going on, as Epstein writes, "in those lively waters outside the boring mainstream."

But the literary world is still better at helping you become cultivated, mastering significant things of lasting importance. To learn these sorts of things, you have to defer to greater minds than your own. You have to take the time to immerse yourself in a great writer's world. You have to respect the authority of the teacher.

Right now, the literary world is better at encouraging this kind of identity. The Internet culture may produce better conversationalists, but the literary culture still produces better students.

It's better at distinguishing the important from the unimportant, and making the important more prestigious.

Perhaps that will change. Already, more "old-fashioned" outposts are opening up across the Web. It could be that the real debate will not be books versus the Internet but how to build an Internet counterculture that will better attract people to serious learning.

54. Unlike an Internet surfer, a book reader would feel that _____.
   A. he is surrounded by helpful people
   B. he is at the top of the academic world
   C. he is hungry for fame and gain
   D. he is getting educated step by step

55. It is implied that in the literary world, there are _____.
   A. academic debates   B. agreed authorities
   C. disdainful readers   D. careless scholars

56. It can be inferred that Victorian England _____.
   A. emphasized submission to authority
   B. produced most of the world classics
   C. witnessed a fast growth of the media
   D. regarded the new as better than the old

57. According to Epstein, "being hip" is being curious about _____.
   A. crucial issues   B. lasting disputes   C. outer space   D. the latest fashion

58. In comparison with literary culture, Internet culture delivers information that is rather _____.
   A. mixed   B. basic   C. vital   D. useful

59. What is suggested about serious learning?
   A. It will be the gap between the two cultures.
   B. It could be available on the Internet.
   C. It may still be the focus of debate.
   D. It should be given greater attention.

Passage Five

America was optimistic almost as a matter of official doctrine right from the outset. Anyone setting up a republic in the 1770s had to be aware that nearly every republic in history had failed, usually under the iron heel of a tyrant or conqueror. No sooner had the American experiment got started than Napoleon repeated the pattern by ruining Europe's frail republics. Yet this one, safeguarded by an ocean, prospered. British visitors in the 19th century, like Frances Trollope and Charles Dickens, found the Americans' self-confidence, national pride and boastfulness almost insufferable, but they had to admit that the Americans got things done. Enterprising chaps like Andrew Carnegie emigrated from gaunt British poverty to accumulate Wagnerian fortunes on the other side of the Atlantic.

In the 20th century, too, a succession of visitors as different as Rudyard Kipling, Winston Churchill and Alistair Cooke loved recharging their spiritual batteries with long trips to America. Cooke even made a career out of praising America's can-do attitude, though with an undercurrent of irony at its excesses. What would he make of its current moods?

Today, recession-related jitters are widespread. Nearly everyone knows someone who has just lost his/her job and can't help speculating whether he/she is going to be next. American gloom comes in both highbrow and lowbrow forms. It has become characteristic of the wealthiest and most highly educated Americans to be pessimistic about their country. They fear the erosion of civil liberties, a loss of competitiveness and an inability to produce new generations of elite scientists.

Lowbrow gloom, sometimes developing into self-contempt, is easy to find just by turning on the TV. Millions watch *The Biggest Loser*, a show in which hideously overweight citizens cast off their last trace of dignity as they compete to shed rolls of fat. In *Das Kapital* Karl Marx made a bitingly ironic remark that the bourgeoisie was becoming so bloated that it would soon be paying to lose weight. The joke's on him; as it turns out, it's the pro-bourgeois American working class that is paying millions to slim down, and taking an abnormal interest in others on the same quest.

60. In Paragraph 1, the case of America in the 1770s is mentioned in order to stress the country's _____.
   A. historical progress
   B. self-confidence
   C. political system
   D. independence

61. Frances Trollope and Charles Dickens recognized that Americans were indeed _____.
   A. successful   B. respectable   C. tyrannical   D. wealthy

62. According to the passage, Alistair Cooke _____.
   A. assisted Americans in fighting several important battles
   B. accompanied Winston Churchill during an American visit
   C. mocked America's extravagant boast of its competence
   D. gave plenty of praise onto Americans' current moods

63. The highbrow gloom in America is characterized by _____.
   A. seeing little promise of the country
   B. feeling uneasy about unemployment
   C. worrying about children's education
   D. doubting one's own competitiveness

64. The author seems to think that the program The Biggest Loser _____.
   A. tells the audience to respect overweight people
   B. leads the audience to a wrong weight loss method
   C. helps the participants to build a competitive spirit
   D. makes the participants lose all of their self-respect

65. As implied by the author, the American working class, similar to the bourgeoisie criticized by

Karl Marx, is now paying for their _____.

A. self-indulgence B. self-deception C. self-possession D. self-satisfaction

Section B (20 minutes, 10 points)

Directions: *In each of the following passages, five sentences have been removed from the original text. They are listed from A to F and put below the passage. Choose the most suitable sentence from the list to fill in each of the blanks (numbered 66 to 75). For each passage, there is one sentence that does not fit in any of the blanks. Mark your answers on your Machine-scoring Answer Sheet.*

Passage One

People were riding horses much earlier than previously thought, new archaeological finds suggest. Scientists have now traced the first conclusive evidence of domesticated horses back to Kazakhstan, about 5,500 years ago. That's 1,000 years earlier than we already knew about, and about 2,000 years before domesticated horses showed up in Europe.

____(66)____ Scientists analyzed the horses' lower leg bones, and found that they more closely resembled those of later known domestic horses rather than those of ancient wild horses. The researchers also developed a new method to identify the chemical signatures of fat from horse milk, and were able to find these traces on Botai pottery fragments. ____(67)____

"The invention of a method to identify the fat residues left by horse milk in ceramic pots is a spectacular and brilliant advance," archaeologists David Anthony and Dorcas Brown of Hartwick College wrote in an e-mail. "If you're milking horses, they are not wild."

____(68)____ For one thing, it meant people could travel much farther, and much more quickly, than before.

"When people began to ride, it revolutionized human transport," Anthony and Brown said. "We still measure the power of our transportation technologies in horsepower, because for millennia, until just about 150 years ago, that was the fastest transport humans had."

____(69)____ They were less nomadic than previous residents of that area, which is why archaeologists have an easier time studying their remains, compared to earlier peoples who moved around so often that they didn't leave large deposits in any one place. ____(70)____

"We'll probably be looking more widely now trying to apply the same techniques to other sites," Brown said. "I wouldn't be surprised if we find even earlier ones. I think even if there are earlier sites, they're still going to be in the neighboring area, where those big grass plains are."

A. The advent of horsemanship was a major advance for civilization, right up there with inventing the wheel and making tools out of iron.

B. Finally, a few of the ancient horse skulls bore physical markings on the teeth that could have been made by the use of a harness with a bit in the mouth.

C. Experts suspect that some of these even earlier groups may have also domesticated horses, though.

D. Comparisons were also made to leg bones from modern and 3,000-year-old domesticated horses and from wild Siberian horses that lived more than 20,000 years ago.

E. The Botai people lived in planned-out villages, with houses partly buried underground.

F. Archaeologists have uncovered thousands of horse bones at the site of the ancient Botai culture in Kazakhstan.

Passage Two

In 2004 and again in 2006, women told pollsters that the concerns that motivated them to decide whether and for whom to vote were centered on nontraditional "women's issues." Women are not single-issue voters, either. __(71)__. In reality, women's voting patterns indicate quite the opposite.

Women are not monolithic in their attitudes about, or votes within, the political system. __(72)__. In the end, women voters ask themselves two core questions when deciding whom to support for president: "Do I like that person?" and "Is that person like me?" The first question is the classic "living room" test. The second is a more complex inquiry that probes whether women believe a candidate cares about, values, confronts, and fears the same things they do.

Party loyalty trumps gender, as indicated by a July 2007 Newsweek survey, which found that 88 percent of men and 85 percent of women say that if their party nominated a woman candidate that they would vote for her if she were qualified for the job. __(73)__: Only 60 percent of men and 56 percent of women believe that the country is ready for a woman president. With regard to race, voters are less hesitant to vote for a qualified African-American candidate of their party, as 92 percent of whites and 93 percent of nonwhites say that they would endorse such a candidate. __(74)__: Only 59 percent of white voters and 58 percent of nonwhite voters believe that the country would elect a black president.

Whereas the contest for president is the most wide-open in decades, one thing is certain: __(75)__.

A. The media's focus on the contentious ones makes it seem as if women only care about one issue on Election Day and that it takes special attention to that issue to compel women to vote

B. Traditionally, women are thought to gravitate more toward the "SHE" cluster of issues — Social Security, Health Care, and Education, while men are considered more interested in the "WE" issues — War and the Economy

C. Like gender, fewer voters doubt that the country is ready for an African-American president

D. Americans express less enthusiasm, however, about the "female factor," when it comes to how they judge their fellow citizens

E. Women, as they have since 1980, will be a majority of the electorate that decides who next occupies the Oval Office

F. When it comes to voting, one woman might vote for all Democrats, another might vote straight-ticket Republican, while a third might take the salad-bar approach to decide her vote

PAPER TWO

PART IV TRANSLATION (30 minutes, 15 points)

Directions: *Read the following text carefully and then translate the underlined segments into Chinese. Write your Chinese version in the proper space on your Answer Sheet.*

The only advice, indeed, that one person can give another about reading is to take no advice, to follow your own instincts, to use your own reason, to come to your own conclusions. (1) If this is agreed between us, then I feel at liberty to put forward a few ideas and suggestions because you will not allow them to fetter (禁锢) that independence which is the most important quality that a reader can possess. After all, what laws can be laid down about books? The battle of Waterloo was certainly fought on a certain day; but is *Hamlet* a better play than *Lear*? Nobody can say. Each must decide that question for himself. (2) Everywhere else we may be bound by laws and conventions—there we have none. Then, how are we to bring order into this multitudinous chaos and get the deepest and widest pleasure from what we read?

(3) It is simple enough to say that since books have classes — fiction, biography, poetry — we should separate them and take from each what it is right that each should give us. Yet few people ask from books what books can give us. Most commonly we come to books with blurred and divided minds, asking of fiction that it shall be true, of poetry that it shall be false, of biography that it shall be flattering, of history that it shall enforce our own prejudices. If we could banish all such preconceptions when we read, that would be an admirable beginning. Do not dictate to your author; try to become him. Be his fellow-worker and accomplice. (4) If you hang back, and reserve and criticize at first, you are preventing yourself from getting the fullest possible value from what you read. But if you open your mind as widely as possible, the signs and hints of almost imperceptible fineness, from the twist and turn of the first sentences, will bring you into the presence of a human being unlike any other.

"We have only to compare" — with those words the cat is out of the bag, and the true complexity of reading is admitted. The first process, to receive impressions with the utmost understanding, is only half the process of reading; it must be completed, if we are to get the whole pleasure from a book, by another. (5) We must pass judgment upon these multitudinous impressions; we must make of these fleeting shapes one that is hard and lasting.

PART V WRITING (40 minutes, 20 points)

Directions: *Write an essay of no less than 200 words on the topic given below. Use the space provided on your Answer Sheet II.*

TOPIC

Unlike such things as technology, fashion, some things never change over time. Name ONE thing that doesn't change and explain why it's changeless.

2014年3月试题精解

第一部分 词 汇

1. 答案:A
    本题考查名词的语义。A 通行;B 路线;C 隧道;D 压力。该句的大意为:这座旧桥不够牢固,重型车辆不能通过。
2. 答案:B
    本题考查介词短语的语义。A 最多,充其量;B 详细而长久地;C 大批量地;D 实际上。该句的大意为:这位孤寡的老妇人是如此的孤独,以至于在超市里她会没完没了地和陌生人聊起她的宠物。
3. 答案:C
    本题考查形容词的语义。A 与众不同的;B 激增的;C 欺骗的,假冒的;D 不起作用的。该句的大意为:发达国家和发展中国家的人民都面临假药带来的危险;这些假药给公共健康造成严重危害。
4. 答案:A
    本题考查动词词组的语义。A 靠(微薄收入)生活;B 离开;C 出行;D 和睦相处。该句的大意为:一年仅靠1万元度日,这一定比我想象的还要艰难。
5. 答案:D
    本题考查名词的语义。A 比率;B 等级;C 规模;D 退潮;衰退。该句的大意为:当父母和孩子们之间的关系处于低潮时,他们之间的爱和尊重需要得到呵护和重建。
6. 答案:C
    本题考查形容词的语义。A 适度的;B 过时的;C 有文化的,受过教育的;D 令人绝望的。该句的大意为:为了拥有知识型的经济和科学素养的人口,发展中国家必须投资于基础科学和短期内无实用价值的研究。
7. 答案:D
    本题考查介词的用法。A 因为;B 通过;C 和,随着;D 在……之后,以……命名。该句的大意为:新西兰人把自己俗称为"鹬鸵",是由本国国鸟的名字而来的。
8. 答案:A
    本题考查副词的语义和题干中的逻辑关系。A 自愿地;B 有选择地;C 强制地;D 必要地。该句的大意为:在大学学习生涯的某一阶段,一些学生或因为自愿或迫于要求而离开课堂。
9. 答案:D
    本题考查动词短语的含义。A 提交;B 分发;C 传承;D 交出,移交。该句的大意为:这些制裁意在迫使利比亚交出两名洛克比空难的嫌疑犯,并且在类似案件的调查中予以配合。
10. 答案:A
    本题考查名词的语义。A 声誉,名望;B 领域;C 突出,卓越;D 权威,权力。该句的大意为:我那时意识到他便是世界知名的发热科专家。
11. 答案:B
     本题考查名词短语的语义。A blessing in disguise 的意思为"塞翁失马;因祸得福"。该句的大意为:劳动党败北是一场灾难,不过,这或许算得上是因祸得福。
12. 答案:A
     本题考查动词的语义。A 获得;B 强加;C 跟踪,追溯;D 编造,伪造。该句的大意为:科学研究显示,乐观的态度在更大的程度上可以由正确的指导而获得。
13. 答案:C
     本题考查动词词组的语义。A 把……计算在内;B 坍塌,跌入;C 存在于……中,在于;D 放慢,止住,控制;勒。该句的大意为:真正的谦逊并不在于忽视我们的优点,而在于对它能够合适的估量。
14. 答案:A
     本题考查名词的语义。A 休假;B 移动;变化;轮班;C 变化;D 狭槽;时段,位置。该句的大意为:公司大约4/5的员工至少每周都有一次无薪假期。
15. 答案:C
     本题考查名词的语义。A 许多,大量;B 大牧场;C (建筑物或机动车的)后部;D 领域,范围。该句的大意为:当他打开行李箱,拿起她的包时,她走到汽车的尾部,静静地站在那儿。
16. 答案:B
     本题考查形容词的语义。A 愤世嫉俗的;B 各不相同的;C 支配的;D 冷漠的。该句的大意为:良好的领导力要求你的身边有看法各异的人,他们可以与你见解不同,而不担心打击报复。
17. 答案:B
     本题考查介词短语的语义。A 值班;B 一经要求(就能够……);C 故意地;D 有记录地,有记载地,公开发表地。该句的大意为:小型的供应商公司往往处于大公司的附近,并且能够一经要求就提供物资。
18. 答案:B
     本题考查形容词语义。A 被忽视的;B 疲惫的;C 被遗弃的;D 被疏远的。该句的大意为:曾经让病人感觉疲惫并且需要长时间方能康复的手术,如今却让他们感觉放松和舒适。
19. 答案:A
     本题考查名词的语义。A 灾难;B 规定,条款;预备;C 竞争,对抗;D 复兴。该句的大意为:反抗会给国家带来灾难:致命的疾病、饥荒、肆虐的野兽和引致颠沛流离的战争。
20. 答案:D
     本题考查动词短语的语义。A 依赖;B 漏水,泄漏;C 排除;D 把……搁置一边。该句的大意为:奥巴马今天再次重申共和党人和民主党人在经济危机面前搁置他们之间的分歧。

第二部分 完形填空

本文主要阐述丈夫对妻子家庭暴力的普遍存在,以及这种家庭暴力普遍存在的原因。
21. 答案:C
     本题考查形容词词义辨析及对上下文语义的联系。A 奇异的,美妙的,极好的;B 外国的;相异的;不相容的;C 暴力的;D 有压力的。本句的意思是:夫妻关系是社会当中最为紧密的一种联系,它深沉、热烈,且常常充满暴力。

22. 答案:D

　　本题考查动词的词义辨析及对语句的理解。A 控制;B 证明;C 假设;D 确定。本句的意思是:尽管夫妻暴力是所有暴力形式中最为常见的一种,但该种暴力的程度却很难确定。

23. 答案:A

　　本题考查介词 than 的使用,than 的意思是"超过""比"。本句的意思是:涉及家庭纠纷的报警电话要多于涉及其他所有暴力行为的电话。

24. 答案:D

　　本题考查形容词的使用以及对"all other forms"的理解。A 记录的;B 犯下的;C 分类的;D 合在一起的。本句的意思是:涉及家庭纠纷的报警电话要多于涉及其他各种暴力行为总和的电话。

25. 答案:A

　　本题考查副词的用法。A 单独地;B 其他;C 它自己;D 只有。本句的意思是:在 1993 年,仅仅纽约警察局就收到了 30 000 个涉及家庭暴力的电话。

26. 答案:B

　　本题考查名词的词义辨析。A 保守的陈述;轻描淡写;B 低估;C 地下;D 供不应求。本句在语义上顺着前句而来,意思是:研究者认为前文提到的 30 000 个涉及家庭暴力的电话数量也依然是一种低估。

27. 答案:D

　　本题考查代词的辨析。本句的意思是:研究者估计每两个家庭中就有一个家庭存在家庭暴力。

28. 答案:B

　　本题考查名词的词义辨析及对语句的理解。A 声望;B 权威;C 等级;D 性情。本句的意思是:在很多社会当中,丈夫一直以来享有合法权利,对不接受他男性权威的妻子进行体罚。

29. 答案:B

　　本题考查动词词组的词义辨析。A 被提及;B 被批准;C 被实施;D 被干扰。本句顺承上句,是说:尽管丈夫一直以来所享有的对不接受他男性权威的妻子进行体罚的合法权利已不再被西方社会所批准接受,但男人的这种行为依然存在。

30. 答案:C

　　本题考查上下文的前后逻辑关系以及连接词的使用。本句与前面几句的逻辑关系是一种递进,前文讲到,丈夫对妻子实施暴力的历史原因,本句则进一步递进,意思是:家庭暴力不仅依然存在,并且,受害者还发现警察不愿对他们提供什么帮助。这几个连接词的意思分别为:A 因此,表示因果;B 然而,表转折;C 另外,表递进;D 与此同时,表伴随。

31. 答案:C

　　本题考查形容词的词义辨析。A 永久的;B 持续的;C 吓人的,威胁性的;D 误解的。本句是说:受虐女性说施虐丈夫仅仅是被警察教训一顿,或者是在监狱中关一晚,但很快他们就又恢复到原来可怕、吓人的方式。

32. 答案:A

　　本题考查名词的词义辨析及对语句的理解。A 受害者;B 儿童;C 社会;D 警察。本句是说:警察认为即使是对受害者造成严重身体伤害的袭击也是私事。
33. 答案:B
　　本题考查动词词义辨析及对语句的理解。A 处理;B 解决;C 许诺;D 关注。本句是说:警察认为即使是对受害者造成严重身体伤害的袭击也是私事,也应该由夫妇双方解决,而不是由警察来解决。
34. 答案:B
　　本题考查介词及介词短语的语义辨析。A 至于;B 与……不同;C 而不是;D 关于。本句是说:与其他类型的暴力犯罪不同的是,相当比例的家庭暴力受害者撤销了对袭击方的指控。
35. 答案:A
　　本题考查固定搭配的用法。在句中,drop charge against someone 是一固定用法,意思是撤销对某人的指控,符合本句意思,即相当比例的家庭暴力受害者撤销了对袭击方的指控。

第三部分　阅读理解
第一小节　阅读理解 A

第一篇:
36. 答案:D
　　本题是细节题,要求考生可以从第一段关于 Mark Kelly 的各种细节(特别是第三句)找出正确的答案。他从事很多种工作,但是各种工作的共性就是他在日本学习期间,需要挣钱谋生,因此 D 为正确答案。
37. 答案:A
　　本题依旧是细节题,要求考生可以从第二段的细节里找到关于外国假牧师在日本供不应求的原因。结合第二段第一句和第三句,不难看出答案应该是 A。
38. 答案:B
　　本题是细节题,考查考生对第二段第一句中"add to the atmosphere"的理解。
39. 答案:A
　　本题是推理题,考查考生对于第三段的主题和细节的把握。主题句是第一句:日本的假牧师要应对许多困难局面。接下来拿 Kelly 先生举例。Kelly 先生所说的两种困难局面都说明对他而言这不是一份容易的工作。
40. 答案:C
　　本题是细节题,考查考生对第四段日本牧师的第一句"It is a real problem...a bad name"的理解。
41. 答案:A
　　本题是细节题,考查考生对第五段第一句的理解:仪式(婚礼)的重点不是宗教,而是形象。也就是 Kelly 接下来解释的:只要有人在婚礼上流泪,就说明仪式是成功的。

第二篇:
42. 答案:C
　　本题是推理题,需要考生结合第一段第二句和第二段中作者表达出来的情绪理解。题干已经提示考生作者有不满情绪,因此只要找出文中细节便可。

43. 答案：D

本题是词汇题，词汇的位置已在题干说明。词汇题可以用"代入法"（将选项逐一放在原文中）和"排除法"（排除在内容和逻辑上不合理的选项）提高对某一词汇的理解能力。

44. 答案：A

本题是细节题，考查考生对于第三段后半段的理解：抗抑郁药可能替代那些真正给人带来幸福的东西。

45. 答案：D

本题是例证题，考查考生对果蝇这个例子说明的道理。第七段说基因改造过的果蝇只需要一次就能学会普通果蝇十次才能学会的东西，这可以说是医药科学带来的奇迹。选项 C 的语气过于肯定，不符合原文的意思。

46. 答案：A

本题是推理题，考查考生对作者在本文最后一句中所发议论的理解。从本句的用词"too crammed""suffer"和"overload"应该可以看出作者对于这种方法是持有负面态度的。

47. 答案：B

本题是推理题，考查考生对全文主旨的理解：不管什么药物都解决不了心理问题。

第三篇：

48. 答案：A

本题是段落主旨题，考查的是考生对第一段的大意归纳：对于校长和老师，学生的考试成绩与他们的利益休戚相关。

49. 答案：D

本题是细节题，考查考生对第三段舞弊事件细节理解。具体而言，就是考查对第一句前半句的理解，破折号后面是对"tubing it"的解释。前半句的意思是这个学校的教育工作者偷看了科学试题后给了学生们非常细致的学习指南，也就是说，学生考试前就知道答案了。

50. 答案：A

本题是推理题，考查考生对第四段第一句的理解：在各种学术舞弊中，没有什么比教育者操纵孩子们的标准化考试更令人震惊的了。言下之意便是教育者很少卷入学术舞弊事件。

51. 答案：C

本题是词汇题，词汇的位置已在题干说明，因此考生须根据此词汇的上下文做出合理猜测。此处教师得失攸关的是他们的利益。

52. 答案：B

本题是细节题，考查的是考生对第五段第二句的理解：休斯敦决定今年利用成绩数据来决定老教师的去留，而纽约则用考试成绩来决定是否让新教师终身留任。二者的共性便是成绩决定教师是否能保有他们的工作。

53. 答案：A

本题是推理题，考查的是考生第六段的理解：主题句是第一句，关键词是"further source of pressure"，也就是学校已然给老师的压力很大，联邦法律更是雪上加霜。因此答案为 A。

第四篇：

54. 答案：D
　　本题是推理题，关键要理解第二段的第一句：读者渐渐地开始学习伟大作家和学者的作品，所以答案是 D。

55. 答案：B
　　本题是推理题，关键要理解第二段最后一句：传播智慧的作者会得到尊重。因此文学世界里有公认的权威，所以答案是 B。

56. 答案：A
　　本题是推理题，出题的地方很明确，在第三段的第三句。本段谈论的是互联网与文学世界的差异。互联网世界强调平等，而文学世界强调服从。第三句说"如果互联网诞生在维多利亚时期的苏格兰，情况就会很不一样，可是互联网诞生在美国"。言下之意就是维多利亚时期的苏格兰强调服从权威。

57. 答案：D
　　本题是细节题，要求考生理解"being hip"在上下文中的意思，答案在第四段最后一句破折号后面对"become hip"的解释说明：互联网还有助于你了解当下世界正在发生的事情。四个选项中只有最近流行的服饰才与世界正在发生的事情对应。

58. 答案：A
　　本题是细节题，要求考生理解因特网文化传播的信息特点，答案在第四段中间"因特网让你消息灵通——让你了解当今要闻、讨论焦点、重要潮流"，这些信息杂糅在一起就是"mixed"。

59. 答案：B
　　本题是推理题，要求考生理解关于严肃学习的信息，考点在最后一段，因特网文化和书本文化不再相互孤立，因特网已经有了传统书本的"前哨"。

第五篇：

60. 答案：B
　　本题是例证题，第一段的第一句中的 optimistic 是整个第一段的核心内容。美国 18 世纪 70 年代的例子是为了说明强调美国的自信和骄傲。其他国家建立共和国都遭受了挫折，只有美国从建国开始就一路顺风，从未失败。

61. 答案：A
　　本题是细节题，Frances Trollope 和 Charles Dickens 去美国之后觉得美国人的自信心爆棚，令人无法忍受，但是他们必须得承认美国人"get things done"，意思是能成事儿。

62. 答案：C
　　本题是细节题，考点信息在文中第二段第二句——Cooke 靠着赞美美国人"能成事儿"的态度建立了自己的事业，尽管他对于他们过剩的自信不乏嘲讽之意。

63. 答案：A
　　本题是细节题，考查考生对第三段第二、三句的理解。美国人的忧郁来自两种形式：一种是来自有文化的阶层；另一种是没有文化的阶层。富有且受过良好教育的美国人属于前者，对他们的国家很悲观。

64. 答案：D

本题是细节题，考查考生对于 The Biggest Loser 节目的理解。这个电视节目是个减肥节目，鼓励超重的选手迎接挑战，这里关键要理解"cast off their last trace of dignity"，意思是扔掉最后一丝尊严。

65. 答案：A

本题是推理题，题干的信息很多，考点在最后一段，美国现在的工人阶级与马克思批判的小资产阶级的共同之处在于他们现在在为自己的放纵买单，都要花钱减肥。

第二小节　阅读理解 B

第一篇：

66. 答案：F

本题的突破口是把握文章第一段和第二段之间的衔接以及第二段的内容概要。所要填入的句子既可以呼应到第一段中提到的最新考古发现，又可以引领第二段整段的内容。

67. 答案：B

本题的突破口是文章第二段的段落结构。第二段中，考生可以从卷面读到的句子有两个，貌似两个句子分别讲到了两个不同方面的内容，但仔细一想，第一句讲的是考古证据一，第二句是考古证据二。这样看来，67 题中所要填入的句子要么是与第二个证据相关的内容，要么是第三个考古证据。选项 B 中"Finally"一词与前一句中的"also"呼应，使得第二段的结构呈现出序列关系。

68. 答案：A

本题的答题关键是把握后一句中代词"it"的指代。根据英语语法，我们知道，"it"所指代的对象必须为第三人称单数物称名词。仔细阅读每个选项，我们可以发现只有选项 A 中"horsemanship"符合这一条件。

69. 答案：E

本题的答题关键是空格后一句中讲到的"they"和"previous residents"两部分，这两部分提示读者填入的句子中一定出现过与古代某一时期的居民相关联的名词。因此选 E。

70. 答案：C

本题的突破口在空格前一句中的"...earlier peoples"，选项 C 中的"these even earlier groups"是对它的呼应。

第二篇：

71. 答案：A

本题的突破口是把握空格后一句中的两个短语："In reality"和"the opposite"。"In reality"这一短语提示读者空格中的句子很可能讲到了在某个问题上的误区或常见错误观点。因此选 A。

72. 答案：F

本题的答题关键是第二段中首句和第二句之间的逻辑关系，这两个句子之间是"一般—特殊"的关系。首先，我们可以理解文章的第一段已经介绍了话题，即女性与选举，这提示我们整篇文章都应围绕这两个关键词展开。第二段的首句却谈到女性与政治体系，貌似离题了，其实是为了从一般到特殊逐渐深入地展开论述。另外,选项 F 中的"when it comes to…"这一句式正是将一般话题引入具体话题的常见句式结构。

73. 答案:D

本题的答题重点是在空格的后一句。后一句用数据分析女性是否会选举女性总统。

74. 答案:C

本题的突破口是空格的后一句,后一句分析了女性是否会选举黑人总统。

75. 答案:E

本题的答题关键是把握最后一段的作用:总结前文的内容,不论女性在总统选举方面有什么样的看法,女性已经成为选民中的一大力量,她们的投票将决定谁入主白宫。

第四部分 翻 译

(1) 译文:

如果我们对此达成共识,我就可以无拘束地提出一些看法和建议,因为你不会让这些看法和建议禁锢你的独立见解,而独立见解正是读者应具备的最重要的品质。

解析:

该句的翻译难点在于主句中的逻辑关系比较复杂,建议考生从语法入手理清主句的关系。另外,考生需要对句首的 this 有准确的理解。

(2) 译文:

我们也许在任何方面都有习俗和规范,唯独在读书方面没有。

解析:

理解该句的关键词是"there"。此处"there"指的不是某地,而是读书这件事。对于"there"的准确理解取决于对文章主题的领会。所以,做翻译时最便捷有效的方法应该是把全文通读一遍,然后再逐句翻译。

(3) 译文:

毋庸讳言,既然书籍有类别之分——比如小说、传记、诗歌,等等,我们就应该从各种不同类别的图书中获取不同的营养。

解析:

本句的理解难点在 say 后面的宾语从句中包含两个从句。建议考生按照句法结构将宾语部分分成 2~3 个部分。另外,对于该句中的"classes",可以根据破折号后的"fiction, biography, poetry"等 3 个列举,想到"classes"此处指的是"书籍的分类或类别"。

(4) 译文:

倘若你未开卷便先行犹豫退缩、说三道四,那么你就在妨碍自己从阅读中最大限度地获取有用价值。

解析:

"hang back"是理解该句的难点。"hang back"中的"back"意为"向后;后退"等,所以"hang back"可以推断为"退缩"或"畏缩不前"等含义。

(5) 译文:

我们必须对各种感受进行梳理和鉴别;把变幻不定的印象固化为明确和持久的感受。

解析：

该句有两个难点，其一是如何理解词组"make of"，此处意为"理解；解释"；其二是对"make of"的宾语和宾语补足语的判断和分析。它的宾语是"these fleeting shapes"，宾补是"one"，当然别忘了"one"后还跟着定语从句。另外，"one"该如何翻译，此处答案并不唯一，除了参考答案中的"感受"，也可以是"印象"。

第五部分　写　　作

题目解析：

本题目考查学生的哲学思辨能力。技术日新月异，时尚捉摸不定，但有些东西却恒定不变,始终如一。题干要求可分为两部分：第一，在"变"中找出"不变"；第二，说明为什么其永恒不变。题目要求已基本上确定了写作的结构，即开篇指出不变的东西，随后，文章的正文部分论述为什么不变。

由于是哲学思辨话题，本身无定论，只要理由充分，能自圆其说便可，因此找出"不变"之物并非难事，难在说理要站得住脚，不能有漏洞。题干关键词为"never"和"changeless"。即所言之物要跨越时空，永远不变，放之四海而皆准，不能在一种情况下不变，而在有些情况下有可能会变。因此，在构思时，可选择全人类普世之道，或者宇宙恒定法则，否则很难做到严丝合缝。如，有考生写"英语考试"永恒不变，就很容易遭到反驳，假设以后取消英语考试，就意味着其论点不成立。

对于一篇200多字的考试作文来说，鉴于时间和篇幅有限，考生最好写两条理由。原因在于，一条理由不够充分，且很难写足字数。而如果列举的理由过多，则无法将每条理由说透彻。因此，两条理由比较合适。

以下所给范文，开篇点明"人类求变之心"为万变其宗，随后，从两个方面解释其不变之由：其一，人类求索革新的热情，乃与生俱来，人皆有之；其二，只有推陈出新，不断求变，人类文明才能得以延续。最后，简单总结文章的主要观点。

范文：

Nations rise. Products improve. Buildings fall and reemerge. And things keep taking on new forms and looks. But underlying all the changes, visible or invisible, is one thing that remains immutable — the human pursuit of change for the better.

The passion for change is hardwired into each and every one of us from the very beginning of human civilization. We become what we are today because the cells in us are in a never-ending process of self-regeneration; our brain is programmed to ask questions and seek solutions; and our heart beats to the rhythm of throbbing pulses of adventures. We keep moving forward, opening new doors, and doing new things because there is that innate passion for change that keeps leading us down new paths and toward better lives. That passion is the lust of human mind, the wick in the candle of learning that never fades.

Also, we human beings never stop exploring because change is the only source of renewal and survival. The entire history of human civilization is a story of relentless struggle against difficulties and unyielding pursuit of better lives. If physicists hadn't toiled in the laboratory to solve tricky cosmic equations, we would still believe that the earth is the center of the universe. If scientists hadn't worked on new vaccines and drugs, fatal diseases like smallpox and polio would have long wiped out the human race. If people hadn't sought new forms of governance, many parts of the world would still be living under the dark reign of feudalism. We change, because we have to.

Human beings are born with the restless genes and energy. No matter how the world beyond us will change, our desire for change is always alive and well, as it is the way for us to clear obstacles on the way toward a better future. (307 words)

中国科学院大学
博士研究生入学考试
英语试题

(2015年3月)

考生须知:

一、本试卷由试卷一(PAPER ONE)和试卷二(PAPER TWO)两部分组成。试卷一为客观题,答卷使用标准化机读答题纸;试卷二为主观题,答卷使用非机读答题纸。

二、请考生一律用HB或2B铅笔填涂标准化机读答题纸,画线不得过细或过短。修改时请用橡皮擦拭干净。若因填涂不符合要求而导致计算机无法识别,责任由考生自负。请保持机读答题纸清洁、无折皱。答题纸切忌折叠。

三、全部考试时间总计180分钟,满分为100分。时间及分值分布如下:

试卷一:

	Ⅰ 词汇	15分钟	10分
	Ⅱ 完形填空	15分钟	15分
	Ⅲ 阅读理解	80分钟	40分
	小计	110分钟	65分

试卷二:

	Ⅳ 英译汉	30分钟	15分
	Ⅴ 写作	40分钟	20分
	小计	70分钟	35分

UNIVERSITY OF THE CHINESE ACADEMY OF SCIENCES ENGLISH ENTRANCE EXAMINATION FOR PH. D PROGRAM
March 2015

PAPER ONE

PART I VOCABULARY (15 minutes, 10 points, 0.5 point each)

Directions: *Choose the word or expression below each sentence that best completes the statement, and mark the corresponding letter of your choice with a single bar across the square brackets on your Machine-scoring Answer Sheet.*

1. _____ you can bring yourself to stop hating her, it sounds like an arrangement that could work out rather nicely.
   A. So far as   B. So long as   C. As well as   D. As often as not

2. The ocean bottom even today is largely unexplored; until about a century ago, the deep-ocean floor was completely _____, hidden beneath waters averaging over 3,600 meters deep.
   A. inevitable   B. indefinite   C. incomparable   D. inaccessible

3. He was a molecular biologist with good hands, impressive ingenuity, and _____ capacities.
   A. intuitive   B. accidental   C. fragile   D. diligent

4. There is nothing secret about what we're doing; it's all perfectly _____.
   A. out of sight   B. on the air
   C. on the horizon   D. above board

5. Under the umbrella of the independent spirit, millions of immigrants came to this country seeking shelter from intolerance, prejudice, and _____.
   A. persistence   B. permanence   C. perspective   D. persecution

6. The junior _____ was impatient for promotion but knew that he would only get it by stepping into a dead man's shoes.
   A. executive   B. explosive   C. captive   D. addictive

7. Since the 1980s, increasingly _____ tools have made it possible to produce, market, and

distribute motion pictures digitally.

    A. predictable   B. disguised   C. ornamental   D. sophisticated

8. People who _____ large amounts of animal fats are more likely to get cancer and heart disease.

    A. congest   B. irrigate   C. consume   D. purchase

9. After the _____ year of 1957, the birth rate in Canada began to decline.

    A. summit   B. peak   C. climax   D. top

10. She has helped thousands of men and women _____ with things that bother them and that they could not talk about with others.

    A. come to the point   B. come to terms
    C. come into force   D. come into contact

11. In this age of globalization, we need to abandon our historical idea of _____ as a single religious or national alliance.

    A. identity   B. registration   C. dignity   D. qualification

12. It is finally realized how foolish it is to develop our economy _____ the environment.

    A. for the sake of   B. on behalf of   C. at the cost of   D. in terms of

13. For the most part, black sportsmen accept that they have advantages, in an unspecified way, over their white _____.

    A. supervisors   B. subordinates
    C. counterparts   D. correspondents

14. The first thing we did was look for errors in our experimental design and for every conceivable _____ that could have led us astray.

    A. exposition   B. scenario   C. illustration   D. scheme

15. The discovery of the sunken ship _____ ancient shipbuilding techniques and trading routes.

    A. made sense of   B. took charge of   C. got around to   D. shed light on

16. Politicians lie, and people with a political agenda _____ the facts to serve them.

    A. slant   B. imitate   C. transfer   D. converse

17. Her strength was her ability to _____ and inspire confidence rather than fear in the people she befriended.

    A. uncover   B. obtain   C. elicit   D. produce

18. As far as the rank and position is concerned, an associate professor is _____ a professor, though they are almost equally knowledgeable.

    A. ranked below   B. adjacent to   C. inherent to   D. subject to

19. Other skeptics point out that such a peaceful rise has no _____ in human history.

    A. reference   B. allusion   C. inference   D. precedent

20. Economists said that their smooth growth this year was suspicious because they were so _____ other economic indicators.

    A. in line with   B. in excess of   C. at odds with   D. in proportion to

PART II CLOZE TEST (15 minutes, 15 points)

Directions: *For each blank in the following passage, choose the best answer from the four choices given below. Mark the corresponding letter of your choice with a single bar across the square brackets on your Machine-scoring Answer Sheet.*

   Plagiarism is widely recognized as a high crime against the project of science, but the explanations for why it's harmful generally __21__ it look like a different kind of crime than fabrication and falsification. __22__, Kenneth D. Pimple claims that plagiarism is not an __23__ that undermines the knowledge-building project of science. Rather, the crime is in depriving other scientists of the reward they are __24__ for participating in this knowledge-building project. __25__, Pimple says that plagiarism is problematic not because it is dishonest, but rather because it is unfair.

   While I think Pimple is right to identify an additional component of responsible conduct of science __26__ honesty, namely, a certain kind of fairness to one's __27__ scientists, I also think this analysis of plagiarism misses an important __28__ in which misrepresenting the source of words, ideas, methods, or results can __29__ the knowledge-building project of science.

   On the surface, plagiarism, while __30__ nasty to the person whose report is being stolen, might seem not to undermine the scientific community's __31__ of the phenomena. We are still, after all, bringing together and __32__ a number of different observation reports to determine the stable features of our experience of the phenomenon. __33__ this comparison often involves a dialogue as well. As part of the knowledge-building project, from the earliest planning of their experiments to well after results are published, scientists are __34__ in asking and answering questions about the details of the experience and of the conditions __35__ which the phenomenon was observed. Misrepresenting someone else's honest observation report as one's own strips the report of accurate information for such a dialogue.

21. A. make   B. get   C. have   D. help
22. A. Therefore   B. So far   C. However   D. For example
23. A. excuse   B. ideology   C. object   D. offense
24. A. competing   B. attracted   C. due   D. craving
25. A. On the other hand B. In other words C. By and by D. In the meanwhile
26. A. besides   B. towards   C. except   D. for
27. A. fellow   B. rival   C. team   D. peer
28. A. chance   B. way   C. reason   D. base
29. A. stimulate   B. construct   C. undermine   D. assess
30. A. surprisingly   B. accordingly   C. potentially   D. necessarily
31. A. knowledge   B. discovery   C. creation   D. evaluation

32.	A. presenting	B. comparing	C. submitting	D. producing
33.	A. So	B. While	C. But	D. And
34.	A. devoted	B. scheduled	C. committed	D. engaged
35.	A. with	B. under	C. for	D. around

PART III READING COMPREHENSION

Section A (60 minutes, 30 points)

Directions: *Below each of the following passages you will find some questions or incomplete statements. Each question or statement is followed by four choices marked A, B, C, and D. Read each passage carefully, and then select the choice that best answers the question or completes the statement. Mark the letter of your choice with a single bar across the square brackets on your Machine-scoring Answer Sheet.*

Passage One

Designating this book (*Handbook of Personality Psychology*) a "handbook" is at once accurate and possibly unfortunate. Handbooks are frequently rather dreary affairs, occasionally useful as sources and for citation but scarcely worth reading.

In fact, this book is highly interesting and readable, comprehensive and authoritative. The domain of personality is covered almost completely, and the material is quite up to date. This book is not a collection of previously published or only slightly reworked papers. It gives clear indication of the careful thought the editors gave to its planning and their firm control over its writing. To begin with, it is wholly refreshing to have a comprehensive work on personality that pays no particular attention to theories of personality. There are no chapters in this volume to review what Freud said or Adler or Rogers or Bandura or anyone else. Theorists such as Freud are mentioned when their views are relevant to topics under discussion, but, blessedly, no summaries of the major theories are included. Instead, the editors present a comprehensive and coherent view of the field of personality today.

The work is presented in eight sections that deal in essence with what personality is, how it is studied, how it develops, its biological and social determinants, how personality works, and what it is useful for. There are 36 chapters extending nearly a thousand pages. The editors chose specific authors for each of the chapters; they chose well and they were remarkably successful in getting the participation of authoritative scientists who generally write quite well.

The handbook lends itself well to its function as a resource volume. Its only obvious deficiency is the lack of a name index, which in these days of information processors should have been possible at modest cost.

Many years ago, I gave up teaching a theories-of-personality course because the dominant textbook was so thorough and well done that it left me with very little to do in the classroom. This handbook would, I think, be a splendid textbook, despite the thoroughness of its coverage, because it leaves the instructor with the challenging but engaging task of integrating the material, which would provide an opening for any instructor with a particular theoretical passion, but many other routes to integration are possible.

36. For *The Handbook of Personality Psychology*, the title of "handbook" may be unfortunate because handbooks _____.
    A. are difficult to compile   B. are often considered boring
    C. can become outdated soon   D. can miss a lot of important information
37. The author likes this handbook partly because it does not _____.
    A. focus on theories of personality   B. relate to previous psychologists
    C. discuss research on personality   D. deal with what is beyond psychology
38. The book talks about Freud only when _____.
    A. his theories are compared with others' B. his contemporaries are mentioned
    C. the discussion concerns his ideas   D. major personality theories are in conflict
39. According to the author, the editors of the book are _____.
    A. particular about the structure of the book
    B. reserved in presenting their own views
    C. defiant of the authority in psychology
    D. successful in their material selection
40. A problem with this handbook is that _____.
    A. it is costly to average readers   B. it is poor in idea development
    C. it has no name index   D. it has too many chapters
41. With respect to being an aid to teaching personality theories, the author thinks that the book _____.
    A. leaves room for the instructor's creativity
    B. presents a challenge to current theories
    C. contains thorough knowledge of personality
    D. provides an integrated system of theories

Passage Two

Our trouble lies in a simple confusion, one to which economists have been prone since the beginning of the Industrial Revolution. Growth and ecology operate by different rules. Economists tend to assume that every problem of scarcity can be solved by substitution, by replacing tuna with tilapia, without factoring in the long-term environmental implications of either. But whereas economies might expand, ecosystems do not. They change — pine gives way to oak, coyotes arrive in New England — and they reproduce themselves, but they do not increase in extent or abundance year after year. Most economists think of scarcity as a labor problem, imagining that only energy and technology place limits on production. To harvest more wood, build a better chain saw; to pump more oil, drill more wells; to get more food, invent pest-resistant plants.

That logic thrived on new frontiers and more intensive production, and it held off the prophets of scarcity — from Thomas Robert Malthus to Paul Ehrlich — whose predictions of famine and shortage have not come to pass. The Agricultural Revolution that began in seventeenth-century England radically increased the amount of food that could be grown on an acre of land, and the same happened in the 1960s and 1970s, when fertilizer and hybridized seeds arrived in India and Mexico. But the picture looks entirely different when we change the scale. Industrial society is roughly 250 years old: make the last ten thousand years equal to twenty-four hours, and we have been producing consumer goods and CO_2 for only the last thirty-six minutes. Do the same for the past 1 million years of human evolution, and everything from the steam engine to the search engine fits into the past twenty-one seconds. If we are not careful, hunting and gathering will look like a far more successful strategy of survival than economic growth. The latter has changed so much about the earth and human societies in so little time that it makes more sense to be cautious than triumphant.

Although food scarcity, when it occurs, is a localized problem, other kinds of scarcity are already here. Groundwater is alarmingly low in regions all over the world, but the most immediate threat to growth is surely petroleum.

42. Economists are prone to _____ .
    A. emphasize the differences between economic growth and scarcity
    B. see economy from an ecological perspective
    C. ignore the environmental impact of economic growth
    D. use different approaches to economics and ecology

43. What does the author think of ecosystems?
    A. They may deteriorate.
    B. They may benefit from the economy.
    C. They are associated with productivity.
    D. They are closely related to technology.

44. What does the passage say about the predictions made by Thomas Robert Malthus and Paul Ehrlich?
    A. They proved to be useful.   B. They have not come true.
    C. They proved to be accurate.   D. They have not drawn enough attention.

45. What happened in the 1960s and 1970s?
    A. Land expansion occurred in Mexico.
    B. Fertilizer began to be used in England.
    C. Hybridized plants were grown in the US.
    D. Food production increased in India.

46. The purpose of mentioning the search engine is to show _____ .
    A. the high speed of modern machines
    B. technological progress

C. popular interest in the Internet
D. the economic impact of information technology

47. The last sentence of the second paragraph implies that _____ .
   A. economic growth has reduced biodiversity worldwide
   B. people and nature should coexist in harmony
   C. people should be proud of their position in nature
   D. economic growth has changed the ecosystem rapidly

Passage Three

Culture is transmitted largely by language and by the necessity for people in close contact to cooperate. The more extensive the communications network, the greater the exchange of ideas and beliefs and the more alike people become — in toleration of diversity if nothing else. Members of a culture or a nation are generally in closer contact with one another than with members of other cultures or nations. They become more like each other and more unlike others. In this way, there develops "national character," which is the statistical tendency for a group of people to share values and follow similar behavior patterns.

Frequently, the members of one culture will interpret the "national characteristics" of another group in terms of their own values. For example, the inhabitants of a South Pacific island may be considered "lazy" by citizens of some industrialized nations. On the other hand, it may be that the islanders place a great value on social relationships but little value on "productivity," and crops grow with little attention. The negative connotation of the label "lazy" is thus unjustified from the point of view of the island culture.

Stereotypes, such as "lazy", "inscrutable," and "dishonest" give people the security of labels with which to react to others in a superficial way, but they are damaging to real understanding among members of different cultures. People react more to labels than to reality. A black American Peace Corps volunteer, for instance, is considered and called a white man by black Africans. The "we-they" distinction applies to whatever characteristic the "wes" have and the "theys" do not have — and the characteristics attributed to the "theys" are usually ones with a negative value.

The distinction becomes most obvious in times of conflict. For this reason, it is often suggested the only thing that might join all men together on this planet would be an invasion from outer space. "We," the earthlings, would then fight "them," the outsiders.

Given the great diversities — real and imagined — among people of the world, is there any foundation for hope that someday all men might join together to form a single and legitimate world government? The outcome will probably depend on the political evolution of mankind.

48. What makes people more tolerant of diversity between different groups?
   A. Extensive communications.   B. Language development.
   C. Close cooperation.   D. Direct interactions.
49. "National character" is built among people who _____ .

  A. like each other   B. share the same values
  C. speak the same language   D. think in the same way

50. To some industrialized nations, the mentioned South Pacific islanders are _____.
  A. idle   B. carefree   C. inefficient   D. well-organized

51. With stereotypes, people tend to _____
  A. react to each other on a regular basis
  B. see different cultures in different ways
  C. take their own culture as the best of all
  D. describe other cultures with labels

52. What is true about the black American Peace Corps volunteer?
  A. He was wronged by his fellow African Americans.
  B. He was considered as a distinguished volunteer.
  C. He was discriminated against by the whites.
  D. He was excluded from the black Africans.

53. It is possible to form a single and legitimate world government only when _____.
  A. people are willing to abandon their "national character"
  B. people of different nations hold similar political views
  C. human beings as a whole have one common enemy
  D. human beings are able to contact beings in outer space

Passage Four

  If gender conflicts continue at their current rate, my partner gloomily observed, men may fade into extinction and women will manage fine without them. What with test-tube babies, cloning, a falling birth-rate, have-it-all career women prevailing like never before, it seems as if old-fashioned, instinct-driven sexual selection was totally out of fashion. But a study from four British universities suggests it is alive and well, and busy shaping the next generation.

  In spite of emancipation, the feminist movement, gender equality, consistent efforts to avoid gender-stereotyping, men still prefer to marry women who are not too brainy. In the study a high IQ hampered a woman's chance of getting married, with a 40 per cent drop in marital prospects for every 16-point rise. The opposite was true for their male classmates. Top-earning men were 8 per cent more likely to be married than their low-earning peers.

  How interesting that we automatically assume that men are put off by cleverness in women. Perhaps the brainy women did not want to get married. Possibly they could not find men clever enough to satisfy them. But these interpretations hardly merit more than a passing thought because this study simply reinforces what we know to be broadly true: that most women do want a committed partner and that most stable marriages occur in a power relation, with the man being the center.

  We usually think of competitiveness as a male activity, and so it is mainly, which is all the more reason for it causing stress in a marriage. Our ancestry certainly included a long phase when the males competed for the alpha role, in which the top male took all the advantages and most of the group matings. Most men nurse secret dreams of being "benign" dictators. No man likes his wife to earn more than he does. We see how fragile are the marriages of those in which the female has the **whip hand** in the shape of fame, success, and wealth. In contrast, marriages where the female status is obviously inferior, including arranged marriages, there is a greater stability.

Women have to accept that coming into our own and achieving the full potential of our (seemingly superior) capacity to use education will undoubtedly make us more inaccessible as partners. More choosy, and therefore less successful.

54. The "test-tube babies" and other things are mentioned in Paragraph 1 to indicate _____.
    A. the development of medical technology
    B. the radical changes of our lifestyle
    C. the decreasing birth rate of human society
    D. the independence of the female gender

55. Conventional sexual selection _____.
    A. gets out-of-date   B. remains active
    C. becomes extinct   D. seems prevalent

56. The statistics in Paragraph 2 illustrate that _____.
    A. women's IQ and their marital probability are in direct proportion
    B. men's IQ and their marital probability are in inverse proportion
    C. women prefer to marry men who are very intelligent
    D. men prefer to marry women who are less intelligent

57. What might be the meaning of "whip hand" in Paragraph 4?
    A. Control.   B. Desire.   C. Intelligence.   D. Commitment.

58. How is marriage related to power, according to the study?
    A. Married men and women all seek power over each other.
    B. A powerful husband is the key to the successful marriage.
    C. A stable marriage depends on the power of the wife.
    D. Rich men tend to hold absolute power over their wives.

59. What might be the title of this passage?
    A. Single Women's Self-reliance.   B. Road to a Successful Marriage.
    C. Why Brainy Women Stay Single.   D. Stereotypes About Marriage.

Passage Five

In *Second Nature*, Nobel Prize-winning neuroscientist Gerald Edelman argues that the brain and mind are unified, but he has little patience with the claim that the brain is a computer. Fortunately for the general reader, his explanations of brain function are accessible, reinforced by concrete examples and metaphors.

Edelman suggests that thanks to the recent development of instruments capable of measuring brain structure within millimeters and brain activity within milliseconds, perceptions, thoughts, memories, willed acts, and other mind matters traditionally considered private and impenetrable to scientific scrutiny now can be correlated with brain activity. Our consciousness (a "first-person affair" displaying intentionality, reflecting beliefs and desires, etc.), our creativity, even our value systems, have a basis in brain function.

The author describes three unifying insights that correlate mind matters with brain activity. First, even distant neurons will establish meaningful connections (circuits) if their firing patterns are synchronized. Second, experience can either strengthen or weaken synapses (neuronal connections). Finally, there is reentry, the continued signaling from one brain region to another and back again along massively parallel nerve fibers.

Edelman concedes that neurological explanations for consciousness and other aspects of mind are not currently available, but he is confident that they will be soon. Meanwhile, he is comfortable hazarding a guess: "All of our mental life... is based on the structure and dynamics of our brain." Despite this optimism about the explanatory powers of neuroscience, Edelman acknowledges the pitfalls in attempting to explain all aspects of mind in neurological terms. Indeed, culture — not biology — is the primary determinant of the brain's evolution, and has been since the emergence of language, he notes.

However, I was surprised to learn that he considers Sigmund Freud "the key expositor of the effects of unconscious processes on behavior." Such a comment ignores how slightly Freud's conception of the unconscious, with its emphasis on sexuality and aggression, resembles the cognitive unconscious studied by neuroscientists.

Still, *Second Nature* is well worth reading. It serves as a bridge between the traditionally separate camps of "hard" science and the humanities. Readers without at least some familiarity with brain science will likely find the going difficult at certain points. Nonetheless, Edelman has achieved his goal of producing a provocative exploration of "how we come to know the world and ourselves."

60. Gerald Edelman would most probably support the idea that the _____.
    A. brain co-functions with the mind   B. brain works like a computer
    C. brain has an accessible function   D. brain sends signals to the mind
61. It was previously felt that perceptions and other mind matters could hardly be _____.
    A. treated as a significant issue   B. studied with scientific methods
    C. separated from brain activity   D. handled with surgical instruments
62. Edelman firmly believes that _____.
    A. brain signals will repeatedly go from one brain region to another
    B. experience will have an ill effect on neuronal connections
    C. distant neurons will help synchronize their firing patterns
    D. mind matters will be explained from a neurological perspective
63. According to Edelman, to provide a thorough explanation of human mind, neuroscience will be _____.

A. responsible B. insufficient C. impractical D. reliable

64. The author disagrees with the idea that the neuroscience-based cognitive unconscious can be _____
    A. clearly explained by Freud's theory
    B. affected by language acquisition
    C. studied relevantly to sexual behavior
    D. examined concerning cultural backgrounds

65. According to the author, *Second Nature* is a good book because _____.
    A. it interests the reader in spiritual activities
    B. it appeals to the reader to study bioscience
    C. it sets the reader probing into human cognition
    D. it presents the advancement of natural science

Section B (20 minutes, 10 points)

Directions: *In each of the following passages, five sentences have been removed from the original text. They are listed from A to F and put below the passage. Choose the most suitable sentence from the list to fill in each of the blanks (numbered 66 to 75). For each passage, there is one sentence that does not fit in any of the blanks. Mark your answers on your Machine-scoring Answer Sheet.*

Passage One

The Santa Ana appeals court upheld an earlier jury verdict awarding $3.2 million in damages to Alexis Sarti who suffered serious nerve damage after a food poisoning episode at a restaurant. 66)

In April 2005, Sarti ate raw tuna at the Salt Creek Grille restaurant. Afterwards, she suffered from sudden paralysis and double vision. She spent the next 49 days in the hospital, and had to drop out of college for more than a year and a half after the food poisoning incident, for medical care and therapy.

  67) Muscles and spasms bother her on a daily basis, although she says she's used to these now. She has recovered somewhat since then. But strenuous activity is out of the question, and what's worse, she expects her situation to deteriorate as she gets older.

Sarti filed a lawsuit against the restaurant, and claimed cross contamination of the tuna with a form of bacteria that exists in raw poultry. 68) The verdict was set aside by Superior Court Judge Derek W. Hunt. The 4th District Court of Appeal in Santa Ana has now overturned Judge Hunt's ruling.

In delivering his decision, Judge Hunt said he was constrained by a 35-year-old appellate decision that prohibits juries from assuming that cross contamination in the restaurants was the result of faulty practices or handling.

The Santa Ana appeals court seems to have disregarded that older appellate decision. __69)__ It has been cited for improper food storage, cross contamination and incorrect handling on three separate instances.

It was clear that the negligent food handling practices at this restaurant were responsible for a deadly cross contamination that resulted in Sarti's food poisoning. __70)__ Still, she has incurred more than a million dollars worth of medical bills, and expects to need more medical care in the future.

A. At the trial, Sarti's attorneys argued that Salt Creek Grille has a record of poor handling practices in its kitchens.
B. Sarti said medical bills totaled about $1 million and she wants to put aside another $1 million for future expenses.
C. Sarti insists that the victory is a moral, rather than monetary one.
D. Once a high school cross country runner, Sarti today is unable to take part in sports like running, or other forms of extreme physical activity.
E. It's a milestone decision that can now be cited across other food poisoning lawsuits.
F. A jury handed down a verdict for $3.2 million, and Salt Creek Grille, which also has branches in New York and New Jersey, appealed.

Passage Two

In today's frenetic workplace, where distractions are constant and competition is often fierce, stress has never been higher. From panic attacks and anxiety to poor sleep, acid reflux, high blood pressure and strokes, stress is causing our bodies to mentally and physically shut down, according to Dr. Tara Swart, neuroscientist and co-author of *Neuroscience for Leadership.*

Instead of telling us what we shouldn't be doing, Swart has noted a few telltale signs we need to watch out for, signs that we're letting stress get to us. Some of the physical signs include fatigue, muscular aches and pains, and flu and colds that are lingering longer — a sign that stress is starting to erode your immune system, she said. __71)__ Other physical symptoms include problems related to the gut and limbic system of the brain — things like heartburn, reflux and irritable bowel syndrome can be signs of stress as well. Sometimes, stress can send us spiraling into survival mode, as Swart calls it. __72)__ Being irritable and moody are also signs that stress is getting to us.

__73)__ Aerobic exercise helps, says Swart, as it releases endorphins (内啡肽) and reduces our cortisol (皮质醇) levels. But other, less physically demanding steps need to be also taken: talking to a friend or psychologist, getting adequate sleep, staying well-hydrated and practicing some type of mindfulness will all help reduce our stress, she said.

__74)__ From Oprah Winfrey to Rupert Murdoch and Arianna Huffington to Russell Simmons, it seems these high-achieving individuals know a thing or two about how to cope with stress. Michael Chaskalson, founder and CEO of Mindfulness Works and author of *Mindfulness in 8 Weeks,* coaches senior people in mindfulness skills to better manage pressures of work. In doing so, he claims his clients become more emotionally alert, more empathic and they have higher levels of concentration and creativity. __75)__ With the right approach, walking, even running (in a mindful way), staring out the window, just taking a break, will help leaders not only perform better, but there's evidence that it will improve an organization's overall health and effectiveness.

A. A lot of mental and emotional issues actually manifest with physical symptoms, she said.
B. We crave high-sugar foods and caffeine, thinking it will make us feel better but actually "it makes us more anxious."
C. It doesn't have to be yoga or meditation, Chaskalson says.
D. Many well-known leaders and CEOs have praised meditation and mindfulness as part of their ongoing success.
E. How to combat all this?
F. Stress makes muscles ache, warns Swart, so watch out for "that feeling when you've been running" where the lactic acid builds up.

PAPER TWO

PART IV TRANSLATION (30 minutes, 15 points)

Directions: *Read the following text carefully and then translate the underlined segments into Chinese. Write your Chinese version in the proper space on your Answer Sheet.*

It happens every semester. A student triumphantly points out that Jean-Jacques Rousseau is undermining himself when he claims "the man who reflects is a depraved animal," or that Ralph Waldo Emerson's call for self-reliance is in effect a call for reliance on Emerson himself.

Our best college students are very good at being critical. In fact, being smart, for many, means being critical. (1) Having strong critical skills shows that you will not be easily fooled. It is a sign of sophistication, especially when coupled with an acknowledgment of one's own "privilege."

The skill at unmasking errors is not totally without value, but we should be wary of creating a class of self-satisfied debunkers — or, to use a currently fashionable word on campus, people who like to "trouble" ideas. (2) In overdeveloping the capacity to show how texts, instructions or people fail to accomplish what they set out to do, we may be depriving students of the chance to learn as much as possible from what they study.

In campus cultures where being smart means being a critical unmasker, students may become too good at showing how things can't possibly make sense. (3) They may close themselves off from their potential to find or create meaning and direction from the books, music and experiments they encounter in the classroom.

(4) Once outside the university, these students may try to score points by displaying the

critical prowess for which they were rewarded in school, but those points often come at their own expense.

Liberal education in America has long been characterized by the intertwining of two traditions: of critical inquiry in pursuit of truth and exuberant performance in pursuit of excellence. (5) <u>In the last half-century, emphasis on inquiry has become dominant, and it has often been reduced to the ability to expose error and undermine belief.</u> The inquirer has taken the guise of the sophisticated spectator, rather than the messy participant in continuing experiments or even the reverent beholder of great cultural achievements.

PART V　WRITING (40 minutes, 20 points)

Directions: *Write an essay of no less than 200 words on the topic given below. Use the space provided on your Answer Sheet Ⅱ.*

TOPIC

Do you agree with the Chinese saying "wealth does NOT last for more than three generations"? Why or why not?

2015年3月试题精解

第一部分　词　　汇

1. **答案：B**
　　本题考查介词短语的语义。A 就……而言；B 只要；C 也，还；D 时常。该句的大意为：只要你能让自己不再憎恶她，这听起来是相当不错的一种做法。
2. **答案：D**
　　本题考查形容词的语义。A 不可避免的；B 不确定的；C 不能比拟的；D 触及不到的。该句的大意为：即便时至今日，海洋底部仍然有大部分区域未被探索；大概在一个世纪以前，人们无法到达深藏于海面下方的、平均深度在 3 600 米以下的海底世界。
3. **答案：A**
　　本题考查形容词的语义。A 直觉的；B 偶然的；C 破碎的；D 勤奋的。该句的大意为：他是一名分子生物学家，有灵巧的双手、令人敬佩的创造性和直觉能力。
4. **答案：D**
　　本题考查固定短语的语义。A 在视野之外；B 在广播；C 在地平线上；D 光明正大地。该句的大意为：我们所做的事情完全是光明正大的，毫无秘密可言。
5. **答案：D**
　　本题考查名词的语义。A 坚持不懈；B 持久，永久；C 观点，看法；D 迫害。该句的大意为：在独立精神的庇护下，数以百万计的移民来到这个国家寻求保护，以免于偏狭、歧视和迫害。
6. **答案：A**
　　本题主要考查词语的辨形。A 执行官；B 爆炸物；C 俘虏；D 上瘾的。该句的大意为：这位初级行政官员急不可待地想晋升，但他知道只有待某人死后或退休后才能谋取其职。
7. **答案：D**
　　本题考查形容词的语义。A 可预见的；B 伪装的；C 装饰的；D 高级的。该句的大意为：自 20 世纪 80 年代以来，越来越高级的工具使得电影制作、发售和推广的数字化成为可能。
8. **答案：C**
　　本题考查动词的语义。A 充满，拥挤；B 灌溉；C 消耗，消费；D 购买。该句的大意为：那些食用大量动物油脂的人更容易患上癌症和心脏病。
9. **答案：B**
　　本题考查形容词的语义。A 最高级的；政府首脑的；B 峰值的；C 高潮的；D 最高的。该句的大意为：加拿大的出生率在 1957 年达到峰值，随后便开始下降。
10. **答案：B**
　　本题考查动词短语的语义。A 说到要点；B 处理，处置；C 生效，实施；D 接触，联系。该句的大意为：她帮助成千上万个男女渡过难关，摆脱了他们难以启齿的烦恼。
11. **答案：A**

本题考查名词的语义。A 身份；B 注册登记；C 尊严；D 资格。该句的大意为：在全球化时代背景下，我们需要摒弃视身份为单一的宗教或民族认同的传统观点。

12. 答案：C

    本题考查介词短语的语义。A 为了；B 代表；C 以……为代价；D 在……方面。该句的大意为：人们终于明白以牺牲环境为代价发展经济是多么的愚蠢。

13. 答案：C

    本题考查名词的语义。A 指导者，上级领导；B 下属；C 对应的人；D 通讯员。该句的大意为：在大多数情况下，黑人运动员会以一种不明确的方式承认他们比白人运动员更具优势。

14. 答案：B

    本题考查名词的语义。A 博览会；B 可能的情况；C 实例；D 计划。该句的大意为：我们首先做的是查找实验设计中的差错，并且想遍任何可能会使我们误入歧途的情况。

15. 答案：D

    本题考查动词词组的语义。A 了解……的意思；B 对……负责；C 抽时间做……；D 使……更清楚。该句的大意为：沉船的发现使人们能够更加清楚地了解古代的造船技术和当时的贸易航线。

16. 答案：A

    本题考查动词的语义。A 使有倾向性；B 模仿；C 转移；D 交谈。该句的大意为：政客们撒谎，抱有政治目的的人会歪曲事实以利己。

17. 答案：C

    本题考查动词的语义。A 揭露；B 获取；C 引发，引出；D 产生。该句的大意为：她的长处是能够引发、激发她的朋友们的信心而非恐惧。

18. 答案：A

    本题考查形容词短语的语义。A 在……之下的；B 毗邻的；C 固有的；D 受制于……的。该句的大意为：就头衔和职位而言，副教授低于教授，虽然他们的学识几乎相同。

19. 答案：D

    本题考查名词的语义。A 参照，参考；B 暗示，提及；C 推论，推断；D 先例。该句的大意为：其他的怀疑论者指出，在人类历史上尚未有过这般和平崛起的先例。

20. 答案：C

    本题考查介词短语的语义。A 符合，一致；B 超过，多于；C 不一致，有差异；D 成比例。该句的大意为：经济学家们认为今年他们的经济发展平稳是可疑的，原因在于其发展与其他经济指数存在很大差异。

第二部分　完形填空

本文主要阐述剽窃对于学术研究的危害。

21. 答案：A

    本题考查动词搭配及对句意的理解。A 使；B 得到；C 有；D 帮助。原文的意思是，剽窃普遍被认为是对科研研究的一种犯罪，但人们对其危害性的解释使它看上去与伪造和篡改这两种行为不同。

22. 答案：D

本题考查连接词与上下文的逻辑关系。A 于是(表结果);B 到目前为止(表时间);C 然而(表转折);D 比如(用于举例说明)。前文提到人们对剽窃危害性的解释使它看上去与伪造和篡改这两种学术不端行为不同。紧接其后,作者就举了一个例子,说明一些学者确实持有这样的观点。

23. 答案:D

本题考查名词的词义辨析及对上下文的理解。A 借口;B 意识形态;C 物体,目标;D 冒犯行为。本句的意思是说,Kenneth D. Pimple 认为,剽窃不是破坏科学知识构建的一种冒犯行为。

24. 答案:C

本题考查形容词的使用以及对句意的理解。A 竞争的;B 被吸引的;C 应得的;D 渴望的。本句的意思是,剽窃这一行为剥夺了其他科学家从事科学知识构建而应得的回报。

25. 答案:B

本题考查连接词词组的语义辨析及句子之间的逻辑关系。A 另一方面;B 换句话讲;C 迟早,终究;D 与此同时。本句的意思是,换句话讲,Pimple 认为剽窃的问题不在于该行为不诚实,而是不公平。

26. 答案:A

本题考查介词的词义辨析及对句意的理解。A 除了……以外(包括后面所提到的内容),还;B 朝……;C 除了……以外(不包括后面所提到的内容);D 为了。本句的意思是,除了诚实这一组成部分外,Pimple 指出了负责任的科研行为的另一组成部分。

27. 答案:A

本题考查名词的词义辨析及对句意的理解。A 同伴;B 对手;C 团队;D 同龄人。本句是顺承前句而来,意思是,负责任的科研行为的另一组成部分就是对科研同行的公平。

28. 答案:B

本题考查名词的词义辨析及对句意的理解。A 机会;B 方式;C 原因;D 基础。本句顺成上句,Pimple 除了将诚实看作科研行为的一部分外,也将对科研同行的公平看作科研工作的一个组成部分。本句的意思是,尽管作者认同 Pimple 的以上观点,但作者认为 Pimple 对剽窃的分析遗漏了很重要的一个方面。

29. 答案:C

本题考查动词的词义辨析及对句意的理解。A 激发;B 构建;C 伤害;D 评估。本句顺承上句,意思是说对某些词语、观点、方法及结果的歪曲会损害科学知识的构建。

30. 答案:C

本题考查副词的词义辨析及对上下文的理解。A 令人感到奇怪地;B 相应地;C 可能地;D 有必要地。本句的意思是,对于那些被剽窃者而言,剽窃行为可能让其感到不愉快。

31. 答案:D

本题考查名词的词义辨析及对句意的理解。A 知识;B 发现;C 创造;D 评价。本句顺承上句,意思是说,尽管对于那些被剽窃者而言,剽窃行为可能让其感到不愉快,但从表面看来,剽窃行为似乎并没有伤害到整个科研群体对这一现象的评价。

32. 答案:B

本题考查动名词的词义辨析及对句意的理解。A 展示;B 比较;C 提交;D 生成。本句是说我们依然会把几个不同的观察报告放到一起进行比较以判断我们所观察到的某一些现象的稳定特征。

33. 答案：C

本题考查连接词的使用及对句子之间的逻辑关系。A 于是，表结果；B 尽管，表让步；C 但是，表转折；D 和，表并列。本句顺承上句，意思是说，对不同观察报告所进行的对比也涉及研究者之间的对话。

34. 答案：D

本题考查动词词组的语义辨析及搭配。A 致力于；B 安排；C 承诺；D 关于。本句的大意是，从开始的实验计划到最后实验结果的发表，科学工作者都在就实验的细节和观察到某种现象时的条件状况进行问答。另外，从词语的搭配来看，在这四个选项中，只有 D 选项 engage 一词可以和介词 in 搭配。

35. 答案：B

本题考查介词的词义辨析及固定搭配的用法。在四个选项中，只有选项 B 介词 under 可以和 condition 搭配，表示"在某种状况下"，符合本句意思：观察到某种现象时的条件状况。

第三部分　阅读理解

第一节　阅读理解 A

第一篇：

36. 答案：B

本题是细节题，要求考生理解第一段的第二句中提到的"手册通常都相当的枯燥"。因此 B 为正确答案。

37. 答案：A

本题是细节题，考点在第二段中第五句中否定意义的表达 "that pays no particular attention to theories of personality"。另外，阅读时应注意到接下来的两句进一步解释了第五句的语义。在阅读过程中，否定意义是特殊信息，会引起读者的注意。本题答题时还应留意题干中的否定词 "not"。

38. 答案：C

本题是细节题，考查考生对第二段倒数第二句中"when their views are relevant to topics under discussion"的理解。本题答题的另一关键是利用题干的人名信息快速检索到原文的位置。

39. 答案：D

本题是推理题，考点在文章的第三段，尤其是第三段最后一句。本题答题时注意选项 A 的干扰性比较大，虽然文中介绍了手册的章节安排，但并未说明这一章节结构具有什么特殊性。

40. 答案：C

本题是细节题，考查考生对第四段的第二句 "Its only obvious deficiency is the lack of a name index" 的理解。

41. 答案：A

本题是推理题，考查考生对最后一段的理解，尤其对第一句的理解。在这一段中，文章作者说明了为什么他(她)多年前要放弃"性格理论"这门课程,这句貌似与文中推荐的《性格心理学手册》这本书无关,但恰恰是通过对比的方法说明该书用于教学时的优势:可以令教师有发挥的空间。

第二篇:

42. 答案:C

本题是推理题,考查考生对第一段第三句的理解,尤其是"... without factoring in the long-term environmental implications ..."中隐含的作者的观点:经济学家并没有考虑到经济发展对环境及生态的长期影响。

43. 答案:A

本题是作者观点题,考查对第一段中作者表达的观点,尤其是第一段第四句的理解。

44. 答案:B

本题是细节题,考查第二段的第一句。这句话中"not come to pass"是"未能成真,未能实现"的意思。题干中的人名信息有助于考生准确定位原文中的相关内容。

45. 答案:D

本题是细节题,考查考生对第二段第二句的理解。题干中的时间信息可以帮助考生快速准确地定位到原文考点的位置。

46. 答案:B

本题是推理题,考查考生对第二段中倒数第三句的理解:如果将人类进化的这一百万年看作24小时的话,那么从蒸汽机到搜索引擎的这段发展也就仅仅为21秒。

47. 答案:D

本题是推理题,正如题干中所提示的,考点在第二段最后一句,该句的大意为:经济发展在如此之短的时间内如此巨大地改变了地球和人类社会,这足以让我们对此慎思谨行,而不是一味欢欣鼓舞。

第三篇:

48. 答案:A

本题是细节题,考查的是考生对第一段第二句的理解,选项A的内容基本与原文保持一致,不难看出为正确答案。

49. 答案:B

本题是细节题,考查考生对第一段最后一句的理解。找到考点是本题的答案关键,因为选项B的用语与原文基本一致。

50. 答案:A

本题是细节题,实际也考查考生对"lazy"一词的理解。选项中只有"idle"与之最接近。

51. 答案:D

本题是细节题,考点在第三段的第一句。"labels"一词的理解是本题答题关键。

52. 答案:D

本题是推理题,考查的是考生对第三段第三句的理解:非洲黑人将他视为白人,因此可以推断选项D"他被排除出了非洲黑人"是正确答案。

53. 答案：C

本题是推理题,考查的是考生对第四段的理解,其中提到的外星人象征着人类共同的敌人。

第四篇：

54. 答案：D

本题是例证题,关键要理解第一段的第一句和第二句:试管婴儿等例证是为了说明女性越来越独立的社会地位。

55. 答案：B

本题是细节题,考点在第一段的最后一句,其中"it"指代的是"old-fashioned, instinct-driven sexual selection"。

56. 答案：D

本题是例证题,关键是理解第二段的第一句。该句的大意是:男人仍旧愿意娶不是那么太聪明的女人。

57. 答案：A

本题是词汇题,要求考生理解"whip hand"在上下文中的意思,尤其是第四段的最后两句呈对比关系,说明女性在婚姻中的强势与否与婚姻的稳定有关:女性强势,婚姻则脆弱;而女性在家庭中地位低于男性的话,婚姻有更大的稳定性。"whip hand"的意思是"执鞭之手",即"支配地位"。

58. 答案：B

本题是归纳推理题,要求考生理解第四段的中心内容。本题也可以运用排除法筛选出选项 B 为最佳答案。

59. 答案：C

本题是主旨大意题,考查读者对全文大意的总结归纳能力。

第五篇：

60. 答案：A

本题是推理题,考点在第一段的第一句。阅读中值得留意的是"little"一词表达的否定意义。

61. 答案：B

本题是长句理解题,考查第二段的第一句。该句中的逗号比较多,考生在阅读时应注意这些逗号与句法成分之间的关系;另外,准确定位句子的主语和谓语动词是阅读长句的关键。

62. 答案：D

本题是细节题,考点信息在文中第四段的第一句。

63. 答案：B

本题是细节题,考查考生对第四段第三句的理解。该句的大意是 Edelman 承认试图从神经学的角度阐释大脑活动的所有方面是非常困难的。

64. 答案：A

本题是推理题,考查第五段的内容。该段的主要内容是本文作者并不同意 Edelman 的观点,因为作者认为弗洛伊德关于无意识的概念与神经科学家们提出的认知无意识的观点并无相似之处。

65. 答案:C

本题是推理题,考点在文章的最后一段,考查读者的总结归纳能力。

第二节　阅读理解 B

第一篇:

66. 答案:E

本题的突破口在于把握文章第一段引领全文的作用,其中第一句概述了 Santa Ana 案件的审判结果。选项中只有 E 选项是总论这一审判结果的历史意义,因此选 E。

67. 答案:D

本题的突破口为文章第二段的主要内容。第二段主要介绍了 Sarti 在食品中毒后遭受的身体机能方面的损伤。选项中只有 D 选项讲到了她身体受到的伤害,即无法像以前那样跑步或进行其他剧烈的体育运动了。

68. 答案:F

本题的答题关键是把握后一句中定冠词 the 在"the verdict"中的使用,这说明前一句中应该已经出现过"a verdict",顺着这个线索浏览选项,不难发现选项 F 在内容上与上下文衔接顺畅,所以为正确答案。

69. 答案:A

本题的答题关键是空格后一句中讲到的代词"It",由于是"cite"一词的宾语,这一代词很可能指的是"供词""记录"等文件,因此选 A。

70. 答案:C

本题的突破口在空格后一句的语义:不包括今后的治疗,受害者 Sarti 目前已经承受了一百多万美金的医疗费用。这句隐含的语义是她这次胜诉与其说是金钱方面的胜诉,不如说是道义上的胜利。

第二篇:

71. 答案:F

本题的突破口是把握空格后一句中的"other physical symptoms",这说明需要填入的内容也是某种生理症状,因此选 F。

72. 答案:B

本题的答题关键是了解第二段的主要内容:压力大时人体出现的症状或反应。另外,空格后的句子讲到了情绪方面的反应,因此要填入的内容有可能也是心理或情绪的变化,因此选 B。

73. 答案:E

本题的答题重点是把握文章第三段的主要内容——应对压力的方法,因此第一句为选项 E。

74. 答案:D

本题的突破口是,空格的后一句列举了名流名人的例子以说明名人减压的方法,因此答案为选项 D。

75. 答案:C

本题的答题关键是把握空格的后一句中用到的"even"一词,意在说明简单易行的运动照样可以减压,没有必要采取一些高大上的方法,因此答案为 C。

第四部分　翻　译

(1) 译文:

具备突出的批判能力表明你不会轻易受骗。这是精明老练的标志,尤其和自己的"特权"得到承认结合起来看,更是如此。

解析:

该句的语言难点是动词短语"coupled with",从名词"couple"的"一对;两三个"等意可推断出"couple with"意为"与……相结合"。

(2) 译文:

我们过度培养这样的能力,即证明文章、教导和人们如何没有达到初衷的能力,或许会剥夺学生们通过学习获取尽可能多知识的机会。

解析:

该句的一个语言难点是理清"how texts, instructions or people fail to accomplish what they set out to do"这一复杂成分的句法结构:这一部分整体上是"show"的宾语,而"what they set out to do"又是"accomplish"的宾语。本句另一语言难点是动词短语"deprive... of",意为"剥夺"。

(3) 译文:

他们可能也扼杀了自己通过课堂上的书本、音乐和实验来发现或建构意义和方向的潜力。

解析:

该句的语言难点是"close oneself off from ...",意为"封锁;隔绝",引申为"扼杀"。

(4) 译文:

一旦走出大学,这些学生或许会试图通过展现超凡的批判能力来出风头,因为在学校时,他们曾因这种能力而得到嘉奖,但这种风头往往让他们自己付出代价。

解析:

该句的语言难点稍多,像"score points","prowess"和"at their own expense"都是理解句子的关键。"score points"意为"得分";"prowess"意为"超凡的技术",而"at their own expense"意为"付出自己的代价"。

(5) 译文:

但在过去半个世纪,对探究的强调占了上风,而且探究常常被简化为揭露错误和破坏信念的能力。

解析:

该句的重点是对"the ability"的后置定语"to expose error and undermine belief"的理解,而其中"undermine"一词不常用,它的意思是"破坏"。

第五部分 写 作

题目解析:

本题目试图探讨的是"富不过三代"的中国谚语。这样一句流传已久的谚语有它存在的理由。在古代,财富的积累受到社会因素的影响很大。在社会动荡的环境下,一代或者两代积累下来的财富,很容易由于时势的影响而散去。另外一个重要的原因是富家子弟多纨绔,创业容易守成难。而且古代的创业环境比较单一,财富积累的途径也比较有限。但是这句谚语在现代社会里理应被重新审视。现代社会政治环境基本稳定,财富受其影响较小。财富的聚集领域和高科技、互联网乃至房地产等领域密切相关。虽然经济环境瞬息万变,在全球化的背景下,包括互联网的冲击都给传统行业带来了巨大的挑战,这是不利于传递财富的因素。但是现代社会也有更多利于创造财富的机会。即使第一代之后企业有所衰退,第二代、第三代仍有可能在新的行业崛起。现代社会的另一个特点是发达的现代教育也使富人阶层的后代有更好的条件去接受最好的教育,掌握管理财富的技能,这使得他们的优势会累积下来。虽有少数富二代仍然挥霍财产,但也有不少富二代起点高,还比普通人更努力。所以财富传递过三代的机会大大增加了。写作的时候可以从这两个角度选取任意一个来创作成文,只要言之有理,证据充分,都有说服力就可以。

范文:

I agree that wealth does not last for three generations. The reasons could be stated as follows.

First, the first generation usually work extremely hard to build the family fortune. Their entrepreneurial spirit and perseverance ensure that the family business runs well. The second generation build upon it, achieve the goals of the first generation, and maintain it. They have usually witnessed the first generation's hard working and would cherish what they have, except for a few "Second-generation Rich" in China after the 1980s who squander the wealth. While the second generation may see the value of hard work, the third generation, because it did not have the same experience of having to work hard, struggle, and earn everything, tend to squander the wealth and lose it. All this tends to make the family wealth that last for three generations very rare.

Moreover, wealth is not an easy thing to maintain. Success won't be easily copied in a changing time. What proved useful in running business in old times may not be feasible in a new era. Everything is changing fast in modern times. Many businesses are springing up like mushrooms after a spring rain, and then disappear very quickly. Many traditional businesses are facing a bleak future in face of the challenges from the Internet. It is difficult to run a family business successfully for three generations in a world of globalization as well.

In a word, the rise and fall in wealth, power and influence of any family is very common. The accumulated wealth of a family usually begins to dissipate after three generations. (266 words)

中国科学院大学
博士研究生入学考试
英语试题

(2016年3月)

考生须知：

一、本试卷由试卷一（PAPER ONE）和试卷二（PAPER TWO）两部分组成。试卷一为客观题，答卷使用标准化机读答题纸；试卷二为主观题，答卷使用非机读答题纸。

二、请考生一律用HB或2B铅笔填涂标准化机读答题纸，画线不得过细或过短。修改时请用橡皮擦拭干净。若因填涂不符合要求而导致计算机无法识别，责任由考生自负。请保持机读答题纸清洁、无折皱。答题纸切忌折叠。

三、全部考试时间总计180分钟，满分为100分。时间及分值分布如下：

试卷一：

Ⅰ 词汇	15分钟	10分
Ⅱ 完形填空	15分钟	15分
Ⅲ 阅读理解	80分钟	40分
小计	110分钟	65分

试卷二：

Ⅳ 英译汉	30分钟	15分
Ⅴ 写作	40分钟	20分
小计	70分钟	35分

UNIVERSITY OF THE CHINESE ACADEMY OF SCIENCES ENGLISH ENTRANCE EXAMINATION FOR PH. D PROGRAM

March 2016

PAPER ONE

PART I VOCABULARY (15 minutes, 10 points, 0.5 point each)

Directions: *Choose the word or expression below each sentence that best completes the statement, and mark the corresponding letter of your choice with a single bar across the square brackets on your Machine-scoring Answer Sheet.*

1. Google is not the only search utility in town, but it comes with such a(n) _____ collection of tools to focus your search that it is the engine of choice for many of us.
   A. comparable   B. formidable
   C. innumerable   D. compatible
2. The defect in David's character has _____ him from advancement in his career.
   A. exempted   B. forbidden
   C. undermined   D. hindered
3. The theory that business could operate totally without the aid of government has proved to be a (n) _____ .
   A. allusion   B. seclusion
   C. illusion   D. confusion
4. The closer one can get to reality, the easier the learning by the student, _____ that the necessary knowledge has been given previously to facilitate comprehension.
   A. so   B. despite   C. such   D. provided
5. I looked at Mum and thought _____ she was as nice as she looked maybe all our lives would have been better.
   A. only if   B. if only   C. even if   D. even though
6. In spite of the attractions, Guide has not adopted this uniform approach, mainly because unifying

rather different types of objects does not _____ simplicity.
   A. make for   B. make up   C. make off   D. make out

7. As a good photographer, you must develop an awareness of the world around you and the people who _____ it.
   A. innovate   B. inhabit   C. integrate   D. inherit

8. Judges must be firm, fair and _____ in their application of the law.
   A. normal   B. virtual   C. consistent   D. incessant

9. The most _____ feature of the building is its enormous dome-shaped roof.
   A. distinctive   B. instinctive   C. definite   D. infinite

10. As quickly as possible, the doctor applies ice packs to your injury. Ice _____ swelling and inflammation.
    A. fastens   B. deters   C. encourages   D. fixes

11. _____ we continue to work hard, we can finish the task ahead of schedule.
    A. As soon as   B. As far as   C. So long as   D. So far as

12. This is such a formidable list that we might be tempted to assume that research and higher education must at least be species of the same genus of activity, even if not actually _____.
    A. ideological   B. identical   C. practical   D. methodical

13. We can _____ broadly between the intention of knowing, and the intention of doing, which correspond roughly to the conventional distinction between pure and applied.
    A. separate   B. extinguish   C. distinguish   D. disguise

14. Of course, there are pictures which can be interpreted in more than one way, and even pictures for which there is no _____ interpretation.
    A. plausible   B. applicable   C. reliable   D. comprehensible

15. His fame proved to be a flash in the pan — his first book was popular but he hasn't written anything _____ since.
    A. innovative   B. descriptive   C. intangible   D. intelligible

16. Many foreign students have the _____ belief that British English is somehow more pure and perfect than American English.
    A. indistinct   B. subjective   C. erroneous   D. communistic

17. The small birds native _____ central and eastern Europe used to migrate southwest to spend the winter in southern France, Spain and northern Africa.
    A. in   B. onto   C. with   D. to

18. A gust of wind blew open the windows and _____ the papers all over the floor.
    A. scattered   B. spit   C. split   D. spread

19. _____ lack of evidence, the prisoner had to be released after staying in jail for six months.
    A. In   B. For   C. On   D. With

20. You could argue that many artists have become more _____ happiness because modern times have seen so much misery.
    A. confident in   B. skeptical of   C. realistic about   D. incapable of

PART II CLOZE TEST (15 minutes, 15 points)

Directions: *For each blank in the following passage, choose the best answer from the four choices given below. Mark the corresponding letter of your choice with a single bar across the square brackets on your Machine-scoring Answer Sheet.*

Explosions. Radiation. Evacuations. More than 30 years after Three Mile Island, the __21__ crisis in Fukushima, Japan, has brought back some of the worst __22__ surrounding nuclear power — and restarted a major debate about the merits and the __23__ of this energy source. Does nuclear energy offer a path away from carbon-based fuels? Or are nuclear power plants too big a threat? It's time to __24__ myth from reality.

One myth is that the biggest problem with nuclear energy is safety. Safety is certainly a critical issue, __25__ the tragedy in Japan is making clear. But for years, the biggest challenge to sustainable nuclear energy hasn't been safety, __26__ cost.

In the United States, new nuclear construction was already slowing down even before the partial meltdown at Three Mile Island in 1979. The disaster __27__ sealed its fate. The last nuclear power plant to come online started __28__ power in 1996 — but its construction began in 1972. Today, nuclear power remains __29__ more expensive than coal- or gas-fired electricity, __30__ because nuclear plants are so expensive to build. __31__ are slippery, but a plant can cost $5 billion. A 2009 MIT study estimated that the cost of producing nuclear energy was about 30 percent higher than __32__ of coal or gas.

Of course, cost and safety aren't __33__. Concerns about safety lead to extensive regulatory approval processes and add uncertainty to plant developers' calculations, both of __34__ boost the price of financing new nuclear plants. It's not clear how much these construction costs would __35__ if safety fears subsided and the financing became cheaper — and after the Fukushima catastrophe, we're unlikely to find out.

21. A. unfolding   B. unyielding   C. unwilling   D. underlying
22. A. spirits   B. crimes   C. nightmares   D. intentions
23. A. faults   B. obstacles   C. objections   D. drawbacks
24. A. separate   B. remove   C. exchange   D. prevent
25. A. if   B. as   C. yet   D. although
26. A. only   B. nor   C. but   D. or
27. A. regularly   B. severely   C. invariably   D. merely
28. A. transcending   B. dispatching   C. delivering   D. saving
29. A. exclusively   B. considerably   C. deliberately   D. conversely
30. A. interestingly   B. roughly   C. mainly   D. surprisingly
31. A. Surpluses   B. Consumptions   C. Deficits   D. Estimates
32. A. those   B. that   C. both   D. either

33. A. unreleased   B. unmatched   C. unrelated   D. unmarked
34. A. which   B. them   C. that   D. whom
35. A. remain   B. fall   C. flow   D. sway

PART III READING COMPREHENSION

Section A (60 minutes, 30 points)

Directions: *Below each of the following passages you will find some questions or incomplete statements. Each question or statement is followed by four choices marked A, B, C, and D. Read each passage carefully, and then select the choice that best answers the question or completes the statement. Mark the letter of your choice with a single bar across the square brackets on your Machine-scoring Answer Sheet.*

Passage One

Starvation probably doesn't sound like a key to living well into old age. But as strange as it seems, calorie restriction, done intermittently, appears to be one of the gateways to lasting long-term health.

The concept has already been proved effective in mice, rats, dogs and monkeys. However, very limited research has been done to evaluate the health impact of calorie restriction in humans. In animals, calorie restriction is associated with longevity, decreased risk for cancer and inflammatory diseases and lower cognitive decline. The challenge has been to translate the concept to the real world in which humans need to eat to get through the day.

A new study tested out a modified version of the concept on humans. Researchers at the University of Southern California have designed what they call a "fasting mimicking diet" that provides all the benefits of starving yourself... with a little less starvation.

The plan lasts for five days a month, with a cycle that's repeated for three months. On Day One, a dieter eats food from the prescribed plan that totals 1,090 calories with 10 percent protein, 56 percent fat, and 34 percent carbohydrates. On Days Two through Five, dieters consume just 725 calories with 9 percent protein, 44 percent fat, and 47 percent carbohydrates.

People on the diet ate vegetable soup, energy bars, energy drinks and low-calorie snack chips, and drank a lot of chamomile tea. They also took vegetable-based dietary supplements. On non-dieting days they ate normally.

It may sound gimmicky, but Vijg, one of the researchers, says existing science already backs up the claim that the plan could effectively improve human health and prolong life. In humans, the diet provided a number of physiological changes that could reduce risk factors for age-related conditions such as reduced blood glucose and insulin levels.

In essence, fasting has the ability to improve stress response on a cellular level. A person on this program is likely to lose weight over time, but researchers say better health in old age is the real benefit. With the right marketing, Vijg believes a fasting mimicking diet could become the next commercially branded diet craze, like Atkins or Paleo. However, it could also have some practical applications in a medical setting. A physician could prescribe the diet to a patient for a specific amount of time before surgery, chemotherapy and other types of treatments and procedures that are known to cause trauma and stress to the body.

36. What is the difficulty in the research of the effect of starvation on humans?
    A. Humans need to eat in real life.
    B. Animals are free from diseases
    C. Humans and animals respond differently to starvation.
    D. Humans and animals have different life expectancy.
37. The modified version of the concept refers to _____.
    A. a diet with fruits and vegetables only
    B. a periodic diet with a little food
    C. a calorie-consistent diet
    D. a diet lasting for five days only
38. What kind of food is NOT allowed on dieting days?
    A. Energy supplements.   B. Sport drinks.
    C. Meat and fish.   D. Food with additives.
39. According to the researchers, what benefits can people get by following the plan?
    A. Nice body shape.   B. Psychological well-being.
    C. Better health in old age.   D. Good relations with others.
40. Atkins and Paleo in the last paragraph most probably refer to brand names of _____.
    A. healthy teas   B. popular diets
    C. fast food   D. weight-reducing medicines
41. What is the best title for the passage?
    A. The Less Calorie, the Better?
    B. Say No to Starvation.
    C. A Proved Method of Weight Management.
    D. Could 5-day Fasting Diet Prolong Your Life?

Passage Two

A sweeping review of NASA's human spaceflight program has concluded that the agency has an unsustainable and unsafe strategy that will prevent the United States from achieving a human landing on Mars in the foreseeable future.

The 286-page National Research Council (NRC) report, says that to continue on the present course under budgets that don't keep pace with inflation "is to invite failure, disillusionment, and the loss of the longstanding international perception that human spaceflight is something the United States does best."

A major argument against returning to the moon was that it didn't pencil out — that there wasn't nearly enough money dedicated to the program. If the goal is a human landing on Mars, the current strategy won't work.

"Absent a very fundamental change in the nation's way of doing business, it is not realistic to believe that we can achieve the consensus goal of reaching Mars," Mitch Daniels, the former Indiana governor and co-chair of the committee, said Wednesday morning in an interview.

A 2009 committee appointed by Obama urged NASA to keep its options open while investing in spaceflight technology and letting the commercial sector handle routine trips to low Earth orbit. But the NRC reviewers argue that NASA and its international partners should focus on the "horizon goal" of Mars and do whatever it takes to get there, step by step, avoiding changes in strategic direction.

NASA officials, aware that critics see the agency as adrift, say they have already been moving in the direction advocated by the NRC. Their strategy targets Mars, just as the NRC report now demands, they say. "All this work will eventually enable astronaut missions to Mars," NASA Administrator Charles Bolden said in a recent NASA white paper.

"NASA's been doing some work, and has been doing some thinking over the last six months, that is in alignment with what the NRC says the top-level goals are," said Greg Williams, a NASA deputy associate administrator.

But Williams was cool to the suggestion of a return to the moon, saying the airless moon offers little help in developing the kind of descent and landing techniques needed on Mars, which has a thin, troublesome atmosphere.

The NRC committee probed the philosophical question of why we send people into space to begin with. The committee concluded that the purely practical, economic benefits of human spaceflight do not justify the costs but that the aspirational nature of the endeavor may make it worth the effort.

42. The review of NASA's human spaceflight program is described as _____.
    A. timely   B. extensive   C. critical   D. notable
43. The National Research Council report implies that _____.
    A. the U.S. plays a leading role in spaceflight
    B. international cooperation requires more budget
    C. the program's chances of success are slim
    D. the public need to give more support to the program
44. According to Mitch Daniels, reaching Mars _____.
    A. lacks funding from the business world
    B. is a project that has made great achievements
    C. is a generally accepted objective
    D. will change the country in various ways
45. A 2009 committee appointed by Obama argued that NASA should _____.
    A. become more commercialized

B. pay more attention to low-Earth-orbit projects
  C. become more realistic with its strategies
  D. make more efforts in different space programs
46. NASA is criticized for _____.
  A. lacking consistent goals
  B. being overambitious
  C. demanding too much fund
  D. having low-quality staff
47. The NRC committee claimed that spaceflight _____.
  A. deserves devotion
  B. brings economic benefits
  C. would have an uncertain future
  D. should use the techniques of moonlanding

Passage Three

Microfinance is an anti-poverty tool. If you make small loans to groups of poor women, they always repay them on time. Microfinance has grown rapidly in many countries. Yet the industry has come under attack for being too commercial.

In Bangladesh the government has **capped the annual interest rate** that microfinance institutions (MFIs) can charge at 27%. In Andhra Pradesh (AP), the Indian state with the most microfinance borrowers, local politicians have bullied the business to a virtual halt. These steps are ostensibly motivated by a desire to defend the poor from getting stuck in a debt. But they are wrong-headed.

Despite charging seemingly high interest rates, MFIs typically have thin margins because of the high costs of making and collecting payments on millions of tiny loans. Pressing them to reduce rates further would jeopardize their ability to attract private capital, inhibiting their growth.

In fact, the poor often use microloans to pay off far more expensive loans from village moneylenders. This suggests that restricting people's access to microcredit by capping rates could have the perverse effect of driving more poor people into the arms of village loan-sharks. That would be good news for these moneylenders, but is surely not the outcome that policymakers want.

Sensible regulation need not be at odds with a thriving microfinance industry. Peru, for example, is ranked as having the best business environment for microfinance, in part because the regulator has successfully set and enforced rules on capital buffers, leading to a more stable environment for the industry. India, in contrast, is yet to decide whether rules governing microfinance are to be set at the national level or by individual states.

Many things can be done. For instance, an association of Indian MFIs is trying to set up a credit bureau which would allow them to track clients' overall indebtedness and credit histories, thus guarding them against lending a person more than she is able to handle. This would be helped enormously if the government sped up its efforts to give all Indians a universal identification number. The Indian government should also allow MFIs to take deposits, which they are currently prevented from doing: this would make them less dependent on capital markets for funding. Actually there are more useful measures for the poor than an interest-rate cap.

48. The microfinance industry is under attack because _____.
    A. it develops too fast
    B. it offers small loans
    C. it over-emphasizes business
    D. it is an anti-poverty tool

49. The underlined phrase in Paragraph 2 most probably means _____.
    A. to set a maximum annual interest rate
    B. to change the annual interest rate
    C. to relax the control of the annual interest rate
    D. to reduce the annual interest rate

50. According to the author, MFIs are not making a big profit because _____.
    A. the interest rates are too low
    B. the handling of numerous small loans is expensive
    C. they fail to attract private capital.
    D. they are under great pressure from the government.

51. According to the author, what would happen if people's access to microfinance is restricted?
    A. The profit of MFIs would be reduced.
    B. Poor people would not be trapped in a debt.
    C. People would only get more costly loans.
    D. Policymakers would be thrilled at the outcome.

52. In paragraph 5, what does the example of Peru and India indicate?
    A. India has been aware of the importance of regulation on microfinance.
    B. The microfinance industry is booming in both India and Peru.
    C. Sensible regulations promote the microfinance industry.
    D. Regulations should be set at the national level.

53. According to Paragraph 6, which measure is **NOT** approved by the author?
    A. Set up capital markets for funding.
    B. Understand the credit histories of the clients.
    C. Give everyone a universal identification number.
    D. Permit MFIs to attract deposits.

Passage Four

Wright, a computer scientist, is plotting an experiment with a humanoid robot called Nao. He and his colleagues plan to introduce this cute bot to people on the street and elsewhere — where it will deliberately invade their privacy. Upon meeting strangers, for example, Nao may use face-recognition software to dig up some detailed information online about them. Or, it may tap into their mobile phone's location tracking history, learn where they ate lunch yesterday, and ask what they thought of the soup.

Wright is one of a number of researchers wondering whether we can trust the robots that are poised to enter our lives. Scientists and scholars argue that if robots become **ubiquitous**, they'll be able to constantly watch and record us. One of the greatest threats, it seems, is to our privacy.

Robots have already been working in factories for decades. Some are now in our homes, cleaning our floors, while others may soon keep a watchful eye on us as security guards or help take care of the elderly. In the last year alone, Google, which is already developing self-driving cars, bought eight robot companies.

Yet despite advances in technology and in artificial intelligence, we're still a long way from intelligent robots. What will empower them, however, is the cloud: the distributed, networked computing in which the Internet lives. By connecting to the Internet, robots can retrieve information and ask for help as they navigate the world, for example.

It would be the next step in a technological evolution already underway. "What we're increasingly seeing now is the existence of computers and sensing devices as part of the infrastructure that surrounds us," says Wright, based at the Oxford Internet Institute at the University of Oxford. With smartphones, the rise of wearable technologies like Google Glass, and the availability of wireless Internet almost everywhere, the Internet is embedding itself deeper into our environment.

"Ultimately, what a robot is or what a robot represents is an increasing presence of computers as more physical objects that we interact with," Wright says. "Those interactions are going to be very rich," he adds. "It's going to be physical and pervasive."

Perhaps that's part of the reason why some of the major web technology firms, such as Google, have been embracing robotics. Some researchers and privacy advocates are concerned that robots could act as physical extensions of these companies, giving them tremendous access into your life.

54. What is true about the humanoid robot Nao?
    A. It is used to intrude into people's privacy.
    B. It has a lot of detailed information in its software.
    C. It can track where people put their mobile phones.
    D. It can help people order in a restaurant.

55. What does the underlined word "ubiquitous" (Paragraph 2) most probably mean?
    A. Unique.   B. Ridiculous.
    C. Commonplace.   D. Powerful.

56. Google is mentioned in Paragraph 3 to _____.
    A. show the latest development of robots
    B. illustrate its contribution to the robotic industry
    C. explain the application of robots on the Internet
    D. demonstrate the widespread use of robots

57. Which of the following statements is true about the cloud?
    A. It is the latest development in artificial intelligence.
    B. It can help develop intelligent robots.
    C. It is a network of Internet-connected computers.

D. It is a navigation tool for world travelers.
58. Some major web technology firms embrace robotics because _____.
   A. robots make human interactions with the Internet more prevalent
   B. robots could advance technological revolution
   C. robots can improve the natural environment
   D. robots can protect the business secrets of companies
59. What is the best title of the passage?
   A. What Is the Underlying Power of Robots?
   B. Robots: Can We Trust Them with Our Privacy?
   C. The Evolution of Robotic Technology.
   D. The Future of Robotic Technology.

Passage Five

New research by Hillary Pennell and Elizabeth Behm-Morawitz at the University of Missouri suggests that, at least for women, the influence of superheroes is not always positive. Although women play a variety of roles in the superhero genre, including helpless maiden and powerful heroine, the female characters all tend to be hypersexualized, from their perfect, seducing figures to their sexy, revealing costumes. Exposure to this, they show, can impact beliefs about gender roles, body esteem, and self-objectification.

Consider, for example, superhero movies like Spider-man or Superman. These action-packed films typically feature a strong, capable, intelligent man fighting a villainous force. The goal of course is to save humanity, but more often than not there is also an immediate need to rescue a fair lady in distress. The female victim is typically delicate, naive, and defenseless, but at the same time sexy and beautiful. What she lacks in strength and cunning she makes up for in kindness and curves. It is not surprising (or insignificant) that she is often the object of the hero's affections.

Pennell and Behm-Morawitz argued that exposure to these stereotypic female victims, whose primary appeal is sexual, may lower women's body esteem, heighten the value they place on body image, and result in less equal gender role beliefs and expectations. However, female characters have come a long way in the superhero genre, and it's possible that the antidote to the helpless fair maiden is the competent, commanding superheroine.

The X-Men films, for example, feature a number of empowering female characters like Storm, Jean Gray, and Dazzler, each of whom wields a unique special ability and displays impressive cognitive and physical competence. Perhaps exposure to this new generation of female heroines will result in more equal gender beliefs, higher body esteem, and greater prioritization of physical competence over appearance.

Still, today's superheroines, like their female victim counterparts, are often unrealistic, sexualized representations of female figures, with large chests, curvy backsides and unattainable hourglass dimensions. Their skin-tight outfits underline their sexuality with plunging necklines and bare skin, and many of their names (e.g., Risque, Mystique, Ruby Summers) connote, shall we say, a slightly less respectable profession than superheroine.

Pennell and Behm-Morawitz thus speculated that while today's powerful superheroines might elevate equal beliefs about gender roles, their sexualized nature might simultaneously have destructive effects on body image and self-objectification.

60. What's the implied meaning of the first paragraph?
    A. Women are either helpless or powerful in superhero movies.
    B. Superhero movies definitely inspire women to become stronger.
    C. Female characters are extremely sexy and appealing in superhero movies.
    D. Superhero movies make women objectify themselves and question their body shapes.

61. Female victims in superhero movies tend to be _____.
    A. formidable and quick-witted
    B. sophisticated and intimidating
    C. pretentious and loathsome
    D. amiable and seductively-shaped

62. According to the author, the image of stereotypic female victims can be improved by _____.
    A. showing more competent and heroic female characters
    B. distinguishing them from the superheroines
    C. turning them into capable and powerful superheroines
    D. strengthening their image as innocent and alluring maidens

63. The film audience in Paragraph 4 will most probably support the idea that _____.
    A. men and women are equal
    B. special abilities are unrealistic for females
    C. women should always be on a diet to stay in good shape
    D. the importance of a strong body should be downplayed compared with that of appearance

64. What is the main idea of the fifth paragraph?
    A. Female roles are dressed in revealing and inviting costumes.
    B. Leading female roles are still stereotyped by alluring bodies.
    C. Many of the superheroines' names are related with undignified jobs.
    D. Sexy maidens remain the typical image of female victims in movies.

65. What is Hilary Pennell and Elizabeth Behm-Morawitz's attitude towards today's superheroines?
    A. Affectionate.   B. Respectful.   C. Objective.   D. Opposed.

Section B (20 minutes, 10 points)

Directions: *In each of the following passages, five sentences have been removed from the original text. They are listed from A to F and put below the passage. Choose the most suitable sentence from the list to fill in each of the blanks (numbered 66 to 75). For each passage, there is one sentence that does not fit in any of the blanks. Mark your answers on your Machine-scoring Answer Sheet.*

Passage One

For centuries, humans have harnessed the power of biological systems to improve their lives and the world. Some argue that biotechnology began thousands of years ago, when crops were first bred for specific traits and microorganisms were used to brew beer. Others define the beginning of biotechnology as the emergence of techniques allowing researchers to precisely manipulate and transfer genes from one organism to another. __66__ Genes are made up of DNA and are expressed into proteins, which do chemical work and form structures to give us specific traits. In the 1970s, scientists discovered and used the power of natural "scissors"— proteins called restriction enzymes — to specifically remove a gene from one kind of organism and put it into related or unrelated organisms. Thus, recombinant DNA technology, or what most experts now label as modern biotechnology, was born.

The pioneers of biotechnology could not have envisioned our current abilities to engineer plants to resist disease, animals to produce drugs in their milk, and small particles to target and destroy cancer cells. __67__ Genomics is based on these tools and is the study of genes and their functions. We have determined the composition of, or "sequenced," the entire set of genes for humans and several other organisms using biotechnology. __68__

Biotechnology, or really any technology, does not exist in a vacuum. It is derived from human efforts and affected by social, cultural, and political climates. Society drives and regulates technology, attempting to minimize the downsides and maximize the benefits. __69__ Recent controversies over the use of genetically engineered organisms in food and agriculture have illustrated that this boundary is not so clear. Not only are there safety concerns about genetically engineered organisms, but there are also cultural differences in acceptance of the products.

International contexts for technologies are important and should be considered. __70__ On the other hand, there are social systems that are affected by new technologies and fears of creating greater divides between rich and poor if technology is not accessible to all sectors of society.

A. The discovery of the structure of deoxyribonucleic acid (DNA) in the 1950s marks the start of this era.
B. Many natural and physical scientists would prefer that the separation between social and ethical concerns and science and technology be well defined.
C. Genomic information is helping us better to evaluate the commonalities and diversity among organisms and human beings and to understand and cure disease, even tailoring treatments to individuals.
D. There are clear indications that biotechnology can benefit the poor and hungry of the world without harming the environment.
E. Biotechnology is not a panacea for global problems, but it is a tool that holds a great deal of promise if used appropriately.
F. However, biotechnology is more than engineering — it is also a set of tools for understanding

biological systems.

Passage Two

Peter Eigen, 65-year-old, chairman of Transparency International, the global anti-corruption watchdog, is proud of a large photograph on his office wall. It pictures him alongside Mwai Kibaki, the Kenyan president, and James Wolfensohn, president of the World Bank.

The picture, taken shortly after Mr. Kibaki's inauguration in January, shows the three men in friendly discussion at a meeting in Nairobi, the Kenyan capital. "This photo is very special because it shows how far Transparency International has come since we set it up 10 years ago," says Mr. Eigen with a smile.

Before leading a group of friends in 1993 to form TI in a one-room Berlin office, Mr. Eigen worked at the World Bank for 25 years. His final position was senior programme manager in east Africa, based in Nairobi. __71__ "I was told that fighting corruption was not part of the bank's mandate," he says.

This led him to leave Kenya and the bank and start campaigning.

The picture shows how things have come full circle. __72__ About 60 people work in the headquarters in west Berlin. TI's annual Corruption Perceptions Index, ranking national corruption levels, has become a benchmark for many governments. __73__ "This would have been unthinkable" a few years ago, Mr. Eigen says.

A series of closed-door meetings in the mid-1990s in Berlin with chief executives from leading German multinationals laid the groundwork for international action. "We moved the executives from being defensive to admitting that there was a big problem. __74__ "

TI's solution was joint pressure from the companies on the government to sign the OECD convention against bribe-paying and, later, the signing of agreements between companies not to use bribery to win contracts.

__75__ Mr. Eigen argues that TI's approach, based on "building coalitions, not on confrontation," has brought results.

A. TI now has a global reach in its information campaigns and lobbying work, supporting national groups in more than 100 countries.
B. Then came the important question: how do we stop bribing without losing business to companies that still do it?
C. One example is the German chapter of TI, which has more than 30 member companies, including Siemens, Lufthans, BASF and Daimler Chrysler.
D. There, he observed not only corruption in his dealings with the government of Daniel Arap Moi, president at the time, but also the unwillingness of the bank to do anything about it.
E. TI has been instrumental in putting corruption on the world agenda, including in the United Nations.
F. TI's approach of working closely with companies to combat corruption contrasts with the tactics of

many other pressure groups.

PAPER TWO

PART IV　TRANSLATION (30 minutes, 15 points)

Directions: *Read the following text carefully and then translate the underlined segments into Chinese. Write your Chinese version in the proper space on your Answer Sheet.*

　　Politicians and the public are quick to blame college faculty members for the decline in learning, but professors — like all teachers — are working in a context that has been created largely by others: Few people outside of higher education understand how little control professors actually have over what students can learn.

　　Here are some reasons:

　　Lack of student preparation. Increasingly, undergraduates are not prepared adequately in any academic area but often arrive with strong convictions about their abilities. (1) So college professors routinely encounter students who have never written anything more than short answers on exams, who do not read much at all, who lack foundational skills in math and science, yet are completely convinced of their abilities and resist any criticism of their work, to the point of anger and tears: "But I earned nothing but A's in high school," and "Your demands are unreasonable." Such a combination makes some students nearly unteachable.

　　Grade inflation. It has become difficult to give students honest feedback. (2) The slightest criticisms have to be cushioned by a warm blanket of praise and encouragement to avoid provoking oppositional defiance or complete breakdowns. As a result, student progress is slowed, sharply. Rubric-driven approaches give the appearance of objectivity but make grading seem like a matter of checklists, which, if completed, must ensure an A. (3) Increasingly, time-pressured college teachers ask themselves, "What grade will ensure no complaint from the student, or worse, a battle over whether the instructions for an assignment were clear enough?" So, the number of A-range grades keeps going up, and the motivation for students to excel keeps going down.

　　Student retention. As the college-age population declines, many tuition-driven institutions struggle to find enough paying customers to balance their budgets. (4) That makes it necessary to recruit even more unprepared students, who then must be retained, shifting the burden for academic success away from the student and on to the teacher. (5) Faculty members can work with an individual student, if they have time, but the capabilities of the student population as a whole define the average level of rigor that is sustainable in the classroom. At some institutions, graduation rates are so high because the academic expectations are so low. Failing a lot of students is a serious risk, financially, for the college and the professor.

PART V WRITING (40 minutes, 20 points)

Directions: *Write an essay of no less than 200 words on the topic given below. Use the space provided on your Answer Sheet II.*

TOPIC

Do you think love can be expressed in different, even opposite ways? Please use specific examples to support your arguments.

2016 年 3 月试题精解

第一部分 词 汇

1. 答案：B
   本题考查形容词的语义。A 可比较的；B 强大的；C 无数的；D 兼容的。该句的大意为：谷歌并非唯一的搜索工具，不过，它强大的工具集合能够专注搜索，因此谷歌是大多数人选择使用的搜索引擎。

2. 答案：D
   本题考查动词的语义。A 免除；B 禁止；C 破坏；D 阻碍。该句的大意为：大卫性格上的缺陷阻碍了他的事业发展。

3. 答案：C
   本题考查名词的语义。A 暗示，提及；B 与世隔绝；C 幻想，错觉；D 混乱，困惑。该句的大意为：那种认为商业运营能够完全脱离政府援助的观点已被证实是一种幻想。

4. 答案：D
   本题考查连词的语义。A 以便……；B 不管，尽管……；C 如此这般；D 如果，假设。该句的大意为：倘若先前学生已经学习了能够帮助理解的必要知识，那么距离现实越近，学习就会变得越容易。

5. 答案：B
   本题考查固定短语的语义。A 只要……就，倘若；B 要是……就；C 即使；D 即使。该句的大意为：我注视着母亲，心想：要是她像她看上去那么和蔼亲切就好了，这样我们的生活也许会变得更好。

6. 答案：A
   本题主要考查固定短语的语义。A 有助于，造就；B 构成，编造；C 匆忙离开；D 理解，辨认。该句的大意为：尽管颇具吸引力，但是吉德并没有采用这种通用的方法，原因在于将不同类型的对象统一起来并不能够促成简化。

7. 答案：B
   本题考查动词的语义。A 改革；B 栖息于；C 使融入；D 继承。该句的大意为：作为一名优秀的摄影师，你必须形成一种意识，留意你所处的世界和栖息在这个世界里的人们。

8. 答案：C
   本题考查形容词的语义。A 正常的；B 虚拟的；C 一致的；D 持续不断的。该句的大意为：法官在实施法律时，必须做到坚定、公正、一致。

9. 答案：A
   本题考查形容词的语义。A 与众不同的；B 本能的；C 明确的；D 无限的。该句的大意为：这幢建筑的最大特色是它那巨大的圆形屋顶。

10. 答案：B

本题考查动词的语义。A 使固定；B 阻止；C 鼓励；D 修理。该句的大意为：医生尽快地将冰袋敷在你的伤处。冰能够防止肿胀和发炎。

11. 答案：C

本题考查固定搭配的语义。A 一旦……就；B 就……而言；C 只要；D 就……而言。该句的大意为：我们只要继续努力工作，就能在计划之前完成任务。

12. 答案：B

本题考查形容词的语义。A 意识形态的；B 相同的；C 实际的；D 有条不紊的。该句的大意为：这一清单令人心生敬畏，以至于有可能让我们觉得研究和高等教育必须至少属于同一类型的活动，即使它们并非真的完全相同。

13. 答案：C

本题考查动词的语义。A 隔离；B 压制；C 区分；D 伪装。该句的大意为：我们可以大致将其区分为了解倾向和行为倾向，大约对应传统观点对纯理论和应用的区分。

14. 答案：A

本题考查形容词的语义。A 看似合理的；B 可应用的；C 可以信赖的；D 可以理解的。该句的大意为：当然，有些画作可以从多角度来理解，而有些画作难以得到合理的解读。

15. 答案：A

本题考查形容词的语义。A 创新的；B 描述的；C 无形的，难以捉摸的；D 容易理解的。该句的大意为：他的名气犹如昙花一现——他的第一本书很畅销，但之后再也没有写出什么有新意的东西。

16. 答案：C

本题考查形容词的语义。A 不清楚的，模糊的；B 主观的；C 错误的；D 共产主义的。该句的大意为：许多外国学生错误地认为，英式英语较美式英语更加纯正、更加完美。

17. 答案：D

本题考查固定搭配的语义。Native to 指的是"来自，产自"。该句的大意为：这种来自欧洲中部和东部的小鸟经常会向西南方向迁徙，在法国、西班牙的南部和非洲北部过冬。

18. 答案：A

本题考查动词的语义。A 使散开，使分散；B 吐唾沫；C 分裂；D 扩散。该句的大意为：一阵风吹开了窗户，纸张散落了一地。

19. 答案：B

本题考查介词的用法和句子内在的逻辑关系。A 在……内；B 由于；C 在……上；D 和，伴随。该句的大意为：由于缺少证据，不得不释放被关押了六个月的那名囚犯。

20. 答案：B

本题考查形容词短语的语义。A 在……有信心；B 对……怀疑；C 对……现实；D 没有能力做……。该句的大意为：你可能会认为艺术越来越怀疑快乐是因为现代社会经历了如此多的灾难。

第二部分　完形填空

本文主要阐述人们对核能源发电站的几个误解及误解产生的原因。

21. 答案:A

本题考查动词现在分词的词义辨析及对句意的理解。A 正在上演的；B 不屈服的；C 不愿意的；D 潜在的。本句的意思是,在三里岛事件发生 30 年后,正在上演的日本福岛核电站危机又将围绕核能的噩梦带回人们的生活当中。

22. 答案:C

本题考查名词的词义辨析及对句意的理解。A 精神；B 犯罪；C 噩梦；D 意图。本句的意思是,发生在日本福岛的这次危机又引发了新一轮有关建立核电站优缺点的辩论。

23. 答案:D

本题考查名词词义辨析及对句意的理解。A 错误；B 障碍；C 反对；D 缺点。本句的意思是,发生在日本福岛的这次危机又一次使人们开始辩论核电站的优点和缺点。

24. 答案:A

本题考查动词的词义辨析以及对句意的理解。A 分来；B 去除；C 交换；D 阻止。本句的意思是,核能源究竟是提供了一种可以替代碳能源的方法,还是给人类带来了潜在危险的威胁,现在有必要将人们的误解和现实进行区分。

25. 答案:B

本题考查连接词的使用以及主从句之间的逻辑关系。A 只要；B 正如同……一样；C 然而；D 尽管。本句的意思是,正如同日本福岛核泄漏灾难所清楚表明的那样,核能源的安全性确实是个关键问题。

26. 答案:C

本题考查连词或副词的使用及句子之间的逻辑关系。A 只有,表条件；B 也不,表递进；C 而,表转折；D 或者,表并列。本句的意思是,多年以来,核能源持续发展所遭遇的最大挑战不是安全性问题,而是成本问题。

27. 答案:D

本题考查副词的词义辨析及句子之间的逻辑关系。本句是顺承前句而来,意思是,甚至在 1979 年三里岛发生部分熔断以前,美国的核电站建设就已经开始放慢速度了。三里岛核电站发生的部分熔断事件更是注定了美国核电站的命运。

28. 答案:C

本题考查动名词的使用及对语句的理解。A 超越；B 派遣；C 输送；D 储存。本句的意思是,美国最后一座核电站虽然 1972 年就开始了建设,但到 1996 年才首次输送电能。

29. 答案:B

本题考查副词的使用及对句意的理解。A 专门地；B 相当地；C 故意地；D 相反地。本句的意思是,在当下,相比较于燃煤发电或燃天然气发电,核电依然是相当的贵。

30. 答案:C

本题考查副词的使用及对上下文的理解。本句的意思是,相比较于燃煤发电或燃天然气发电,核电依然相当贵,其主要原因在于建设一座核电站耗资巨大。四个选择"A 有趣地,B 大约地,C 主要地,D 让人吃惊地"中,只有 C 符合句意。

31. 答案:D

本题考查名词的词义辨析及对句意的理解。A 剩余额；B 消耗；C 负债；D 估计。本句的意思是,尽管对建设一座核电站需要多少花费进行估算很难有个准确数字,但可以花到 50 亿美元。

32. 答案:B

本题考查代词的使用及对句意的理解。A 那些;B 那个;C 两者;D 任何一个。本句的意思是,根据 MIT 2009 年的一个研究估算,核能产生电能所需花费要比以煤或者天然气发电的花费高 30%。

33. 答案:C

本题考查过去分词转换来的形容词词义辨析及对句意的理解。A 未发行的;B 不匹配的;C 不相关的;D 未标记的。本句是说,花费和安全性并非不相关。

34. 答案:A

本题考查定语从句中关联词的使用。本句是一个非限制性定语从句,意思是,出于对安全的考虑,规章制度的通过过程更加昂贵,核电站开发商的盘算更加不确定,而这两点又使为建设新核电站所进行的融资费用增加。which 在本句中指代前面所提到的两点,是个关联代词,引导非限制性定语从句。

35. 答案:B

本题考查动词的词义辨析及对句意的理解。A 保持;B 降低;C 流动;D 摇摆。本句的意思是,如果人们的恐惧消退并且融资比以前价格低,人们不知道建设核电站的费用能下降多少。

第三部分　阅读理解

第一小节　阅读理解 A

第一篇:

36. 答案:A

本题是细节题,要求考生可以找出研究饥饿对人类健康影响的困难,从第二段最后一句可以看出:现实世界中人类需要吃东西生存,要把(饥饿状态对人类健康有益)这个理念传达给大众不是件容易的事情。关键点:... challenge has been to translate the concept to the real world ...

37. 答案:B

本题是细节指代题,要求考生理解第三段第一句中 a modified version of the concept 的意思,这个理念在第三段和第四段中都有详细解释,即阶段性节食。关键点:... fasting mimicking diet ... with a little less starvation.

38. 答案:C

本题是细节题,要求考生理解第五段中节食者可吃的食物。第五段列举的各种食物中,鱼和肉是未提及的。

39. 答案:C

本题是细节题,要求考生理解节食计划的好处。第六段第二句说明,这种计划能改变体质,从而降低一些随着年龄增长而带来的健康风险。关键点:... reduce risk factors for age-related conditions ...

40. 答案:B

本题是细节题,要求考生掌握最后一段提到的两种产品品牌是什么。关键点:... could

become the next commercially branded diet …

41. 答案:D
    本题是主旨题,要求考生总结归纳全文大意。

第二篇:

42. 答案:B
    本题是细节题,实为词汇题,要求考生理解第一段中对美国航空航天局载人航天飞行计划评论的描述。只需理解第一句中 review 前面的形容词 sweeping,其意为"影响广泛的,全面的"。

43. 答案:A
    本题是推理题,要求考生理解第二段引号内美国国家科学研究委员会报告(NRC)的原话隐含的意思。关键点:… human spaceflight is something the United States does best.

44. 答案:C
    本题是细节题,要求考生理解第四段中 Mitch Daniels 说的关于到达火星的这一段,这段的大意为:国家(目前)在做事的方式上缺少根本性的改变,(而一味地)认为我们可以完成到达火星这一大家共识的目标是不现实的。关键点:… the consensus goal of reaching Mars.

45. 答案:D
    本题是细节题,要求考生理解第五段第一句的语义。关键点:… urged NASA to keep its options open while investing … and letting …,这说明在不同的空间项目可以采取不同的方案。

46. 答案:A
    本题是细节题,要求考生理解美国国家研究委员会批评美国国家航空航天局(NASA)不专注。考点在第五段的最后一句,其中情态动词 should 暗示了批评的口吻,言下之意 NASA 目前的目标不够专注。

47. 答案:A
    本题是细节题,要求考生理解美国国家研究委员会对载人航天飞行计划的看法。考点在最后一段,关键点:… but that the aspirational nature of the endeavor may make it worth the effort.

第三篇:

48. 答案:C
    本题是细节题,要求考生理解小额信贷受到攻击的原因是过于商业化,关键点在第一段最后一句:Yet the industry has come under attack for being too commercial.

49. 答案:A
    本题是细节题,要求考生理解第二段画线部分的意思,关键在于理解 cap 这个词引申的意思。另外,第三段中讲到了对于小额信贷来说降低利率的弊端有哪些,由此也可以推断出政府试图限制小额信贷的利率。

50. 答案:B
    本题是细节题,要求考生理解小额信贷机构不盈利的原因是运营成本太高。答案在第三段第一句的后半段。关键点:… because of the high costs of making and collecting payments on

millions of tiny loans.
51. 答案:C
本题是推理题,要求考生理解限制人们小额信贷的后果是迫使穷人转向利率更高的高利贷者借贷。关键点:... could have the perverse effect of driving more poor people into the arms of village loan-sharks...

52. 答案:C
本题是例证题,要求考生理解秘鲁和印度两个例子说明的观点,即明智的法规不会与小额信贷产业起冲突。关键点:... need not be at odds with a thriving microfinance industry.

53. 答案:A
本题是细节题,要求考生理解最后一段中作者提到的促进小额信贷的各种办法。可以运用排除法来做题。选项中除 A 以外,都在文中有所提及。

第四篇:

54. 答案:A
本题是判断题,要求考生理解人形机器人用于刺探人们的隐私。考点在第一段的第二句,关键点:... it will deliberately invade their privacy.

55. 答案:C
本题是词汇题,要求考生理解第二段画线部分词汇的意思。根据第二段的第二句,可以了解如果这些机器人变得 ubiquitous 的话,他们将一直观察并记录我们的一举一动。选项 C 为正确答案。

56. 答案:D
本题是例证题,要求考生理解谷歌公司这个例子与其他几个例子都是用来说明机器人运用广泛。

57. 答案:B
本题是细节题,考点在第四段的第二句。要求考生理解目前我们离智能机器人还很遥远,但是云(cloud)是可以用来开发机器人技术的。关键点:... we're still a long way from intelligent robots. What will empower them, however, is the cloud...

58. 答案:A
本题是细节题,要求考生理解各大网络公司纷纷专研机器人学的原因是机器人与互联网的互动更加广泛。关键点:... It's going to be physical and pervasive.

59. 答案:B
本题是主旨题,要求考生理解全文大意。

第五篇:

60. 答案:D
本题是推理题,要求考生理解超级英雄电影对妇女的影响是使妇女们把自己降格为物件,质疑自己的性别角色,甚至对自己的身体自尊。关键点:Exposure to this, they show, can impact beliefs about gender roles, body esteem, and self-objectification.

61. 答案:D

本题是细节题,要求考生理解超级英雄电影中女性受害者常常被刻画成柔弱、单纯、无助,然而又楚楚动人。她们不强壮不狡猾,于是用善良和曲线(性感的身体)来弥补。关键点:What she lacks in strength and cunning she makes up for in kindness and curves.

62. 答案:A

本题是细节题,要求考生理解作者认为柔弱的女性角色可以通过刻画能干的、善于发号施令的女性超级英雄来改善。关键点:… it's possible that the antidote to the helpless fair maiden is the competent, commanding superheroine.

63. 答案:A

本题是推理题,要求考生推理出第四段的电影观众会支持男女平等的观念。关键点:…Perhaps exposure to this new generation of female heroines will result in more equal gender beliefs, higher body esteem, and greater prioritization of physical competence over appearance…

64. 答案:B

本题是段落大意题,要求考生理解第五段的段落大意,主题句是第一句:… today's superheroines, like their female victim counterparts, are often unrealistic, sexualized representations of female figures.

65. 答案:C

本题是作者态度题,要求考生理解 Pennell 和 Behm-Morawitz 两位作者对于如今超级女性英雄的态度,两位作者在最后一段中非常中肯地评价了现如今的女性超级电影,既有好的一面(might elevate equal beliefs about gender roles),也有不好的一面(their sexualized nature might simultaneously have destructive effects on body image and self-objectification),因此是较为客观的态度。

第二小节　阅读理解 B

第一篇:

66. 答案:A

本题的突破口是把握文章第一段的结构:以生物技术的起源为引子,以时间为线索概要地介绍人类发现和研究基因的过程。空格后的时间节点 1970s 也是提醒我们这里的逻辑顺序有可能为时间顺序。

67. 答案:F

本题的突破口是空格后一句中讲到的"these tools"。其中指示代词"these"的使用表明空格中的句子应该包含"tools"这一单词。把握了这一线索,即可快速锁定选项 F。通过分析选项 F 与上下文之间的内容衔接,可以进一步确定 F 为正确答案。

68. 答案:C

本题的答题关键是把握前一句中讲到了基因组学目前已经取得的进步,那么接下来可能会探讨这一科学进步的意义,因此选 C。

69. 答案:B

本题的答题关键是空格后一句中讲到的"this boundary",这说明空格的句子中应包含"boundary"这一语义。因此选 B,选项 B 中的"separation"正是"boundary"的同义词。

70. 答案:E

本题的突破口在空格后一句中的"on the other hand",这说明两句话之间有某种程度的转折关系,因此答案为选项 E。

第二篇：

71. 答案：D

本题的突破口是了解第三段的主要内容是介绍 Peter Eigen 是如何放弃世界银行的一名高级项目经理这一职位而白手起家成立一家反腐败公司的。根据主要内容,可以推断空格中的内容可能是和他经历的某件涉及腐败的事情有关,因此选 D。

72. 答案：A

本题的答题关键是把握第五段的主要内容是公司的发展现状,尤其值得注意的是文章所用的时态的变化。时态也可以是答题的一个重要线索。

73. 答案：E

本题的答题重点是空格的前一句讲到了该公司提供的年度腐败指数的影响力,后一句讲到这在几年前还是难以置信的事情。同时考虑前后两句,可以判断出空格中句子应该也是谈论到公司的影响力。因此答案为 E。

74. 答案：B

本题的突破口是空格前一句中讲到"a big problem",接下来很可能就是告诉读者这个重要的问题到底是什么。因此选 B。

75. 答案：F

本题的答题关键是把握空格后一句解释了该公司的策略是公司之间的合作,而不是对抗。"coalitions"一词与选项 F 中的"working closely"相呼应。

第四部分 翻 译

(1) 译文：

因此,大学教授遇到的学生往往都是这样的:除了会在试卷上写简单答案之外,从不动笔写任何东西,不怎么读书;缺乏基本的数理技能,却对自己的能力信心满满,还拒绝接受任何针对其作业的批评,甚至到了大哭大闹的程度。

解析：

理解该句的难点在于能把握"to the point of anger and tears"是"resist"的状语,用以形容学生们对批评的抵制到了"哭闹和恼怒的程度"。

(2) 译文：

稍加批评,就得施以各种赞美鼓励来缓和,以防引发对立情绪、无视老师的要求,或情绪完全崩溃。

解析：

该句的词汇难点是"be cushioned by"。如果能够从"cushion"的名词词义"垫子"引申出"用垫子加以保护或缓冲"之意,那么整个句子的理解就简单多了。

(3) 译文：

由于时间压力,越来越多的大学老师自问:"给学生什么样的成绩才能保证他们不抱怨,更糟糕的是,才不会因为作业要求是否清晰而引发纷争?"

解析：
  该句有两个难点：一是能从句法结构上辨别出"no complaint"和"a battle"的并列关系，均为动词"ensure"的宾语；二是能看出"over"表示原因。

（4）**译文：**
  因此，就不得不招进更多不合要求的学生，还不得不留下他们，从而将争取学业成功的负担从学生身上转嫁到了老师身上。

解析：
  该句的语言点是动词短语"shift away/on"，意为"转移走/转移到"。

（5）**译文：**
  如果有时间，教师可以进行单独辅导。但是学生的整体能力决定了在课堂上能够严格要求他们的程度。

解析：
  该句比较长，从句法结构分析句子主干有助于整句的理解。除此之外，还有两个词汇难点："rigor"和"sustainable"。"rigor"意为"严厉"；"sustainable"意为"可以忍受的"。

第五部分 写 作

题目解析：
  题目试图探讨的是爱可以用不同的,甚至相反的方式来表达。此题目初看上去比较简短，但内涵深刻。需要仔细审题："不同的,甚至相反的方式"是指的什么方式？"爱"的定义是什么？定义不同,对爱的表达方式就会不同。世界上有很多种爱：父母之爱、恋人之爱、朋友之爱，等等。不同的爱有不同的表达方式；就是同一种爱，在不同的环境下，也会有不同的表达方式。但是它们的出发点都是爱，都是为了被爱者的利益。联系实际生活来看，有时候表面的严苛，可能是为了长远的好处，这一点在父母对待孩子的教育上尤其明显。当然，写作的时候也可以反对这一说法，坚持说爱就要用易于被人接受的方式来表达。写作的时候，要注意把握好度。有的考生有点走极端，把一些父母对孩子的过分冷漠也当成了爱而大肆赞扬。还要注意正确理解题目中的"different"之意。有考生把"different"理解成为男女间追逐各种不同的爱，与不同的人交朋友，于是在作文中反对滥情。这些都是没有很好地理解题意。

范文：

  When it comes to love, we always think of tenderness and warmness, support and encouragement. But criticism and harshness, in certain situations, are also love. Love is a feeling hidden in humans' hearts, and the ways to express it could be varied according to different people. I agree that love can be expressed in different ways.

  Eagles throw their kids from the edge of the mountain to teach them how to fly. Hens cover their children under their wings to keep them warm. Both of them are expressions of love, but in opposite ways. Sometimes love can be expressed in a direct and warm way. Lovers' sweet words are intoxicating, and they encourage each other with everything.

  But love can also be expressed in a harsh way. Our parents are not always affectionate if we do something wrong and refuse to admit, correct or change. Their harsh scolding is love in our upbringings. Our supervisors always push us to read more literatures and do more experiments, although we feel very tired after a strenuous day. They even remind us, in a serious and criticizing tone, what needs to be improved in our research. Through this process each of us has learned a lot and become a better self. These are also love, love out of responsibility, although expressed in a different, opposite way.

  No matter how love is expressed, the intention behind it, whether it is out of sincere affection, is all we care. (244 words)

中国科学院大学
博士研究生入学考试
英语试题

(2017 年 3 月)

考生须知:

一、本试卷由试卷一(PAPER ONE)和试卷二(PAPER TWO)两部分组成。试卷一为客观题,答卷使用标准化机读答题纸;试卷二为主观题,答卷使用非机读答题纸。

二、请考生一律用 HB 或 2B 铅笔填涂标准化机读答题纸,画线不得过细或过短。修改时请用橡皮擦拭干净。若因填涂不符合要求而导致计算机无法识别,责任由考生自负。请保持机读答题纸清洁、无折皱。答题纸切忌折叠。

三、全部考试时间总计180分钟,满分为100分。时间及分值分布如下:

试卷一:

	Ⅰ 词汇	15 分钟	10 分
	Ⅱ 完形填空	15 分钟	15 分
	Ⅲ 阅读理解	80 分钟	40 分
	小计	110 分钟	65 分

试卷二:

	Ⅳ 英译汉	30 分钟	15 分
	Ⅴ 写作	40 分钟	20 分
	小计	70 分钟	35 分

UNIVERSITY OF THE CHINESE ACADEMY OF SCIENCES ENGLISH ENTRANCE EXAMINATION FOR Ph. D PROGRAM
March 2017

PAPER ONE

PART I VOCABULARY (15 minutes, 10 points, 0.5 point each)

Directions: *Choose the word or expression below each sentence that best completes the statement, and mark the corresponding letter of your choice with a single bar across the square brackets on your Machine-scoring Answer Sheet.*

1. Research marches onward, but we're still _____ something as simple as the flu.
   A. in the course of   B. with the exception of
   C. on the brink of   D. at the mercy of
2. Although there are plans to _____ additional pensions, this will not affect anyone retiring before 1998 and will only marginally affect those retiring by 2009.
   A. break down   B. scale down   C. boil down   D. narrow down
3. Parents often fall into the trap of offering other food in order to _____ the child to eat.
   A. tempt   B. manipulate   C. incense   D. escort
4. What is perhaps of great importance is the fact that she challenged the decision of her employers and won the case _____ .
   A. in the extreme   B. to the point   C. against all odds   D. around the corner
5. Learning is unique and dependent on many factors, many of them internal and _____ to the individual.
   A. intrinsic   B. narrative   C. primitive   D. emphatic
6. If we cannot _____ exactly what we are supposed to be managing, how can we manage it?
   A. knock on   B. pin down   C. let go   D. get over
7. Studies have proved that smart people tend to be smart across different kinds of _____ .
   A. institutions   B. occasions   C. characters   D. realms
8. Toyota said on Tuesday that it will _____ its annual year-end sales event early.
   A. give away   B. fix on   C. kick off   D. bring up

9. My mother would rather put honesty first in her _____ of values, which is important for our growth.
   A. inventory   B. hierarchy   C. observation   D. identification
10. They have reduced _____ in the labor market by allowing employers and prospective employees to connect more easily than ever before.
    A. incentive   B. budget   C. aggression   D. friction
11. Physical exercise has the capacity to be used to attempt to control emotional feelings, to _____ the calories consumed in food and to control body size.
    A. make up   B. pass on   C. work off   D. mark down
12. The news that the president had submitted his resignation caused a great _____.
    A. sensation   B. stimulation   C. devotion   D. deterioration
13. It's nice to have close friends and family you can _____, but it lifts a huge weight off your shoulders when you know that you could survive on your own if you had to.
    A. cope with   B. count on   C. conform to   D. commit to
14. Astronauts' dietary requirements are different from those of their gravity-bound _____ on Earth.
    A. counterparts   B. equivalents   C. correspondences   D. candidates
15. For a moment he was speechless, still too astonished to _____ what it all meant, then he sat heavily and leaned forward, putting his hand down on the summons button.
    A. break down   B. search for   C. take in   D. see after
16. The world _____ credit to Prince Henry, known as Henry the Navigator, for the development of craft that made oceanic exploration possible.
    A. owes   B. pays   C. admits   D. gains
17. People with more timid personalities must be encouraged to _____ and to give orders.
    A. get through   B. play safe   C. take charge   D. stand by
18. These pollutants can be _____ hundreds and even thousands of kilometers by large air masses.
    A. conveyed   B. conjectured   C. conjured   D. conserved
19. Dr Howard Martin gave fatal doses of painkillers to terminally ill patients out of _____ and acted in their best interests.
    A. suspicion   B. curiosity   C. compassion   D. prejudice
20. The workload can be evened out, instead of the shop having busy times and _____ periods.
    A. prosperous   B. memorable   C. discrete   D. slack

PART II CLOZE TEST (15 minutes, 15 points)

Directions: *For each blank in the following passage, choose the best answer from the four choices given below. Mark the corresponding letter of your choice with a single bar across the* square brackets on your Machine-scoring Answer Sheet.

Suppose you are there in the museum, with the head-sized smartphone permanently positioned in front of your nose. According to a new study published in *Psychological Science* this week, you are doing it all wrong. That tiny camera you are using to carefully __21__ your art viewing experience is actually __22__ your art memory, not preserving it.

The study, __23__ by Fairfield University's psychological scientist Linda Henkel, claims that museum goers have worse memories __24__ objects and specific object details __25__ they used a camera to record paintings, archeological relics or historical artifacts __26__. It's a phenomenon Henkel calls the "photo-taking impairment effect."

"When people __27__ technology to remember for them — counting on the camera to record the event and thus not needing to __28__ to it fully themselves — it can have a negative __29__ on how well they remember their experiences," Henkel explains in a description of the study.

To reach her conclusion, Henkel __30__ an experiment at Bellarmine Art Museum at Fairfield University, __31__ she recruited undergraduate students to __32__ the institute and take note of specific objects on display. The subjects could either photograph the items or just observe them — it was __33__ them. Then the following day, the students' memories were tested.

The results proved that the camera-happy participants __34__ worse than the persons who relied on their simple observation skills.

"Research has suggested that the sheer __35__ and lack of organization of digital photos for personal memories discourages many people from accessing and reminiscing about them," Henkel states.

21. A. describe   B. memorize   C. document   D. present
22. A. impairing   B. compiling   C. activating   D. adapting
23. A. sponsored   B. conducted   C. managed   D. arranged
24. A. to   B. in   C. for   D. by
25. A. where   B. whereas   C. when   D. how
26. A. in advance   B. in essence   C. at hand   D. on display
27. A. rely on   B. account for   C. lay out   D. stick to
28. A. view   B. add   C. benefit   D. attend
29. A. suggestion   B. impact   C. inference   D. feedback
30. A. set up   B. put up   C. made up   D. ran up
31. A. which   B. when   C. where   D. as
32. A. march   B. tour   C. scan   D. survey
33. A. just for   B. far from   C. all about   D. up to
34. A. struggled   B. fared   C. failed   D. recited
35. A. volume   B. scale   C. shape   D. size

PART III READING COMPREHENSION

Section A (60 minutes, 30 points)
Directions: *Below each of the following passages you will find some questions or incomplete statements. Each question or statement is followed by four choices marked A, B, C, and D. Read each passage carefully, and then select the choice that best answers the question or completes the statement. Mark the letter of your choice with a single bar across the square brackets on your Machine-scoring Answer Sheet.*

Passage One

Everyone knows that English departments are in trouble, but it is difficult to appreciate just how much trouble until you read the report from the Modern Language Association (MLA).

The report is about Ph. D. programs, which have been in decline since 2008. These programs have gotten both more difficult and less rewarding: today, it can take almost a decade to get a doctorate, and, at the end of your program, you're unlikely to find a tenure-track position.

The core of the problem is the job market. The MLA report estimates that only sixty per cent of newly-minted Ph. D. s will find tenure-track jobs after graduation. If anything, that's wildly optimistic: the MLA got to that figure by comparing the number of tenure-track jobs on its job list with the number of new graduates. But that leaves out the thousands of unemployed graduates from past years who are still job-hunting.

Different people will tell you different stories about where all the jobs went. Some critics think that the humanities have gotten too weird—that undergrads, turned off by an overly theoretical approach, don't want to participate anymore, and that teaching opportunities have disappeared as a result. Others point to the corporatization of universities, which are increasingly inclined to hire part-time, "adjunct" professors, rather than full-time, tenure-trackprofessors, to teach undergrads. Adjuncts are cheaper; perhaps more importantly, they are easier to hire.

These trends, in turn, are part of an even larger story having to do with the expansion and transformation of American education after the Second World War. Essentially, colleges grew less élite and more vocational. Before the war, relatively few people went to college. Then, in the nineteen-fifties, the Baby Boom pushed colleges to grow rapidly, bulking up on professors and graduate programs. When the boom ended and enrollments declined, colleges found themselves overextended and competing for students. By the mid-seventies, schools were seeking out new constituencies — among them, women and minorities — and creating new programs designed to attract a broader range of students.

Those reforms worked: about twice as many people attend college per capita now as they did forty years ago. But all that expansion changed colleges. In the past, they had catered to élite students who were happy to major in the traditional liberal arts. Now, to attract middle-class students, colleges have had to offer more career-focused majors, in fields like business. As a result, humanities departments have found themselves drifting away from the center of the university.

36. What does the word "appreciate" mean in Paragraph 1?
    A. Enjoy.　　　　B. Overlook.　　　　C. Investigate.　　　　D. Understand.
37. What has made Ph. D. programs unpopular?
    A. They no longer save your time.
    B. They cannot guarantee a secure job.
    C. They are competitive and time-consuming.
    D. They are not subsidized by the government.
38. The MLA report about the employment rate is too optimistic because it _____.
    A. overestimates the job market　　　　B. fails to account for former graduates
    C. does not include all kinds of jobs　　D. excludes newly-graduated PhDs
39. University job openings are diminishing due to the fact that _____.
    A. the scale of universities is shrinking
    B. adjunct professors are likely to take full-time jobs
    C. fewer undergraduates want to major in humanities
    D. some theoretical approaches have been proven wrong
40. According to Paragraph 5, the American educational institutions _____ over the past decades.
    A. have resulted in tenure-track professors
    B. have attracted more male and élite students
    C. have been expanding to overseas countries
    D. have begun to offer a variety of vocational programs
41. The final paragraph suggests that current liberal arts majors _____.
    A. are more desirable than ever before　　B. will cater to middle-class students
    C. are less appealing than business majors　D. are as competitive as business majors

Passage Two

We're in the middle of an epic battle for power in cyberspace. On one side are the traditional, organized, institutional powers such as governments and large multinational corporations. On the other are the distributed: grassroots movements, dissident groups, hackers, and criminals. Initially, the Internet empowered the latter. It gave them a place to coordinate and communicate efficiently, and made them seem invincible. But now, the more traditional institutional powers are winning, and winning big. How these two sides fare in the long term, and the fate of the rest of us who don't fall into either group, is an open question — and one vitally important to the future of the Internet.

In the Internet's early days, there was a lot of talk about its "natural laws" — how it would transform traditional power blocks, empower the masses, and spread freedom throughout the world. The international nature of the Internet circumvented national laws. Anonymity was easy. Censorship was impossible. Police were clueless about cybercrime. And bigger changes seemed inevitable. Digital cash would undermine national sovereignty. Citizen journalism would topple traditional media, corporate PR, and political parties. The ease of digital copying would destroy the traditional movie and music industries. Web marketing would allow even the smallest companies to compete against corporate giants. It really would be a new world order.

This was a utopian vision, but some of it did come to pass. Internet marketing has transformed commerce. The entertainment industries have been transformed by things like MySpace and YouTube, and are now more open to outsiders. Mass media has changed dramatically, and some of the most influential people in the media have come from the blogging world. There are new ways to organize politically and run elections. Facebook and Twitter really did help disrupt governments.

But that is just one side of the Internet's disruptive character. The Internet has emboldened traditional power as well.

On the corporate side, power is being consolidated, a result of two current trends in computing. First, the rise of cloud computing means that we no longer have control of our data. And second, we are increasingly accessing our data using devices that we have much less control over: iPhones, iPads, Android phones, Kindles, ChromeBooks. Unlike traditional operating systems, these devices are controlled much more tightly by the vendors, who limit what software can be run, what they can do, how they're updated.

42. In the Internet battle, the grassroots movement _____.
    A. experienced an epic failure
    B. gradually became invincible
    C. previously beat institutional forces
    D. distributed power to dissident groups

43. According to the author, in the future a key Internet issue will be _____.
    A. which side has the technological resources
    B. what happens to those who remain neutral
    C. which side is good at communications
    D. what financial resources are available

44. "Natural laws" refers to _____.
    A. the fast expansion of Internet
    B. the traditional power structure
    C. national laws to regulate the Internet
    D. lack of control on the Internet

45. Lack of surveillance over the Internet would likely _____.
    A. strengthen national security
    B. devastate the traditional film industry
    C. provide more information to the police
    D. handicap the development of small companies

46. Online media has _____.
    A. made the utopian vision impossible
    B. won more support for the government
    C. made some ordinary people become famous
    D. excluded outsiders from the entertainment industries

47. We now have less control over the data we use because _____.

A. cloud computing is highly confusing
B. there is no limit to updating software
C. corporate giants are in a dominant position
D. it is difficult to assess data in electronic devices

Passage Three

Since the dawn of civilization, mankind has been obsessed by the possibility that it will one day be extinguished. The impact of an asteroid on earth and the spectre of nuclear holocaust are the most prevalent millennial fears. Now some scientists are increasingly leaning towards the view that a new nightmare must be added to the list. Their concern is that intelligent computers will eventually develop minds of their own and destroy the human race.

The latest warning comes from Professor Stephen Hawking. He told an interviewer this week that artificial intelligence could "outsmart us all" and that a technological catastrophe is a "near certainty." Most non-experts will dismiss his claims as a fantasy rooted in science fiction. But the pace of progress in artificial intelligence, or AI, means policy makers should already be considering the social consequences.

According to a recent survey, half the world's AI experts believe human-level machine intelligence will be achieved by 2040 and 90 per cent say it will arrive by 2075. Several AI experts talk about the possibility that the human brain will eventually be "reverse engineered." Some prominent tech leaders, meanwhile, warn that the consequences are unpredictable. Elon Musk, the pioneer of electric cars, has argued that advanced computer technology is "potentially more dangerous than nuclear threats."

That said, the risk that computers might one day pose a challenge to humanity should be put in perspective. Scientists may not be able to say with certainty when, or if, machines will match or outperform mankind.

But before the world gets to that point, the drawing together of both human and computer intelligence will almost certainly help to tackle pressing problems that cannot otherwise be solved. The growing ability of computers to crunch enormous quantities of data, for example, will play a huge role in helping humanity tackle climate change and disease over the next few decades. It would be folly to arrest the development of computer technology now — and forgo those benefits — because of risks that lie much further in the future.

There is every reason to be optimistic about AI research. There is no evidence that scientists will struggle to control computers, even at their most advanced stage. But this is a sector in which pioneers must tread carefully — and with their eyes open to the enduring ability of science to surprise us.

48. According to Paragraph 1, _____.
    A. human civilization will some day disappear
    B. intelligent computers will threaten mankind one day

C. natural disasters will lead to human extinction

D. artificial intelligence will control the human mind

49. The underlined word "catastrophe" can be interpreted as _____.

    A. revolution   B. advancement   C. challenge   D. disaster

50. Professor Stephen Hawking believes that artificial intelligence _____.

    A. will be much smarter than humans   B. only appears in science fictions

    C. should not be overdeveloped   D. will have negative social impacts

51. AI experts contend that _____.

    A. humans may be threatened by artificial intelligence

    B. the implications of AI development is still unknown

    C. the human brain will not be subject to machine intelligence

    D. computer technology can cause massive destruction

52. With the help of computer intelligence, human beings can _____.

    A. solve technical problems   B. conduct vast data analysis

    C. forecast weather precisely   D. prevent fatal diseases

53. The author suggests that we should _____.

    A. restrict AI development due to the potential risks

    B. be optimistic about AI and maximize the benefits

    C. cautiously develop AI with an open attitude

    D. suspend AI research at its most advanced stage

Passage Four

Ariella Rosengard of the University of Pennsylvania didn't set out to scare anyone. She just wanted to investigate a little-understood part of the immune system by studying how viral proteins interact with it. At first, Rosengard worked with a common virus called vaccinia. But vaccinia rarely makes people sick, and she began to worry that it wouldn't tell her much about the human immune system. So she turned to a closely related, far more fearsome virus: smallpox.

Smallpox virus isn't easy to come by. Officially, it resides in only two places — secure labs in the United States and Russia. But Rosengard didn't need the virus itself. Scientists have made its genetic code freely available on the Internet, giving her the data she needed to synthesize a key smallpox protein in the lab. Test-tube studies showed that it works far better than the corresponding vaccinia protein at blocking a key step in the human immune response. The discovery may help explain why smallpox kills, and it could lead to new treatments.

But when Rosengard published her report last month in the Proceedings of the National Academy of Sciences, a slightly defensive commentary appeared with it. The article said it would be unlikely to use the work as a blueprint for making vaccinia more like smallpox. It acknowledged, however, that "the idea that bioterrorists might be tempted to attempt such an experiment has been suggested as a reason for considering it unwise to publish observations of this nature."

Rosengard rejects the idea that basic science like hers should be put under wraps. "Think how many brilliant minds would not be able to participate in finding a cure," she says. "You can't predict the mind of a madman. The best defense against any virus is understanding how it functions."

Most biologists would agree. But these days, they find themselves grappling with a dilemma, as their tradition of openness clashes with the fear that well-intentioned research could be misused to develop bioweapons. As much as scientists fear aiding their enemies, they get unnerved when government officials talk about restricting their freedom to publish. One thing's for sure — the problem won't just go away. The Government has proposed a dramatic increase in funding for basic research on potential biowarfare agents. This means that many more scientists will study deadly germs, and they'll inevitably want to publish what they find.

54. Why did Ariella Rosengard decide to study smallpox?
   A. Because smallpox is becoming more important and complicated.
   B. Because smallpox is more familiar to scientists today.
   C. Because the smallpox virus can be obtained more easily.
   D. Because smallpox can reveal more about the immune system.

55. How did she obtain the smallpox protein?
   A. She made it from information available online.
   B. She relied on secure labs for a sample.
   C. She developed it by using vaccinia virus.
   D. She received help from government.

56. Smallpox is deadly probably because _____.
   A. it kills vaccinia in the human immune system
   B. it stops the reaction of the human immune system
   C. it causes the human immune system to attack proteins
   D. it reproduces quickly in the human immune system

57. According to the commentary mentioned in Paragraph 3, Rosengard's report _____.
   A. would be criticized
   B. would help control smallpox
   C. would mislead researchers
   D. would lead to more publications about smallpox

58. Rosengard thinks that basic science _____.
   A. should have a long-term perspective   B. should receive more financial support
   C. should focus on academic research   D. should develop in an open manner

59. According to the final paragraph, biologists are worried about _____.
   A. a loss of motivation among researchers   B. funding from the government
   C. their freedom to publish   D. the prospects of their research

Passage Five

One of the largest earthquakes ever recorded hit on Boxing Day 2004. The resulting tsunami devastated huge swaths of the Indian Ocean coastline and left an estimated quarter of a million people dead across Indonesia, Sri Lanka, India and Thailand. Aid agencies quickly arrived to help battered and traumatised survivors.

Mental health care was a massive part of the emergency response but the World Health Organization (WHO) promptly did something it has never done before or since. It specifically denounced a type of psychological therapy and recommended that it shouldn't be used. The therapy was a single session treatment called "psychological debriefing," which involved working with disaster victims to encourage people to supposedly "process" the intense emotions by talking through them in stages. It was intended to prevent later mental health problems by helping people resolve difficult emotions early on. The only trouble was that it made things worse. Studies had shown that people given post-disaster psychological debriefing were subsequently more likely to suffer mental health problems than people who had had no treatment at all.

Guidance from the world's most influential health authority had little effect, and the therapy was extensively used. The reluctance to do things differently was tied up with some of the least-appreciated facts about our reactions to disaster. In our trauma-focused society, it is often forgotten that the majority of people who experience the ravages of natural disaster, become the victims of violence or lose loved ones in tragedy will need no assistance from mental health professionals.

Most people will be shaken up, distressed and bereaved, but these are natural reactions, not in themselves disorders. Only a minority of people — rarely more than 30% in well-conducted studies and often considerably less — will develop psychological difficulties as a result of their experiences, and the single most common outcome is recovery without the need of professional help. But regardless of the eventual outcome, you are likely to be at your most stressed during the disaster and your stress levels will decrease afterwards even if they don't return to normal. Your body simply cannot maintain peak levels of anxiety.

These are important facts to bear in mind because, from the point of view of the disaster therapist, psychological debriefing seems to work — stress levels genuinely drop. But what the individual therapist can't see is that this would happen more effectively, leaving less people traumatised, if they did nothing.

60. In Paragraph 1, the underlined word "battered" means _____.
    A. bruised   B. shocked   C. tortured   D. destroyed
61. In Paragraph 2, "psychological debriefing" is close to _____.
    A. neurotherapy   B. behavior therapy   C. physical therapy   D. psychotherapy
62. What can be inferred from Paragraph 2?
    A. The emergency response did not involve psychological debriefing.
    B. Mental therapy reduced the incidence of emotional problems.

C. Psychological intervention caused more serious emotional problems.

D. Psychological intervention was not recommended by the WHO.

63. Psychological debriefing was still widely used because _____.

    A. it was proved to be highly effective by survivors

    B. the WHO reminded people to get assistance from mental health professionals

    C. professionals paid a lot of attention to the necessity of psychological intervention

    D. the majority of survivors developed mental disorders

64. Paragraph 4 indicates that _____.

    A. most survivors will get over trauma without professional assistance

    B. one third of survivors will have mental illnesses after disasters

    C. it is difficult for survivors to return to normal levels of mental health

    D. peak levels of anxiety will lead to mental disorders

65. According to Paragraph 5, we should bear in mind that _____.

    A. psychological debriefing mainly deals with stress levels

    B. psychological debriefing has little effect

    C. more professional aid should be given to survivors

    D. stress levels are the key to mental breakdowns

Section B (20 minutes, 10 points)

Directions: *In each of the following passages, five sentences have been removed from the original text. They are listed from A to F and put below the passage. Choose the most suitable sentence from the list to fill in each of the blanks (numbered 66 to 75). For each passage, there is one sentence that does not fit in any of the blanks. Mark your answers on your Machine-scoring Answer Sheet.*

Passage One

In the mid-1990s, three senior female professors at M.I.T. came to suspect that their careers had been hampered by similar patterns of marginalization. __66__ After performing the investigation and studying the data, the committee concluded that the marginalization experienced by female scientists at M.I.T. "was often accompanied by differences in salary, space, awards, resources and response to outside offers between men and women faculty, with women receiving less despite professional accomplishments equal to those of their colleagues." The dean concurred with the committee's findings. And yet, as was noted in the committee's report, his fellow administrators "resisted the notion that there was any problem that arose from gender bias in the treatment of the women faculty. Some argued that it was the masculine culture of M.I.T. that was to blame, and little could be done to change that." __67__

The committee's most evocative finding was that the discrimination facing female scientists in the final quarter of the 20th century was qualitatively different from the more obvious forms of sexism addressed by civil rights laws and affirmative action, but no less real. Not everyone agrees that what was uncovered at M. I. T. actually qualifies as discrimination. 68 Even if female professors have been shortchanged or shunted aside, their marginalization might be a result of the same sorts of departmental infighting, personality conflicts and "mistaken impressions" that cause male faculty members to feel slighted as well. "Perceptions of discrimination are evidence of nothing but subjective feelings," Kleinfeld scoffs.

 69 In February 2012, the American Institute of Physics published a survey of 15,000 male and female physicists across 130 countries. 70 "In fact," the researchers concluded, "women physicists could be the majority in some hypothetical future yet still find their careers experience problems that stem from often unconscious bias."

A. In almost all cultures, female scientists received less financing, lab space, office support and grants for equipment and travel, even after the researchers controlled for differences other than sex.
B. Judith Kleinfeld, a professor emeritus in the psychology department at the University of Alaska, argues that the M. I. T. study isn't persuasive because the number of faculty members involved is too small and university officials refuse to release the data.
C. But broader studies show that the perception of discrimination is often accompanied by a very real difference in the allotment of resources.
D. Yet women pursuing tenure track must leap hurdles that are higher than those facing their male competitors, often without realizing any such disparity exists.
E. In other words, women didn't become scientists because science — and scientists — were male.
F. They took the matter to the dean, who appointed a committee of six senior women and three senior men to investigate their concerns.

Passage Two

We've all heard about endangered animals. Creatures like the critically endangered black rhinoceros are famous. But what are the most endangered plants? They might not be as exciting or loveable as animals, but they are just as important to the ecosystem — and humanity relies on that ecosystem.

Here are three of the most threatened plants today. 71 These plants occupy some of the most inaccessible, remote parts of our planet. They are threatened by habitat destruction, illegal collection, poaching, and competition with invading species.

Attenborough's pitcher plant is known only from the relatively inaccessible summit of Mount Victoria in Palawan in the Philippines. There are thought to be only a few hundred of them. 72 Attenborough's pitcher plant is one of the biggest, with pitchers up to 30 cm in height that can trap insects and rats. It was only discovered in 2007 when a team of botanists, tipped off by two Christian missionaries, scaled Mount Victoria. 73

The suicide palm is a gigantic palm found only in remote parts of north-west Madagascar. It lives for about 50 years, then flowers only once, and dies soon after. Suicide palms were discovered in 2005 by a cashew plantation manager during a family outing, and formally described in 2008. With trunks reaching 18 m in height, and huge fan-leaves up to 5 m across, the palms can be seen on Google Earth. __74__

The coral tree, with its bright red flowers and spiny trunk, occurs only in the remote forests of south-east Tanzania. __75__ However, the forest patch was cleared to grow biofuels, and the species was feared to have gone extinct again until it was re-rediscovered in 2011. There are now fewer than 50 mature individuals in the wild, in a single unprotected location.

A. Pitcher plants are carnivorous plants that trap animals in liquid-filled bowls called pitchers.
B. They are almost all classed as critically endangered by the International Union for Conservation of Nature (IUCN).
C. It was declared extinct in 1998, but rediscovered in 2001 in a small patch of forest.
D. As a result, the population has dropped more than 95% over the last 20 years.
E. There are only about 90 in the wild.
F. It is named after British natural history broadcaster David Attenborough.

PAPER TWO

PART Ⅳ TRANSLATION (30 minutes, 15 points)

Directions: *Read the following text carefully and then translate the underlined segments into Chinese. Write your Chinese version in the proper space on your Answer Sheet.*

The first edition of Thomas Kuhn's "The Structure of Scientific Revolutions" appeared in 1962. (1) His vision revolutionized the way we think about science, and it has given us a new way to look at change in "science" itself. (2) Whereas previous visions of science saw science as an accumulation of all that had been learned over history, Kuhn envisioned science as having, at any one time, a worldview, or "paradigm(范式)", of its environment.

Kuhn(库恩) postulated that most scientists engage in "normal science" that often results in solid, but relatively incremental gains, which nevertheless accumulate and collectively contribute to move research and subsequent scientific knowledge forward. When anomalies arise, some individual(s) step out of the paradigm, and propose a new principle or law. (3) If the scientific community accepts the proposed change, then science experiences a "paradigm shift", and new science proceeds from that new paradigm.

Paradigm shifts are important, and a necessary part of life. Things do change, and we have to adjust and adapt to that change. Perhaps not surprisingly, important paradigm shifts often come from the young. (4) It usually takes a long time to effect a paradigm shift—often as much as 20-25 years—which, perhaps not so coincidently, is about the life of a generation.

(5) A relatively recent white paper emanating from MIT justifiably argues that the intersections of arrays of scientists, engineers, mathematicians, as well as individuals with a host of many other professional talents, will be the next Kuhnian scientific revolution and in fact, the "Third" biomedical revolution. This new revolution is broadly known as Convergence.

PART V   WRITING (40 minutes, 20 points)

Directions: *Write an essay of no less than 200 words on the topic given below. Use the space provided on your Answer Sheet II.*

TOPIC

"Stay hungry, stay foolish" is a quote from Steve Jobs. How do you understand this statement? Please give reasons or examples to illustrate your points.

2017年3月试题精解

第一部分 词 汇

1. 答案：D
   本题考查介词短语的含义。A 在……过程中；B 除……之外；C 在……的边缘；D 任凭……摆布。该句的大意为：研究不曾止步，而我们对类似流感这般简单的疾病仍然难以控制。

2. 答案：B
   本题考查动词短语的含义。A 故障，分解；B 缩减；C 归结到；D 缩小范围。该句的大意为：尽管有计划缩减额外退休金数额，但是这并不会影响于1998年前退休的职工，也仅仅会对2009年退休职工造成很小的影响。

3. 答案：A
   本题考查动词的含义。A 吸引，诱使；B 操作，操控；C 使激怒；D 护送，陪同。该句的大意为：家长们常常陷入困境，通过给予别的食物来吸引孩子好好吃饭。

4. 答案：C
   本题考查固定短语的含义。A 非常，极度；B 中肯，切题；C 困难重重；D 即将到来。该句的大意为：最重要的或许在于，她敢于质疑雇主的决定，并且克服重重困难，最终获得胜利。

5. 答案：A
   本题考查形容词的含义。A 本质的，固有的；B 叙事的；C 原始的；D 强调的。该句的大意为：学习具有唯一性，取决于多种因素，这些因素于个体而言既是内在的，也是与生俱来的。

6. 答案：B
   本题主要考查动词词组的含义。A 敲击，撞击；B 确定；C 放开，释放；D 恢复，解决。该句的大意为：如果我们无法准确指出有待管理之处，那么我们该如何进行管理？

7. 答案：D
   本题考查名词的含义。A 机构，制度；B 场合，机会；C 性格，角色；D 领域，范围。该句的大意为：研究表明，聪明的人容易在各个不同的领域都表现得很聪明。

8. 答案：C
   本题考查动词短语的含义。A 放弃，分发；B 确定，固定；C 开始；D 提出，养育。该句的大意为：周二，丰田汽车公司宣布将提前开展其一年一度的年终促销活动。

9. 答案：B
   本题考查名词的含义。A 存货；B 层级，等级；C 观察；D 识别，鉴别；身份认同。该句的大意为：我的母亲宁可将诚实放在其价值观体系的首位，这对于我们的成长很重要。

10. 答案：D
    本题考查名词的含义。A 刺激，动机；B 预算；C 侵略，侵犯；D 摩擦。该句的大意为：让雇主和潜在雇员之间的联系较从前变得更加容易，通过采用这一方式，他们减少了劳动市场中的摩擦。

11. 答案：C

本题考查动词短语的含义。A 构成，编造；B 传递；C 发泄，排除；D 降低价格，记下。该句的大意为：体育运动有以下作用：可以用于控制情绪，排除食物中所消耗的卡路里，并且控制体重。

12. 答案：A

本题考查名词的含义。A 感觉，轰动；B 刺激；C 奉献；D 恶化。该句的大意为：总统已经提交辞呈的消息引发了巨大的轰动。

13. 答案：B

本题考查动词短语的含义。A 处理，应付；B 指望，依赖；C 符合，遵照；D 交付，致力于。该句的大意为：有亲密的朋友和家人可以依靠固然很好，但是当你知道在不得已的情况下，你可以独立生活，那时你便会卸下一身重担。

14. 答案：A

本题考查名词的含义。A 对应的人或物；B 等价物；C 信件，一致；D 候选人。该句的大意为：宇航员的饮食要求与地球上受引力作用的饮食要求是不一样的。

15. 答案：C

本题考查动词词组的含义。A 分解，故障；B 搜寻；C 吸收，领会；D 照顾，照料。该句的大意为：他一时说不出话来，仍十分惊讶，不知这一切意味着什么。他心事重重地坐了下来，身子向前倾斜，将手放在传票徽章上。

16. 答案：A

本题考查固定短语的含义。由 A 组成的短语 owe credit to 指"感激，归功于"；B 支付；C 承认；D 获得。该句的大意为：世界应感谢被称为"航海家亨利"的亨利王子，原因是他发展了海船技术，使远洋航行成为可能。

17. 答案：C

本题考查动词短语的含义。A 通过，完成；B 谨慎行事；C 掌管，负责；D 袖手旁观。该句的大意为：必须鼓励那些更加腼腆的人担起责任和发号施令。

18. 答案：A

本题考查动词的含义。A 传播，输送；B 推测；C 用魔法变出，想象；D 保全，保护。该句的大意为：这些污染物会因为强大的气团而被传播至百里，甚至千里之外。

19. 答案：C

本题考查名词的含义。A 怀疑，猜疑；B 好奇；C 同情，怜悯；D 偏见，损害。该句的大意为：霍华德·马丁医生说，出于怜悯，他采取最佳治疗方法，给绝症晚期的病人服用致命剂量的止痛剂。

20. 答案：D

本题考查形容词的含义。A 繁荣的，兴旺的；B 难忘的，值得纪念的；C 离散的，不连续的；D 松弛的，萧条的。该句的大意为：工作量可以均衡分配，商店就不会有旺季和淡季之分。

第二部分　完形填空

本文主要阐述对相机的依赖对我们记忆力的负面影响。

21. 答案：C

本题考查动词的词义辨析及对语句的理解。A 描述；B 记忆；C 记录；D 展示。原文的意思是,事实上,你所用来记录你参展经历的相机正在损坏你的记忆,而不是保持你的记忆。

22. 答案:A

  本题考查动词的词义辨析及对句意的理解。A 损伤;B 编辑;C 激活;D 改编。这句话前后语义对立,后半句提到不是保持记忆,那么整句的意思是,使用照相机会损坏你的记忆,而不是保持你的记忆。

23. 答案:B

  本题考查动宾搭配,动词 conduct 的宾语为 the study。A 资助;B 实施,进行(研究、实验等);C 应付;D 安排。原文的意思是,这项研究由费尔菲尔德大学(Fairfield University)的心理科学家 Linda Henkel 实施完成。

24. 答案:C

  本题考查介词的使用及固定搭配。"have a memory for (of) sth."表示对某事的记忆。

25. 答案:C

  本题考查关联词的词义及对句意的理解。A 在……地方;B 然而;C 在……时候;D 以……方式。本句的意思是,当参观博物馆的人们用相机来记录他们所看到的绘画、古迹以及其他历史文物的时候,他们对所看到物品及物品细节的记忆反而比不用相机记录时还要差。

26. 答案:D

  本题考查介词词组的用法。A 提前;B 本质上;C 手头;D 展示。本句的意思是,对博物馆中所展示的绘画、古迹以及其他历史文物用相机进行记录。

27. 答案:A

  本句考查动词词组词义辨析。A 依赖;B 解释;C 展开;D 坚持。本句的意思是,人们依赖于科技手段来记住所看到的事件。

28. 答案:D

  本句考查的是动词与 to 的搭配。A 看,看待(及物动词);B 增加(及物动词与不及物动词);C 有益于(及物动词);D 关注(不及物动词)。本句的意思是,人们依赖于相机来记住事件,于是就无须自己来关注事件。

29. 答案:B

  本句考查名词的词义辨析。A 建议;B 影响;C 干扰;D 反馈。本句的意思是,当人们依赖于科技,即用相机来记录所看到的事件而不是靠自己去全面关注事件时,这会对人们关于其所经历事件的记忆产生负面影响。

30. 答案:A

  本题考查动词词组的词义辨析。A 建立,安排;B 建造,修建;C 组成,补足;D 积欠。本句的意思是,Henkel 教授在费尔菲尔德大学(Fairfield University)的一家博物馆安排进行了一场实验。

31. 答案:C

  本题考查定语从句中关联词的使用。从上下文可以看出,这一句是非限制性定语从句,修饰前面所提到的费尔菲尔德大学。本题此处需要的是一个关联副词来连接,在定语从句中做地点状语,意思是,Henkel 教授在该大学招募大学生参与实验。

32. 答案:B

  本题考查动词的词义辨析。A 前进,行军;B 观光,参观;C 扫描;D 调查,勘测。本句的意思是,Henkel教授招募大学生参加实验,在实验中,她让这些大学生参观这家博物馆并对所展示的具体物品进行记录。

33. 答案:D

本题考查固定词组的语义。A 仅仅为了;B 远远没有达……;C 都是关于……;D 多达,直到,在于……,由……决定。本句的意思是,大学生被试究竟是靠相机拍摄还是仅仅靠自己的观察来记录他们所看到的具体物品,这由被试自己决定。

34. 答案:B

本题考查动词的词义辨析。A 挣扎;B 进展;C 失败;D 背诵。本句的意思是,研究结果证明,使用相机的被试与依靠自己观察技能进行记忆的被试相比,其记忆成绩更糟。

35. 答案:A

本题考查名词的词义辨析。A 量;B 尺度;C 形状;D 尺寸。本句的意思是,研究表明仅仅是用来记录个人经历的数码照片的数量与这些照片的缺乏组织性就阻碍了人们对这些信息的提取和回忆。

第三部分 阅读理解
第一节 阅读理解 A

第一篇:

36. 答案:D

本题是词汇题,要求考生可以从第一句的上下文理解 appreciate 的意思:即"理解,明白"。第一句中的"knows"与"appreciate"是同义词。

37. 答案:B

本题是细节题,要求考生理解第二段(语言学的)博士项目自2008年以来一直走下坡路的原因,答案就在第二句,即攻读博士时间长,还不太可能找到终身职位。

38. 答案:B

本题是细节题,要求考生理解美国现代语言协会(MLA)关于就业率的报告太乐观的原因,即没有把过去毕业的、依然在找工作的博士考虑进去。关键点:... But that leaves out the thousands of unemployed graduates ... 。

39. 答案:C

本题是推理题,要求考生理解工作机会越来越少的原因,即有些评论家认为教师的职位越来越少是因为人文学科的理论性让很多大学生不愿意以文科为专业。关键点在第四段的第二句话:... undergrads, turned off by an overly theoretical approach, don't want to participate anymore。

40. 答案:D

本题是细节题,要求考生理解美国教育机构在过去的几十年间的教育更加倾向职业教育而不是精英教育。关键点:Essentially, colleges grew less élite and more vocational。

41. 答案:C

本题是推理题,要求考生理解最后一段关于目前人文学科的事实,即人文学科不如商科热门。关键点在该段的最后一句话:人文学科已经不再是大学的中心。

第二篇：

42. 答案：C

本题是推理题，要求考生理解草根运动从前在互联网之战击败过政府组织机构，尤其要理解起初互联网给予过草根力量。关键点：the Internet empowered the latter。

43. 答案：B

本题是细节题，要求考生理解作者认为未来关于因特网的力量双方，关键取决于那些中立的人。关键点在第一段的最后一句。

44. 答案：D

本题是推理题，要求考生理解"自然法则"的意思。破折号后对自然法则有所解释，接下来的几句都是对于这种状态的例证：匿名很容易，监控不可能，警察对网络犯罪一筹莫展，这些都是反面例证。关键点：The international nature of the Internet circumvented national laws。本题也可以用排除法来分析四个选项。

45. 答案：B

本题是细节题，要求考生理解对互联网缺乏监管对于各行业的影响，要看懂第二段的后半部分。关键点：... would destroy the traditional movie and music industries。

46. 答案：C

本题是细节题，要求考生理解互联网市场对商业模式以及对于大众媒体的改变。关键点：... some of the most influential people in the media have come from the blogging world。

47. 答案：C

本题是细节题，要求考生理解我们对于自己的个人信息和资料没有掌控权的原因是因为大机构通过云计算和各种应用掌握了我们的数据。关键点：... these devices are controlled much more tightly ...。

第三篇：

48. 答案：B

本题是主旨大意题，要求考生理解第一段的中心意思，即有朝一日人工智能将毁灭人类。关键点：intelligent computers will eventually develop minds of their own and destroy the human race。

49. 答案：D

本题是词汇题，要求考生根据上下文理解 catastrophe 的意思。这个词可以根据第一段的中心意思以及第二段开头的 warning 一词猜出 catastrophe 应为否定语义。

50. 答案：A

本题是词汇题，要求考生理解第二段开头两句中史蒂芬·霍金对人工智能的看法，即霍金警告人类人工智能比人类要聪明得多，技术灾难是肯定的事。关键点在于理解"outsmart"一词的意思为"比……更聪明"。

51. 答案：A

本题是主旨大意题，要求考生理解人工智能专家对这项技术的看法。第三段的人工智能专家观点基本一致，那就是人工智能对于人类可能造成极大的负面影响。考生需根据所举例子进行归纳大意。

52. 答案：B

本题是细节题，要求考生理解人类在计算机的帮助下可以获得各种好处，其中一种好处是进行庞大的数据分析。关键点：... crunch enormous quantities of data ...。

53. 答案：C

本题是推理题，要求考生理解作者对于人工智能的态度。最后一段第一句作者的评论说我们有各种理由对人工智能的研究抱有乐观态度，然而第三句又说这是一个开拓者们必须小心谨慎的地方。因此，作者的态度是既乐观又谨慎。关键点：... reason to be optimistic... pioneers must tread carefully ...。

第四篇：

54. 答案：D

本题是推断题，答题关键：在第一段的最后讲到，她开始担心牛痘和免疫系统的关系不太大，因此她决定选择与免疫系统关系紧密也更可怕的一种病毒——天花。

55. 答案：A

本题是细节题，题眼在第二段的第三句。科学家们已经在网上公开了天花的基因密码，这使她可以在实验室合成天花蛋白。因此选项 A 为最佳答案。

56. 答案：B

本题是细节题，答题关键在于理解第二段倒数第二句提及的"at blocking a key step in the human immune response"，即，和牛痘相比，天花病毒更厉害，是因为天花会阻止免疫系统的反应。

57. 答案：A

本题是推断题，题眼在文章的第三段，尤其值得注意的是一些否定语义的词汇，例如 defensive, unlikely, unwise。这些词汇均表明该评论对 Rosengard 的实验报告持批评态度。

58. 答案：D

本题是细节题，答题关键是第四段的第一句。这句表明了 Rosengard 的态度，她认为像她这样的基础科学的研究不应该受限制。

59. 答案：C

本题是细节题。最后一段的第三句中提到政府官员们说要限制科学家们发表论文的自由，这令他们烦恼不已。

第五篇：

60. 答案：A

本题是词汇题，考查 battered 一词在上下文中的语义。本题的答题关键是将 battered 和 traumatised（受创伤的）一起考虑，这两个词的语义很接近。

61. 答案：D

本题是概念题，可以根据第二段的语义判断，也可以根据关键词 psychological 来判断选项 D 为最佳答案。psychological debriefing 可以理解为"心理疏导"或"心理解说"。

62. 答案：D

本题是细节题，题眼在第二段的第二句：世界卫生组织特地通告废除一类心理治疗，认为不得使用该心理治疗方法。

63. 答案：C

本题是推断题，答题关键在理解第三段的最后一句：他们忘记大多数并不需要心理健康专家的帮助。

64. 答案：A

本题是推断题，题眼在第四段的中间：最常见的结果就是无须专业帮助的情况下就可以康复。

65. 答案：B

本题是推断题，值得注意的是，第五段中的一些用词，例如 psychological debriefing seems to work 和 this would happen more effectively, leaving less people traumatized, if they did nothing, 均表明整篇文章的态度和立场：心理疏导起不到什么作用。

第二节 阅读理解 B

第一篇：

66. 答案：F

本题的答题关键是空格后一句中提到 committee 时用到了 the committee, 这说明前面已经出现过 committee。根据这一线索，可以断定选项 F 为正确答案。

67. 答案：E

本题是第一段的最后一句，答案关键在于充分理解前文(尤其是上一句)的语义。选项 E 的语义与前文最接近。

68. 答案：B

本题的关键是空格的前一句中提到 Not everyone agrees that...，接下来很有可能要举例说明。另外，第二段的最后仅提到了一个人名 Kleinfeld, 说明前文中一定交代了 Kleinfeld 是谁、什么背景等信息。

69. 答案：C

本题的答题关键是理解文章脉络：从 MIT 的一个案例开始，渐渐讲到女性从事科研时受到的性别歧视或边缘化是一个普遍现象。因此选项 C 中 broader studies 是值得注意的用词。

70. 答案：A

选项 A 中 In almost all cultures 呼应了上文中提到的 across 130 countries, 因此为正确选项。

第二篇：

71. 答案：B

本题答题的关键是第二段句子的主语均指向 three of the most threatened plants, 主语均为复数。因此选项 B 为正确答案。

72. 答案：A

本题的答题关键是植物名 Attenborough's pitcher plant, 选项中只有 A 和 F 与之呼应。另外，空格后一句中提到的 one of the biggest 为省略语，意思是 one of the biggest carnivorous plants that trap animals。

73. 答案：F

本题的解题思路与第 72 题一致，充分利用该段的关键词 Attenborough's pitcher plant。

74. 答案：E

本题可以分析第四段的内容，前文就这一濒临灭绝的植物已经做了详细的说明，可能没有涉及的信息包括其在世界上的现存数目。

75. 答案：C

本题的答题关键是留意空格后的句子中用到了 re-rediscovered，这提示了我们文章已经用过 rediscovered 一词。因此答案为 C 选项。

第四部分　翻　译

（1）译文：

他看问题的眼光彻底改变了我们对科学的思考方式，给了我们一个全新的方式来看待"科学"自身的变化。

解析：

原文的句子比较容易理解，考生在翻译时采取直译法即可。

（2）译文：

过去，人们对科学的看法是把科学当作人类在历史长河中所学全部知识的积累过程，而库恩则把科学看成在任一时刻对环境的一种世界观，或"范式"。

解析：

理解该句的重点是要能判断出这是一个表示转折关系的主从复合句，主句和从句用了一对近义词短语 "saw... as... "和 "envisioned... as... "。如果有考生不认识 envision，也可以从 "saw... as... " 中得到启发。该句的另一个分析要点是主句中的两个插入语部分（at any one time 和 or "paradigm"）要单独处理，这样可以连贯地理解主句。

（3）译文：

如果科学界认可了所提出的变化，那么科学就将经历"范式转移"，而新的科学将按照新的范式向前发展。

解析：

该句的 "If... , then... , and... "的结构可以译成"如果……，那么……，而……。"

（4）译文：

引发范式转移通常需要很长时间——往往长达 20～25 年——而也许不算太巧的是，这大约相当于一代人。

解析：

该句翻译需要考生颇费心思的地方或许是 "perhaps not so coincidently" 这个插入语，对它最简单的处理方法是按字面逐字翻译，建议大家试一试。

（5）译文：

最近出自麻省理工学院的一份详情报告理由充分。它认为各类科学家、工程师、数学家以及个人与众多其他专业人才的交汇将成为下一场库恩意义上的科学革命，事实上也就是"第三次"生物医学革命。

解析：

该句的翻译难点有三，一为 "emanating"；二为 "arrays of"；三为 "a host of"。根据 "white paper（白皮书）"，考生或许可以猜出 "emanating from" 和 "from" 基本同义；而 "arrays of" 和 "a host of" 也是同义词短语，意为"大量的"。

第五部分 写 作

题目解析：

"Stay hungry, stay foolish"是2005年史蒂夫·乔布斯在斯坦福大学的演讲中所引用的一句话。这句话的含义很丰富。对"stay hungry"的一种理解是，我们要对一切保持强烈的好奇心和旺盛的求知欲，永不满足，永无止境地追求卓越。"Stay foolish"则可以理解为要用像初学者那样谦虚的心态去看待新事物。要有一种空杯心态：清空已经知道的东西，去不断地从事物的最初开始来理解新技术、新事物。尤其是我们现在学的东西几年之后很容易就落后了，要有不断学习的心态。我们的知识永远都是不够的，一些人学到一些知识和技术以后很容易就固化了，不再更新自己的知识，但在如今日新月异的科技面前，我们需要打开自己的心智，进行新的探索。有时候甚至要像一个傻瓜那样敢于从新的角度去审视世界，这样才能看到更多，不断地创新。"Stay foolish"另外一种理解则是：永远保持对成功、对理想的渴望，拥有雄心，敢于犯错，不怕别人耻笑自己在追求理想过程中一些看似不自量力的"愚蠢"行为，做自己钟爱的事。

范文：

Steve Jobs once said, "Stay hungry. Stay foolish," in his Stanford commencement address to call for the young people to be ambitious in this world. The quote is really thought provoking and means much to me.

To begin with the first part of Job's quote, "stay hungry" means to have a hunger for success, to be curious about the new things, and to be never satisfied with what we have achieved. In such a world where the knowledge explosion brings abundant and overwhelming information, we seem to have acquired enough knowledge about the world, and we have created plenty of inventions to facilitate our lives. Given this situation, it is easy for us to become complacent, or lazy, about learning. Job's message to us is not to become satisfied with our current level of understanding, but rather to continue our quest for more.

"Stay foolish" means to try everything and not to be afraid of making mistakes. In order to be innovative, sometimes we need to have a child-like attitude towards the new things and explore the world in a way we never see it before. Through making mistakes does a child learn. Jobs' message to us is to remain "child-like," almost naïve, in our wonder of the world and the knowledge it has to offer. Since we are facing a fast-developing world and it is not easy to predict what will happen in the next decade, we need to be open to new technologies and always desire for better achievements. It is through our curiosity and foolishness that advances in technology and services will develop. For instance, Artificial Intelligence is here and our world and our lives will be redefined by it in the future. We must embrace it and desire to learn more about it.

In short, Jobs' quote may serve as a guide for how we conduct and lead our lives in today's world. Since knowledge is updated very fast in many fields, we need to keep learning all the time. We know how much we *do* know, but we often do not comprehend the scope of our ignorance while facing new uncertainties. Therefore, we need to be both ambitious and innovative. We need to stay hungry and stay foolish.